| DATE DUE | | | |
|---|---|---|---|
| Dec 3 '75 | | | |
| Dec 15 '75 | | | |
| Nov 12 8 | | | |
| | | | |
| | | | |
| | | | |
| | | | |
| | | | |
| | | | |
| | | | |
| | | | |
| | | | |

*The Dynamics of Reading*

*David H. Russell*

---

# The Dynamics of Reading

EDITED BY *Robert B. Ruddell*
*University of California at Berkeley*

WITH CONTRIBUTIONS BY *Isabel Lewis, Virginia Reid, and James R. Squire*

GINN–BLAISDELL A XEROX COMPANY
WALTHAM, MASSACHUSETTS | TORONTO | LONDON

Library of Congress Catalog Card Number: 76-96468
PRINTED IN THE UNITED STATES OF AMERICA.

# *Preface*

*The Dynamics of Reading* grew primarily out of Professor Russell's intense interest in the effects of literature and secondly from his personal philosophy "that at least once every seven years one should undertake a task different from what one has been doing – that one should have a sort of mental sabbatical leave." Thus the present text followed as a natural sequence from his previous works, *Children Learn to Read* and *Children's Thinking*.

The central concern of this book is the effect of reading from the perspective of Holbook Jackson's reference to "the reader as artist." As Professor Russell suggests early in the discussion, "depending on the curiosity and purpose of the reader" the book may be interpreted to possess at least six objectives:

First, to draw the sciences and humanities closer together by offering a theoretical framework to bridge the gap between psychology and literature.

Second, to study the effects of communication from the standpoint of social psychology.

Third, to examine the impact of literature on the individual.

Fourth, to investigate the reading process and specific factors influencing personal response.

Fifth, to synthesize and interpret empirical research and authoritative data on the effects of reading.

Sixth, to derive implications and recommendations for clinical and classroom practice at various developmental levels from the literary and research backgrounds, and to provide a basis for understanding literature programs and experiences for young people.

The first three objectives are guidelines for Part One, which establishes the literary and psychological framework central to *The Dynamics of Reading*. The discussion relies heavily on autobiographies, personal documents, and anecdotal information which demonstrate the effect literary experience has had on widely known authors and personalities. Psychoanalytic processes in reading are also presented in depth, with particular concern for Freud's basic theories as related to literary interpretation. A discussion of literary criticism in relationship to reader response concludes the first part of the text.

Part Two, Research Backgrounds, focuses on the fourth and fifth objectives. Research related to the personality of the reader, reading difficulties, the reader's environment, content of material, levels of comprehension and appreciation, the nature of meaning and understanding, studies of reader interests and effects, the influence of television, and immediate literary response, is dealt with in detail. This discussion reflects one of the Russell hallmarks – the ability to synthesize and summarize significant research in a meaningful and interesting fashion.

The final section of the text develops the sixth objective and has as its initial focus the application of the earlier discussion to curriculum development. A second focus, growing out of the first, deals with an overview of literary programs and experiences for young readers. Chapters 9, 10, and 11, as well as the latter part of Chapter 3, offer valuable suggestions for developing literary experiences and responses with young people, leading to the enhancement of personal and social understandings.

This text should be of value to upper division and graduate students of reading and literature at any level. It should also serve as a valuable resource for teachers of teachers and scholars who are constantly concerned with the impact and effects of reading.

At the time of Professor Russell's untimely death, Chapters 1, 2, and 4 to 9 were near completion. In Part One, however, the third chapter, entitled "Psychoanalytic Points of View," and the last two chapters in Part Three, dealing with "Children and Literature" and "Teaching Literature – High School and College," had not been initiated, except for brief outlines and occasional references in other chapters. Discussions with Mrs. Elizabeth F. Russell led to the decision to ask three persons who had known Professor Russell's professional contributions and writings and had understood his personal philosophy toward the importance of studying the effects of literature to complete the remaining chapters of the manuscript. These individuals were: Dr. Isabel Lewis of the Mt. Diablo Public Schools, Concord, California, a specialist in literature and language arts, and a former student of Professor Russell, whose doctoral work had as its central focus the development of personal values in children through literature; Miss Virginia Reid of the Oakland Public Schools, Oakland, California, who had worked extensively in the field of children's literature, was past chairman of the Elementary Section of the National Council of Teachers of English, and had worked closely with Professor Russell in various professional activities; and Dr. James Squire, formerly executive secretary of the National Council and presently editor-in-chief of Ginn and Company, a specialist in the field of literary response and the application of literature, particularly at high school and college levels, and who was closely associated with Professor Russell in professional activities. Thus, Chapter 3 was completed by Dr. Lewis, Chapter 10 by Miss Reid, and Chapter 11 by Dr. Squire. These individuals labored diligently in completing the remaining chapters of the Russell text. Their efforts, and my own, in effect represent a memorial to a dear friend and colleague – David H. Russell.

I should also like to acknowledge the help of Mrs. Elizabeth F. Russell, who was most helpful in providing available information on the original manuscript; Dr. Marion Anderson who offered suggestions to parts of the work; and Mr. Charles Cooper, the first recipient of the David H. Russell Graduate Fellowship at the University of California at Berkeley, who has aided me in completing the detailed index. My role has been essentially that of editing and offering suggestions to the manuscript and serving as catalyst and resource to the three individuals who have given so generously of their time in bringing to full realization Professor Russell's significant manuscript.

It seems most appropriate to conclude with a final paragraph from the preface of one of Professor Russell's earlier texts:

> First, I have clung to the idea that a book can be both scientific and readable: Many of the quotations and anecdotes given here are not strict evidence, but I hope that they add interest and occasional enlightenment. Second, I have dared to believe that providing a basis for the understanding of children's thinking may eventually help many people to think more clearly. In a world plagued at times by anti-intellectualism, in an atmosphere where thought is too often not only neglected but mistrusted, solid bases for good thinking need to be laid down. We still want men to be spiritually and mentally free – to arrive at their own convictions and solutions by their own thinking. Perhaps this analysis will contribute to that end. Finally, I have hope that the book will aid all who work with children to understand them better and to help them more in their problem solving in creative thinking, and related behaviors.

ROBERT B. RUDDELL
*Berkeley, California*
*June 1969*

# Contents

## Part One Literary Backgrounds



## Part Two Research Backgrounds

*The Dynamics of Reading*

*Part One*

# Literary Backgrounds

# CHAPTER 1 | Some Problems in the Dynamics of Reading

Reading, like much human behavior, is a function of the total personality. Imaginative literature permits the reader to be both spectator and participant. As spectator he brings to his reading a uniqueness which means he will perceive selectively in accordance with his needs, goals, defenses, and values. As participant he will respond in relation to his selective perception with varying degrees of acceptance or rejection of the ideas stated and implied. In the process the total person may be involved. "Not only does the eye find what the mind is seeking; the mind finds what the heart is seeking."[1] In the total involvement, responses may be entities of scientific merit because they are observable ways of behaving. The reader, as well as the writer, may be studied in various ways.

Like any other piece of writing, this book can be perceived in different ways, depending upon the experience, the interests, and the needs of the reader. The content deals with the reader more than the author. It is concerned with the interpretation which occurs during thoughtful reading, as when members of a high school class, after reading Salinger's *Catcher in the Rye*, give such estimates of the main adolescent character as "Holden is a bum"; "He's a crazy mixed-up kid"; "He's a sensitive boy"; "Holden Caulfield should have minded his parents"; and "He's almost like myself." The book explores the possible effects of reading on the reader, an idea discussed by Mr. Gerald Gardiner, Q.C., counsel for the defense who had published in England an unexpurgated edition of *Lady Chatterley's Lover.* In the famous censorship trial held in No. 1 Court at the Old Bailey in the fall of 1960, part of his opening address to the jury contained these words:

> It is quite true that the book includes what is called four-letter words, and it is quite plain that what the author intended was to drag these words out of the rather shameful connotation which they had achieved since Victorian times. . . .

[1] Shrodes, Caroline. "The Dynamics of Reading," *Etc.: A Review of General Semantics, 18*:21–23, 1961.

The author thought that if he used what had been part of our spoken speech for about six hundred years, he could purify. . . . Whether he succeeded or not in his attempt to purify these words by dragging them into the light of day, there is nothing in the words themselves which can deprave or corrupt. . . .

Whole parts of the book may (and I do not doubt will) shock you; but there is nothing in the book which will in fact do anybody any harm. No one would suggest that the Director of Public Prosecutions would become depraved by reading the book, nor counsel, nor witnesses; no one would suggest that the judge and jury would become corrupted; it is always someone else, it is never ourselves![2]

The reaction to an adolescent character in a story and the questioning that a book can "deprave and corrupt" are only two examples that may be included in the complex topic of the effects and the dynamics of the reading act. Every child or adult who has ever read for himself knows that books have the gift of companionship. They bring ideas and new points of view. They poke fun at some of our peculiar notions. They bring joy and deep-running laughter. They fill the hollow of our loneliness. We also want to know why books, stories, or poems do – or sometimes do not – have these qualities. We want to find out the relationships among various factors in the reader, the situation, the printed material, and responses during and after reading. Depending, then, on the curiosity and purpose of the reader, this book can be perceived and interpreted in several different ways:

To some, its contents will be an approach to a general problem, an attempt to bridge the gap between psychology and literature which is one part of the current division between the sciences and the humanities.

To others, the book may be a study in social psychology on the effects of communication, and as such can be placed alongside investigations of the influence on the audience of television, movies and other mass media.

To other readers, it will be an exploration of the impact on the individual of reading stories, poems, and other forms of imaginative literature. The discussions will attempt to analyze the elusive, intuitive, emotional response which is sometimes labeled aesthetic, and about which we know so little, especially in children.

To some readers it may be an investigation of the process of reading from a fresh slant. As such, it will go beyond the study of eye movements or methods of reading instruction to report our limited evidence about the dynamics of the act, the emotional factors which may influence whether a person finds in reading an answer to his needs and whether he becomes a habitual reader.

To more literal students of reading it may provide an organized summary of published research on the influences of reading on the individual

[2] Bedford, Sybille. "The Last Trial of Lady Chatterley," *Esquire,* 55:132–55, April 1961.

or group, plus the original reports of several other researches on the effects of reading. Where possible the book relies upon empirical data and therefore presents accumulated knowledge plus suggestions for further research.

To some parents, teachers, and therapists it may give a few hints on ways of sharing literature with young people so that their self- and social understandings may be enhanced.

This book, then, may serve its readers in various ways. For example, it may be one basis for a study of censorship. It may be an introductory approach, from a psychological point of view, to the literary criticism which was stimulated by I. A. Richards and now goes beyond his theories. It may be interpreted as a critique of psychoanalytical concepts of literature or as an extension of some current methods of content analysis of literary materials. It may add to knowledge of the comprehension factor in reading in school classrooms or therapeutic uses of printed materials in hospitals and clinics. The reader ultimately will determine whether or not any of the goals are reached. In the words of Emerson, " 'Tis the good reader that makes the good book," but brief expositions of the goals or possibilities listed above may serve as an introduction to the theme of the dynamics of reading.

While describing the book's possible goals, this writer would also suggest what his book is *not* about. It is not concerned with the craft or technique of reading, rapidly or otherwise. It is not a reading list of selected classics on the "hundred best books" because the best books are usually best for some readers but not for others. It is not a history of literature, a summary of plots, nor a wily guide to the art of bookmanship. Although dealing with the process and art of reading, and discussing the literary critic as reader, the book is not one of literary criticism. The concern is less with art or method than with effect. The book is not about reading for practical purposes as when a boy follows directions for making a model airplane or a suburbanite gets help on a do-it-yourself project. It is concerned with results from what Thomas de Quincey called the "literature of power" as distinct from the "literature of knowledge." In recreational and contemplative reading ideas may penetrate more deeply than the reader realizes at the time. Hence, the central theme may be described as "the reader as artist" for "there is artistry in perception, in point of view, and in attitude."[3]

Until recently, reading materials have been broadly categorized as contributions to knowledge or to recreation. Writing has been informative, hortatory, or amusing. In the following pages an attempt is made to go below these superficial descriptions and, with emphasis upon the reader, to analyze the effects of reading upon the person engaged in it.

[3] Jackson, Holbrook. *The Reading of Books.* New York: Scribner, 1947, p. 24.

## *Psychology and Literature*

In the second half of the twentieth century the gap between what C. P. Snow calls "the two cultures" of science and the humanities seems to be widening and to be widest between the humanities and the physical sciences. In some ways the social sciences including psychology may be in an intermediate position, a pontoon helping to bridge the gap. Of the many bridges that could be built, perhaps the joining of psychology and literature can be based on as solid a structure as any now available. Psychology and literature have both been concerned with human nature, with the same emotions, ideas, and imagery. The two disciplines have had common goals in developing insights about man's behavior, but divergent approaches to the common goals. Today's high school or college student moving from his morning class in English to his afternoon science laboratory may never connect the two activities; but sometimes the social studies instructor in history, economics, or psychology will indicate a relationship between scientific and intuitive thought, a lacework of coherence which the able student may fashion for himself from different strands. The similarities and differences of the two worlds exemplified by English and psychology may both be productive in extending our knowledge of human aspiration and behavior. The psychological search for verifiable facts about the human organism may be stimulated and enriched by a comedy or tragedy, an essay or character sketch, an incident or a novel. The wall between the two may be breached, the chasm spanned.

The positive relationships between literature and psychology may be stated in a number of ways. Both attempt to describe human lives in terms of overt action and in relation to personality. The development of psychological science has often confirmed insights long achieved by writers. Forster[4] has written, "Psychology is not new, but it has newly risen to the surface. Shakespeare was subconsciously aware of the subconscious." Reciprocally, psychological knowledge has aided modern writers in developing their characters and plotting the course of their conflicts and problems. This knowledge has aided biographers in assessing the roles of heredity and environment, in studying genius, and in appraising the relationship of the individual to social movements. Thomas Mann's work reveals more knowledge of psychology than do the Robin Hood stories, and John Steinbeck's work has more psychological insight than that of Charles Dickens.

In *Modern Man in Search of a Soul* Jung[5] suggests that psychological research may help to reveal the factors that make a person artistically cre-

[4] Forster, E. M. *The Development of English Prose Between 1918 and 1939.* Glasgow: Jackson, 1945, p. 9.

[5] Jung, Carl G. *Modern Man in Search of a Soul.* London: Routledge and Kegan Paul, 1933.

ative and to explain the formation of a work of art. The characteristics of the creative person are not the concern of this book, but the characteristics of his written product are a main factor in any study of the effects of reading. Studies which probe themes in literature, which analyze the use of literary symbols in psychological terms, and which attempt to deduce the author's motivation from evidence in his writings are all spans in the bridge between psychology and literature.

Jung urged caution in building such spans, especially in making deductions about the artist from the work of art. He described these inferences as "never conclusive" and at best "lucky guesses." He also pointed out that the most fruitful source of obtaining reciprocal insights was not in the so-called psychological novel with its detailed exposition of motive and character, but in the literary work barren of psychological explanation. He stated that, "an exciting narrative that is apparently devoid of psychological exposition is just what interests the psychologists most of all," and quotes Rider Haggard's stories and Melville's *Moby Dick* in support of his statement. It is probably not necessary to accept Jung's "hinterland of man's mind," however, to find psychological insights in novels of family, love, crime, and society, in undidactic poetry, and in drama. Such insights do not necessarily depend upon a subconscious factor unrelated to overt experience. Analysis of a variety of materials, especially with children and adolescents who have much experience still to be savored, may be undertaken not on the hypothesis of a racial unconsciousness, but on the assumption of different values and accruals at different levels of psychological insight. Some empirical data on such levels are now available.

Any optimistic statement of the common interests of psychology and literature must be tempered by a realistic appraisal of the differences in their methods. Although both are concerned with human life and thought, their approaches differ markedly. "Literature is not watered down psychology; psychology is not methodized literature."[6] Psychology may deal with specific facts such as eye blink and the learning of nonsense syllables, but literature is supposed to mean more than it says. The psychologist looks for logic and order in a situation; the artist, unfettered in imagination, knows that life does not proceed according to rules or logic. Like other sciences, psychology seeks verifiable general laws while literature may deal with the fugitive truths of a specific person in a specific situation. Psychologists prefer observations which can be replicated, while the serious writer deals with analogy, metaphor, and perhaps intentional ambiguity. Members of departments of English refer to a long history of discerning writing and subtle thinking about imagery, emotion, character, and conflict. Psychologists must rely on relatively crude and

[6] Adams, Robert M. "Literature and Psychology: A Question of Significant Form," *Literature and Psychology*, 5:67–72, 1955.

isolated tests and experiments, not yet sufficiently developed to cope with man's understanding and use of some of the profound ideas and values of our culture. Literary works are not treatises on psychology. They embody stimuli, often of an intensive nature, out of which psychological insights may arise.

One of the complicating factors in establishing common ground for literature and psychology has been the considerable interest in literature of several branches of psychoanalytic thought. Although few American psychologists today support a Watsonian brand of behaviorism, they are less likely than many European psychologists to be influenced by psychoanalytic theory and they therefore tend to reject what they may call the "mythological terrain" of psychoanalytic concepts of literature. As discussed more fully in Chapter 3, Freud himself was interested in folklore and literature, and the tradition has been preserved in different schools of psychoanalysis. Rank, Reik, Bergler, and Fromm have all been interested in the problem. Freudian concepts have markedly influenced many American novelists and critics, and at least one newsletter, *Literature and Psychology,* for some years illustrated psychoanalytical interest in literary works ranging from Homer to Kafka. Psychologists reared in the experimental tradition have been unable to accept the assumptions and conclusions resulting from psychoanalytical analyses of literary text and author's personality, about which Jung also had reservations.

The publication of Freud's *The Interpretation of Dreams* in 1900 and his monograph entitled *Leonardo da Vinci* a decade later suggested the possiblity of psychoanalyzing historical and literary characters. The experiences of doctors in dealing with shell shock and other neuroses in World War I and the appearance in English of Freud's *General Introduction to Psychoanalysis* in 1920 opened many possibilities for writers of novels, plays, and biographies to incorporate psychoanalytic concepts into their work. Many of the more scholarly writers and literary critics stressed the close connection between a writer and his literary work. In a discussion of Poe, Krutch[7] declared, "The forces which wrecked his life were those which wrote his books." Mumford[8] wrote a psychological study of Melville and later concluded that, "it is better to make mistakes in interpreting the inner life than to make the infinitely greater mistake of ignoring its existence and import."

The enthusiasms of the 1920's for psychoanalytic interpretations of literary works diminished appreciably in the succeeding decades. Critics writing more recently have complained about the lack of authenticity in psychoanalytic interpretations of authors' lives, particularly in the lack of hard evidence in the case of persons no longer living. Literary production

[7] Krutch, Joseph. *Edgar Allan Poe.* New York: Knopf, 1926.

[8] Mumford, Lewis. "The Task of Modern Biography," *English Journal,* 23:1–9, 1934.

cannot be equated with dreams, and good authors may write for something more than catharsis. Literature is not a symptom but an art. Although production may be therapy for the writer, the results may have many more deep meanings for the reader.

The extremes of psychoanalytic theories of literature do not invalidate an attempt to find relationships between literature and psychology. The two may be combined in assessing a literary work or in attempting to predict its effects. As Adams[9] said:

> One cannot today read Lucretius to learn the literal structure of the universe, or Sir Davies to learn anatomy. One may still read Dr. Johnson to learn of the armed resistance of the stoic heart, or Shakespeare to see anatomized the pangs of jealousy.

It is not necessary to subscribe to Freud's concepts of infantile sexuality, symbolization, and ego or to Jung's "collective unconscious" to explore relationships between literature and psychology. Freud himself did not always attempt to extract information about the author's personality from a novel, such as *Gradiva*, and a writer's motivation may be money or fame as well as an Oedipus complex. Because motivation is many-sided and behavior is complex, psychology and literature can be complementary in the study of human behavior. The psychological interpretation of literary material and the analysis of the writer have already been mentioned; a third topic emphasized in this work is the role of the reader himself in the total reading situation.

## *The Effects of a Communication*

One possible view of the reader from the standpoint of the social psychologist is as a receiver of a communication or message. The effect of a story, passage, or poem on the reader may be compared to the effects on the decoder in any communication situation. Sound or communication engineers and military signals officers have been concerned for some time about the accuracy with which a message is received, and some social psychologists have been interested in the impact of public speakers, radio, advertising, television, and other media on their audiences. Do these media really change the ideas of the person listening or seeing? Do the horror comics affect the child, and does a steady television fare composed chiefly of crime and violence influence the adolescent or adult toward crime and violence in his thinking or overt behavior? Similarly, can the myth, fairy tale, play, or novel exert a permanent influence on the listener or reader?

[9] Adams, Robert M. "Literature and Psychology: A Question of Significant Form," *Literature and Psychology*, p. 71.

The effects of reading on personality and character have been accepted from philosophical and hortatory writing as least as far back as the ancient Greeks; the empirical evidence for such effects is scanty. Plato wrote, "We should do our utmost that the first stories that they hear should be so composed as to bring the fairest lessons of virtue to their ears." Since Plato's time many good men have testified to the influence of literature in their lives, but personal anecdote does not constitute scientific evidence. We are interested in Abraham Lincoln's remark on first meeting Harriet Beecher Stowe, "Is this the little woman whose book made such a great war?" We are probably pleased with Winston Churchill's testimony to the power of literature:

> I began to learn by heart many of those passages of poetry which have been a great treasure and comfort to me during my life – heroic poetry and famous tales and legends of the past. The committing of passages to heart, and the recording of them, is the most valuable part of education and sinks more deeply into the composition of the child than a lot of chatter-patter that is hurriedly spread over him in order to pass some examination.

But the opinions of such stout characters do not constitute solid data which can be checked, verified, and generalized.

Most teachers, and especially teachers of English, hope that literature affects personality and character, but many have gnawing doubts and wavering convictions in the matter. Their point of view is well summarized by the critic Granville Hicks:[10]

> Literature does affect the lives of its readers. How and why, we do not know, and the effect certainly cannot be measured. But it is there, and even the blank-faced boy or girl in the aisles in front of us may be touched in ways that baffle definition. We cannot control the effect of literature, cannot be sure that it is what the author wanted or what we think he wanted. . . . We bring the student and the book together and let the thing happen . . . rejoicing most of the time if anything at all happens that is perceptible.

Because there is often doubt that anything happens to the reader and because the effects of reading have not been explored as fully as some of the effects of the mass media, it is worthwhile to turn to this evidence from social psychology. A summary of the research made by Hovland[11] suggests that the four elements affecting the communication situation are:

1. The surface characteristics of the material read.
2. The content of ideas communicated.
3. The traits of the reader.
4. The environment or occasion for the reading.

[10] Hicks, Granville. "Assumptions in Literature," *English Journal,* 25:709–17, November 1936.

[11] Hovland, Carl I. "Effects of the Mass Media of Communication," *Handbook of Social Psychology,* Vol. 2 (G. Lindzey ed.). Cambridge, Massachusetts: Addison-Wesley, 1954, pp. 1062–1103.

In another article Klapper[12] suggests that the "process of effect" is "highly complex and not easily predictable." In an early study[13] of the effects of mass media he hypothesized the following:

1. "The major portion of mass media content today is devoted to material generally regarded by critics as being in poor taste. Material in good taste is nevertheless presented by all media."
2. "The audience reached by 'poor material' is much greater than that reached by 'good material.' . . . However, much of the audience for 'poor material' consumed no communicational material whatever prior to the advent of the mass media."
3. "Reading activity is correlated with degree of education. Movie viewing and radio listening are related to age. Radio (and television) draw from all cultural and age levels. Persons on various culture levels use each medium to satisfy their already established tastes. Thus mass media content largely selects its own audience." (The last statement assumes that free choice of type and material is possible.)
4. Since the mass media may be used as instruments for furthering already established behavior patterns, the media's content may be harmful to neurotics and other maladjusted persons.
5. Mass media can and do stimulate the development of good taste, especially with persons already predisposed to such development.
6. Each of the media may stimulate its audience to use related media. (A possible division between verbal and pictorial media, however, has been noted in later studies.)
7. Print, radio, screen (and television) each have unique advantages and disadvantages ascribed to them by various writers.
8. Escapist materials (defined as communications providing emotional release by diverting the user from his own problems or anxieties) are probably used less by persons who are highly socially aware. Such material "does not greatly change people's interests, but is rather used by individuals in accordance with their existing interests and behavior patterns."
9. "All mass media can and have been used effectively in persuasion. . . . attitude changes more often consist of modification than of conversion. . . . The condition believed to render persuasion most effective is monopoly propaganda position."
10. All mass media have been observed to *fail* in attempted persuasion. Failure may be reduced by offering new ways to answer existing needs, offering tangible and social rewards, exploiting prestige,

[12] Klapper, Joseph T. Studying Effects of Mass Communication, *Teachers College Record*, 57:95–103, November 1955.

[13] Klapper, Joseph T. *The Effects of Mass Media.* New York, Bureau of Applied Social Research, Columbia University, October 1950. (Mimeographed).

employing "repetition with variations," and supplementing mass media appeal by direct face-to-face contact.

These ten hypotheses have been suggested and in part verified by experiments with various types of mass media. Some of them seem applicable to the reading of literature in various forms.

In his study of the influences of television, Schramm[14] has presented somewhat more direct evidence of the effects of the newest of the mass media:

> When we talk about the effect of television, we are talking about how children use television. A child comes to television seeking to satisfy some need. He finds something there, and uses it . . . some increment of this choice enters into [his] funded experience, and ultimately into [his] understanding, values and behaviors.

As a result of eleven studies in different communities in the United States and Canada, Schramm avoided "good" and "bad" labels, but believed that any effect depends upon the nature of the child, the type of television program, and the kind of situation in which it was viewed. He defined the chief needs for which children go to television as the needs for *fantasy* and for *reality experiences,* and found the content of television programs to be directed overwhelmingly to the fantasy needs of children. Television, however, may affect learning, especially in the preschool years, and tends to raise the vocabulary scores of televiewers about one grade above nonviewers in the first grade. By the teens, when most children are using considerable amounts of printed materials, heavy televiewing is associated with lower school achievements. The emotional effects of television are more striking than its cognitive effects.

If results of careful studies of the effects of the mass media can be applied to the impact of reading, there is considerable hope for influencing people with various types of printed material. In a magazine-reading nation magazines may be classified as mass media. Wood[15] describes their effects as follows:

> For over 200 years American magazines have disseminated information and opinion. They have reported, commented, advised, entertained . . . they have influenced both the life of the nation and the lives of millions of individuals. . . . Magazines have affected American social, political, and economic thought. They have made their influence felt in government, commerce, and industry. They have stimulated the minds and imaginations of American readers, formed many of their ideas, affected their actions, fashioned their ethical and social concepts. . . .

Such exuberant statements must be considered in the light of more ob-

[14] Schramm, Wilbur L., Jack Lyle, and Edwin B. Parker. *Television in the Lives of Our Children.* Stanford: Stanford University Press, 1961.

[15] Wood, James Playstead. In James F. Fixx, *Magazines in the United States.* New York: Ronald Press, 1956, p. 376.

jective evidence. Elsewhere this writer has summarized some seventy researches on the impact of reading, and most of these are discussed in Part Two, entitled "Research Backgrounds." Studies of the communication process in social psychology suggest many hypotheses for parallel studies of the dynamics of the reading act. In turn, the old and new researches reported and the discussion in this book may be regarded as one contribution to social psychology concerned with the communication process.

## *The Impact on the Individual*

The eminent conductor, Bruno Walter,[16] once stated that "There is a certain fierce strength to be derived from music." Can literature have a similar effect? In *The Musical Experience* Sessions states that the roles of composer, performer, and listener overlap. Each contributes creatively if the total effect of the music is of high quality. Walt Whitman[17] has said "All music is what awakes from you when you are reminded by the instruments." Is the listener to music like the reader of a book? Can a parallel be drawn between music and literature in their demands and affects on the reader?

An autobiography, biography, and other writing occasionally testify to the influence of a poem, a book, or other imaginative literature on the individual. A few examples of such testimony are given in Chapter 2 as interesting anecdotes rather than historical or psychological evidence. Such writers as Jackson[18] have approached reading with emphasis upon the reader and a wide range of examples of possible effects. He states that reading evokes emotional responses, including boredom, but books "can help us to recover from ourselves, from our inner lives, qualities, treasure, which might otherwise go unheeded." Books "induce that sort of refreshment of the soul which corresponds with religious experience." But Jackson also states that in the testimonies to the power of books in the past "There is little attempt to go below the surface or to analyze the effect of reading on individual temperaments, the assumption being that books are good for you whoever you are."

The enthusiasms of the habitual and sophisticated reader must be subjected, if possible, to more exact analysis. No one experiment can analyze the breadth and charm of Jackson's appreciations or the ardor of other writers discussing certain books. Their reactions, however, can provide a

[16] "Bruno Walter; Poet of Conductors," *The New York Times Magazine,* September 9, 1956.

[17] Whitman, Walt. "*A Song for Occupations,*" Part 4, *Leaves of Grass,* (H. W. Blodgett and S. Bradley, eds.) New York: New York University Press, 1965, p. 215.

[18] Jackson, Holbrook. *The Reading of Books.* New York: Scribner, 1947, pp. 21, 33, and 37.

basis for accepting or rejecting such hypotheses as the following: "Not every 'good book' is good for every child"; "although reaction to literature is personal, response may be heightened by participation in group activities such as discussion, dramatization, or choral speaking"; and "feelings and ideas derived from literature will become permanent only if they are reinforced by other family, school or community activities."

The available evidence on the kinds of effects literature may have on the individual is meager. The data are even more meager in relation to such hypotheses as the three given above, but some of this evidence is summarized in Part Two and Chapter 9 of this book. We have discovered many facts about eye movements in reading, reading interests, and methods of reading instruction, but we do not know much about the effects of reading or, more objectively, the responses which are part of the reading act. Van Doren[19] has said that "The important thing about a poem is the reader," and Pasternak[20] stated that the biography of a poet is found in what happens to those who read him. Such insights may yield dividends in further exploration by empirical means. We need to know more about the factors influencing human behavior, and the parent and the English teacher need to know how reading will affect children and youth. One hypothesis, for example, is that children and adolescents will become habitual readers, in competition with other activities, only if reading fills some basic needs for information, for enjoyment, for escape, or for answers to deep-laid anxieties. Only as it contributes to personality will reading be given a place as part of an enduring pattern of activities. Only then will it go beyond the status of the superficial diversion to become part of the permanent activities of the individual.[21] Studies labeled "research" on such matters may be no more valid than the subtle insights of critic or teacher, but formal studies may help more people to understand and use some of the processes of response to writing.

Observations and research both suggest that the responses of the individual are usually determined by a group of factors rather than a single cause. The child's reaction to a film or story may be influenced by his age, sex, and previous experiences. The attitude he brings to the story about space travel or a foreign land may influence what he gets from the story. His personality traits, such as his readiness to accept or reject others' ideas and his general susceptibility to the influences of others, his "persuasability," may affect his responses to the printed message. Clusters of personality traits, rather than any single measures we now have, seem to be associated with particular types of response. These and other find-

[19] Van Doren, Mark. *The New York Times,* Book Review Section, April 19, 1953, p. 2.

[20] Pasternak, Boris. *Safe Conduct.* New York: New American Library (Signet Book), 1959.

[21] Russell, David H. "Some Research on the Impact of Reading," *English Journal, 47*:398–413, October 1958.

ings are analyzed in Chapter 5 to add to our knowledge of the possible impact on the reader.

## *Comprehension and Interpretation in Reading*

When John Q. Citizen picks up his evening newspaper or current magazine he hopes, probably unconsciously, to be informed about his community, his nation, or international matters, or to be amused by some facet of life therein. (He probably realizes that his chances of being amused by international affairs are much less than they are by the comic strip artist or syndicated columnist.) Later, especially if he does not switch on the television set, he may turn to do-it-yourself directions for a weekend project or to a pamphlet or book dealing with some aspect of his occupation or interests. In most of these activities he is concerned with the literal comprehension of what he reads. He wants to know the facts in the latest scandal, the events in Britain in relation to the Common Market, or the correct way to build a hothouse frame. But as he reads about a political speech or a new set of taxes he may find himself becoming angry. As he reads about juvenile delinquency he may experience a twinge of anxiety about his own family. As he reads a particularly well written story or book he experiences delight in the humor, the imagery, the language, or the train of ideas it starts. The news story, magazine article, or chapter in a book may evoke various kinds of emotion or thoughtful reaction beyond what is printed. His reading may include emotional response and various thinking processes which go beyond the specific meanings of the page to some sort of creative response, unique perhaps to John Q. himself.

These phenomena of the reader at his daily work or in the comparative peace of an evening or weekend at home suggest that it is worthwhile to distinguish two types of response to print. *Comprehension* is the process of getting meaning from the printed page as the author presents it, and *interpretation* occurs when the reader goes beyond literal meaning to add his own ideas and emotions. The two often overlap, and the first is usually a basis for the second. The first may be termed more accurately literal comprehension, the second is more an original discovery response and may be called creative reading.

Although creative reading involves more originality, it is not necessarily a better or higher type of reading than the first. In mixing the garden spray or ordering the hi-fi component from a catalogue, the householder wants to read as exactly and accurately as possible. Indeed, it may be useful to distinguish four levels[22] at which we often read:

1. Word identification – recognizing the words on the page without attaching much meaning to paragraph or passage.

[22] Russell, David H. *Children Learn to Read* (2d ed.). Boston: Ginn, 1961, p. 455.

2. Casual skimming – getting the main idea of a report or news story, sometimes to explore whether we want to read it more carefully.
3. Reading for literal comprehension – noting exact details, grasping a sequence of events, following a set of directions, and other activities of adhering to the printed text.
4. Creative reading – for implied and inferred meanings, for appreciative reactions, for critical evaluations of what is read, and sometimes for individual changes in ideas and personality.

The bulk of our reading is undoubtedly in the first three categories, but the most important reading we do may be in the fourth category, and is the concern of this book.

The distinguishing mark in these overlapping categories is not likely to be the material read so much as the purposes of the reader, conscious or unconscious. The same magazine article or story may be read for pleasure, for information, or for dreaming over. A factual article on nuclear fission is unlikely to evoke imaginative response, and a story of a southern town such as Harper Lee's *To Kill a Mockingbird* is not the best basis for factual, sociological data. However, the writer can never tell what the reader's response to his ideas will be. Perhaps the chief determiner of the responses or effects is the attitude or purpose with which the reader approaches the print. An early formulation of reactions to reading was proposed by Lind[23] from adults' reports of their childhood reading. She listed the following purposes or uses:

Reading as an escape – including fantasy, not always concealed.

Reading as temporary diversion – some identification with characters involving momentary thrill, sadness, and other emotions.

Reading in relation to objective interests – specific uses or instrumental effects.

Reading as organizing influence on personality – enjoying biography, and getting clues to one's own vocational interests, with some integrating effects.

Another early list of possible causes or effects of reading was given by Waples, Berelson, and Bradshaw[24] in *What Reading Does to People.* They listed five possible results of reading:

1. The instrumental effect – gaining greater competence in solving practical problems.
2. The prestige effect – relieving feelings of inferiority by reading material that increases self-approval.

[23] Lind, Katherine N. "Social Psychology of Children's Reading," *American Journal of Sociology, 41:*454–69, January 1936.

[24] Waples, Douglas, Bernard Berelson, and Franklyn R. Bradshaw. *What Reading Does to People.* Chicago: University of Chicago Press, 1940.

3. The reenforcement effect – strengthening one's attitudes or beliefs on controversial topics.
4. The respite effect – reading for escape and relaxation from tension.
5. The esthetic effect – enjoying beautifully written materials.

Unfortunately, Waples provided no quantitative data on the circumstances stimulating such effects, or on the frequency with which they can be observed in different kinds of readers.

Such formulations, however, are hypotheses which can be explored in the use of books in school, hospital, reading group, or other circumstances. Reading need not always be used, much of it simply should be enjoyed. But reading for enjoyment, in the broad sense, may be listed as one of the possible outcomes or effects of reading. Similarly, reading to inculcate moral lessons or to provide therapy for warped personalities may seem to be a hopelessly utilitarian approach to literature; nevertheless these additional benefits may sometimes go along with the appreciation of good writing. Accordingly, the fourth way of looking at the dynamics of reading may be through the eyes of teacher, clinician, or therapist who hope for such specific effects of literature as influencing ideas and values or increasing self-insight and social awareness.

## *Influencing Individuals Through Reading*

The therapist in Brown County Clinic or the English teacher in George Washington High is seldom satisfied when patient or student knows the author, the literary period represented, or the plot of a story, narrative poem, or novel. Somehow or other, therapist or teacher hopes to influence ideas and lives. The task is enormous in the case of a patient living within himself or the high school junior whose activities center on his basketball team, but still the responsible adult keeps trying. Every clinic worker tries for a positive influence on an individual's mental health, vague as that concept may be. At any educational level, from primary grades through college, the instructor attempts to involve the student in some of the most vivid experiences of man. These may be described, for example, in the relatively simple terms of Stevenson's "Land of Counterpane" (most children have been ill), in a novel of a teen-ager such as *Johnny Tremain,* by Wolfe in *Look Homeward, Angel,* by Camus in *The Stranger.* In every case, the teacher or therapist is not so much interested in the exact meaning of the phrase or the type of literary device used as in some sort of emotional impact on the reader, some contribution to a changing or growing system of ideas and values.

The use of books to increase self-understanding and social adjustment, described more fully in Chapter 9, may range from classrooms of normal children to deeply disturbed patients undergoing clinical treatment. The scientific basis of bibliotherapy is not yet fully established, although a theoretical basis has been provided by Shrodes,[25] and the method is practiced in a number of hospitals and clinics. The difference between classroom teaching and therapeutic treatment may be largely one of degree, for both have common goals of increasing self-understanding. In addition, the teacher of literature to a class or group may aim at part of a wide spectrum of desirable outcomes of acquaintance with literature and may therefore use a wider variety of writing to move toward the broader goals of understanding.

In both clinic and classroom there must be a basic search for information, a literal comprehension of facts and ideas upon which to build appreciative or self-referent reactions. The child, adolescent, or adult must, first of all, be able to read the material. Given this basis, the therapist and teacher tries for emotional as well as intellectual perceptiveness, for a wholeness and immediacy in comprehension, interpretation, and response. The rational and systematic are combined with the social-psychological in attitudes and feelings. Loban, Ryan, and Squire[26] write of literature for self-understanding, literature as imaginative illumination, and literature as balanced perspective. They suggest that the teacher must help students to perceive beauty in form which closely parallels content, to understand development in the structure of the narrative or logic of the characterization, and to explore meanings below the surface as found in theme, connotative use of words, imagery and other literary devices. But such intellectual awareness must be accompanied by genuine response in terms of search for further meaning, suspending judgment, weighing evidence, and fusing cognitive and connotative responses. Such experiences do not occur automatically in reading any more than they do in other behavior. They may occur when the teacher sets the stage and arranges for a few moments of quiet contemplation of idea or issue. Then self-insight, illumination, and some grasp of the universality of character or problem may occur.

Because children, adolescents, and adults differ so widely in their experience and their maturity of thought, a wide range of materials is needed in evoking response. One elementary schoolchild may find meanings in a simple story of family life in a reading textbook, another may be ready for the tug-of-war which, like Tom Sawyer, we all feel occasionally, between respectability as represented by Aunt Polly and the raffish life exemplified by Huck Finn. Some adolescents go through a short interval when a "'teen-age" novel such as Felsen's *Bertie Comes Through* or Daly's

[25] Shrodes, Caroline. *Bibliotherapy: A Theoretical and Clinical Experimental Study.* Unpublished Doctoral dissertation (University of California, Berkeley, 1949).

[26] Loban, Walter, Margaret Ryan, and James R. Squire. *Teaching Language and Literature.* New York: Harcourt, Brace, 1969.

*Seventeenth Summer* may strike them with telling impact. Some more mature classmates, and the same adolescents who earlier enjoyed Felsen or Daly, may be ready for the young person's problems of *The Red Badge of Courage,* the career decision of *Arrowsmith,* or the social problems of *A Raisin in the Sun.* In the high school and college years many students will be ready to react to some of the great literature of all time, or can be helped in attaining such readiness, but even here the problem of differences in ability and experience mean varied responses to the same masterpiece. One hallmark of a work of art is that it may be ambiguous or many-sided, that it may evoke a wide variety of responses in different people.

In the past, teachers have varied in their points of view on teaching the interpretation of literature. Many English teachers, especially at the high school and college level, have conceptualized their job largely as the teaching of the history, the types, and the criticism of literature. At the other end of a possible scale, a few teachers have emphasized the therapeutic values of literature in discovering solutions to one's own problems. One assumption has been the scholarly one – that adolescents should study literature as literature, that they should know some great writers and literary works and tell why they are great. The second assumption has been that good literature can influence personality, character, and behavior, that it can add meaning to such words as friendship, loyalty, courage, honesty, justice, faith, and truth. Perhaps the good teacher combines both approaches.

A good summary of the latter point of view in teaching English literature has been given by Rice:[27]

> If through literature a student can be helped to see reality and to attain maturity and depth in his feelings and ideas about life as well as some sense of human values and aspirations through time, he will have something against which to measure the present and determine what to do other than simply what the other kids on the block are doing. For example, Ring Lardner's short story "Haircut" can make a person who has grown up with and thoughtlessly accepted crude humor and brutality turn his eyes searchingly upon himself and his neighborhood. What he sees may be upsetting, but man must turn his eyes upon himself and examine his habits, his optimisms, his dreams, his rebellions.

The point of view of Rice and of this book is not that literature must be regarded as a grim assault on the individual's ideas, adjustments, and values. It does not always have to do good or change lives. The aim of teaching literature is not to develop a pseudo-psychological vocabulary of Oedipus complex, sibling rivalry, social mores, or patterns of parental rejection. Reactions to writing may be positive, negative, or indifferent. As early as the second grade children can be moved out of the indifferent

[27] Rice, Leonard W. "The Place of Literature in General Education," *Rhode Island College Journal, 1:*119–26, March 1961.

category to see something of the meaning or possible interpretations below the surface. Reading can be taught, not only as a world-identification skill, but as a meaning-getting process, with both literal and implied meanings involved. As their experience broadens, both children and adolescents can be helped to read creatively—to find beauty, humor and irony, to judge, to project, and to infer. We can do more to utilize the dynamics of reading behavior.

# CHAPTER 2 | Autobiographical Anecdotes

Many novelists, poets, and critics, like generals, feel a compulsion to write their memoirs. The records of literary people often include references to their childhood reading. Not all avid readers become writers, but it seems that most writers were once avid readers and like to recall how reading influenced them.

## *The Psychological Moment*

Such reports of events long past do not constitute evidence in the strict empirical sense but may give more insight into the effects of reading than many carefully controlled experiments. Memories of events forty or fifty years ago are easily distorted by time; nevertheless many of us, writers or not, can remember that "first fine careless rapture" when we raced through a book, excitement mounting with every chapter. A nine-year-old closes *The Wind in the Willows* and says with a sigh of regret for the end, "I think that is the best book I ever read." A fourteen-year-old discovers for himself some of the Sherlock Holmes stories and thinks there have never been better stories written. Many people somewhere between the poet and the general have had an illuminating, emotional, imaginative, indelible, and cataclysmic experience when reading. The results or memories may be hard to verify, but these intuitive effects of reading suggest phenomena which can be analyzed and perhaps studied experimentally.

Such experiences do not necessarily involve the world's great literature. *War and Peace* may be a profound experience for a mature reader but so may a Nancy Drew adventure or a Tarzan novel at a certain stage of development. The electric reaction to a story or poem may be response to trash, but the encounter was at the right time for the individual. There may be a psychological moment when writing matches reader. Many people have a favorite book that is remembered from childhood or youth, a book important less for itself than because it was read in a magic, unrecapturable time. We may reread the book years later and find the magic gone; fortunately some books have the capacity for maturing along with the reader.

At the age of sixty-seven Charles Darwin[1] wrote about his changing tastes as follows:

> Up to the age of thirty, or beyond it, poetry of many kinds, such as the works of Milton, Gray, Byron, Wordsworth, Coleridge, and Shelley, gave me no great pleasure, and even as a schoolboy I took great delight in Shakespeare, especially in the historical plays. . . . But now for many years I cannot endure to read a line of poetry: I have tried lately to read Shakespeare and found it so intolerably dull that it nauseated me. . . . On the other hand, novels which are a work of the imagination, though not of a very high order, have been for years a wonderful relief and pleasure to me, and I often bless all novelists.

Darwin accuses himself of a "loss of the higher aesthetic tastes" possibly injurious to the intellect "and more probably to the moral character, by enfeebling the emotional part of our nature." However, he was still able toward the end of his life to enjoy history, biography, and travel.

The matter of timing or readiness in one's reading may mean the difference between enjoyment and frustration, a developing love of reading or disgust, and a dislike of all books. We do not expect an elementary schoolchild to enjoy Thomas Mann or Jean Jacques Rousseau. However, the recommendation that children should occasionally have a chance to read a piece of literature they do not thoroughly understand may have some validity. The point is illustrated in an autobiographical note by R. G. Collingwood,[2] written when he was Waynflete Professor of Metaphysical Philosophy at Oxford:

> One day when I was eight years old curiosity moved me to take down a little black book lettered on its spine "Kant's Theory of Ethics" . . . as I began reading it, I was attacked by a strange succession of emotions. First came an intense excitement. . . . Then, with a wave of indignation, came the discovery that I could not understand them. . . . Then, third and last, came the strangest emotion of all. I felt that the contents of this book, although I could not understand it, were somehow of my business: a matter personal to myself, or rather to some future self of my own. It was not unlike the common boyish intention to "be an engine-driver when I grow up."

Of course not all eight-year-old boys grow up to be professors of metaphysical philosophy; nor is Kant recommended fare for all children. But the passage illustrates the point that we cannot be sure what happens in the reading process especially in the early years, with the most unlikely amalgam of reader and material.

[1] Barlow, Nora (ed.). *Charles Darwin's Life and Letters (rev. ed.)* London: Colliers, 1958.

[2] Collingwood, R. G. "An Autobiography 1939," in Margaret Bottrall (compiler), *Personal Records.* New York: John Day, 1962, pp. 72–73.

## *Personal Documents*

Personal documents such as diaries, letters, autobiographies, and biographies are sometimes of considerable interest to historians, sociologists, and psychologists as well as the merely curious. The quantity of such writing is almost overwhelming. Matthews[3] has issued separate bibliographies of *American Diaries* and *British Diaries,* the latter, for example, containing over two thousand entries up to 1942. Collections of letters by the famous or near famous are being edited and published every year. Kaplan's[4] *A Bibliography of American Autobiographies* up to 1945 lists over six thousand entries and does not include unpublished manuscripts or journals, diaries, or collections of letters. Biographies are standard items on publishers' lists. Allport[5] has suggested that such documents either "intentionally or unintentionally yield(s) information regarding the structure, dynamics and functioning of the author's mental life." He later adds that the many reasons for which persons write include exhibitionism, literary delight, relief from tension, therapy, monetary gain, and desire for literary immortality.

This chapter includes examples from several kinds of these personal documents, but the chief source lies in autobiographical anecdotes. These various types of writing are probably more alike than different, although on the surface differences are evident. For example, a diary is usually written for oneself, and an autobiography may be set down with an eye to publication, but diaries, too, may be published. Letters are directed to a reader or small group of readers and are likely to be influenced by the relationship between the correspondents. But both letters and autobiographies are likely to be more patterned, more influenced by a consistent point of view, than the day-to-day jottings of the diarist. On the surface, autobiography and biography differ in that one is usually witten in the first person, the other in the third person. A good autobiography is supposed to be subjective, a biography objective. On closer examination of the two kinds of writing, this distinction breaks down. Both involve selection of facts guided by the writer's view of the important or by an image he is trying to create. The characteristics developed by the biographer may be as subjective as those claimed by the autobiographer, as witnessed in the variety of traits emphasized by several biographers of the same person, such as Mary, Queen of Scots, or Queen Victoria. Because of the similarities among the different types of writing, it seems reason-

[3] Matthews, William. *British Diaries.* Berkeley and Los Angeles: University of California Press, 1950.

[4] Kaplan, Louis. *A Bibliography of American Autobiographies.* Madison: University of Wisconsin Press, 1961.

[5] Allport, Gordon. *The Use of Personal Documents in Psychological Science.* New York: Social Science Research Council, 1945.

able for the purpose of this chapter to utilize several sources of personal document, with emphasis upon autobiography.

The disadvantages in the use of personal documents should be noted as an aid to critical reading and thinking rather than a reason for elimination of sometimes weak evidence. Allport, for example, lists such psychological problems as the "unrepresentativeness of the sample" of writers and the fact that the validity of their statements is undetermined. He adds that the writers may be guilty of self-deception, oversimplification, and errors of memory. They may indulge in the "riding of hobbies." Perhaps most important is the arbitrariness of their selection of data, their limitation to terms they think are important or that contribute to the total picture. This last characteristic of autobiographical writing becomes particularly important when the writer attempts to associate cause and effect.

However, personal writing can contain unmatched resources, giving intimate descriptions of behavior. Allport states that such material contributes to a "concrete psychology" because it describes experiences of love, beauty, religious faith; of pain, ambition, fear, jealousy . . . fantasies and friendships." He adds that it gives information about the ego – the course and development of personality. Finally, biographical material may yield hunches or hypotheses about human behavior, providing specific data and inferential knowledge which may eventually lead to the prediction and general law desired by the scientists.

Accordingly, in autobiography and especially in biography, a conflict is likely between the demands on personal writing as an art and as a science. The biographer particularly must balance sympathetic insight with carefree scholarship. The student of autobiography should know something about the psychology of introspection, and the user of biography be aware of the point of view of the writer, whether Freudian, behaviorist, fictional, or debunking. Inconvenient facts can be ignored or minimized and equivocal facts interpreted to suit a theory, but these dangers are probably less in a reasonably overt or objective situation such as describing one's use of books than in self-analysis. Some of the best writing in autobiographies is about childhood years. Accounts of the pleasures of childhood, including reactions to stories and other literature, may have a quality of frankness possible when there are no axes to grind. The following sections give personal accounts of what reading has meant to the individual, with emphasis upon the influence of certain reading in the formative years.

## *Some of the Classic Autobiographies*

The first biographies were recorded in the form of autobiographies in Egyptian tombs five thousand years old or on the clay tablets and stone slabs of Assyria and Babylon dating back to 1400 B.C. The art of biography begins at least with Plutarch, who was born about the middle of the first century and who wrote his biographies in pairs, matching such warriors as Alexander and Julius Caesar, such orators as Demosthenes and Cicero. Plutarch was impartial, inaccurate by modern standards, and hero-worshipping. He stressed personal anecdotes and used the specific to prove the general. Plutarch's influence was not really felt until the days of the Renaissance, also the time of the first autobiography still widely read today. Benvenuto Cellini (1500–1571) was the son of a man who combined musicianship and engineering in the service of the Medici. The boy's early tutoring was accordingly on the flute, which he disliked, and his vocational education began when he became an apprentice to a goldsmith at the age of fifteen. By the age of sixteen he had been in at least one sword fight in the streets of Florence. In describing his boyhood he does not tell of learning to read and write. In his later years he got comfort from reading parts of the Bible in prison, but reading was not an important part of a life devoted to the other arts.

Boswell's *Life of Johnson* contains so many firsthand references that it seems almost autobiographical. Because Boswell was some thirty years younger than Johnson, he obviously could not record directly Johnson's earliest activities and conversation. The date of the beginning of their friendship was 1763 when Johnson was over fifty years of age. Early in his biography, however, Boswell[6] defends his short record of Johnson's childhood and youth because Johnson "from time to time obligingly satisfied my inquiries by communicating to me the incidents of his early years." Johnson learned to read in a Dame School in Lichfield and was a successful scholar there and in later schools. From the beginning he was an omnivorous reader with a marvellous memory. This reading was of an unorganized variety. Boswell[7] says:

> He used to mention one curious instance of his casual reading, when a boy. Having imagined that his mother had hid some apples behind a large folio upon an upper shelf in his father's shop, he climbed up to search for them. There were no apples; but the large folio proved to be Petrarch, whom he had seen mentioned in some preface, as one of the restorers of learning. His curiosity having thus been excited, he sat down with avidity, and read a great part of the book.

Of this miscellaneous reading in "all literature" Boswell further comments:

> He might, perhaps, have studied more assiduously, but it may be doubted whether such a mind as his was not more enriched by roaming at large in the fields of literature than if it had been confined to any single spot. . . . May there not be the same difference between men who read as their taste prompts and men who are confined in cells and colleges to stated tasks?

[6] Boswell, James. *Life of Johnson.* London: Oxford University Press, 1953, p. 19.

[7] Boswell, James, *Ibid.*, p. 44.

When writing of the years at Oxford, when Johnson was almost twenty, Boswell added a few recollections of childhood.

> He told me that from his earliest years he loved to read poetry, but hardly ever read any poem to an end; that he read Shakespeare at a period so early that the speech of the ghost in Hamlet terrified him when he was alone; that Horace's Odes were the compositions in which he took most delight. . . . He had a peculiar facility in seizing at once what was valuable in any book, without submitting to the labour of perusing it from beginning to end.

*The Autobiography of Benjamin Franklin* is usually considered one of the half dozen best known classics of the type. As a boy Ben had only a few months' schooling in Boston but records at an early age that "all the little Money that came into my hands was ever laid out in Books." His first purchase was Bunyan's *Pilgrim's Progress.* Franklin[8] wrote of a time a little later when

> There was also a Book of Defoe's called *An Essay on Projects,* and another of Dr. Mather's called *Essays to do Good* which perhaps gave me a Turn of Thinking that had an Influence on some of the principal future events of my life.
>
> This "Bookish Inclination" at length determined my Father to make me a Printer.

It is no surprise to anyone who has read Franklin's *Autobiography* to recall that the adolescent Ben, with his sense of practicality, also used his reading to good, utilitarian purpose. He describes how he discovered the third volume of the English journal, *The Spectator.*

> 'I bought it, read it over, and was much delighted with it. I thought the Writing excellent and wished if possible to imitate it.' After a few days wrote on the same topic and "then I compared my Spectator with the Original, discover'd some of my Faults and corrected them."[9]

There are many other references to Franklin's constant reading throughout the *Autobiography* but, as he grows older, less mention of specific effects or uses – and this may be true of others.

In one of the most introspective of autobiographies (in complete contrast to Cellini), Adams continually writes of the influences which affected him. In the first chapter of *The Education of Henry Adams,* covering the first ten years of his life from 1838 to 1848, he is affected not so much by stories or books as by his famous family ("his education was chiefly inheritance") and by the contrasting, even antithetical environment of Quincy and Boston. In the next six years he attributes most influence to his father and his father's friends, especially Charles Sumner. The young Henry detested school, had a "passionate hatred of school meth-

[8] Ferrand, Max (ed.). *Benjamin Franklin's Memoirs.* Berkeley and Los Angeles: University of California Press, 1949.

[9] Ferrand, Max (ed.). *Ibid.,* p. 36.

ods," and considered his school years from ten to sixteen as completely wasted.

Because of the influence of his Bostonian environment, one of Adams's[10] comments on it is included:

> Politics offered no difficulties, for there the moral law was a sure guide. Social perfection was also sure, because human nature worked for good, and three instruments were all she asked – Suffrage, Common Schools and Press. On these points doubt was forbidden. Education was divine and man needed only a correct knowledge of facts to reach perfection.

Adams believed his education was one-sided and makes the point that a literary education may result when other areas are neglected. He[11] says of his immediate family:

> The children reached manhood without knowing religion and with the certainty that dogma, metaphysics, and abstract philosophy were not worth knowing. So one-sided an education could have been possible in no other country or time, but it became, almost of necessity, the more literary and political.

And so, the years up to sixteen, before he went to Washington with his father, the Vice-President, Henry Adams writes of many hours spent in reading and of books as "the source of life." He read Thackeray, Dickens, Tennyson, Macaulay, Carlyle, and others as their books appeared, but the best times were spent with imaginative writing:

> "The happiest hours of the boy's education were passed in summer lying on a musty heap of Congressional Documents in the old farmhouse at Quincy, reading *Quentin Durward, Ivanhoe,* and *The Talisman* and raiding the garden at intervals for peaches and pears. On the whole he learned most then."[12]

Adams disliked all the schools he attended in his first sixteen years and felt that his education came from other sources. This feeling of no profit from formal education continued during 1854–1858 when he attended Harvard College, "a mild and liberal school." With the possible exception of hours spent in the study of James Russell Lowell and the lectures of Louis Agassiz, he felt that college "taught little, and that little ill, but it left the mind open, free from bias, ignorant of facts." (Reforms under President Eliot were to come later.) After Harvard, Berlin University was also a disappointment to Adams, but a subsequent visit to Rome meant much ("the month of May, 1860, was divine") in terms of tradition, art, and ideas. Then back to Boston, Washington, and war. Henry Adams was one writer who read widely but who records few specific literary works which influenced his early life and "education."

[10] Adams, Henry. *The Education of Henry Adams.* Boston: Houghton Mifflin, 1918.

[11] Adams, Henry. *Ibid.,* p. 35.

[12] Adams, Henry. *Ibid.,* p. 39.

## *Reminiscences of Writers: Early Childhood*

As Edel[13] has pointed out in *Literary Biography*, in recent years there have been detailed definitions of the craft of fiction but a singular lack of study of the theory and practice of biography, including autobiography. Studies by such men as Harold Nicolson, Donald Stauffer, and Wayne Shumaker tend to be neglected. Some of the practical problems of the writing of biography have been analyzed by the historian, John A. Garraty,[14] in *The Nature of Biography*. But there is little general acceptance of principles involved in such matters as sampling, the search for significant facts, the interrelationships of personality and biography, the conflicting claims of biography as an art or a science (Virginia Woolf called it a *craft*), or the relations between biography and autobiography and biography and criticism. Because of such doubts and difficulties, this section is entitled "Reminiscences" and is an anecdotal account of unsystematic reading and recording rather than a coherent view of biography and autobiography as art or science or both. Isolated examples or illustrations of the dynamics of reading are presented; that is, what the reading of certain books has meant to varied individuals who themselves became writers.

Perhaps children are most impressionable when they are very young and have not learned to read. The influence of the storyteller has been a powerful one for many individuals and in many cultures. The boy born in humble circumstances who became the foremost poet of his people tells of such influences in Robert Burns'[15] letter written in 1787 to Dr. Moore:

> In my infant and boyish days, too, I owe much to an old woman who resided in the family, remarkable for her ignorance, credulity and superstition. She had, I suppose, the largest collection in the country of tales and songs concerning devils, ghosts, fairies, brownies, witches, warlocks, spunkies, kelpies, elf-candles, dead-lights, wraiths, apparitions, cantraips, giants, uncharted towers, dragons, and other trumpery. This cultivated the latent seeds of poetry.

At a later time the story had not lost its power. In one of the best known American biographies, Paine[16] wrote of Mark Twain's early childhood:

> It was Jennie, the house-girl, and Uncle Ned, a man of all work – apparently acquired with the improved prospects – who were in real charge of the children and supplied them with entertainment. Wonderful entertainment it was. That was a time of visions and dreams, small gossip and superstitions. Old

[13] Edel, Leon. *Literary Biography*. Garden City, New York: Doubleday Anchor Books, 1959.

[14] Garraty, John A. *The Nature of Biography*. New York: Knopf, 1957.

[15] Burns, Robert. In *Library of Masterpieces of Autobiography*, Vol. 4. (George Iles, ed.). New York: Doubleday, 1913, pp. 46–47.

[16] Paine, Albert Bigelow. *Mark Twain, a Biography*. New York: Harper, 1912, p. 15.

tales were repeated over and over, with adornments and improvements suggested by immediate events. At evening the Clemens children, big and little, gathered about the great open fireplace while Jennie and Uncle Ned told tales and hair-lifting legends. Even a baby of two or three years could follow the drift of this primitive telling and would shiver and cling close with the horror and delight of its curdling thrill.

Robert P. Tristram Coffin[17] tells how he imitated his father's declamation, and also how some of the classics became part of himself:

But ducks and geese and turnips weren't the only things Peter's father had on his farm. He had books, too. He had a whole room full of them. His favorite book was the Shakespeare one, but he could say a lot of *Paradise Lost* too. He used to go on for hours. Peter got the habit from him. He could say a lot of poetry at a stretch too. And he started out reading every minute he could. . . . The Shakespeare book was worn loose at its back by Peter and his father. The boy would lie on his elbows and listen to his father speaking in Gaunt's voice about England and Kings and death. Kings and death were favorite subjects of his father, when he got heated up and solemn. Peter had rather hear his father read Shakespeare than strum his guitar and sing Belle Brandon, even. And Peter loved that song. Peter's father had said Shakespeare to him long before he knew what half the words were about. Peter knew from the first, though, that they were about something fine. They sounded like a south gale making the pines roar on a January night. They sounded like the thunder of the mile of surf on Pond Island ledges. They came up from something deep.

> "For God's sake, let us sit upon the ground
> And tell sad stories of the death of kings:
> How some have been deposed, some slain in war,
> Some haunted by the ghosts they have deposed,
> Some poisoned by their wives, some sleeping killed;
> All murdered: for within the hollow crown
> That rounds the mortal temples of a king
> Keeps Death his court. . . ."

That was the way Peter dreamed the world was going to be. Strange and deep and sad, and yet like a kind of music. Some day he would know all about it. Now it was enough to hear his father's deep voice going on and on like a prophecy in the night.

It was those books on the farm that had got Peter started off thinking and acting books out underneath the tall trees, and the story-stick had come out of them. And part of every breath that Peter drew.

Padraic Colum[18] too has paid his respects to the oral tradition:

There in my grandmother's house, I heard stories before I read them and songs and scraps of poetry before I had to learn any at school. I was fortunate, I believe, in getting this sort of oral knowledge which left me with an interest in legends and traditions.

In such lines Colum and other writers suggest that early influences

[17] Coffin, Robert P. Tristram. *Lost Paradise*. New York: Macmillan, 1934, p. 258.

[18] Colum, Padraic. Autobiographical Sketch in *The Junior Book of Authors* (2d ed.). New York: H. W. Wilson, 1951, p. 76.

helped develop interests which lasted a lifetime. Put another way, early exposure to literature can produce both immediate emotional response and a more permanent interest which may have utility in the years to come. In the *Poetic Principle,* Poe argued that "All excitements are, through a psychological necessity, transient," and believed that half an hour was the time limit for "that degree of excitement which would entitle to be so called at all." But the effects of some poems and other literature may last a lifetime. It is perhaps logical to expect that these effects may be especially true of people who themselves become writers for children and youth.

## *Anecdotes by Writers of "Juveniles"*

It is doubtful if there should be separate categories of books for children and books for adults. Children are not a separate species, and many books which are beloved by children are equally accepted by grown-ups. As Hugh Lofting,[19] author of the *Dr. Doolittle* stories, has put it, "Practically all children want to be grown up and practically all grown-ups want to be children." It is still true, however, that many of the authors of books classed as "juveniles" or "teen-age stories" have paid tribute to the power of books in their early lives. Some of these writers do so in short autobiographies in *The Junior Books of Authors* and *More Junior Authors.* In brief accounts many testify to the effects of having a parent read aloud the classics of childhood. Others learned to read at an early age and began to enjoy books at a time when their peers were largely engaged in play. Mary Jane Carr,[20] author of *Children of the Covered Wagon,* tells how her father used to read to his nine children on winter evenings. "He read both poetry and prose, always from the classics, and long before I was able to understand the meaning of the words, I loved the rhythm and music of poetry." Some of the authors cannot remember when they learned to read and can testify with Ben Franklin[21] about "my early Readiness in learning to read (which must have been very early, as I do not remember when I could not read)."

Some writers of books for the young were themselves influenced by literature at a later age. Robert Louis Stevenson was an invalid much of his childhood and was undoubtedly influenced by his faithful nurse, Alison Cunningham, and the stories she read to him. But it was when he was a young man writing in the south of France that he came across a book of

[19] Lofting, Hugh. Autobiographical Sketch in *The Junior Book of Authors.* New York: H. W. Wilson, 1935, p. 238.

[20] Carr, Mary Jane. Autobiographical Sketch in *The Junior Book of Authors* (2d ed.). New York: H. W. Wilson, 1951, p. 66.

[21] Ferrand, Max (ed.). *Benjamin Franklin's Memoirs.* Berkeley and Los Angeles: University of California Press, 1949, p. 18.

childhood verses by Kate Greenaway. These inspired him to write about his own childhood in *A Child's Garden of Verses.* Similarly James Daugherty,[22] the author and illustrator, testifies to the influence of a book when he had spent about two years in Europe at the age of eighteen to twenty. He testifies, "In London I first read Walt Whitman and took fire from his vision of America, and shook the dust of Europe permanently from my feet and returned to the States."

The testimony to the influence of books appears briefly in many other autobiographical sketches. For example, Marcia Brown,[23] author and illustrator, notes that "Reading was the main entertainment of our family, the public library being a second home. Fairly tales – Anderson, Perrault, Grimm and the *Arabian Nights* – were favorites and still are." Miss Brown has since illustrated a child's book of the *Arabian Nights.* The biography of Wesley Dennis,[24] author and illustrator of many horse stories such as *Misty of Chincoteaque* and *King of the Wind,* declares his belief in the influence of the movies. "One day he saw a newsreel that changed his whole life. It was of a polo game and the young Wesley did not rest until he found out all about it." Robert Heinlein,[25] writer of science fiction for both adults and youth (*Red Planet, Rocket Ship Galileo,* and so on) states, "As a youngster I was addicted to the stories of Jules Verne and H. G. Wells; as an oldster I try to emulate them." Although such direct influences seem to be rarer than the more general influences of hearing and reading stories, Carol Brink[26] contributes one more example of a one-to-one influence. "The book children love best, however, is *Caddie Woodlawn.* . . . It is based on the stories I loved so much when I was a little girl, the stories of my grandmother's girlhood."

Here again what the psychologist would call the sample is not typical of all people. These are men and women who grew up to be authors and illustrators of books for children and teen-agers. The elements of cause and effect are mixed, but there is no question of the influence of the oral tradition and early reading on the minds and hearts of some boys and girls. Examples such as those given rank second only to those describing the influence of natural surroundings and the outdoor environment on youthful development. It may be that children who grow up to be writers are more sensitive to such influences, or it may be that adults who write

[22] Daugherty, James. Autobiographical Sketch in *The Junior Book of Authors.* New York: H. W. Wilson, 1935, p. 113.

[23] Brown, Marcia. Autobiographical Sketch in *More Junior Authors.* New York: H. W. Wilson. 1963, p. 32.

[24] Dennis, Wesley. Biographical Sketch in *More Junior Authors* (Muriel Fuller, ed.) New York: H. W. Wilson, 1963, p. 64.

[25] Heinlein, Robert A. Autobiographical Sketch in *More Junior Authors.* New York: H. W. Wilson, 1963, p. 159.

[26] Brink, Carol. Autobiographical Sketch in *Junior Book of Authors* (2d ed.). New York: H. W. Wilson, 1951, p. 46.

for youth have selective memories about their childhood. Whatever the case, belief in the influence of books is clearly documented.

## *Reminiscences: Utilitarian Effects*

We read newspapers, magazines, and books for the information they give. Permanent, even lifetime effects of reading may relate to interests and to choice of career. Such effects combine emotional response plus a certain commitment to idea and ideal. One chain of circumstances in such an effect involved John Muir, the naturalist, and Charles Darwin, the scientist. Muir claimed that his whole life was changed and directed by reading one book, Darwin's *The Origin of Species.* Darwin[27] himself paid a tribute to the influence of one book on his choice of a future career:

> Early in my school days a boy had a copy of the *Wonders of the World* which I often read, and disputed with other boys about the veracity of some of his statements; and I believe that this book first gave me a wish to travel in remote countries, which was ultimately fulfilled by the voyage of the *Beagle.*

In the American setting, about 1900, of a small Illinois village and farm, Mark Van Doren[28] related how his brother Carl's future career was influenced by one book: "Carl's teacher had given him at nine, the year I was born, no less a prize than Green's *History of the English People* in four volumes . . . which had a great deal to do with his becoming what he was when he grew up, a professional reader and writer."

Carl Van Doren in *Three Worlds* also mentioned the influence of Green's *History;* in addition, he wrote of more general utilitarian values of reading. Because of his reading, a background of a prairie farm and village was no handicap in later years at the University of Illinois and in New York literary circles. Van Doren, like many others, pays tribute to reading as experience:

> I can barely remember when I could not read, and except in the most crowded seasons (on the farm) I read hours a day. . . . We read greedily and uncritically. A book was a book, and it was interesting or it was not. We liked Dickens and Mark Twain best and David Copperfield and Huckleberry Finn best of all . . . Reading was simply experience otherwise denied us. We traveled without leaving Hope. When later we did leave, life was not so strange as we expected. Books had enlarged the village.[29]

In a setting quite different from the Illinois prairie, Lewisohn[30] com-

[27] Darwin, Charles. In *Library of Masterpieces of Autobiography,* Vol. 3. (George Iles, ed.). New York: Doubleday, 1913, pp. 8–9.

[28] Van Doren, Mark. *The Autobiography of Mark Van Doren.* New York: Harcourt, Brace, 1958.

[29] Van Doren, Carl. *Three Worlds.* New York: Harper, 1936, pp. 49–50.

[30] Lewisohn, Ludwig. *Up Stream.* New York: Boni and Liveright, 1922, pp. 132–33.

ments on the utilitarian value of reading in developing one's own writing style, not in mere imitation, but in some understanding of what makes good imaginative writings:

> What I needed next was a method. I had never studied closely the technique of modern fiction. A very sure instinct led me to Henry James, to the clear, brimming stories of his middle years: "The Lesson of the Master," "Broken Wings," "The Altar of the Dead." I soon knew what, for my purpose I needed to know. I didn't, I must say in justice to myself, imitate Henry James at all. But no one with the craftsman's insight can read these stories — I lingered over about fifteen — without learning from that close and scrupulous master the essential secrets of imaginative narrative.

Maugham[31] had little conventional schooling but, as a youth, travelled widely and read voraciously. His craftsmanship in writing seems to have been due, in part at least, to his reading while he was living in Paris. He makes it clear he did not imitate directly but that he was influenced by de Maupassant.

> It was the novels and short stories of Guy de Maupassant that had most influence on me when I set myself to write. I began to read them when I was sixteen. . . . Though he does not enjoy now the reputation that he did then it must be admitted that he had great merits. He was lucid and direct, he had a sense of form, and he knew how to get the utmost dramatic value out of the story he had to tell. I cannot but think that he was a better master to follow than the English novelists who at that time influenced the young.

In addition to specifics such as vocational choice, elements of experience and techniques of writing, books may have an effect on interests and tastes which come somewhere between utilitarian and emotional responses. A number of the testimonies quoted here suggest the development of criteria or standards which influenced the habits of a lifetime. H. L. Mencken[32] learned to read at an early age and gives a negative example, probably not so much of a "natural taste" as one acquired in his family environment:

> But pretty soon I was again feeling the powerful suction of beautiful letters . . . and before Christmas I was sweating through the translation of Grimms' *Fairy Tales* that had been bestowed upon, "for industry and good deportment" at the closing exercises of F. Knapp's Institute on June 28. This volume had been put into lame, almost pathological English by a lady translator, and my struggles with it awoke in me the first faint mutterings of the critical faculty. Just what was wrong with it I couldn't of course make out, for my gifts had not yet flowered, but I was acutely and unhappily conscious that it was much harder going than "The Moose Hunters," and after a month or so of unpleasantly wrestling with it, I put it on the shelf. There it remained for more than fifty years. Indeed, it was not until the appearance of "Snow White" as a movie that I took it down and tried it again, and gagged at it again.

[31] Maugham, W. Somerset. *The Summing Up.* New York: Doubleday, Doran, 1938, p. 163.

[32] Mencken, H. L. *Happy Days.* New York: Knopf, 1947, pp. 160–62.

I was born, in truth, without any natural taste for fairy tales, or, indeed, for any other writing of a fanciful and unearthly character. The fact explains, I suppose, my lifelong distrust of poetry. No doubt the same infirmity was responsible for the feebleness of my appetite for the hortatory and incredible juvenile fiction fashionable in my nonage – the endless works of Oliver Optic, Horatio Alger, Harry Castlemon and so on. I tried this fiction more than once, for some of the boys I knew admired it vastly, but I always ran aground in it. So far as I can recall, I never read a single volume of it to the end, and most of it finished me in a few pages.

Of course, not all families influenced tastes in positive imitation. C. S. Lewis,[33] medieval scholar, critic, and author of children's books, says of his parents: "What neither he [his father] nor my mother had the least taste for was that kind of literature to which my allegiance was given the moment I could choose books for myself. Neither had ever listened for the horns of elfland."

Coffin[34] gives another example of the fact that not everyone agrees to the utility of books, specifically or generally, even in families that produce poets and other writers. He describes the attitude of his older brother, Edward, when they were still both boys:

"Books," said Edward, "are about as much use as a last year's crow's nest." He would pry into Peter's drawers and unearth one of the books he had written. He would read it aloud to Peter and poke fun at him. "No more use than a trimmed nightie."

Contrary to Edward Coffin's point of view, some writers have found excitement and utility in the most workaday materials. Erskine Caldwell[35] illustrates the point:

Of my three most prized material possessions – typewriter, cigarette-making machine, and dictionary – I valued the dictionary by far the highest and would have certainly endeavored to hold on to it the longest. I not only consulted it frequently, but in my free time I read the dictionary instead of reading novels and magazines; in my estimation, nothing had been written that was as fascinating, provocative, instructive, and fully satisfying as a book of words and their alluring meanings.

In contrast to the imaginative work, a factual book, whether dictionary or text, may sometimes have considerable impact on the reader in satisfying curiosity and in directing future interests. Perhaps Carl Sandburg's[36] comments are as typical as any of the hundreds of writers who attest to the effects of informational materials. In *Always the Young Strangers* he writes of the depression days before the turn of the century

[33] Lewis, C. S. *Surprised by Joy.* London: Geoffrey Bles, 1955, p. 12.

[34] Coffin, Robert P. Tristram. *Lost Paradise.* New York: Macmillan. 1934, p. 23.

[35] Caldwell, Erskine. *Call It Experience.* New York: Duell, Sloan and Pearce, 1951, p. 134.

[36] Sandburg, Carl. *Always the Young Strangers.* New York: Harcourt, Brace, 1953, p. 225.

when he was a young adolescent and helped the family by earning twelve dollars a month on a milk delivery wagon. But he still found time to read some of his sister Mary's high school texts:

> The great book Mary brought home – great for what it did to me at that particular time, opening my eyes about law, government, history, and people – was *Civil Government in the United States* by John Fiske. Here for the first time I read answers to many questions: What are taxes? Who has the taxing power?, etc. This led to other reading, the Constitution of the United States, the Magna Carta, the speech of Ben Franklin on the Constitution, political columns in a local newspaper.

As well as developing particular interests through factual books, Sandburg is typical of many writers in describing other effects which merge from the utilitarian into the imaginative. He suggests that poetry can give a certain "comfort" and that fiction based on fact may lead to experiences of emotion tinged with imagination. He writes of when he was in the sixth grade in Galesburg with a good teacher:

> We read Gray's "Elegy in a Country Churchyard." I learned it by heart and never forgot five or six of the verses. They had a music that stayed with me and was many times a comfort. . . .
>
> Best of all was the American history series by Charles Carleton Coffin. *The Boys of '76* I read three or four times and some chapters a dozen times. The book made me feel I could have been a boy in the days of George Washington and watched him on a horse, a good rider sitting easy and straight, at the head of ragged soldiers with shotguns. I could see Paul Revere on a horse riding wild and stopping at farm houses to holler the British were coming.[37]

Thus, in one short passage, Sandburg illustrates the three responses of obtaining reassurance through familiar literature, identifying with characters in a story, and evoking mental images of persons and places. Factual benefits and emotional responses are often not far apart.

## *Imaginative Response*

What we have called the utility of books finds expression in various ways, and there are many types of imaginative response to fiction, poetry, and even factual material. We call these responses fantasy, escape, wish-fulfillment, identification, and imagery. Sometimes the response results in childish terrors, sometimes in lifetime purposes. In a letter to Thomas Poole, written in 1807, Coleridge[38] describes a mixture of identification, escape, and delusions:

> So I became fretful, and timorous, and a tell-tale; and the schoolboys drove

[37] Sandburg, Carl. *Ibid.*, pp. 114–15.

[38] Coleridge, S. T. in Margaret Bottrall (compiler), *Personal Records.* New York: John Day, 1962, pp. 24–25.

me from play, and were always tormenting me. And hence I took no pleasure in boyish sports, but read incessantly. I read through all the gilt-cover little books that could be had at that time, and likewise all the uncovered books of Tom Hickathrift, Jack the Giant Killer and the like. And I used to lie by the wall, and mope; and my spirits used to come upon me suddenly, and in a flood; . . . and then I was accustomed to run up and down the churchyard, and act over again all I had been reading on the docks, the nettles, and the rank grass. At six years of age I remember to have read Belisarius, Robinson Crusoe, and Philip Quarles; and then I found the Arabian Nights' Entertainments, one tale of which (the tale of a man who was compelled to seek for a pure virgin,) made so deep an impression on me, (I had read it in the evening while my mother was at her needle,) that I was haunted by spectres, whenever I was in the dark; and I distinctly recollect the anxious and fearful eagerness with which I used to watch the window where the book lay, and when the sun came upon it, I would seize it, carry it by the wall, and bask, and read. My father found out the effect which these books had produced, and burnt them.

Different writers have pointed out that imaginative writing has more power to move the reader, to evoke emotional response, than factual or oratory writing. In telling of the ways in which fiction touches us, Stevenson[39] first gives an intellectual analysis of what may happen but then describes how he surrendered to the imaginative in drama and especially in comedy:

The most influential books, and the truest in their influence, are works of fiction. They do not pin the reader to a dogma, which he must afterward discover to be inexact; they do not teach him a lesson, which he must afterward unlearn. They repeat, they rearrange, they clarify the lessons of life; they disengage us from ourselves, they constrain us to the acquaintance of others; and they show us the web of experience, not as we can see it for ourselves, but with a singular change – that monstrous, consuming *ego* of our being, for the nonce, struck out. To be so, they must be reasonably true to the human comedy; and any work that is so serves the turn of instruction. But the course of our education is answered best by those poems and romances where we breathe a magnanimous atmosphere of thought and meet generous and pious characters. Shakespeare has served me best. Few living friends have had upon me an influence so strong for good as Hamlet or Rosalind. The last character, already well beloved in the reading, I had the good fortune to see, I must think, in an impressionable hour, played by Mrs. Scott Siddons. Nothing has ever more moved, more delighted, more refreshed me; nor has the influence quite passed away.

Reading was an imaginative experience of a healthier sort than Coleridge's for C. S. Lewis[40] at an early age:

Of the books that I read at this time very few have quite faded from memory, but not all have retained my love. Conan Doyle's *Sir Nigel*, which first set my mind upon "knights in armour," I have never felt inclined to reread. Still less would I now read Mark Twain's *Yankee at the Court of King Arthur*. . . .

[39] Stevenson, Robert Louis. "Books Which Have Influenced Me," *Little Masterpieces of Autobiography*, Vol. 4. (George Iles, ed.). New York: Doubleday, 1913, pp. 148–49.

[40] Lewis, C. S. *Surprised by Joy*. London: Geoffrey Bles, 1955, pp. 20–21.

Much better than either of these was E. Nesbit's trilogy, *Five Children and It, The Phoenix and the Wishing Carpet,* and *The Amulet.* The last did most for me. It first opened my eyes to antiquity, the "dark backward and abysm of time." I can still re-read it with delight. . . .

It will be clear that at this time – at the age of six, seven and eight – I was living almost entirely in my imagination; or at least that the imaginative experience of those years now seems to me more important than anything else.

A little later, when attending his first preparatory school, a place like something out of Dickens or Orwell, Lewis[41] suggests an experience that may be fairly common. After some of the good books of a well-stocked home library, the only fare at a school without a library was largely trash.

My reading was now mainly rubbish. . . . I read twaddling school stories in *The Captain.* The pleasure here was, in the proper sense, mere wish-fulfillment and fantasy; one enjoyed vicariously the triumphs of the hero. When a boy passes from nursery literature to school-stories he is going down, not up. *Peter Rabbit* pleases a disinterested imagination . . . but the story of the unpromising boy who became captain of the First Eleven exists precisely to feed his real ambitions.

Fortunately, imaginative response, with its tremendous scope, can go far beyond wish-fulfillment. Paine tells of an incident which evoked Mark Twain's imaginative response and, indeed, influenced his intellectual interests for the rest of his life. As a young man learning the printer's trade, Mark Twain was simply walking along the street one day. As Paine[42] describes it:

There came into his life just at this period one of those seemingly trifling incidents which, viewed in retrospect, assume pivotal proportions. He was on his way from the office to his home one afternoon when he saw flying along the pavement a square of paper, a leaf from a book. At an earlier time he would not have bothered with it at all, but any printed page had acquired a professional interest for him now. He caught the flying scrap and examined it. It was a leaf from some history of Joan of Arc. The "maid" was described in the cage at Rouen, in the fortress, and the two ruffian English soldiers had stolen her clothes. There was a brief description and a good deal of dialogue – her reproaches and their ribald replies.

He had never heard of the subject before. He had never read any history. When he wanted to know any fact he asked Henry, who read everything obtainable. Now, however, there arose within him a deep compassion for the gentle Maid of Orleans, a burning resentment toward her captors, a powerful and indestructible interest in her sad history. It was an interest that would grow steadily for more than a half a lifetime and culminate at last in that crowning work, the *Recollections,* the loveliest story ever told of the martyred girl.

The incident meant even more than that: it meant the awakening of his interest in all history – the world's story in its many phases – a passion which became the largest feature of his intellectual life and remained with him until

[41] Lewis, C. S. *Ibid.*, p. 40.

[42] Paine, Albert Bigelow. *Mark Twain, a Biography.* New York: Harper, 1912, pp. 81–82.

his very last day on earth. From the moment when that fluttering leaf was blown into his hands his career as one of the world's mentally elect was assured.

Perhaps such an event was more than imaginative response and could be classified as one of those times when reading seems to have some sort of integrated impact on total personality and intellectual output. There are simpler examples of writing leading to imaginative response in the form of imagery. In his autobiographical *John Mistletoe,* Christopher Morley[43] tells of one example of imagery included here, not because it is esoteric so much as for its unique, homely quality. He writes:

> That, I think, was Mistletoe's fullest introduction to the joys of secret reading. Its nearest competition was hearing the *Jungle Book* read aloud when it first appeared in 1894, and being given a paper-bound piracy of *Treasure Island* to read when in bed with an ear-ache, a hot baked onion crackling and stewing under his cheek. (*Treasure Island* still smells faintly of onions in his mind.)

Not all imagery is so idiosyncratic. Lewis's description of reaction to a poem may be more typical of the wide range of pictures and feelings evoked by poetry. Lewis[44] describes his experience in these words:

> Much the most important thing that happened to me at Campbell [another boys' school] was that I there read *Sohrab and Rustum* in form under an excellent master whom we called Octie. I loved the poem at first sight and have loved it ever since. As the wet fog, in the first line, rose out of the Oxus stream, so out of the whole poem there rose and wrapped me around an exquisite, silvery coolness, a delightful quality of distance and calm, a grave melancholy. . . .

Mountains and prairies, log cabins and palaces, sober adult and merry child, melodies and harmonies, delicious smells and prickly touches all may be evoked by writing, especially if it relates to experiences of childhood and youth. Such memories and images may be part of a more highly charged response.

## *"The Whole World Changed"*

Among other topics, Chapter 8 discusses reading as impact, as a tremendous occasion affecting not only information and experience but influencing personality, beliefs, and values. The content of reading matter is often commonplace and easily forgotten, but a few times in one's life it may provide excitement, shock, realization. Here is some idea stated or illustrated towards which one has been stumbling but which is now clearly delineated and integrated. Here is some half-formed belief which

[43] Morley, Christopher. *John Mistletoe.* Garden City; New York: Doubleday, Doran, 1931, p. 17.

[44] Lewis, C. S. *Surprised by Joy.* London: Geoffrey Bles, 1955, p. 56.

suddenly becomes crystal clear and which may influence one's life for years to come. Here is some idea so tremendous that one must continue to explore and analyze it for a long time.

Such impelling forces or conversion experiences may be unusual in the general population, but occur occasionally in the reminiscences of persons who are or become writers. Perhaps these experiences have occurred with most literate people, but writers are more articulate about them. Certainly these moments have come to many types of persons reading many kinds of material. In *John Mistletoe*, Christopher Morley[45] comments on the phenomenon:

> . . . then one thinks of the moment when some young high school girl, some eager college boy, some fashionable young matron, find their ways for the first time into some book of genuine truth and beauty, see the world momentarily anew and feel the glow of that immortal heat when we know ourselves collaborators with Destiny in the endless fashioning of life. What does it matter in what particular volume they first encounter that moment of millenium? It may be some little Everyman copy of *Walden*, some play like Ibsen's *Wild Duck*, some liberalizing essayist like Matthew Arnold, or some marvelous old-timer like Thomas Fuller – hard to find, but worth search.

Under the pseudonym of Peter Porcupine, the English journalist, William Cobbett,[46] describes such an awakening as "a sort of birth of intellect," an experience here related to reading some of Jonathan Swift:

> Two pennyworth of bread and cheese, and a pennyworth of small beer, which I had on the road, and one halfpenny that I had lost somewhere or other, left three pence in my pocket. With this for my whole fortune, I was trudging through Richmond, in my blue smock-frock and my red garters tied under my knees, when, staring about me, my eye fell upon a little book, in a bookseller's window: *Tale of a Tub:* price 3*d.* The title was so odd, that my curiosity was excited. I had the 3*d.* but, then, I could have no supper. In I went and got the little book, which I was so impatient to read, that I got over into a field, at the upper corner of Kew Gardens, where there stood a haystack. On the shady side of this, I sat down to read. The book was so different from anything that I had ever read before; it was something so new to my mind, that though I could not at all understand some of it, it delighted me beyond description and it produced what I have always considered a sort of birth of intellect. I read on till it was dark, without any thought about supper or bed. When I could see no longer, I put my little book in my pocket, and tumbled down by the side of the stack, where I slept till the birds of Kew Garden awakened me in the morning; when off I started to Kew, reading my little book.

Two excerpts from C. S. Lewis[47] illustrate the impact of a tremendous reading experience at two different times. When he was doing his first

[45] Morley, Christopher. *John Mistletoe.* Garden City; New York: Doubleday; Doran, 1931, p. 291.

[46] Cobbett, William. *Life and Adventure of Peter Porcupine,* in Margaret Bottrall (compiler), *Personal Records.* New York: John Day, pp. 49, 50.

[47] Lewis, C. S. *Surprised by Joy.* London: Geoffrey Bles, 1955, pp. 22–23.

reading at home he tells of the influence of one of Beatrix Potter's charming and apparently simple stories:

> The second glimpse came through *Squirrel Nutkin;* through it only, though I loved all the Beatrix Potter books. But the rest of them were merely entertaining; it administered the shock, it was a trouble. It troubled me with what I can only describe as the Idea of Autumn . . . in this experience also there was the same surprise and the same sense of incalculable importance. It was something quite different from ordinary life and even from ordinary pleasure; something, as they would now say, "in another dimension."

From this early period of his life, Lewis[48] had also developed an interest in Norse mythology, but for years, away from home in poor schools, this interest was dormant. But the ground was prepared, however, and the tremendous experience was possible. One day it happened. Lewis speaks metaphorically:

> This long winter broke up in a single moment. . . . Spring is the inevitable image, . . . I can lay my hand on the very moment; there is hardly any fact I know so well, though I cannot date it. Someone must have left in the schoolroom a literary periodical. . . . My eye fell upon the headline and a picture, carelessly, expecting nothing. A moment later, as the poetry says, "The sky had turned around." What I had read was the words *Siegfried and the Twilight of the Gods.* What I had seen was one of Arthur Rockhorn's illustrations to that volume. . . . There arose . . . the knowledge . . . that I was returning at last from exile and desert lands to my own country.

In another setting and in a chapter entitled "Larval Stage of a Book Worm" Mencken describes[49] the impact of *The Adventures of Huckeberry Finn:*

> If I undertook to tell you the effect it had upon me my talk would sound frantic, and even delirious. Its impact was genuinely terrific. I had not gone further than the first incomparable chapter before I realized, child though I was, that I had entered a domain of new and gorgeous wonders, and thereafter I pressed on steadily to the last word. My gait, of course, was still slow, but it became steadily faster as I proceeded. As the blurbs on the slip-covers of murder mysteries say, I simply couldn't put the book down.

Examples of reading as intense experiences affecting one's innermost depths can be accumulated, but perhaps Carl Van Doren[50] describes as well as any the possibility that the phenomenon can also occur after childhood and adolescence. He tells of his experience when he was a student at the University of Illinois:

> Then, random in the library, I discovered Marlowe, and the glory of great verse changed my world as if mountains had sprung up out of the prairie. . . . Here was a poet who did not make me feel he was older and wiser than I, only

[48] Lewis, C. S. *Ibid.,* p. 74.

[49] Mencken, H. L. *Happy Days.* New York: Knopf, 1947, p. 167.

[50] Van Doren, Carl. *Three Worlds.* New York: Harper, 1936, p. 76.

that he had words of light and fire for my cloudy thoughts and smoky feelings. . . . It was really an ear I found in him, not a voice. . . . I began to read poetry, and for three or four years I suppose I read as much of it as any boy alive.

## *A Nonconclusion*

While some of us have been told in childish hymn that little drops of water make a mighty ocean, we have also been warned by the proverb that "One swallow does not make a summer." Literary biography and autobiography are specialized genres, and people who grow up to be successful authors do not constitute a random sample of the human race. Writers of personal documents such as letters, diaries, and autobiographies may be both consciously and unconsciously deceptive. Theodore Roosevelt wrote what have been called "posterity letters," Andrew Carnegie wrote what he hoped was a motivating guide to ambitious youth, and some autobiographies are overtly propagandistic, worthily so in Clifford Beer's *A Mind That Found Itself* and notoriously evil as in Hitler's *Mein Kampf*. The selection of passages from autobiographies (the selection itself being a subjective matter) does not allow a generalized set of conclusions about the influence of literature on youth and their future development.

In the study of literary creativity, however, the individual case may be as telling as the all-embracing conclusion. Psychologists are not yet at the stage where they are willing to generalize broadly about the creative person and the influences which affect him. Rather, the individual instance may give more insight, especially in accounts of happenings during childhood and youth. In most of the autobiographies (and biographies) quoted here the most entertaining chapters are those which describe childhood and adolescence. The writer is less ego involved about the events of his youth than about the decisions made in his adult career. There is a comparative detachment about the reading done in one's first years and there is an abiding vividness in early recollections of encounters with books. Although it has been fashionable in recent years to have had an unhappy childhood (the influence of Freud?), there is often in literary accounts an occasional spirit of enjoyment, an account of openness to sensation, a curiosity, an importance of adventures, secrets, and books which come close to the truth about childhood experiences. These events, delights, influences are not true of everybody; they are a fairly accurate description of how reading affected one person.

Furthermore, even if not entirely accurate, the account of the effects of childhood reading may have psychological significance. The content of the written memories is significant not primarily as absolute truth but as it is important to the writer and a stimulus to the reader. In his biography,

*Sherwood Anderson,* Howe[51] warns "From Anderson's autobiographical volumes it is possible to extract almost anything but reliable information." Anderson was determined to create a public legend about his boyhood and family, but he also reveals unconsciously, as do other autobiographers, the factors influencing his development. Howe concludes, "If they [Anderson's writings] often deviate from factual accuracy, they as often penetrate to psychological truth."

Similarly, in comparing the boyhoods of Mark Twain and Sinclair Lewis, Schorer[52] has pointed out that Lewis was often inaccurate in details of his early life: "Young Clemens did not suffer from a lack of friends or from the brutal taunts of boys who were not his friends or from the long stretches of dull monotony that plagued the young Lewis and led him, in later life, to gloss them with factitious recollections of a 'normal boyhood.' "

He adds that Lewis's chief boyhood pleasures were solitary pleasures, notably reading, in a village which was "rare and bare and gawky." In his high school years his diary contains many references like "Wasted a lot of time reading tonight." His reading matter was miscellaneous and probably lacked in impact and specific influence. In addition, Lewis's statements illustrate the point that a writer may have inaccurate or camouflaged memories about his reading as well as about his family and social relations with peers. Schorer[53] quotes Lewis's adult statement: "When I was a boy, in the prairies of Minnesota, there was no book which had for me a more peculiar and literal enchantment than *Walden* of Thoreau." Because the book is never mentioned in Lewis's early diaries, Schorer suggests that Lewis was "imposing on the Minnesota years a maturity of taste and judgment that came only later."

Although anecdotes of childhood and youth are often factually inaccurate, they may be psychologically meaningful. Because of their early circumstances or adult motivations, Sherwood Anderson and Sinclair Lewis colored descriptions of their encounters with literature with adult motivations, revealing influence or impact of a permanent sort because they believed, or wanted to believe in it. And so with James, Stevenson, Van Doren, and others quoted here, the belief – the acceptance that literature influenced them in these ways – became an important motivation in their lives.

Thus we have evidence of the intuitive sort that the reader adds part of himself to the ideas of the printed page. He hears more, sees more, and sometimes imagines more than the bare bones of the printed text. His ex-

[51] Howe, Irving. *Sherwood Anderson.* ("American Men of Letters Series.") New York: Wm. Sloane, 1951, pp. 18–19.

[52] Schorer, Mark. *Sinclair Lewis: An American Life.* New York: McGraw-Hill, 1961, p. 22.

[53] Schorer, Mark. *Ibid.,* p. 25.

perience with a short story, essay, novel, or poem is probably unique, for to no one else will the factual or imaginative writing mean quite the same thing. He may hear the music, delight in the form, get clues to his own vocation, respond with visual or even olfactory images, and see new worlds opening. Does this happen only to people who later become writers themselves? Probably not; rather, these are phenomena shared, in lesser degree perhaps, by most literate children and youth, and even by some adults. In succeeding chapters, the facts and circumstances are explored in the relatively sophisticated and individual responses of the literary critic and then, more generally, in terms of empirical research on the personality of the reader, the content of the material, and reactions to it which are true of most people.

Edna Ferber has remarked that autobiography is often more embarrassing for the reader than for the writer. Certainly, masses of trivia are accumulated in the thousands of autobiographies written (and printed!) in the United States alone. However, in the best of these volumes, especially in accounts of childhood and youth, some gold can be mined – in examples of self-analysis, in revelation of personality and how it was formed by reading. In autobiography are some hints, not conclusions, about the effects of many kinds of writing on the perceptive reader.

# CHAPTER 3 | Psychoanalytic Points of View

## (ISABEL LEWIS)

Literature can stimulate both conscious and unconscious response in the reader. It can produce pleasure and knowledge in the conscious mind and, in addition, can influence the unconscious, which is moved by the hidden psychological meaning of the work as the reader perceives it with his inner self. The response of the unconscious is more profound and appealing because of the variety of emotions which may be touched, and because powerful instinctual needs can be satisfied. The study of the relationships of psychology to literature deals with deep-lying personal feelings and images. Psychoanalytic points of view provide theories and operational frameworks for interpreting literary works and for explaining the impact of literature on the reader through his use of literary material for his own unconscious purposes.

There is some resistance to analyzing literature in terms of psychological knowledge because the approach requires subjective interpretation of the written material and an effort to establish psychology as a scientific discipline. A possible additional reason may be the threatening nature of the material itself when interpreted psychoanalytically, as will be discussed later. Some critics have felt that study of literature from a psychoanalytic viewpoint stresses emotional expression to the exclusion of intellectual content, and that great literature is concerned with higher concepts than the elemental impulses attributed to the hidden nature of man. However, the literature which has stirred readers and sustained interest over long periods contains some universal appeal to the emotions. Richards[1] declared that "Among the experiences which are by the nature of the case hidden from observation are found almost all those with which criticism is concerned."

Literature which has value to the conscious mind speaks with addi-

[1] Richards, I. A. *Principles of Literary Criticism.* New York: Harcourt, Brace, 1934, p. 112.

tional meaning to levels of the mind which do not reveal themselves in consciousness. Studies of individual readers and groups have validated statements by Freud and others concerning the power of the unconscious in determining response to literature. According to Lesser:[2]

> While the nature of the conscious cognitive activity which occurs in reading fiction has not always been correctly understood, the very existence of unconscious intuitive understanding is usually overlooked or alluded to cursorily . . . though the part the unconscious plays is large and crucially important.

Much has been written in analysis of the psychological mechanisms of the writer as he gains relief from anxiety through expression of his unconscious conflicts. The reader also bases his selection of and relationship to literature on the satisfaction of his hidden needs. Freud has described these processes in his statement, "the unconscious responds to the unconscious." Neither the writer nor the reader is likely to be aware of the forces disguised in the written material, but the greatest literature gratifies the deepest needs of the primitive unconscious.

Although it would be difficult to interpret the unconscious meanings of literature and the reader's response to it without using psychological insight, employing only one system of psychology would be unjustifiable. Freud first proposed the theory of the unconscious mind with all its dimensions of primitive needs, irrational forces, and mystical directions, and made the early psychoanalyses of literature. A number of other psychiatrists, however, including Jones, Bergler, Jung, Rank, Fromm, and Reik, have applied their respective systems of study of the human psyche to the interpretation of literature. A satisfactory approach to finding relationships between psychoanalytic concepts and literary works examines samples of insights adduced by psychoanalysts in addition to contributions made by psychologists, writers, and critics.

Although psychological mechanisms found in literary works are defined and applied in order to discover the various possible meanings for different readers, the use of psychoanalytic vocabulary is not intended as a means of teaching readers to interpret their reading interests. Especially in teaching children, such information can be useful to the teacher in selecting suitable books and in understanding pupil responses, but it would not be appropriate for introduction into class discussion.

Before examining the psychoanalytic explanations of the impact of literature, several key terms will be defined and an overview of Freudian theory presented in order to clarify major concepts and to supply a background for the reader's convenience. This summary of theory is designed to provide a framework for the later discussion of the nature of the impact of literature on the reader, the types of impact, the causes of impact, and the use of literature in the classroom.

[2] Lesser, Simon O. *Fiction and the Unconscious.* Boston: Beacon Press, 1957, p. 235.

## *Psychoanalytic Theories*

Freud's original perception and exploration of the unconscious mind formed the foundation for understanding the unconscious and its manifestations in both normal and abnormal personality development. Later psychoanalysts have modified or expanded Freud's concepts, but, for the most part, have included his basic principles, accepting that concealed, unrecognized motives and emotions exert strong control on everyday life.

Freud[3] called the conscious "the conception which is present to our consciousness and of which we are aware." The unconscious conception is "one of which we are not aware, but the existence of which we are nevertheless ready to admit on account of other proofs and signs," and which contains latent ideas which are consciously forgotten or repressed, but which constantly seek expression. Freud described the total mental life of man in dynamics of three elements, the Id, the Ego, and the Superego. The unconscious comprises by far the greater part of the mind, and it is there that the Id is hidden. The Id is the "dark, inaccessible part of our personality," and is the repository of chaotic, primitive instincts, retained from ancient animal experience.

At birth the child is the expression of the Id, containing "everything that is inherited," its only purpose the gratification of its needs and desires. It craves protection from hunger, pain, and aloneness, all means of self-preservation, and is completely ruthless and unaware of needs of others in its urge toward self-satisfaction. Thomas Mann[4] wrote, "It knows no values, no good or evil, no morality. It even knows no time." The impulses of the Id are powered by the libido, or psychic energy. The libido is the center of pleasure, and in the child is manifest in self-satisfying physical activities. In adults the libido may be expressed through sexual relationships, through creativity in art, music, or literature, and in other achievements.

As the child comes into contact with other individuals having their own purposes, a part of the Id relates to reality and becomes the Ego, the conscious element of the mind. The Ego recognizes that if the Id releases its impulses without control, the forces of society, religion, and law will destroy or cripple the self. The Ego, then, mediates between the "the reckless claims of the Id and the checks of the outer world." Some neuroses develop from the irreconcilable conflicts between the Ego and the Id.

The third and highest mental level in man is the Superego, an unconscious force which conflicts with the Id. The Superego is a modified portion of the Ego, developed by experiences with the world of reality. The

[3] Freud, Sigmund. "A Note on the Unconscious in Psycho-Analysis," *Collected Papers*, Vol. 4. New York: Basic Books, 1959, p. 23.

[4] Mann, Thomas. "Freud and the Future," *Art and Psychoanalysis* (William Phillips, ed.). Cleveland: World Publishing Co., 1963.

Superego is recognized as the conscience and is formed by the rules imposed on the child by the authority figures in his life, most strongly by the interdictions of the father. The Ego is the only conscious part of the mind and labors to satisfy the cravings of the Id while conforming to the restrictions of the Superego. Adult personality stresses, especially those produced by guilt, can result from conflict between the Ego and the Superego.

Because society refuses to accept the expression of the powerful, irrational, self-gratifying impulses of the Id, these impulses are repressed into the unconscious. However, they retain their original strength and need, and continually seek means of satisfaction. Freud was convinced that the unconscious was inaccessible except by specific means. Because no one can deliberately bring to awareness any item from the unconscious, it can only be tapped through hypnosis, psychoanalysis, or interpretation of dreams. Dreams are fantasy reality for the unconscious, and psychoanalysts have related them to imaginative expressions of some writers. Freud found that wit is also an expression of the repressed material in the unconscious, similar to dream structure.

The dream reveals a fulfillment of a concealed wish, but the wish may be represented by an obscure allusion, a symbol, or even a statement of the opposite. Whereas the dream is projected by the Id in an effort to gain fulfillment through fantasy of desires not permitted by reality, humor is a conscious activity of the Ego serving the Id by using distortion to fulfill forbidden desires; but in both mechanisms the individual is not aware of the repressed material. The unconscious transference of wish fulfillment from dream fantasy or wit to writing and reading is the basis of psychoanalytic interpretation of literature.

An aspect of Freudian doctrine which is essential to psychoanalytic understanding of literature is the Oedipus complex, referring to the legendary Greek king, Oedipus, who unknowingly killed his father and married his mother. In Sophocles' play, *Oedipus Rex*, the careful disclosure of the murder and incest is developed in a manner similar to psychoanalysis. Freud[5] stated that, "Falling in love with one parent and hating the other forms part of the permanent stock of the psychic impulses which arise in early childhood." He considered the Oedipus legend and others of similar nature to be corroboration of the universal validity of his hypothesis of infantile psychology. The story expresses the wish fulfillment of childhood. Freud stated that the urges of the child continue in the adult, repressed but insistent.

The Oedipus complex has been a controversial theory since Freud proposed it, and he himself commented that none of his research had aroused such bitter opposition. However, many critics have discerned portrayals

[5] Freud, Sigmund. "The Interpretation of Dreams," *The Basic Writings of Sigmund Freud*. New York: Random House, 1938, p. 306.

of the complex in popular writing. Freud perceived the tragedy of *Hamlet* to be "rooted in the same soil," expressing the hesitation of Hamlet to avenge his father's death because he had himself wished just such an event and loved his mother with the same desires as the man who took his father's place with her.

In *Totem and Taboo*[6] Freud compared the psychology of primitive man as revealed in folklore with the psychology of modern man, and especially of unhappy people. The study indicated to him that the myths and taboos of primitive man and the religion and morality of modern times are expressions of complexes relating to fathers and mothers, originating in the need for repression of hatred of the father in the male child, of the mother in the female, and the desire for incest with the parent of the opposite sex.

A number of critics have contradicted Freud's emphasis upon the Oedipus complex and have produced interpretations of the same literature with other symbolic significances. These interpretations of literary works are also of value, especially when used to supplement those of Freud, and some significant ones will be considered later in this chapter.

Some additional Freudian concepts which are found in interpretations of writing include the delineation of stages in the psyche of the child which evolve through relationships with the outer world, especially parents, and which continue to influence the personality of the adult. These phases have been termed the oral period, the anal period, the oedipal period, and the latent period. The oral period is experienced mainly during the first year of life and begins under the control of the Id when the child is dependent upon gratification of bodily needs, particularly hunger for survival. The infant's relationship with his mother is most significant in forming attitudes that may remain constant throughout life. The nature of his attitudes will be determined by the degree to which she satisfies his needs. The two phases of the oral period – the first passive, dependent stage, and the later aggressive, sadistic stage – influence individual and cultural elements of adult life.

The Ego has begun to develop during the oral period and must gain more control in the next stage, the anal period, which covers roughly the second and third years of the child's life. During this period the child is more active, receives more prohibitions, and as a result feels ambivalence – or love and hatred at the same time – toward his parents. The emphasis of his instinctual impulse has shifted from the oral needs to the anal area. Excretory functions represent power and pleasure to the child, but he is forced by parental pressure to repress them and their affects. The requirement to learn cleanliness and to part with that which he values arouses hostility. As a result of his need to cooperate and follow rules he begins

[6] Freud, Sigmund. "Totem and Taboo," *The Basic Writings of Sigmund Freud*. New York: Random House, 1938.

to incorporate into himself the standards and beliefs of authorities around him, thus developing the Superego.

The oedipal period is evident during the fourth, fifth, and sixth years of age, when the child's major impulses focus on the genital area. It is at this time that the child feels a possessive love for the parent of the opposite sex, and resentment for the other parent.

From about seven years of age until the onset of puberty the child experiences a time of relief from the powerful urges moving him until this time. This period of rest from instinctual pressure, known as the latent period, permits sublimation, or rechanneling of some of the conflicts of the earliest periods. At this time the child begins his formal education, develops relationships with people outside the family, forms bonds of loyalty to a group, class, or gang, and is stimulated to intellectual growth. While the earlier needs are quiescent, the child develops a busy fantasy life concerning his growth in power.

Freud maintained that the pattern of the adult personality is structured by the psyche of the child. In the well-adjusted adult these previous levels remain, but are hidden in the unconscious and need some subtle expression. The disturbed adult who failed to grow beyond a phase of childhood, or the person who has regressed to an early period because of some traumatic experience, will manifest symptoms of that period where he is still functioning. Such symptoms are usually disguised, so that the individual, and often those around him, cannot be aware of their origin, but they can be found abundantly in literature.

According to Freud, there is a need for all people, normal or neurotic, to review the conflicts of the early psychological periods in an effort to seek better solutions for the unsolved problems of the past. He labeled the tendency of the unconscious to examine constantly and to relive the haunting phases of childhood as the repetition compulsion. The unconscious attempts to relieve anxiety by continuing to repeat situations in search of outcomes more satisfying than those found in the original trauma. These efforts are realized in the form of dreams, real life confrontations, and the reading and writing of material related to the conflict. The repetition compulsion is advanced as a major motivation in the selection and enjoyment of literature. Lesser[7] has stated that "the meanings grasped below the threshold of awareness may make a disproportionate contribution to the pleasure we receive from reading fiction: they satisfy some of our deepest and most urgent needs – needs which though unacknowledged are never relinquished."

This condensation of some fundamental Freudian principles which are applicable to understanding literature is necessarily limited and does not attempt to reveal the many amplifications that were made by Freud and others. The basic hypotheses are summarized to provide a framework of

[7] Lesser, Simon O. *Fiction and the Unconscious.* Boston: Beacon Press, 1957, p. 224.

definitions in order to examine the interpretations made by a variety of writers concerning reader response to literature. This does not mean that Freud's doctrines are considered the most valid, but that they are frequently the basis for other psychological interpretations.

## *Psychological Mechanisms*

Certain relationships between the goals and processes of psychotherapy and those of imaginative reading have been observed by some therapists and literary commentators. In both experiences the aim is the increase of well-being, of feelings of satisfaction, and of self-realization. Freud defined the task of psychotherapy as the uncovering of repressions in order to develop insight into problems and to discover better judgments which would provide for accepting or rejecting the material which was formerly hidden and conflictual. Rogers,[8] whose approach to therapy is very different from that of Freud, has listed corresponding goals for therapy. These include increase in insightful statements, the incorporation of previously denied experience into the self-structure, and changes in perception and acceptance of the self. Other systems of psychology, such as those of Jung and Adler, though built on different understandings of the psyche, adduce similar goals for therapy.

In both psychology and reading, the event, that is, the psychological trauma or the written description on the printed page, is not so important as the individual's interpretation of the meaning of the event.[9] The unique perception of each individual determines his personal response to experiences in the life situation or in reading.

The processes by which therapy takes place also correspond to experiences which may occur in reading, and are related to the aims of therapy. Shrodes[10] explained that "The processes involved in the aesthetic experience parallel in substance and function to the primary phases of psychotherapy, are (1) identification, including projection and introjection, (2) catharsis, and (3) insight."

Identification is a major mechanism of psychological development and adjustment as set forth in Freud's theories of personality and therapy. Although not all psychologists agree on a definition of the process or its importance in personal development, the term has become a part of the language and is used frequently, if somewhat loosely, in both psychologi-

[8] Rogers, Carl. *On Becoming a Person.* Boston: Houghton Mifflin, 1961, p. 75.

[9] Combs, Arthur W. "Phenomenological Concepts in Nondirective Therapy," *Journal of Consulting Psychology, 13:*198, July–August, 1948.

[10] Shrodes, Caroline. *Bibliotherapy: A Theoretical and Clinical Experimental Study.* Unpublished doctoral dissertation (University of California, Berkeley, 1949), p. 36.

cal terminology and literary criticism. It has been used chiefly to apply rather imprecisely to any of three concepts, described by Bronfenbrenner[11] as "(1) *behavioral* (acting like one's parent), (2) *motivational* (wanting to be like one's parent), and (3) *emotional* (being effectively involved, positively or negatively, with one's parent)."

Freud's[12] use of the term in psychoanalysis is more definite and begins with the psychological incorporation of the loved object into the infant's own body during the oral period. This is the prototype of identification which later assumes such psychic importance through the formation of the self-concept by introjecting or absorbing into the unconscious the qualities and standards of parents and other authoritative or desired figures, and the mores of society. The infant identifies with the loved person, not by striving to be like that figure, but by feeling that it *is* the figure. By developmental means the older child is impelled to become like those with whom it identifies. For all people the incorporation of psychological characteristics continues throughout life as new experiences and personalities are encountered. According to English and Pearson,[13] "Identification is one of the successful means of instinct repression, where the energy of the instinct can find outlet by imitation of the behavior of a loved or admired person."

When there have been errors in identification because of lack of an appropriate figure, or because of other environmental deficits, the Ego does not properly develop and must constantly seek for completion of the self-image. In therapy as well as in reading the individual is able to find new ways of perceiving himself and new sources of identification. A defense mechanism which operates in the opposite manner from introjection is projection, by which the individual relieves his own inner conflicts by displacing his unacceptable impulses and fears onto someone or something else. Therapy and literature both deal with introjection and projection.

Catharsis is an important aspect of therapy and may also be facilitated through reading experiences. It may begin with ventilation of emotions and progress through an elimination of disturbing impulses and fears. Catharsis can bring release of tension, feelings of relief, and increase in general spontaneity. It is effective because it makes provisions for absolving feelings of guilt, shifting of responsibility, expressing inhibited or forbidden topics, gaining relief from shame, and obtaining release from loneliness. In therapy, catharsis is skillfully directed from conscious confession to ventilation of unconscious problems. The reader can gain the

[11] Bronfenbrenner, W. "Family Structure and Development," *Newsletter*, Division of Developmental Psychology, American Psychological Association, Fall 1958, pp. 1–4.

[12] Freud, Sigmund. "Three Contributions to the Theory of Sex," *The Basic Writings of Sigmund Freud.* New York: Random House, 1938.

[13] English, Spurgeon O., and Gerald Pearson. *Common Neuroses of Children and Adults.* New York: W. W. Norton, 1937, p. 270.

effects of catharsis by identifying with characters, vicariously experiencing their actions and emotions through which he receives relief from tension for reasons similar to those in therapy.

Insight, or perception of the inner nature of one's self, is the third psychotherapeutic process which also takes place in reading. Through catharsis and identification it is possible for the individual to develop insight into himself and his characteristics. Catharsis frees him temporarily from certain prohibitions so that he is able to examine his inner self with fewer restrictions and discern formerly unrecognized tendencies. Through identifications the individual can see himself in others and thereby apprehend some of the forces which produce facets of his personality. Such insight may lead to the uncovering of childhood experiences and feelings and to the realization that they are continuing to influence behavior and emotions resulting in consequent reevaluation of attitudes and patterns of action. Through incorporation of some of the qualities and behavior of the one with whom he identifies, the individual may improve his self-image and perceive different means of solving his problems. This insight can increase Ego strength. It is possible for anxieties and guilt to be relieved, unsatisfied needs to receive some gratification, and the concept of self to be enhanced through the processes of catharsis, identification, and insight.

## *Variables Affecting the Impact of Reading*

A number of variables which influence the impact of reading have been identified. Lists of such elements tend to overlap and include the same general factors, any of which can be important in determining the reader's response to specific writing. These variables include physical, intellectual, and emotional factors.

The physical environment in which reading takes place influences the quality of response, because the extent to which it is favorable or unfavorable to perception and concentration can modify the reader's reactions. Such conditions as proper lighting, optimum temperature, and comfortable seating influence the receptivity of the reader. The location for reading should provide freedom from interruptions and apprehension of interruption, and opportunities for occasional rest from concentration of eyes and thought. Technical aspects of the written material itself can be important in determining reader interest. The quality of the paper and printing, the size of print, and the ease of handling the book are considerations that may facilitate or interfere with reading response.

Intellectual traits of the reader influence the type and quality of his response to literature. The individual's general intelligence, size of vocabulary, and level of reading skills and abilities are basic in determining the amount and kind of reading he will do, and, up to a point, his reaction to the content. A number of studies support the hypothesis that readers with very inadequate skills will be discouraged by the inability to comprehend meaning and will reject the task. Satisfactory competences which permit the reader to relate to the written material are necessary for involvement with the content. The reader must be able to perceive, that is, see and recognize the words used in the written material. Comprehension, or understanding of the meaning intended by the author is necessary, and the degree of realization of this faculty is related to the reader's mental maturity and background of experience. In addition, the reader's interest in the subject matter, his ability to interpret beyond literal meanings, and his involvement in the content will influence his response. Emotional or personal characteristics of the reader are of crucial importance in determining response to reading. The reader's health, energy, eyesight, and emotional state are important primarily in terms of sense perception but are also related to reception of content. The span of attention and concentration must reach certain minimal periods of time in order to achieve sufficient identification and intensity. Attitudes and values of the reader exert powerful influences upon his selection and interpretation of literature.

Two early empirical studies by Richards,[14,15] which are described more fully in Chapter 7, provided information about interpretation of reading and listed some common errors of readers. The errors included difficulties with meaning, with imagery, and with sensuous perception of form, sound, and rhythm. Other errors were in the area of attitudes: stock responses, sentimentality, inhibitions, doctrinal beliefs, technical presuppositions, and critical preconceptions. Later studies, stimulated by those of Richards, also found that there were wide varieties of reader interpretations, indicating the importance of individual characteristics in response to literature.

## *Psychoanalytic Processes in Reading*

The purposes, conscious or unconscious, for which a reader turns to a book are perhaps the most powerful influences on his response to reading. According to statements of Mirrielees,[16] Lind,[17] Russell,[18] and others, the

[14] Richards, I. A. *Practical Criticism: A Study in Literary Judgment.* New York: Harcourt, Brace, 1929.

[15] Richards, I. A. *Interpretations in Teaching.* London: Kegan Paul, Trench, Trubner, 1937.

[16] Mirrielees, Lucia B. *Teaching Composition and Literature.* New York: Harcourt, Brace, 1952, p. 468.

reasons for reading can be grouped under three broad categories: practical, emotional, and aesthetic. Types of reading causes or effects have been proposed by Waples, Berelson, and Bradshaw,[19] as follows:

1. The instrumental effect – discovering information for a definite purpose.
2. The prestige effect – offering relief from inferiority feelings and increasing self-respect.
3. The reinforcement effect – providing reinforcement of predispositions of the reader, or conversion to another attitude.
4. The aesthetic effect – enjoying vicarious satisfaction from literary art.
5. The respite effect – finding pleasant distraction and escape from anxiety.

Rogers[20] has commented that through literature the reader becomes involved in the problems of the characters and sees the situation through the vision of another being. The impact of reading comes through the penetration of the reader into the mind of the writer or of the character. The reader enjoys and suffers, he wonders or knows, he looks with the eyes of the writer.

According to Wellek and Warren,[21] reading serves to relieve us from the pressure of emotions by providing them with a focus, thereby releasing tension and bringing peace of mind. These writers then question if such relief is desirable, if such catharsis prevents the discharge of the emotions on more useful purposes. They also ask, in line with Plato's admonition that tragedy and comedy "nourish and water our emotions when we ought to dry them up," whether literature does relieve emotional pressures or, in fact, incites them to further activity.

These questions may not be susceptible to positive answers; in any case as Carlsen stated:[22]

> Yet literature has always held a mirror up for the reader to see himself sharply and clearly. Literature, by its very nature, is selective and suggests integrations, connections, insights into experience, and values which the individual might not otherwise find for himself. At its best, literature confronts the reader with the basic, eternal problems of human beings.

---

[17] Lind, Katherine N. "Social Psychology of Children's Reading," *American Journal of Sociology, 41:*454–69, January 1936.

[18] Russell, David H. *Children Learn to Read.* Boston: Ginn, 1961, p. 26.

[19] Waples, Douglas, Bernard Berelson, and Franklin Bradshaw. *What Reading Does to People.* Chicago: University of Chicago Press, 1940, pp. 74–80.

[20] Rogers, Carl. *On Becoming a Person.* Boston: Houghton Mifflin, 1961, p. 286.

[21] Wellek, René, and Austin Warren. *Theory of Literature.* New York: Harcourt, Brace (Harvest Books), 1956.

[22] Carlsen, G. Robert. *Books and the Teen-Age Reader.* New York: Bantam Books, 1967, p. 15.

The psychoanalytic interpretation of the impact of literature is concerned with the emotional characteristics and psychological needs of the reader. Each reader responds in his individual manner, unique because of his own experiences and searchings. The "reader as artist" creates the story for himself from the elements given by the author. He adds bit by bit as the plot progresses and deletes or emphasizes aspects that have most impact upon him. He builds the author's work into an answer to his own problems. Lesser[23] believed that "we read because we are beset by anxieties, guilt feelings, and ungratified needs. The reading of fiction permits us, in indirect fashion, to satisfy these needs, relieve our anxieties and assuage our guilt."

Analyses of the unconscious expressions of the writer are rarely supported by the author himself. In most cases it is not justifiable to attribute the thoughts or feelings, good or bad, of characters to their originator. But it is not necessary for the emotions and ideas of characters to belong to their creator in order for the reader to identify with and internalize them for his own.

Not enough evidence concerning the impact of literature has been accumulated to establish a valid scientific theory of the reader's response. It is only possible to construct a tentative typology which is founded on certain basic assumptions regarding human nature, the formation of personality, and human interaction. Psychoanalysis provides a systematic structure of theory and knowledge dealing with these factors. Literary works which have appealed to readers over hundreds of years also are concerned with these factors. Interpretation of the enduring literature according to the theory of psychoanalysis indicates some of the kinds of response the words evoke in readers.

Freud[24] begins an examination of literary works with the suggestion that the play of the child is the first trace of imaginative activity. The child creates a new world or reorders the external world to his own pattern. He takes his play seriously although he realizes that it is not reality. The writer expresses himself in the same way; "he creates a world of phantasy which he takes very seriously; that is, he invests it with a great deal of affect, while separating it sharply from reality." As the child grows to adulthood, he ceases to play, but he still needs and wants the pleasure he derived from play. "Really we never can relinquish anything; we only exchange one thing for something else." The adult substitutes phantasy for the concrete play of childhood. He builds daydreams as a continuation of play, but he knows that they are not as socially acceptable and must be kept secret. He recognizes that the content of his phantasies,

[23] Lesser, Simon O. *Fiction and the Unconscious.* Boston: Beacon Press, 1957, p. 39.

[24] Freud, Sigmund. "The Relation of the Poet to Day-Dreaming," *Collected Papers.* Vol. 4. New York: Basic Books, 1959, p. 173.

although perhaps dealing with the same desires as child's play, are no longer innocent.

Nocturnal dreams are of the same stuff as daydreams, dealing with material, ideas, and feelings that cannot be expressed openly, built around the wish, the desire, as in play the child reconstructed a world more pleasing to him. Freud believed that all dreams are wish fulfillment, improving upon an unsatisfactory reality, but often distorted or symbolized in disguised form. The imaginative writer expresses the wish of the unconscious, but, as in dreams or phantasies, the true meaning of the wish and its fulfillment is disguised or hidden in symbol. The reader, however, is not lost in this private world, even though neither he nor the writer is consciously aware of the secret map. Because "the unconscious responds to the unconscious" the reader responds to the concealed wish and secures gratification from its literary fulfillment.

A number of critics have discussed this hypothesis formulated by Freud. Lowenfeld[25] agreed with Freud's tracing of the creative act from the play of childhood. He stated that in the identification of the writer with his characters there can be seen an element of magic, the conspicuous feature of children's play which imitates the real world in phantasizing a more pleasing way of life. "The tendency quickly to identify is a basic feature of the world of magic. The artist, susceptible to magic to a strong degree, is able to charm others so that they in turn feel themselves one with him."

Read[26] has analyzed the elements in dream-formation which are relevant to literary works. He described the genesis of one of his own poems in a vivid dream and defined it in Freudian terminology as "the manifest content of a dream whose latent thoughts have been turned into sensory images or visual scenes." Read believed that "poetic inspiration has an exact parallel in dream-formation." He suggested that although the dream process cannot be found in every poem, "every authentic image is conceived in the unconscious." It is an unconscious impulse that creates the dream and the poem, and "That impulse seeks in the poem, no less and no otherwise than in the dream, its desired satisfaction."

In a comparison of history with literature, Toynbee[27] likened history to the drama and the novel. He stated that the three forms of writing grew out of mythology, "a primitive form of apprehension and expression in

[25] Lowenfeld, Henry. "Psychic Trauma and Productive Experience in the Artist," *Art and Psychoanalysis* (William Phillips, ed.). Cleveland: World Publishing Co., 1963, p. 304.

[26] Read, Herbert. "Surrealism and the Romantic Principle," *Criticism: The Foundation of Modern Literary Judgment* (Mark Schorer, Josephine Miles, and Gordon McKenzie, eds.). New York: Harcourt, Brace, 1948, pp. 110–12.

[27] Toynbee, Arnold J. *A Study of History.* New York: Oxford University Press, 1947, p. 44.

which – as in fairy tales listened to by children or in dreams dreamt by sophisticated adults – the line between fact and fiction is left undrawn."

Fraiberg[28] analyzed Kafka and his work in terms of the dream process. She wrote that Kafka "established his human fellowship in his writings through the fraternity of the dream . . . it is the creation through the device of the private dream in a world of collective memory where each man can know his fellow." She warned that although Kafka left a record which provides opportunities for examining relationships between his dreams and his writings, we must be cautious in interpreting the symbols he used. Every symbol may have multiple meanings, and even those designated as "universal" by Freud have their meanings determined by the dreamer, the writer, or the reader.

Not all critics agree with Freud's analogy of creative writing to daydreaming. Phillips,[29] for example, stated that such a comparison is inadequate and misleading. He believed with Freud that in literature the reader can tap the Id and its secret material without being overwhelmed by it, but he did not consider the process necessarily analogous to that of daydreaming.

Edel[30] pointed out that "An important distinction must be drawn between the material most readers can grasp in a novel and that part of it which becomes, in effect, a part of our personal mental dream-state." Readers can read with equal skills, discuss and criticize in agreement about the plot or characters. "But the question recurs: do we *experience* the book in the same way?" Some readers will shiver with horror while reading a book which may bore others, or may weep or exult with characters who amuse others. "Between the book *read* and the book *felt* there lie all the differences of opinion that divide reader and reader, critic and critic."

In the opinion of Freud, dreams contain the "unconscious tendencies present ever since his childhood in the mind of the dreamer, but ordinarily *repressed* and excluded from his conscious life." In the dream some part of the unconscious emerges in a disguised form and brings some freedom from the repression; in like manner "the true enjoyment of literature proceeds from the release of tensions in our minds." The writer enables us to "enjoy our own day-dreams without reproach or shame."

Freud said that much study remains to be done before we can delineate the processes by which the writer arouses the reader's emotional reactions, but we do know that the writer is able to transport us and to

[28] Fraiberg, Selma. "Kafka and the Dream," *Art and Psychoanalysis* (William Phillips, ed.). Cleveland: World Publishing Co., 1963, pp. 21–53.

[29] Phillips, William. *Art and Psychoanalysis*. Cleveland: World Publishing Co., 1963, p. xvi.

[30] Edel, Leon. *The Psychological Novel 1900–1950*. New York: Lippincott, 1955, p. 100.

arouse emotions in us of which we were not aware and had not suspected we were capable of having. He enables us to throw off the heavy burden of reality and life in a world we never made by giving us a world more like our phantasies in which we can identify with one or more of the characters. The daydreamer is ashamed of his phantasies, but by identification with a selected character he can live through some of his repressed impulses. The lack of gratification of need is the most threatening situation faced by the child and continues in the unconscious Id as a danger which constantly seeks solution. Because the infantile desires are never relinquished, we seek to satisfy them by many disguised paths, in play, in dreams, in literature. We seek answers by reading about people who have lived through situations similar to ours and by trying to fit their solutions to our needs.

Identification is the first relationship that the individual makes with another person. The infant identifies with the mother and for a time does not recognize their separate existence. As the child grows older, identification with others is one of the most important ways in which the personality is developed. Identification is ambivalent in nature, reflecting a tenderness or a need to destroy. The reader can identify with a character he admires and would like to imitate, with one he perceives as very much like himself, or with one whose qualities are repugnant to him.

Reading remedies some of the deficiencies of experience and satisfies inner needs. The process is an expression of Freud's statement that in each person the unconscious is sensitive to the unconscious of another. Good literature, and sometimes literature that critics consider bad, deals with the problems and emotional needs in the unconscious of the reader. Bergler,[31] after years of observing patients and their reading, stated that "Unconsciously, the reader and the writer understand each other. The mechanism of unconscious identification on two levels (unconscious *and* conscious) is the basis for the reader's 'interest' in every type of literature; only a naive aesthete believes otherwise."

One of the discoveries of psychoanalysis which has been most strongly resisted is the revelation that hidden in the unconscious of each person are unacceptable impulses and fears, which are unknown or not admitted. According to Lesser,[32] "in number and intensity these are the impulses which are most important among those which seek and secure satisfaction in the reading of fiction." Freud[33] explained that one of the most crippling demands made by civilization upon the erotic life of man is the prohibition of incest, which causes an intense loss of pleasure and results in conflicts that are centered in guilt and anxiety. Freud intended "to repre-

[31] Bergler, Edmund. *The Writer and Psychoanalysis*. Garden City: New York: Doubleday, 1950, p. 170.

[32] Lesser, Simon O. *Fiction and the Unconscious*. Boston: Beacon Press, 1957, p. 41.

[33] Freud, Sigmund. *Civilization and Its Discontents*. London: Hogarth, 1939, p. 74.

sent the sense of guilt as the most important problem in the evolution of culture, and to convey that the price of progress in civilization is paid in forfeiting happiness through the heightening of the sense of guilt." He stated that guilt may eventually overwhelm civilized man, and that symptoms of such suffering are seen in the depression, anxiety, and desperate ambitions of modern man. Lesser[34] spoke to this point in the following statement:

> Repressed tendencies can only secure expression when they are sufficiently disguised so that their connection with a repudiated impulse is not perceived by the censorious ego and when they do not threaten to lead to action. Great fiction can easily satisfy these conditions. The kind of tendencies which would be disavowed are usually disguised and are invariably displaced onto others.

According to Trilling,[35] psychoanalysis is the only systematic account of the human mind which is subtle and complex enough to stand beside the psychological insights that have accumulated through centuries of literature. Analytic therapy uses a rational approach to deal with the polar extremes of practical reality and neurotic illusion. Both the poet and the neurotic deal in fantasy; Trilling finds as a difference that the poet has control over his fantasy while the symptom of a neurotic is that he is possessed by it.

It is possible that there are periods when the writer is also possessed by his fantasy until he resolves the material into literary form. Perhaps it is in his rational thought (the Ego?) that he achieves a perspective that the neurotic fails to do. Or perhaps he has greater freedom to find successful alternatives because he is not dealing *directly* with his own problems. It may be that the reader, too, becomes possessed by the fantasy in the book and secures relief from his tensions only when the character with whom he has identified finds a solution for their common problem. It may be hypothesized that the creative processes of literature involve the psychoanalytic therapy system, with the reader (as well as the writer) as both patient and physician.

Trilling believed that psychoanalysis may be inadequate in dealing with artistic meaning and value, but supports the rich ambiguity in literature and the connective links between apparent and latent meanings in viewing a work of art. He concluded that Freudian psychology shows man to be a complex and dignified creature, and is the one mental system which "makes poetry indigenous to the very constitution of the mind" and the mechanisms by which art makes its effect.

Through identification with characters in literature the reader becomes

[34] Lesser, Simon O. *Fiction and the Unconscious.* Boston: Beacon Press, 1957, p. 42.

[35] Trilling, Lionel. "Freud and Literature," *Criticism: The Foundations of Modern Literary Judgment* (Mark Schorer, Josephine Miles, and Gordon McKenzie, eds.). New York: Harcourt, Brace, 1958, p. 172.

actively involved with their feelings and actions. He performs, vicariously, the hero's deeds, both noble and reprehensible. He obtains gratification of his hidden impulses, and through participation with the character, finds the reward or the punishment earned by these impulses. The satisfaction of release of the buried desire is balanced by the swift, sure justice that follows in the story, so that guilt is not necessary. The catharsis experienced through the identification enables the Ego to exert more control over the unacceptable impulses of the Id. Aristotle wrote of the cathartic experience to be found in tragedy, "the imitation of noble actions," which brings satisfaction through suffering. Trilling has suggested that both writer and reader can obtain catharsis in that sense and, in addition, can secure a "sense of active mastery" of the problems of life.

Lesser[36] believed that the Aristotelean concept of catharsis involves a shift in the reader's response from the experience of being chiefly a participant to that of being largely a spectator. The first step in the cathartic experience is the gratification of hidden impulses through identification with the selected character. The second step is the perception and acceptance of the inevitable outcomes of the action of the character. At this point, the imminence of the unavoidable and deserved consequences, the reader usually begins to disengage himself from his identification with the character and his behavior. Occasionally, the reader is unable to escape from the bonds of identification and continues to undergo vicariously the sufferings and destruction of the protagonist, leaving a feeling of dissatisfaction and tension until the story can be reviewed and softened in the conscious mind.

The usual shift of the reader to the role of spectator is an important aspect of the cathartic experience. It is then that the reader may feel that he has had a narrow escape from disaster, and in relief may congratulate himself that he did not behave in the unacceptable manner of the character who is receiving the inevitable and merited punishment. Lesser felt that the catharsis gained from great literature is broader than that described by Aristotle. He said that at the conclusion of a great tragedy,

> we feel purged not only of pity and fear but of the desires to which the tragic hero has yielded and whose gratification is responsible for his suffering. This feeling is only explicable on the assumption that we, too, have vicariously satisfied those desires. Having done so, we now feel relieved and fulfilled, momentarily free of tension and anxiety.

In real life we cannot obtain the freedom from tension that literature can engender. If we actually indulge the buried impulses, the gratification we enjoy is spoiled by guilt or fear of punishment. If we continue to repress the powerful impulses of the Id, we suffer from conflict and anxiety. Through reading we can gain satisfaction, over and over, without

[36] Lesser, Simon O. *Fiction and the Unconscious.* Boston: Beacon Press, 1957, pp. 238–268.

guilt, fear, or threat to the Ego. We are purged and purified by identification with the hero and by the withdrawal to watch the final just judgment of his unacceptable behavior.

The reader turns to books to obtain relief from tensions and guilt, but another purpose is the search for knowledge about himself. This insight is gained on both cognitive and affective levels. Reading provides information about and an understanding of facts, relationships, and appreciations covering the world of the present and that of the past. It also gives opportunities to share unconsciously in the roles and events of an infinite variety of experiences. This combination of conscious knowledge and covert emotional wisdom can give the reader insight into his own needs and may help him to find new solutions to his problems.

As the reader encounters a number of different characters with whom he identifies he can explore various aspects of his own personality and experiment with different ways of handling them. Readers tend to prefer certain types of literature, whether it be a detective story, biography, drama, or any other type. In this way the reader can seek over and over the answers he needs in similar situations, much as "the criminal returns to the scene of the crime." He can "try on for fit" the roles of protagonists who go beyond his own tendencies in expressing impulses, and the roles of those who are more prudent than he would like to be. Somewhere in the range of possible life styles the reader may find a pattern that satisfies his search.

Insights may occur in varying degrees. To discover that others have undergone the same difficulties which we face, to perceive that the raging impulses which we control with such tension are felt and sometimes yielded to by others gives us consolation and courage, and relieves our guilt. In literature we are enabled to face and work through our worst fears about ourselves and to find some security in accepting our nature and some better ways of dealing with it, with the minimum amount of effort and conflict. The insight which ensues may be predominantly unconscious, yet it serves to strengthen and reassure the anxious self. After much reading, insight may accumulate large conscious components so that the individual can understand more of his inner nature and determine with awareness effective solutions to his conflicts.

## *The Hero*

It is through identification with a selected character, usually the hero, that the reader obtains catharsis and insight. Freud believed that in fiction as in the dream the goal is wish fulfillment and that the real essence of the wish and the fulfillment is carefully hidden in symbol. One clue is the universal presence of the hero, a character who is the center of the story, who evokes the sympathy of the reader, and who ultimately triumphs over all his vicissitudes either through victory or through death, according to the inevitable consequences of his actions. Freud wrote, "this significant mark of invulnerability very clearly betrays – His Majesty the Ego, the hero of all day-dreams and all novels."

Another element that points to the Ego as hero is the tendency for the hero to be beloved and aided by the "good" characters in the book, whereas his enemies are manifestly the "bad" characters. In the unconscious are childhood longings of which we are only dimly aware; many more of the most powerful desires are below the surface of consciousness than are above. A somewhat extreme example of the compulsion to identify with a hero is found in Thurber's "The Secret Life of Walter Mitty." The story portrays the escape of an unfulfilled man into a world of fantasy. It reveals the unconscious longing of the man to be independent and heroic and shows how he uses minute details to make his daydreams complete.

As the child progresses through stages of development he acquires and enhances facets of his personality through identification with heroes. In discussing developmental values in books, Brooks[37] defined developmental value as the element which "supplies vicariously a wealth of experience that may aid a reader in his choice of modes of behavior." Some books are more useful for the purpose than others and may be seen to possess developmental value if they provide situations or characters which stimulate in the reader perception of new, more satisfying behavior patterns or reinforcement of desirable attitudes already held. Havighurst[38] expressed the opinion that identification is a means of development of aspects of personality, and that identification is especially the basis of the development of the conscience. The sequence of identification begins with parents and includes heroes read about, along with real life figures.

DeVoto[39] perceived the hero as the adult with whom the child in each reader wishes to identify. In all novels there is the meeting between the unconscious child in the writer and the unconscious child in the reader, but in great literature there will be a hero embodying the maturity of an adult who is no longer controlled by the desires and fears of a child. "None of us has ever completely silenced the little monster from whom he grew, but sometimes in a mature novel we can break all the chains that bind us to him." A novel may be the only place where a reader can be the hero, the mature adult he will never be in his own person.

The reader can also identify with the protagonist who represents the

[37] Brooks, A. R. "Developmental Values in Books," *Youth, Communications, and Libraries* (Frances Henne, ed.). Chicago: American Library Association, 1949, pp. 49–61.

[38] Havighurst, Robert J. *Human Development and Education.* New York: Longmans, Green and Co., 1953, p. 161.

[39] DeVoto, Bernard. *The World of Fiction.* Boston: Houghton Mifflin, 1950, p. 44.

elements in the reader's personality which he cannot admit to consciousness. He can confront the immoral or illegal impulses he will never express in real life and repudiate them or realize that "there but for the grace of God go I." He can project his unacknowledged errors and lack of success onto the fictional character without feeling more inadequate. Through reading he can get a second chance and still another to succeed in tasks which have previously frustrated him. In the victory or defeat of the hero the reader can experience triumph, or justify his own failure. In the words of DeVoto,

> None of us has ever killed a giant or kissed a princess awake and we know we never will. But, oh, yes, Lord, we all want to. . . . That is why people read the humblest fiction. We can kill the giant. And in precisely the same way on higher planes of fiction we can experience a moment of love or friendship or achievement purer and more intense than we have ever managed to feel by ourselves — but the substance remains the same as giant-killing.

In some ways the hero of a book is more real to us than people around us. Proust commented that in real life people are too opaque, too difficult to know and understand. They live behind their masks and mislead themselves and others as to their real natures. In fiction the characters can be more real, more intense and revealed, for "we have made them our own, since it is in ourselves that they are happening." We become the hero; hearing, seeing, and feeling with him in all his action.

According to Foss,[40] the destiny the reader perceives in the hero is only a single strand of his being, an abstraction of the universal abundance of life, separated out for clarity of understanding. We can comprehend a fragment of the hero's expression, but not all the complexities of personality he represents. Foss wrote that in literature "The plot becomes the mere manifestation and realization of the hero's life," and that when seen clearly the hero "represents in metaphorical extension more than himself and turns out to be the destiny of his fellow man." He also points out that other characters in the story are not separate personalities but are extensions of the inner life of the hero personifying his secret wishes or fears. It must also be remembered that not all heroes are human; in some stories the hero is an animal or a supernatural being. Especially in children's stories animals are the protagonists involving the reader in identifying or analogizing.

The hero is the personification and illustration of the recommended values of the story. He is the embodiment of the ideas, feelings, and characteristics the writer wishes to portray. The conventional hero usually has one or more of the following characteristics: strength, with physical strength exemplified by Beowulf, mental by Ulysses, or moral by Balder, Christ, and Galahad; virtue with Galahad, Lohengrin, and Percival as

[40] Foss, Martin. *Symbol and Metaphor in Human Experience.* Lincoln, Nebraska: University of Nebraska Press, 1949, pp. 128–29.

examples; ability, or a variety of skills, as in war, with Lancelot as an illustration, or in magic, with Merlin; and courage, as expressed by Beowulf. The hero is often of royal or noble birth, may have supernatural ancestry and thereby be a changeling, or may be a remarkable personality of unknown parentage. Freud suggested that the superior, unusual qualities and status of the hero reflect the unexpressed longings or even secret convictions of the unconscious.

In traditional literature the hero is usually confronted with certain circumstances which are extraordinary but have typical heroic patterns. He is frequently allied with the forces of good and is often a leader. The hero is customarily placed in a difficult situation in which he is victorious, the obstacle is impossible to overcome and no one could triumph, or it is his fate to be defeated. In another case he chooses to achieve one desired goal at the sacrifice of other goals. In cases of failure he meets defeat courageously and gloriously, and may kill or seriously injure his foe in doing so. In other situations the apparent defeat of the hero serves to redeem his cause.

The hero may fight against a prophecy and succeed, bringing reassurance to the reader that he, too, can oppose or even overcome fate. He may fulfill a favorable prophecy, providing assurance that fate may support one with heroic qualities. He may oppose or fulfill a prophecy leading to his death or destruction of his goals. Such a conclusion enables the reader to satisfy a need for justice, or to relieve guilt by perceiving that if fate is against one, not even heroic efforts will succeed. This releases the reader from feelings of guilt at failure since even a hero fails if he is doomed by forces outside himself. In meeting unusual difficulties with magnificent exploits, the hero dramatizes for us the unconscious problems of our more mundane lives.

Some modern literature is considered by critics to center around an antihero. He personifies attributes that are opposite to those of the traditional hero. He may be weak of body and spirit, and is easily discouraged; his goals are self-seeking; his honor and skills are marketable to expediency; and he finds no reason to resist evil or even to expect good. Some of the works of Camus, Sartre, and Moravia are among those considered notable for their antiheroes.

## *The Art of the Reader*

The hero, the embodiment of the book's values, must have characteristics that are related in some way to the reader in order for identification to take place. The hero is vital in the story and so is the congruence or "fit" of some of his qualities with some of the reader's values, feelings, experiences, perceptions, and desires. If the attributes of the hero match closely the qualities sought by the reader, reinforcement of the reader's ideas and values, or satisfaction of unfilled needs takes place. If the "fit" is less congruent but still intense in some areas, the reader is likely to identify with those areas and ignore, deny, or accept the others. Where too many significant values of the reader conflict with those of the hero, the reader may feel guilt or hostile rejection. In some cases where the hero manifests only the desired characteristics, the reader may react with envy if he thinks there is no chance that he could acquire them, not even by the "eucatastrophe" or good catastrophe, of Tolkien[41] or the deus ex machina which may have saved the hero. The self-image of the reader may be so inadequate that fantasizing the longed-for qualities or vicariously living through the desired experiences by identification with the hero, cannot be accepted by the Ego.

Other variables influence whether and how much the reader will identify with the hero, perceive life with his eyes, and use him as a model. Studies by Bergler and others indicate that setting is of minor importance in affecting reader response to writing. The reader who identifies with a character transports himself into the setting, or, more frequently, transposes the hero into the setting chosen by the reader. Lesser[42] stated that empirical evidence on response to fiction indicates that "among the deeper reverberations stirred up by reading, setting seldom appears to play an important part." Psychoanalysts who have observed the reaction of patients to literature have noted that the patients nearly always respond chiefly to the behaviors and relationships of the characters. The plot and action of fiction are also subsidiary to the role taken by the hero or character with whom the reader identifies. The plot must be relevant to the message expressed by the life of the hero and must flow so as to reveal his character.

The approval of the hero by society or by the reader's peers increases the tendency to identify because it provides another opportunity for wish fulfillment. In some cases the reader may consciously reject the hero who does not meet his approval, but may unconsciously identify in order to satisfy unacceptable impulses. When a reader identifies with a part of the hero, he may come to accept some other aspects of the character that he had previously rejected.

Among the causes of identification are opportunities to experience pleasurable events or to possess desired qualities through vicariously living as the hero. Such identification may bring relief from anxieties or from feelings of inferiority, or may produce heightened tension that the reader finds stimulating. The reader can be distracted from the problems of his real world by becoming involved in a fictional world. The sources of

[41] Tolkien, J. R. R. *The Tolkien Reader.* New York: Ballantine Books, 1966, p. 68.

[42] Lesser, Simon O. *Fiction and the Unconscious.* Boston: Beacon Press, 1957, p. 70.

reader identification with characters in books are likely to be multiple, springing from both the unconscious and conscious minds, and being built upon the experiences of a lifetime. After completing a book, the reader can continue for a time to participate in the fictional experience and to see the world through the eyes of the hero. Unless forbidden by the Ego, even the most unlikely possibility of achieving some of the qualities and gratifications of the hero may make the identification satisfactory and further fantasy enjoyable.

McLuhan has said that "the medium is the message" and it is thus that the hero is the message, the model expressing the qualities the writer wishes to express and those the reader is seeking. As the reader identifies with the model he interprets the being of the model, the message, in his own life. Walt Whitman observed that, "All music is what awakes from you when you are reminded by the instruments." In like manner the hero reminds the reader of himself – his longings, his fears, his failures, his triumphs, his determinations.

By identification with the model we discover the important things about ourselves that we had put away or forgotten, or had lost the capacity to perceive, and find more satisfactory understanding of ourselves. We recognize the hero and his actions as remembrance of things past or as discovery of new extensions of our feelings. Whether the memory of the hidden self that is called up by reading is the individual repository of impulses, the Id of Freud, or the recollection of the racial past, the collective unconscious of Jung, the reader responds to countless different personalities with real and familiar identification.

In the process of identification the reader forms an image of the hero and merges his own impulses and emotions with those of the fictional or biographical character. Wellek and Warren[43] emphasize that an image may include more than the usual picture. They wrote that "In psychology 'image' means a mental reproduction, a memory, or a past sensational or perceptual experience, not necessarily visual." The reader may express the image with "gustatory, olfactory, thermal, pressure, color, auditory, or muscular" responses. William James[44] believed there is evidence that specific perceptions produce "widespread bodily effects by a sort of immediate physical influence antecedent to the arousal of an emotion or an emotional idea." He related physical effects of perception to literature by stating that poetry, drama, or heroic narrative can stimulate a "cutaneous shiver which like a sudden wave flows over us" and may induce a swelling of the heart and effusion of tears.

The conscious enjoyment and suffering that the reader feels through

[43] Wellek, René, and Austin Warren. *Theory of Literature.* New York: Harcourt, Brace (Harvest Books), 1956, p. 186.

[44] Lange, Carl G., and William James. *The Emotions.* Baltimore: Williams and Wilkins Co., 1922, p. 20.

identification are even more strongly experienced in the unconscious, according to psychoanalytic theories of literature. As the reader projects his impulses and introjects those of the model, he achieves catharsis, which opens the way for development of new insights, feelings, and behaviors. Jung[45] believed that "No psychic value can disappear without being replaced by another of equivalent intensity." As the reader perceives, compares, and interprets his vicarious experiences, he is able at times to make application to his own life of the understandings obtained. Through wide reading, or by reading the right book at the right time, the reader may find such profound or comprehensive insights that they reach the conscious mind, and he may then be able to generalize his understandings to apply to more effective behaviors of his real life.

The art of the reader is that he is reader and creator at the same time. He is affected by the work and in turn changes it into his own conceptual pattern. The story molds the reader and is molded by him. Concrete objects or ideas are taken from the writing and shaped by the imagination or unconscious perceptions of the reader into the individual personal embodiment of his wishes. He uses the material he finds in literature to communicate, explain, and clarify certain feelings and to conceal others. The unconscious experiences of reading may break down repressions, modify personality patterns, and suggest new solutions for old problems. The inner understandings may progress to conscious discernment and enable the reader to realize some of his hidden needs and impulses and deliberately to incorporate some of the insights into real life situations. A graphic representation of the relationship between the response of the reader to literature and the processes by which the response takes place may be seen in the following interaction model.

*Interaction Model of Reader Response*

| THE READER | THE LITERATURE | THE PROCESS | CONCEPT DEVELOPMENT |
|---|---|---|---|
| Perception | Character | Identification | Model |
| Interaction | Plot Development | Catharsis | Interpretation |
| Creation | Solutions | Insight | Generalization |

The art of the reader enables him to use his reading to enhance his understandings and to discover new insights. The reader perceives familiar feelings, values, and relationships through identification with a character that he takes for a model for his reading response. Through interaction of his emotions with the experiences of the model in the development of the story he undergoes catharsis, thereby experiencing relief from anxiety and

[45] Jung, C. G. *Modern Man in Search of a Soul.* New York: Harcourt, Brace, 1933, p. 209.

relaxation of tensions. He interprets his vicarious experiences and the resulting emotions in terms of his own buried impulses and unexpressed longings and creates an identification that is relevant to his individual needs. He may gain deeper understanding of himself and his relationships with others through a sudden or lengthy evolving of insight into the behavior of the hero. He may sometimes recognize that he has shared impulses, feelings, and values with the model. If the reader attains profound conscious insights into the hero's nature, he may generalize into his own life and value system some of the meanings he perceived in the message of the story as exemplified by the model.

## *Psychoanalytic Interpretations of Literature*

There are numerous sound and accepted methods of interpreting the wealth of literature available to the reader. Regardless of the approach which a critic feels is most relevant to his material, he is necessarily reminded to deal with the psychological implications of a written work because of the explosive impact of Freudian theory upon interpretation.

A number of familiar and accepted methods of literary criticism will be described in Chapter 4. The present chapter, however, focuses on the psychoanalytic interpretation of literature. This discussion is not an attempt to present a complete examination of the method, but is intended to provide illustrations of how the method is used by some critics. Nor is it implied in this chapter that the psychoanalytic approach is the only, or even the best, means of literary interpretation. Regardless of the approach a critic feels is most relevant to his material he is necessarily reminded to deal with the psychological implications of literature because of the explosive impact of Freud's writings upon interpretation. DeVoto[46] stated that "no other scientist has ever had so strong and so widespread influence on literature." Freudian themes and symbols are found abundantly in poetry, drama, and fiction.

Not all psychological interpretations of literature refer to the structure of the Id, Ego, and Superego, or to the developmental phases of Freudian theory, but most of them are based on Freud's discoveries concerning the human psyche. Freud himself wrote extensively about the psychoanalytic interpretation of literature, especially with reference to the personality of the author as revealed in his works. Other critics have followed the pattern set by Freud in using psychoanalytic criteria for the interpretation of literature. Jung and Adler also have influenced literary criticism with elaborations from their respective psychoanalytic systems.

Lesser[47] believed that other psychologies have not dealt with the un-

[46] DeVoto, Bernard. *The World of Fiction.* Boston: Houghton Mifflin, 1950, p. 44.

[47] Lesser, Simon O. *Fiction and the Unconscious.* Boston: Beacon Press, 1957, p. 15.

conscious forces which determine to a great degree the destiny of man. These are powerful, basic human needs which have been significant in great literature. Lesser expressed the opinion that:

The supreme virtue of psychoanalysis, from the point of view of its potential utility for literary study, is that it has investigated the very aspects of man's nature with which the greatest writers of fiction have been preoccupied: the emotional, unconscious or only partly comprehended bases of our behavior.

Psychoanalytic interpretations of literature deal with "universal" themes appearing in varieties of literature. The themes of birth, death, family relationships, achieving adulthood, and obtaining power, are found in literature from the earliest times. In ancient myths, heroic sagas, and fairy tales are seen the common themes of life that are expressed throughout the historical development of literature. Secret emotions and repressed conflicts are explored in disguise in early fantasy and in modern writing. Symbols discerned by Freud in dreams have their parallels in literature. On the psychoanalytic level they express the instinctual needs of all humanity. Symbols may be deeply concealed, or may appear clearly to the reader.

The oedipal theme delineated by Freud as an important unconscious directive of man's decisions and relationships has been perceived in many great works by psychoanalytic critics. The oedipal impulses develop early in the child and are among those which are never completely relinquished by the Id. The male child competes with the father for the love and possession of the mother but senses that he can never succeed in the same manner that the father has. The theme frequently appears in literature as the expression of the boy's longing for his mother and his desire to defeat the father or to identify with him completely and thereby take his place with the mother. It is sometimes expressed, especially in contemporary literature, as an opposite impulse, with portrayal of the denial of the wish, as a rejection of the powerful mother and a desire for identification with the father as a means of safety from the disavowed impulse. In a larger sense the theme is often found in the literature of all ages as a picture of man's struggle against overwhelming odds. Freud[48] postulated that:

It can scarcely be mere coincidence that three of the masterpieces of literature of all time, the *Oedipus Rex* of Sophocles, Shakespeare's *Hamlet,* and Dostoevsky's *The Brothers Karamazov,* should all deal with the same subject, a father's murder. In all three, too, the motive for the deed, sexual rivalry for the woman, is laid bare.

*Hamlet* has been the subject of controversial study for many years. T. S. Eliot[49] objected to the general tendency among critics to consider

[48] Freud, Sigmund. "Dostoevsky and Parricide," *Art and Psychoanalysis* (William Phillips, ed.). Cleveland: World Publishing Co., 1963, p. 13.

[49] Eliot, T. S. "Hamlet and His Problems," *Selected Essays: 1917–1932.* New York: Harcourt, Brace, 1932, p. 125.

Hamlet, the man, as a primary problem and the play itself as secondary. Yet the character of Hamlet emerges as Eliot's outstanding objection to the artistry of the play. He found that he could not reconcile the degree of disgust which Hamlet displays toward his mother with her negative and insignificant character. "Hamlet (the man) is dominated by an emotion which is inexpressible, because it is in *excess* of the facts as they appear." It is this imbalance that has long intrigued both critic and reader.

Our emotional response to Hamlet is far greater than the reasons given in the play. Hamlet[50] himself suggests that there may be revelations in the drama when he speaks of the art of playing,

> whose end, both at the first and now, was and is, to hold, as 'twere, the mirror up to nature; to show virtue her own feature, scorn her own image, and the very age and body of the time his form and pressure.

Some writers, like Eliot and earlier critics such as Hanmer and Samuel Johnson, feel that Shakespeare failed to provide adequate material; others look to the circumstances to show how they could cause Hamlet to delay on the grounds of common sense. Hamlet has been explained as a man suffering from the shock of what has occurred before the play opens, as an overall neurotic personality, and as a man who is actually insane. He has been called a master philosopher, a symbol of all humanity, and a juvenile delinquent. There is material in the play to support all these interpretations and still we are faced with the problem: Why does the character of Hamlet have such an emotional impact and imaginative appeal that causes us to attempt such various rationalizations?

Ernest Jones' psychoanalytic solution offers a plausible resolution of the difficulty. Perhaps its main distinction from other criticisms of Hamlet lies in the statement, "If we ask, not what ought to produce such soul-paralysing grief and distaste for life [in Hamlet], but what in actual fact does produce it, we are compelled to go beyond this explanation and seek for some deeper cause." Previously critics either justified or condemned the character of Hamlet on the basis of what they were able to make of actual material presented in the play. Jones deals with psychoanalytic principles of human personality that have been systematized to apply to particular cases. According to this method, Shakespeare, in giving a believable picture of the character he created, also furnished material that makes the personality conform to general psychological precepts. Jones stated, "I would suggest that in this Shakespeare's extraordinary powers of observation and penetration granted him a degree of insight that it has taken the world three subsequent centuries to reach."[51]

Trilling accepts Jones' analysis of an oedipal situation as the source of

[50] Shakespeare, William. *Hamlet.* Act III, Scene ii, 18–39.

[51] Jones, Ernest. *Hamlet and Oedipus.* New York: Doubleday, n.d. (Originally published by W. W. Norton, 1949).

Hamlet's failure to avenge his father's death. In fact, he says, such an interpretation adds a new point of interest to the play. He does not, however, think that this is a total explanation of the meaning of *Hamlet,* or wholly accounts for the impact the play has on the audience.

The role of the mother in a damaging relationship with her son is, of course, most often associated with Iocaste in the *Oedipus Rex* of Sophocles. Iocaste enters in the role of queen, a figure to whom the citizens turn to settle the quarrel between their enraged king, Oedipus, and Creon, the wise man. She scolds her husband and her brother, calling them "poor, foolish men" who should be ashamed to quarrel when the state is in danger. Her presence and her words seem to reduce the two most powerful men in the community to the status of foolish boys, who must explain and justify their actions to her. As she dismisses Creon and asks Oedipus to go to his chambers, her manner is more that of mother to child than queen to king. It is ironic that she should here assume the position which subsequent events prove to be her true role.

As Oedipus releases Creon and turns to confide in Iocaste, "for none of these men deserves my confidence as you do," Iocaste seems a source of strength, capable of overcoming his doubts with calm reason. By a strange paradox, understandable by psychoanalytic theory, in each of Iocaste's attempts to reassure Oedipus she uses the very evidence which will most clearly threaten him. Instead of dispelling his fears, she continues to offer further proofs to justify them. Her unawareness of the implications of her remarks seems proof of her innocence, yet the facts she brings forth so easily and so lucidly may also indicate that she is unconsciously aware of Oedipus' identity. This idea is further suggested by her compulsive need to think only in the present. She strongly advises Oedipus: "A man should live only for the present day." In the end when Iocaste fully recognizes the truth, and understands that there are no further avenues of escape from reality, she hangs herself. In this way she again abandons her son just as she had when he was an infant, leaving him to die in the wild hills of Kithairon.

Psychoanalytic interpretations can be of value in searching for the meaning of any literature which moves us profoundly, and can be used not only in dealing specifically with characters but also with situations. A classical example of this possibility occurs in *The Odyssey,* where the hero's experience can be seen as symbolic of his search for self. The first four books deal chiefly with Telemachus, the son of Odysseus. The growth of the boy through the problems of childhood and adolescence is paralleled by the experiences of his father in a dreamlike world of witches and giants. The adventures of Odysseus begin when he first appears as the prisoner of the witch, Calypso, whose name means "concealer." She suggests the figure of a possessive mother who seeks to conceal and hold her son, by force if necessary, and prevent him from living his own life.

Calypso may be the symbol of the overwhelming, clutching mother. Under the direction of the goddess Athena, representing wisdom, Odysseus escapes in a symbolical rebirth from the concealing, womblike control of Calypso. He reaches the land of the Phaeacians, which is like the protected world of the child with no decisions or responsibilities and where the people are like children without worry or need to care for themselves or to control themselves. Odysseus feels the need to grow beyond such childlike immaturity and to develop self-control through decision making and striving in the real world.

The further adventures of Odysseus are manifestations of childhood fears, the repetition compulsion expressed in the need to work through again and again the unsolved problems of the unconscious. In his wanderings he encounters the temptations of the Sirens and the Lotus Eaters, the danger of being killed by the Cyclopes and the escape by hiding under the belly of a sheep, the ordeal of Scylla and Charybdis, and the descent into Hades where he meets his mother and enters the abode of the dead as a means of dying and returning to life. All of his adventures and the figures he meets can be interpreted in the symbols of Freudian theory.

Odysseus continues to seek his destiny as a man and sets out for home. As in all of the story, each aspect of his journey is symbolic. On many occasions he sails over the sea, the symbol of the source of life and of birth. While he is asleep, he is carried by the Phaeacians and placed by a phallic olive tree near a cave, representing his desire to escape from the womb, and from childhood, and to assume his manhood. When Odysseus arrives home in Ithaca, the real world, he finds that he must fight to regain his right to a position that he has neglected in his search for maturity. With the success of this final struggle Odysseus achieves full command of his situation and is able to assume his mature role as husband, father, and ruler of men.

In the book, the use of places, people, and happenings as symbols of self-development parallel the growth of the inner self of Telemachus, Odysseus' son. While Odysseus seeks to regain a self that was lost, his son develops from boy to man and achieves an identification with the father on an adult level. It is interesting that the young Telemachus is faced with the struggle Hamlet had already lost at the beginning of the play. Telemachus must find a means to prevent a horde of suitors from forcing his mother to desert his father, representing his own desire for her. But where Hamlet's mother had conceded with untimely haste, arousing her son's guilt for his secret incestuous impulses, Penelope, the mother of Telemachus, stands as a representation of woman's fidelity. Her steadfastness in the role of ideal wife and mother sets the barrier that definitely precludes any possibility of the son's usurping the place of the father. As a result Telemachus does not have to confront Hamlet's dilemma, and both husband and son are able to achieve maturity and, in a sense, merge into one character.

It is not surprising that so many literary works from *Beowulf* and *Theseus* to D. H. Lawrence's *Sons and Lovers* have been psychoanalytically interpreted as dealing with oedipal impulses. Freud[52] explained that the fate of Oedipus is so moving to us because it could have been our own. He believed that "It may be that we were all destined to direct our first sexual impulses toward our mothers, and our first impulses of hatred and violence toward our fathers; our dreams convince us that we were."

In literature which treats of oedipal urges the reader finds gratification of powerful instinctual impulses. At the same time, in much of the literature, he can purge himself of those impulses and satisfy the Superego by sharing the horror and punishment which result from fulfilling the buried desires. When Oedipus realizes his guilt, he gouges out his eyes in an act similar to the amnesia of a child as he blinds himself to painful memories. With the inevitable punishment of Oedipus, the plague is lifted from his people and they are restored to health. According to Freudian theory, the reader correspondingly recovers his psychic health through the unconscious purging and punishing of his secret impulses, and this benefit accounts for the continuing enjoyment of such literature over the centuries.

Among writers who have used the oedipal theme in their works are Swift, Dostoevsky, Henry James, Maugham, Hawthorne, and Melville. Jung pointed out that the Freudian theory of the oedipal conflict failed to deal adequately with the female aspect of the Oedipus motif. Some literature, however, is seen by some readers as portraying the girl's search for the love and approval of the father, and on a deeper level to represent the incestuous impulses of the female toward the father. Books by de Beauvoir and Sagan have suggested symbolism of this sort.

Not all literature providing relief from oedipal impulses deals with the theme as gratification and punishment. Some works, such as *Odysseus*, reveal a satisfactory resolution of the conflict, giving hope and a model to the reader. Some stories, especially contemporary works, shout a denial of the incestuous drive. Children's stories are especially open in aggressive treatment of the family triangle. In some the killing of the unwanted father is clearly depicted, as in *Jack and the Beanstalk*, *Peter Pan*, and Kipling's *Jungle Book*. Other children's stories, such as *Hansel and Gretel*, reveal a denial of the incestuous impulse and a satisfaction in revenge upon the dominating, unloving mother. The Oedipus theme is not confined to the western world but is found in literature of other lands, races, and degrees of civilization.

Symbols of other aspects of Freudian theory are found in early and recent literature. Dodgson's *Alice in Wonderland* is filled with symbols

[52] Freud, Sigmund. "The Interpretation of Dreams," *The Basic Writings of Sigmund Freud*. New York: Random House, 1938, p. 308.

appropriate for psychoanalytic interpretation. The images range from expressions of the desire to return to the womb to an almost literal portrayal of the progression of the unconscious through various stages of psychic development. There are also disguised jokes about current and traditional beliefs. The Cinderella theme is universally popular because it gives the reader consolation for humiliation and assurance of ultimate success. The reader identifies with the heroine, sharing in her suffering and rejoicing in her eventual prosperity. Robinson Crusoe, with his orderliness and cleanliness, has been labeled an example of the "anal personality." Silas Marner and Scrooge have been considered representations of the same fixation. Such symbolic expressions of stages in the development of the psyche are believed to give the reader with unsatisfied needs from the matching stage, vicarious gratification of his desires.

Melville's *Moby Dick,* considered the greatest American novel, has been popular for analysis by critics. Leverenz[53] and others have seen in the great white whale the image of the cold, indifferent mother, who will not relate emotionally except in an aggressive way during a crisis. Leverenz commented that *Moby Dick* is essentially a Rorschach test; that each reader sees in it what he unconsciously feels. Ishmael at first perceived the whale as the figure of his father, with whom he had never had a good relationship. Early Puritan sermons reveal fear of the father figure, which later diminished and became directed toward the mother. Leverenz believed that mother conflict has been increasingly at the heart of American literature. He analyzed Henry James's "The Beast in the Jungle," Frank Norris's *The Octopus,* Albee's *The Zoo Story,* and Mailer's *Why Are We in Viet Nam,* in terms of the reader's aroused fear of the overwhelming, castrating mother. Best-selling contemporary books which reveal oral aggressive feelings toward the mother figure are *Generation of Vipers* by Wylie and *Portnoy's Complaint* by Roth.

Lesser[54] reviewed the opinions of several writers concerning the psychoanalytic interpretations of *Moby Dick.* He refers to Murray as perceiving in Ahab the representation of the primitive urges and values which are repressed in the Id. To Murray, Moby Dick is the object of Ahab's rage and hatred because it is the Superego which first symbolizes the parents and their prohibitions of pleasure. The whale, or Superego, is not limited to parents, however, and further incarnates the restrictions of society, and finally the intimidations of a Supreme Ruler. Mumford saw Ahab becoming "the thing he hates," an extension of the threat of the whale and destroying the self, as the Superego destroys the Ego if the Id is not controlled. According to Arvin, Ahab is heroic in his attack upon the

[53] Leverenz, David. *A Psychoanalysis of American Literature.* Unpublished doctoral dissertation (University of Californa, Berkeley, 1969).

[54] Lesser, Simon O. *Fiction and the Unconscious.* Boston: Beacon Press, 1957, pp. 118–20.

world's restrictions which inhibit happiness and creativity, although his approach is wrong. "He is our hatred enobled."

These examples of interpretation of reader response to *Moby Dick* are limited and omit many others that are available. This is also true of other literature mentioned in this chapter. The interpretations of works examined in more detail are also incomplete and omit many explanations of symbolism which are adduced by originators of the criticism to support their theses.

Goethe's *Faust* is a work which has been analyzed in a variety of styles. Rexroth[55] commented that "*Faust* is a kind of immense psychoanalytic session." He perceived Faust as the destroyer of love and the exponent of the business or work ethic which is stifling to creativity. He stated, "*Faust,* as a moral tract, is as dangerous as the hydrogen bomb."

Other viewpoints have seen Freudian symbols in the play. Several critics have pointed out the difference in quality and meaning between the first and second parts of the drama. The first appears to be a clear statement about Faust as a man seeking his own pleasures, and about the results of his self-centered actions on those he exploits. This phase can be considered the search of the Id for infantile impulse gratification.

The second part of the play is more difficult to interpret and contains various psychological symbols and literary allusions. In this section Faust is not as clear-cut in his characteristics, showing ambivalence in his attitude toward women, and seeming to move from emphasis on sexual satisfaction to a striving for power, and finally seeking higher spirituality. He is involved in relationships with many figures and enlarges his sphere of desires. This may represent the development of the Ego and the final control of the Superego.

The drama, especially the second part, is rich with psychoanalytic symbols and hidden meanings. Mephistopheles, the devil, represents the dark, negative aspect of Faust – the Id. Faust indulges himself in the hedonistic rewards offered by Mephistopheles and destroys an innocent girl and her family by his lust, but later seeks a more acceptable way of life. The play contains many symbolic references to the need for rebirth and finding a better self.

Through the magic of Mephistopheles, Faust descends into the underworld where the Mothers, who are the preservers of life and controllers of creativity, enable him to experience love for Helen, which lifts him from his base past. The second part of the play depicts the confused fantasy in which the Ego overcomes the Id and produces the Superego. The references to the Mothers, representing Eternal Womankind, are expressions of the gratification and the denial of the oedipal impulses. In the end, Mephistopheles, the Id, is defeated and the regenerated Faust is promised

[55] Rexroth, Kenneth. "Goethe," *Saturday Review,* 52:21, April 19, 1969.

a future in heaven. The play overflows with Christian, pagan, and magical symbolism. Wayne[56] quoted the opinion of Burckhardt that:

What you are destined to discover in *Faust*, you will have to discover intuitively. *Faust* is a genuine myth, *i.e.*, a great primordial image, in which every man has to discover his own being and destiny in his own way.

Jung[57] agreed with Burckhardt, the historian, that *Faust* deals with a primordial image. Jung saw the drama as the representation of the archetype of the great teacher, the savior or redeemer who "lies buried and dormant in man's unconscious since the dawn of culture." When people develop problems they seek a counselor or physician. When a whole society is involved in serious difficulties it calls for a teacher or savior, in reality or in fiction. The reader finds in *Faust* the archetypal image of the guide or wise man he needs to head him to a better way of life.

Jung's theories of psychoanalysis differed from those of Freud in basic assumptions which resulted in dissimilar ways of perceiving the human psyche. Freud believed that the unconscious of each individual is the basis of his personality, whereas Jung averred that "Ideas spring from a source that is not contained within one man's personal life. We do not create them; they create us." He felt that impulses, dreams, thoughts, and beliefs are timeless and appear in one human mind as a single part of the whole racial psyche.

According to Jung, the reader finds pleasure, catharsis, or insight in literature, not because it satisfies the needs of his own unconscious, but because it speaks to the collective unconscious. The reader responds to symbols that express meanings to him through his memory of primitive processes. Jung did not interpret symbols as representations of impulses in the individual but as instinctual expressions of primitive nature which can only be analyzed through the study of myths, legends, fairy tales, religion, and language. To Jung the cry of Faust, "The mothers – mothers – how very strange it sounds!" does not refer to his repressed incestuous impulses but to the archetypal mother symbol, the natural, instinctive origin of life, the unconscious beginning which is the foundation of consciousness, and stands for his desire for rebirth to find a higher level of being.

Jung perceived primordial experience as the source of the appeal of many books in addition to *Faust*, including Haggard's *She*, the poetry of Blake, and Dante's *Inferno*. He believed that to attribute the importance of great literature to personal factors is to miss completely its meaning to the reader. Great art is impersonal but profoundly moves the reader because it involves in the *participation mystique* the healing experience of the collective psyche of mankind, of all human existence.

[56] Wayne, Philip (trans.). *Faust*, Part II. Baltimore: Penguin Books, 1949, p. 18.

[57] Jung, C. G. *Modern Man in Search of a Soul*. New York: Harcourt, Brace, 1933, p. 171.

Adler, another early pupil of Freud, attributed the instinctual needs of the unconscious to an innate urge for power, rather than to the desire for pleasure postulated by Freud. He found the dominant need in the human psyche to be that of self-assertion. In literature the reader identifies with the character who represents the power he seeks, or who justifies his lack of power, or helps him deny or socialize his craving for power. The reader finds literature a means of protesting his subordinate position and vicariously asserting his psychic strength, and an avenue for learning social adaptation.

From this small sampling of various theories of psychoanalysis and the interpretations which they supply it can be seen that there are quite diverse responses to books that are widely read. All the interpretations, however, have some vital points in common. They all deal with symbols, although each theory assigns different meanings to them. More importantly, they all assume that the reader responds to literature on the basis of unconscious impulses and needs.

## *Myths and Fantasy*

Out of the depths of time, close to the dim beginnings of man's struggle to civilization, glow the myth and legend – the origin of literature, according to Toynbee.[58] At first spoken or sung, later written, it was used for many of the same purposes as modern literature. It offered explanations for the curious, morality for the young, comfort for the old, consolation for the unhappy, escape for the miserable, and a model for the unsure. It also provided beauty and understanding and a common background of proverbs, values, and history that contributed to group solidarity. From the myth and legend developed the fairy tale, fantasy, poetry, biography, and the novel. They have similar characteristics, although the differences cannot be minimized. Some authors have emphasized the differences between myth and legend, stating that a myth is invented and focuses upon gods or supernatural heroes, whereas a legend is based on history and focuses upon mortal beings. Because a story considered to be a myth may be discovered to be historically based, and therefore a legend, the distinction appears to be unsure for application. Freud[59] supported the contention that modern literature developed from myths and legends. He wrote that the material of literature

> is derived from the racial treasure-house of myths, legends, and fairy tales. The study of these creations of racial psychology is in no way complete, but it seems

[58] Toynbee, Arnold J. *A Study of History.* New York: Oxford University Press, 1947, p. 44.

[59] Freud, Sigmund. "The Relation of the Poet to Day-Dreaming," *Collected Papers,* Vol. 4. New York: Basic Books, 1959, p. 182.

extremely probable that myths, for example, are distorted vestiges of the wish-phantasies of whole nations – the age-long dreams of young humanity.

The influences of myths and legends and their place as prototypes of literature to which the reader responds with unconscious mechanisms are best studied in English literature. Chinese literature, although prolific, is not available from early periods. The first writings are from the School of Confucius, which reflect an advanced culture. Almost no writings are available from early periods of ancient societies, except for Homer. The only literature which reveals the cultural development of the society is English, beginning with *Beowulf* and continuing with historical development and the emergence of many literary forms. This phenomenon may be due to two factors: the age of the older cultures, such as China and India, in comparison with that represented in *Beowulf*, and the invention of the printing press. By starting with *Beowulf* and following the development of literature paralleling the progress of the culture, it might be possible to observe the unfolding of the unconscious responses of readers through the periods of evolution and any changing effects.

Folktales are the vehicles which carry the wisdom and beauty of mankind's accumulated memories of experience. Speculations about the origins of folktales include theories that they are remnants of nature myths or of religious beliefs and rituals. Some folktales have been found almost intact in widespread locations. There are 345 variants of the Cinderella story already discovered in different societies. This and other evidence seem to indicate that folktales are expressions of basic human needs and beliefs. According to Arbuthnot,[60] psychoanalytic explanations of many folktales interpret them as "symbols of emotional fantasy," representing unconscious urges. She suggested that a more plausible theory is that folktales grew out of "the dreams and nightmares of the storytellers," which she related to realistic situations. In terms of Freudian definition of dreams and literature, however, the theory would still refer to unconscious impulses. Arbuthnot preferred the psychological interpretation that folktales provide "a satisfaction for . . . unconscious frustration and drives." She saw them as "splendid dreams which symbolize *wish fulfillment* for each succeeding generation."

The types of stories designated as folktales include fables, or talking beast stories, religious tales, realistic stories, and tales of magic. The fairy tales of magic and marvels have enchanted men of all ages through the centuries. They provide the reader with opportunities for wish fulfillment in unreal, magical worlds. Sometimes the women – queens, mothers, fairy godmothers – are beautiful beyond description, gracious and generous, expressing the ideal, desired mother. Sometimes they are wicked stepmothers, evil witches, or cold selfish queens, who are cruel, jealous, and

[60] Arbuthnot, May Hill. "Time for Fairy Tales Old and New," *The Arbuthnot Anthology of Children's Literature.* Chicago: Scott, Foresman, n.d., p. 3.

self-centered, representing the rejecting, aggressive mother, and, at the same time, the denial of unconscious love. According to psychoanalytic theory, boy readers can enjoy stories in which father figures are defeated as evil men, animals, or monsters. For example, in *Jack and The Beanstalk,* Jack lives happily with his mother after killing the giant and bringing back his wealth. Girls can find satisfaction in stories like *Cinderella,* in which the unappreciated daughter wins the handsome prince and is publicly recognized as more beautiful and desirable than the mother and sisters who had scorned her. Other tales which have been interpreted as appealing to the unconscious incestuous impulses of the reader include *Snow White and the Seven Dwarfs* and *Little Red Riding Hood.*

Tolkien[61] agreed with Freud that the values of fairy tales to readers is the satisfaction of "certain primordial human desires." He believed that these wishes which lead readers to seek the magic of fairy tales include the desire "to survey the depths of space and time," to swim in the sea and fly as a bird, and to escape from a harsh, cruel world. By withdrawal from the real world the reader can recover a clear view, see his world with new perceptions. Tolkien emphasized the consolation the reader finds in the inevitable happy ending in the fairy tale, the eucatastrophe which denies final defeat, insures joy and victory, and affirms a strong faith in the future.

Modern fairy tales are expressed as fantasy and science fiction. Fantasy arouses response in the reader because he can find there a new world of freedom and magic for himself, where good overcomes evil, where sorrow and death are confronted and understood, where supernatural forces support and save those with faith and integrity.

The aim of science fiction is to "point up a moral for the world of today" by predicting "the world of tomorrow," according to Ellison.[62] Science fiction may be based on genuine scientific knowledge, or upon pseudoscience. It travels the past and the future, and worlds of Earth or anywhere in the universe. Although it provides pleasure and escape, much science fiction speaks to the reader of philosophy and politics, of happy anticipation or fear of the future. Howe[63] evaluated the impact of Orwell's *1984* by emphasizing that the book "appalls us because its terror . . . is particular to our century; what haunts us is the sickening awareness that in *1984* Orwell describes tragedies of our society that we could have prevented."

Two other modern literary categories include the psychological and the stream of consciousness novel. In earlier novels the reader became involved in a story through identification with one or more characters. He

[61] Tolkien, J. R. R. *The Tolkien Reader.* New York: Ballantine Books, 1966, pp. 57–66.

[62] Ellison, Harlan. "Introduction," *Nine by Laumer.* New York: Berkeley Publishing Co., 1967, p. 2.

[63] Howe, Irving. *Politics and the Novel.* Cleveland: World Publishing Co., 1957, p. 236.

projected and ventilated on an unconscious level. In the psychological novel the reader is not entertained by a story, but enters the mind of the character who is being revealed at the time in order to feel with him. Edel[64] believed that in the psychological novel the reader "walks not only with but *as* the character." Humphrey[65] stated that meaning comes to the reader most forcibly in the stream of consciousness novels. Jung and O'Connor, however, suggested that the unconscious of the reader responds with more strength and more effect to literature which does not attempt to reveal the psychic nature of the character so openly.

## *Literature and Culture*

Literature interacts with the culture with both receptive and directive effects. It reflects and, at the same time, helps to mold and transmit cultural values. In reflecting the existing values it helps to perpetuate and reinforce them among the people of the society and to transmit them to the next generation. Downs[66] stated that

> Throughout history, the evidence is piled high that books, rather than being futile, harmless and innocent, are frequently dynamic, vital things, capable of changing the entire direction of events — sometimes for good, sometimes for ill.

Literature is social history, according to Wellek and Warren.[67] They described literature as "a source book for the history of civilization." Readers form their impressions of important personages, of the historical past, and of other countries and cultures through the literature they read. Wellek and Warren averred that

> The writer is not only influenced by society: he influences it. Art not merely reproduces life but also shapes it. People may model their lives upon the patterns of fictional heroes and heroines. They have made love, committed crimes and suicide according to the book.

The myths and legends of early history served to transmit the values of the culture to the young and to reinforce them for the adults. According to Róheim,[68] the myth "is only conceivable on a superego level" and "the

[64] Edel, Leon. *The Psychological Novel 1900–1950.* New York: Lippincott, 1955, p. 33.

[65] Humphrey, Robert. *Stream of Consciousness in the Modern Novel.* Berkeley: University of California Press, 1954, p. 22.

[66] Downs, Robert B. *Books That Changed The World.* New York: New American Library of World Literature, 1956, p. 7.

[67] Wellek, René, and Austin Warren. *Theory of Literature.* New York: Harcourt, Brace (Harvest Books), 1956, p. 102.

[68] Róheim, Géza. "Myth and Folk Tale," *Art and Psychoanalysis* (William Phillips, ed.). Cleveland: World Publishing Co., 1957, p. 344.

fully developed superego represents the real father . . . [but] also stands for society." Arbuthnot[69] believed that "folk tales were the *cement of society*, the carriers of the moral code." From folktales people learned belief in rewards for practicing the virtues of courage, kindness, and hard work. They likewise learned that the evils of selfishness, deceit, and harm to others are inexorably punished. The drama of the stories made the lessons meaningful to the listeners or readers and helped to unify society "with a common body of moral and social standards."

The earliest English epic, *Beowulf*, taught the values of the culture by encouraging the listener to fight courageously against adversities and by providing at the same time a philosophy permitting the acceptance of failure without guilt. Comparison of *Beowulf* with a series of books which were widely read in the United States during the early part of this century, indicates cultural changes in the values of the superego of the society. *Beowulf* encourages the reader to struggle until utter disaster prevents any other further effort, whereas in the Horatio Alger, Jr., books any regression in the forward thrust of the protagonist breaks the reader's enchantment. The Alger hero struggles against obstacles, but he constantly rises to a better position, and the reader safely anticipates certain success.

In the opinion of Downs and others, literary works of fiction, nonfiction, and political philosophy have had tremendous impact on national events. Downs considered Paine's *Common Sense* and Stowe's *Uncle Tom's Cabin* the instruments that triggered two major wars in our country. Wellek and Warren[70] suggested that literature has had an important influence on the rise of modern nationalism. They wrote:

> Certainly the historical novels of Walter Scott in Scotland, of Henryk Sienkiewicz in Poland, of Alois Jirásek in Czechoslovakia, have done something very definite to increase national pride and a common memory of historical events.

The effect of literature upon the culture cannot be proven, but can only be inferred by social or legal changes. Two recent books have apparently resulted in social change. *The Other America*, by Harrington, was described in *Time*[71] as a "key impetus for the poverty program" and has stimulated national awareness of problems of the poor. Nader's *Unsafe at Any Speed* produced legal action on automotive safety and changes in automobile construction.

Literature is in turn powerfully affected by factors in the culture.

[69] Arbuthnot, May Hill. "Time for Fairy Tales Old and New," *The Arbuthnot Anthology of Children's Literature.* Chicago: Scott, Foresman, n.d., pp. 3–4.

[70] Wellek, René, and Austin Warren. *Theory of Literature.* New York: Harcourt, Brace (Harvest Books), 1956, p. 102.

[71] Wellek, René, and Austin Warren. "The Tortured Role of the Intellectual in America," *Time,* May 9, 1969, pp. 48–49.

Social changes and technological advances influence reader response to books. An example is seen in the change in the portrayal of the Negro since the rise of the civil rights movement. The literary stereotype of the Negro has improved as national attitudes have changed. Wallace's *The Man* probably would not have been accepted before the development of a political climate in which it is possible that a Negro could become president of the United States. Technological advances have reflected the prophecies of science fiction and have stimulated more acceptance of it by readers as related to life. Radio and television have helped to make fantasy more acceptable.

Two men whose works have radically affected their societies were Einstein and Freud. Einstein's "General Theory of Relativity" revolutionized concepts of gravity, light, space, energy, and mass. Application of his theories have had inestimable impact on our society and on the world; for example, in the development of television, motion-picture sound tracks, the electric eye, and the atomic bomb. Einstein's effect upon science and our society extended beyond the practical results of his theories. The imaginations and inventiveness of other men were freed by his daring. Downs[72] quoted Banesh Hoffman, a scientist, who concluded:

> The importance of Einstein's scientific ideas does not reside merely in their great success. Equally powerful has been their psychological effect. At a crucial epoch in the history of science Einstein demonstrated that long-accepted ideas were not in any way sacred.

The influence of Freud can be seen in much modern literature, and he himself stated that his theories were supported in part by the literature of the ages. Downs[73] wrote:

> In exploring the unknown regions of the mind, Freud formulated ideas and terms that have now become part of our daily living. Virtually every field of knowledge – literature, art, religion, anthropology, education, law, sociology, criminology, history, biography, and other guides of society and the individual – has felt the effects of his teachings.

## *Psychological Implications for the Classroom*

The use of literature in the classroom has multiple objectives, as do other subject areas of contemporary education. Literature is especially effective in facilitating the growth of the learner in the two main fields of learning, the cognitive domain and the affective domain. Under these two general headings may be subsumed some specific aims. The cognitive domain includes skill development and is exemplified by problem solving, concept

[72] Downs, Robert B. *Books That Changed The World*. New York: New American Library of World Literature, 1956, pp. 174–175.

[73] Downs, Robert B. *Ibid.*, p. 192.

formation, interpretation, generalization, and application of principles. The affective domain embraces the enhancement of insight, self-concept, relationship with others, and competence in dealing with emotions.

The development of each of these areas is considered a professional aim, and there is current emphasis on the importance of feelings and emotions as influences on the acquiring of knowledge. Although these two categories of educational objectives are analytically distinct in purpose, activity, and method of teaching, they subtly interact in theory and practice in the learner's response and in the achievement of goals.

Evidence from research indicates that the emotional state of the learner is a critical factor in the learning situation. The development of knowledge is in some degree dependent upon emotion. Interest in learning, understanding of meaning, ability to perform, and retention of information are related to the feelings of the learner. Russell[74] believed that "Emotions and attitudes not only help determine what reaches consciousness but act as directive forces in most thinking processes." He stated that evidence indicates "emotional factors enter into all cognitive processes in varying degrees." Gates and Witty are among other writers who have found that reading ability is related to emotional factors. Studies between emotional or personality factors and learning include those of Thistlethwaite,[75] who showed the influence of attitudes and emotions on tests of logical thinking; Mumford,[76] who found that emotional problems can prevent development of ideas and that fear of failure can lead to failure in problem solving; and Diethelm,[77] whose research showed that the pupil's level of performance may be inhibited by anxiety. Russell concluded that "since emotional difficulties are often closely connected with learning difficulties," the teacher needs to be aware of the emotional needs of the pupils in planning for instructional activities.

One of the aims of education is to enable children to develop adequate means of dealing with their own and others' emotions and needs. Children in school have already seen or been involved in real life dilemmas. They have developed fears and conflicts which interfere with learning. They have met disapproval and rejection, and may be unable to meet the expectations of self, parents, and teachers. Even the child who appears to be well adjusted and successful may be working below his real capacity because of anxieties about feelings of inferiority or about conflicts concerning parents or siblings.

[74] Russell, David H. *Children's Thinking.* Boston: Ginn, 1956, pp. 165–99.

[75] Thistlethwaite, D. L. *Effect of Attitudes and Beliefs upon Reasoning.* Unpublished master's thesis (University of California, Berkeley, 1948).

[76] Mumford, Sheila. *Factors Involved in Problem-Solving with Special Reference to the Problem of Insight.* Unpublished doctoral dissertation (University of London, 1937).

[77] Diethelm, O., and M. R. Jones. "Influence of Anxiety on Attention, Learning, Retention, and Thinking," *Archives of Neurology and Psychiatry,* 58:325–36, 1947.

The psychological mechanisms found in response to reading are applicable to children in the classroom. In fact, there is the possibility that children are more sensitive to reading response than are older persons. Havighurst[78] pointed out that the child's conscience develops through identification with the parents and is modified by a sequence of identifications which includes "heroes read about." Other writers have referred to the developmental value of books in providing vicarious experiences for children in order to develop insight and to stimulate new thinking and behavior patterns. Wellek and Warren[79] hypothesized that the effect of reading is stronger and more direct for children than for adults.

Because young people are probably more powerfully influenced by books than are adults, owing to their lack of experience in reading, some caution in the selection of books for psychological development is recommended. Few teachers are trained in bibliotherapy, and amateur psychiatry can be hazardous in the classroom. It is dangerous to diagnose and prescribe for seriously disturbed children.

It is important to avoid literature that arouses anxieties for children that are greater than can be dealt with in the classroom. Attitudes and behaviors which are agreed upon as desirable, such as consideration for others, can be selected as a basis for study without unduly threatening children with psychological problems. Psychoanalytic terms are likely to be disturbing and confusing if used in the elementary school classroom, and also if applied directly in any way to individuals at any grade level. For some people certain terms have unpleasant associations and destroy pleasure in a book for which they have been used as interpretation.

In some cases the response to a book is on such a deep unconscious level that the reader is unable to perceive it consciously. In contrast, a student who has perceived an important insight may not wish to have attention drawn to his emotional response. The hidden meanings of a work are concealed because they might arouse anxiety if more clearly seen. As in the dream, the conscious mind can accept material on one level and recognize its secret message only in the unconscious. Lesser[80] warned that hidden levels of meaning should be dealt with

> only when it is desirable to make students aware that there are closer connections they appear to realize between 'great' literature and their own problems and experience; or when they are puzzled by aspects of a story which can only be explained by taking account of unconscious sources of motivation.

Lesser also believed, however, that "every mode of analyzing literature should take cognizance of the fact that literature speaks to the uncon-

[78] Havighurst, Robert J. *Human Development and Education.* New York: Longmans, Green and Co., 1953, p. 151.

[79] Wellek, René, and Austin Warren. *Theory of Literature.* New York: Harcourt, Brace (Harvest Books), 1956, p. 102.

[80] Lesser, Simon O. *Fiction and the Unconscious.* Boston: Beacon Press, 1957, p. 301.

scious" whether or not the teacher is aware of the process. Since it is probable that pupils respond unconsciously to literature in some psychological manner, the teacher needs some techniques to help literature "work its magic and change the hearts of men." Lesser[81] stated that all evidence

> points to the desirability of building the English program around books which are on students' level of sensibility and concerned with their deepest interests and problems; of seeking a proper balance between intensive and extensive reading; and of concentrating upon literature itself, using any and every kind of information which will help to illuminate it, but never letting the focus of attention shift to the information more than momentarily.

Many teachers hope that literature can have beneficial effects on pupils' personality and character and can help to solve some of their emotional problems, but have doubts about the manner in which reading can assist in the process. Reported research studies dealing with the psychological effects of literature in the classroom are meager, limited in scope, and often indeterminate in result. A few have provided evidence of effects on specified attitudes or values, when particular techniques of presentation have been used. Because such effects on personality are subtle and complex, they are difficult to measure and evaluate statistically. They are more likely to be inferred from differences in expressed attitudes or changes in behavior.

Some studies of personal responses of students to literature have been reported. Russell's[82] summary of research noted that few studies provide specific evidence of the effects of reading upon personality. Some of these studies are discussed in other chapters of this book. Interesting results were obtained by Webster,[83] referred to elsewhere in this book, in her study of personal problems of children in the first grade. Half of the pupils interviewed were fearful of dogs or of the dark. After hearing and discussing stories with positive attitudes toward dogs and darkness, the children reported that their fears had been significantly reduced. Reports from parents and observation of the behavior of the children supported the findings from the children.

A study by Lewis[84] pointed out the importance of teaching method in using literature to bring changes in emotional values. Eleven short stories portraying the desirability of nurturance and the undesirability of aggressiveness and selfishness were heard and read by two groups of 54 children over a period of six weeks. After the reading, one of these groups freely

[81] Lesser Simon O. *Ibid.*, p. 301.

[82] Russell, David H. *Children's Thinking.* Boston: Ginn, 1956, pp. 165–99.

[83] Webster, Jane. "Using Books to Reduce the Fears of First Grade Children," *Reading Teacher, 14:*159–62, 1961.

[84] Lewis, Isabel R. *Effects of Reading and Discussion of Stories on Certain Values.* Unpublished doctoral dissertation, (University of California, Berkeley, 1967).

discussed the stories and their personal responses, without critical comment by the teacher. The second group heard and read the stories but drew pictures of an event in each story instead of discussing. A third group discussed the same values from each story but without reading the stories. The remaining group did not hear or read the stories nor did they discuss the values. A semiprojective test of values was administered to all the subjects before and after the experiment.

The findings supported the basic assumption that literature affects personal values, although differently in the two reading groups. Reading without discussion produced significant increase in aggressive feeling and projected aggressive behavior, and decrease in nurturant feeling and projected nurturant behavior. Discussion of the values without reading the stories resulted in no significant changes but indicated a trend toward increased aggressiveness. Reading followed by discussion of personal response to the stories significantly reduced the aggressive feeling and projected behavior from the reading level, and produced a trend toward increase in nurturance. There were no significant changes in any of the attitudes for the group which had no reading or discussion.

An interpretation of the findings in line with psychoanalytic theory is that the children responded to the stories on an unconscious level and needed the opportunity to explore their feelings in order to develop insight. Reading stories dealing with aggressiveness, selfishness, and nurturance, without discussion, increased awareness of the values and negative feelings about them through concretizing of the issues involved and emotional identification with the characters. It appears that the children were limited in this condition to personal feeling experience with ventilation. Free discussion, with acceptance of the feelings of all participants by the teacher, following the reading decreased the heightened negative feelings by providing for expression of feelings without anxiety, resulting in catharsis, and for opportunities for group feeling interaction leading to internalization of values suggested by the stories and adopted by the group. According to reports of teachers' observations there was a decline in aggressive behavior and a noticeable increase of nurturance in the group which followed reading with discussion. Discussion of the values without reading the stories did not result in the expression of change of values. Without the stories as focal points for discussion, the pupils did not develop the emotional identification with the characters which would effect change. Implications for teaching found in this study indicate that it is important to select literature which offers children opportunities to identify with characters who represent desirable values, and that the techniques of teaching literature should provide opportunities for children to express emotional values verbally since the exploration of feelings in an environment that reduces anxiety permits the modification of values in a positive direction.

Other studies point to the importance of classroom atmosphere and social climate in encouraging group interaction and reducing aggressive expression. Miel[85] noted that nondirective teaching with much student participation was more effective in producing change in attitudes in groups than was authoritarian leadership. Waples, Berelson, and Bradshaw[86] stated that discussion of the meaning of literature increases the influence of reading. Taba[87] concluded that reading enhances sensitivity in human relations more effectively when it is followed by discussion. Elkind[88] and Lind[89] found that group interaction in class discussion after reading stimulated and reinforced identification and attitude change.

There are a number of valuable sources of guidelines to assist the teacher in developing an emotional climate in the classroom which will increase group interaction, feeling interpretation, and personal insight in discussion of reading. Some of these books are discussed in later chapters. Books by Taba,[90] Crosby,[91] Rogers,[92] and Heaton[93] provide helpful suggestions for planning procedures for open-end discussions. Heaton offers the following question sequence to aid the understanding and interpretation of emotional relationships in stories and personal responses:

> What happened to the people?
> How did they feel about it?
> Has anything like this happened to anyone you know or to you?
> What could you or anyone else have done to change the situation?
> What conclusion can we draw?

Research suggests that the attitude and emotional response of the teacher affects the quality of children's learning. Russell said that the teacher who provides an accepting atmosphere so that the child is free to express his feelings and fantasies without fear of criticism "not only gains a greater understanding of the child but contributes to his mental health."

[85] Miel, Alice. *Changing the Curriculum: A Social Process.* New York: Appleton-Century, 1946.

[86] Waples, Douglas, Bernard Berelson, and Franklin Bradshaw. *What Reading Does to People.* Chicago: University of Chicago Press, 1940, pp. 74–80.

[87] Taba, Hilda (ed.). *Reading Ladders for Human Relations.* Washington, D.C.: American Council on Education, 1947.

[88] Elkind, D. "Students Face Their Problems," *English Journal, 38:*489–503, 1949.

[89] Lind, Katherine. "The Social Psychology of Children's Reading," *Americal Journal of Sociology, 41:*454–69, 1936.

[90] Taba, Hilda (ed.). *Reading Ladders for Human Relations.* Washington, D.C.: American Council on Education, 1947.

[91] Crosby, Muriel (ed.). *Reading Ladders for Human Relations.* Washington, D.C.: American Council on Education, 1963.

[92] Rogers, Carl. *On Becoming a Person.* Boston: Houghton Mifflin, 1961.

[93] Heaton, Margaret M. *Feelings Are Facts.* New York: National Conference of Christians and Jews, 1951.

The teacher needs to show the pupils her concern for their feelings, to help the children learn how to get their feelings out into the open, and to make it clear that she understands and accepts their feelings. She needs to be careful not to betray confidences, not to moralize, not to use sarcasm when children reveal their feelings. She must be sensitive to withdrawal because of fear, to signs of anxiety aroused by the story or by discussion, and irrelevant comments or behavior covering feelings of inadequacy in dealing with insights. The effective teacher is tactful, accepting, alert to the reactions of the children, and responsive to their emotions by providing explanations, reassurance, or change of focus.

Sources of lists of books which are valuable in influencing psychological response in young people are found in Chapters 10 and 11. A well-known source is *Reading Ladders for Human Relations,* fourth edition, edited by Muriel Crosby and published in 1963 by the American Council on Education. It describes books that can help the reader to develop greater sensitivity to the needs of others and to gain insight into his own experiences and emotions. Carlsen's[94] *Books and the Teen-Age Reader* provides comprehensive references to books meeting many psychological needs, and analyses reader response to each type of literature.

## *Conclusion*

The illustrative sampling of psychoanalytic interpretation of literature examined in this chapter embraces the insight shown in Rumi's statement that "a tale, fictitious or otherwise, illuminates truth." Not only does literature illuminate truth but it also persuades the reader to accept its message as truth and to share its fantasies and values. Some critics and psychologists believe that reading affects the reader on both conscious and unconscious levels. They see literature as the repository of hidden personal and cultural dreams, fears, and desires. Psychoanalytic theories indicate the mechanisms of interaction between reader and literature which produce specific responses of a psychical nature. The discoveries and theoretical analyses of Freud, especially, provide statements and hypotheses for considering the impact of reading in psychological terms.

The processes involved in psychotherapy are considered to be parallel with those which take place in the reader in response to literature. They have been described as identification, catharsis, and insight. These phases are not discrete in sequence but are sometimes simultaneous or overlapping. Identification involves empathy with another, gratification of unconscious impulses, projecting onto another undesirable traits found in the self, or introjection into the self the desired qualities of the character.

[94] Carlsen, G. Robert. *Books and the Teen-Age Reader.* New York: Bantam Books, 1967.

Catharsis may begin with ventilation of emotions and progress to relief from anxiety and guilt, and to increase of spontaneity. Through identification with a character, usually the hero, the reader may develop insight into his inner needs and characteristics. Insight can provide understanding for acceptance of the self or direction toward possible solutions for adjustment or change. After "walking in the moccasins of the hero" while experiencing the story, the reader may continue to share some of the virtues and values of the character with whom he identified.

There is little evidence from research to support assumptions of psychoanalytic response to literature, and there is much controversy about Freudian theories of human personality. It appears, however, that literature does appeal to unconscious motives and emotions. Each reader brings to literature his own perceptions and inner needs and will respond in terms of his individual experience. Teachers need to be aware of psychoanalytic interpretations and to be accepting of the feelings of pupils who are affected by literature in personal and differing ways.

# CHAPTER 4 | Literary Criticism as Response

Literary criticism is a form of response differing in degree more than in kind from the responses discussed in other chapters of this book. Criticism may be more skilled or sophisticated than other reactions, but is still a personal reaction. Oscar Wilde called all criticism a form of autobiography.

Like many complex human activities, literary criticism extends along some sort of continuum; for example, the scale may range from mechanical counting to subtle interpretation. We can study Shakespeare's use of the comma or his ethical values. The book reviewer for the daily newspaper meets his deadline, and a Shelley and Matthew Arnold write about their theories of poetry. Not unexpectedly, there is some evidence of a practical sort that the declarations of literary scholars, over which they may have labored for many months, are more penetrating, diverse, and complex than are the first reactions of students or the usual judgments of teachers.[1] It seems unwise, however, to attribute a high degree of wisdom and insight to all writing that may be categorized as literary criticism. Doctoral dissertations in English have included such titles as *The Imagery of Edward Taylor's Preparatory Meditations* and *The Syntax of Substantive and Non-Finite Satellites to the Finite Verb in German.* Eminent literary scholars have written on such topics as *The Nature of Literature, Theory of Literature and Society and Self in the Novel.* Somewhere along the continuum of writing may appear Alexander Pope's *Essay on Criticism,* Coleridge's notes on the *Lyrical Ballads,* or D. H. Lawrence's *Why the Novel Matters.* Depending on individual preference, one may also include the more recent writing of Forster, Eliot, Richards, Wellek, or Schorer. Literary criticism, like many other human perceptions, varies widely with the writer and the reader, and who can say which sort of interpretation is best? Pope expressed it aptly:

> Tis with our judgments as our watches, none
> Go just alike, yet each believes his own.

[1] Scribner, Marion J. *The Responses of Students, Teachers and Critics to Selected Poetry.* Unpublished doctoral dissertation (University of California, Berkeley, 1960)

In other lines Pope points out some of the dangers inherent in writing such as that contained in this chapter. It is written by an amateur for amateurs, not literary scholars. It is included in a book on the dynamics of reading because such a broad and fertile area of response to literature could not be excluded. It contains no original analysis of literary works. It is an introduction to literary criticism not an example of *explication de texte* applied to some poem or novel but in terms of reader reaction. Perhaps, then, it may be defended, again in the opening lines of Pope's *Essay on Criticism,*

> 'Tis hard to say, if greater want of skill
> Appear in writing or in judging ill;
> But, of the two, less dang'rous is the offence
> To tire our patience, than mislead our sense.

Criticism of a literary work is based on the assumption that a successful piece of writing has an accessible meaning. This chapter does not attempt to give the meaning or meanings of representative works but tries the "less dang'rous" task of describing how literary criticism functions as a form of response. In such a description there may be some psychological bias, but Mairer and Reninger's attempt at a psychological interpretation of literary criticism, from a behavioristic point of view, was only moderately convincing.[2]

The term literary criticism is an inclusive one. Wellek and Warren[3] point out that it is possible to distinguish between literary theory, literary history, and literary criticism. Literary theory is "the study of the principles of literature, its categories, criteria and the like." Literary history, of course, is concerned with literary works in some sort of chronological order, and literary criticism may be narrowly concerned with the concrete literary work of art, studied in isolation or as part of a chronological series. Although Wellek and Warren stress these distinctions, they believe that in practice the activities overlap. Literary theory must include references to individual literary works, and literary criticism must use some of the questions, concepts, and generalizations of literary theory. Although the term literary criticism is herein the most frequently used of the three, it sometimes includes the categories of theory and history. As suggested below, the approach may create certain dilemmas in the study of an individual work of literary art (should the teacher introduce Wordsworth's "Ode on the Intimations of Immortality" by giving the historical setting on some of Wordsworth's theory of poetry?), but it may also illustrate the advantages of an eclectic approach to literary response. The chief

[2] Mairer, N. R. F., and H. W. Reninger. *A Psychological Approach to Literary Criticism.* New York: D. Appleton and Co., 1933.

[3] Wellek, René, and Austin Warren. *Theory of Literature.* New York: Harcourt, Brace (Harvest Books), 1956.

concern of this volume is the effects of the work upon the reader, correlated with other factors including the characteristics of the work itself.

## *The Individual Nature of Response*

Perhaps the chief characteristic of the response of the literary scholar, particularly at the intuitive, interpretive end of the scale, is its individuality. Different critics find different symbolism and meaning in the same poem, short story, or other work of imagination. Even such an apparently simple poem as Robert Frost's "Stopping By Woods on a Snowy Evening" – which Ciardi has described as "probably the best known lyric in the English language" – has been given a variety of interpretations by different writers. It has been analyzed as representing a journey through life and as a tribute to the New England sense of duty. At least one critic has seen it as a choice between estheticism and moral action while another believes, in psychoanalytic terms, that it depicts the death wish.

Such variation in interpretation has been viewed with horror by certain writers. Mairer and Reninger in *A Psychological Approach to Literary Criticism*[4] write not only of "The present chaos in literary theory" but also of "the appalling confusion in critical practice." They deplore a body of criticism in which personal opinions are often diametrically opposed to one another and have made criticism "meaningless" because such opinion has been "confused with objective critical judgment." They therefore call for a "scientific" approach to literary study but are not too convincing when they base this in part on Mairer's theory of productive thinking or reasoning as "the ability to combine spontaneously the essentials of two isolated experiences in such a manner as to reach a goal." Mairer and Reninger would, accordingly, stress a research approach to problems of literary judgment, applying some of the methods of psychology and the other social sciences, and even the natural sciences, to literary scholarship. They argue, not for the same interpretation of a literary work by everyone, but for a consistent set of guiding principles, definitions, and theories which will require consistency of analytical method by various critics. Perhaps they would agree with some of the applications of methods of psychology to literary interpretation given in Chapter 3.

Although the attempt to bring order into a field which may be regarded as chaotic is an enticing one, there are problems in equating literary study with "scientific" criticism. Wellek and Warren believe that literary criticism goes beyond research in the usual scientific connotation. They state that the term *research* suggests certain preliminary operations involving search but not "those subtle concerns with interpretation, char-

[4] Mairer, N. R. F., and H. W. Reninger. *A Psychological Approach to Literary Criticism.* New York: D. Appleton and Co., 1933.

acterization, and evaluation which are peculiarly characteristic of literary studies."[5]

In his essay on Galsworthy, D. H. Lawrence put it this way:

> Literary criticism can be no more than a reasoned account of the feeling produced upon the critic by the book he is criticizing. Criticism can never be a science: it is, in the first place, much too personal, and in the second, it is concerned with values that science ignores. . . . A critic must be able to *feel* the impact of a work of art in all its complexity and its force.[6]

Perhaps even more important than these definitional approaches is the philosophical position that responses to any work of art must always be of an individual nature and that any attempt to establish norms or categories or rules essentially destroys the meaning of such responses. If criticism could achieve the exactitude and lawfulness usually attributed to science (but not accepted by many modern physicists, for example), the result might easily be only *one* opinion about any example of literature. If the rules of literary criticism could be programed for the computer, there would be no need of literary critics, and teachers of literature would become what one man has called "disc jockeys of culture."

Some problems of literary scholarship are amenable to the scientific approach, and for others the scientific method gives few results, or at least the tools have not yet been developed which make analysis profitable. It is the bias of the writer that the latter group of problems is smaller than we sometimes think. For example, the literary scholar, suspicious of empirical approaches, sometimes claims that the subtle intuitions of the writer and scholar, the "characterization and evaluation" mentioned by Wellek and Warren, are too intangible or too complex to be analyzed scientifically, but that the psychological approach to some of these problems is already well begun. McKinnon, Barron,[7] and some of their colleagues at the University of California have made studies of the creative process in writers and others groups of creative workers. The report of the Allerton Conference in 1963[8] suggested other overlapping areas of literary criticism and psychological research. Indeed, much of the scientific study of human perception in psychological laboratories corroborates and extends the insight of the literary scholar about the many factors that cause individual differences in sensory and cognitive response. The total effect of scientific experimentation in perception is probably that of

[5] Wellek, René, and Austin Warren. *Theory of Literature.* New York: Harcourt, Brace (Harvest Books), 1956, p. 27.

[6] Lawrence, D. H. "John Galsworthy," *Selected Literary Criticism* (Anthony Beal, ed.). New York: Viking Press, 1932, p. 118.

[7] McKinnon, Donald W., and others. *The Creative Person.* Berkeley: University of California Extension Division, 1963.

[8] *Proceedings of the Allerton Park Conference on Research in the Teaching of English.* (R. W. Rogers, director). Champaign, Ill.: National Council of Teachers of English, 1963.

reinforcing and explaining, in part, the wide variations in individual variations in individual reaction and judgment. The implications of these wide differences in response for literary critics and for teachers of literature would seem to be a freeing influence on their work.

## *The Work of the Critic*

Parents, teachers, or psychologists may sometimes wonder how a literary critic operates. One of the chief reasons for individual variation in critical response is, of course, the purpose of the critic and the theory of criticism, conscious or largely unconscious, which guide his work. Here the extremes are easy to state. Much of the newer criticism would confine itself to the *interna* of the work of art itself; in contrast, some critics and teachers would include historical setting, the life of the writer, the probable purpose of the writer, the ethical implications and other *externa* — the kind of material derided in the question, "How many children had Lady Macbeth?" Eliot wrote, "To divert interest from the poet to the poetry is a laudable aim," but he also pleads for consideration of the historical tradition. "No poet, no artist of any art, has his complete meaning alone. His significance, his appreciation is the appreciation of his relation to the dead poets and artists."[9] By the 1960's this appeal was outmoded for many of the younger critics.

> Textual criticism is now triumphant in most universities. Biography is irrelevant; social background is irrelevant; nothing matters but the work of literature, and this the student scrutinizes with the care and precision of a microbiologist examining a segment of tissue.[10]

One critic is interested in the effects of literature on ethical values, another with literature for its own sake.

The varying purposes of critics sometimes conceal the common strands which run through much critical writing and which represent agreements about the work of the critic. At the cliché-level, the critic must have an open, vigilant and responsive mind. Whether he stays "inside literature" or emphasizes setting and effect, he must be able to detect the "contrived façade of novelty" and to evaluate in terms of some of the qualities of unity, atmosphere, selection, pattern, focus, intent, and psychological distance. "He should be a man of eminently sceptical good will."[11]

[9] Eliot, T. S. "Tradition and the Individual Talent," *The Egoist, 6,* No. 4, Sept.–Oct. and Nov.–Dec., 1919. Reprinted in *Selected Essays.* New York: Harcourt, Brace, 1932.

[10] Hicks, Granville. "Gestation of a Brain Child," *Saturday Review, 45,* January 6, 1962.

[11] Enright, D. J., and Ernest de Chickera (eds.). *English Critical Texts.* New York: Oxford University Press, 1962.

In somewhat more specific terms, Cowley[12] has described at least two functions of the critic. The first is to select works of art worth writing about, with emphasis not on the well-known classics but on the new or the neglected. His second function is "to describe or analyze or interpret the chosen works" as a basis for judgments which must often be implied. He says that he himself tries to start with "a sort of innocence," not ignorance of the author's life or the circumstances of writing, but rather a lack of preconceptions and an attitude of asking questions. He adds, "I always start and end with the text itself, and I am willing to accept the notion of the textual or integral critics that the principal value of a work lies in the complexity and unity of its internal relations."

To put the case in other functional terms, the activities of the critic will vary with the work of art being studied and with the purpose of the critic which, as suggested above, may range on a wide spectrum. Just as writers as various as Chaucer, Shakespeare, Milton, Donne, Keats, and Faulkner require differences in critical approach, so the intention and audience of the critic require variations in what he does. The teacher-critic may desire to move his class from enjoyment of mere violence or dramatic action to some of the writing in which violence and action are fused with other qualities, as in Hemingway's *The Killers* and Kipling's *The Man Who Would Be King.* The literary scholar summing up five or ten years' work may have more complex and subtle aims. However, common elements run through different teaching and critical writing and a simplified approach to the problem suggests that the competent critic does three things:

1. He prepares the reader (or the listener) for experiencing the work. This may consist of an introduction to the sources – the artist's theory or experience. For example, the eleventh or twelfth grade class may not have met Wordsworth's theory of poetry as an expression of nature or the influence of Freud on twentieth century writing. It may involve an account of the setting in which the work was produced; as Frost believed, "a poem is best read in the light of all the other poems ever written."
2. He begins an explication of some of the characteristics of the material studied – the structural elements and technical qualities of the work as a whole. Here the wise scholar, and especially the teacher-critic, may do best if he enables his audience or class to discover some of these qualities for themselves. This entails close reading of (or attentive listening to) a text to arrive at elements of pattern and unity, to recognize the use of such devices as image, metaphor, and symbol. As suggested above, there the attempt is to get "inside literature."

[12] Cowley, Malcolm. "Criticism: A Many-Windowed House," *Saturday Review 44:* 10–11, 46–47, August 12, 1961.

3. He expresses meaningful judgments about the work. The reader of the book review in the newspaper or the weekly magazine wants to know how his favorite reviewer evaluates the book. The more leisurely and perhaps more scholarly critic is careful to suggest how valuable the ideas in the work are in their own right and how effectively these ideas of the author have been communicated. This function relates to the main theme of this book – the response of the reader or audience. Therefore the effect of the work is of interest, as when Sir Philip Sidney writes of poetry as an influence on character, or Shelley is concerned with its social implications. It may involve the studies of Richards or other psychological approaches to interpretation as exemplified in Chapter 3.

Lest the three functions seem disparate it is well to suggest that the critic is not just a judge in a position superior to the writer. He himself must be judged by what he writes about literature just as a judge's right to be on a bench depends on his knowledge of law.

> If he's up against something the size of Shakespeare, he's the one being judged. The critic's function is to interpret every work of literature in the light of all the literature he knows, to keep constantly struggling to understand what literature as a whole is about. Literature as a whole is not an aggregate of exhibits with red and blue ribbons attached to them, like a cat-show, but the range of articulate human imagination as it extends from the height of imaginative heaven to the depth of imaginative hell. Literature is a human apocalypse, man's revelation to man, and criticism is not a body of adjudications, but the awareness of that revelation, the last judgment of mankind.[13]

The three main functions of the critic, however, put his endeavors in fairly workaday terms. They are perhaps skewed more to the *use* of literature than to the *delight* of literature. However, they do not neglect such topics as the unity of a work of art. Rather they suggest that the student must know some of the nature and the ways of integrating the qualities that make for unity. They do not emphasize some of those characteristics of writing such as sincerity, clarity, force, and beauty which are often talked about, nor do they rule out these sometimes nebulous qualities. Schorer and his coeditors[14] have suggested that critical writings through the years tend to give most place to *source*, *form*, or *end* but that these are a matter of emphasis, not separate topics. A brief look at the history of literary criticism accordingly gives more depth to a discussion and enriches a concept of criticism as dynamic response which may be described and applied in such a wide variety of ways.

[13] Frye, Northrop. *The Educated Imagination.* Toronto: Canadian Broadcasting Corporation, 1963, p. 44.

[14] Schorer, Mark, Josephine Miles, and Gordon McKenzie (eds.). *Criticism: The Foundation of Modern Literary Judgment.* New York: Harcourt, Brace, 1948.

## *Varieties of Literary Criticism*

Recent years have seen a shift in literary criticism to the study of symbol, of myth, of form as revealing meaning. But this change in emphasis is only one of the alterations in a continuous development of critical theory in a historical sense. Because critical interpretation is associated with individuals, especially with the development of movements or schools of thought in comparatively modern times, the casual reader of criticism may get an impression of discontinuity. Wellek,[15] Wimsatt and Brooks,[16] and other historians of literary ideas, however, stress their continuity. In the words of Wimsatt and Brooks, "Plato has a bearing on Croce and Freud." The Idea, not the Hero, is important. Nevertheless, criticism, especially in its earlier days, must be summarized partly in terms of individuals.

The first extant writing of the western world that specifically concerns itself in literary criticism is the early Platonic dialogue *Ion* which discusses the kind of knowledge involved in the criticism of a poem or in the poem itself. Wimsatt and Brooks describe the dialogue as "a thorough going, radically naive inquiry into the nature of poetic composition as a department of verbal meaning and power." The dialogue is between Socrates and Ion, a rhapsodist or public reciter and interpreter of passages from the *Iliad* and the *Odyssey.* The speakers conclude that composing poetry is not the same ability as giving a rationale for it – the artist is not necessarily a critic. Plato's belief in the power of poetry and his "mistrust" of the effects of literature also show in his famous passage from *The Republic,* "We should do our utmost that the first stories that they hear should be so composed as to bring the fairest lessons of virtue to their ears." Plato thus accepted as fact the idea that literature influences conduct, and may even have given a bit of comfort to the censors.

Aristotle's rebuttal to Plato on certain points exceeded the range of the dialogue *Ion.* His theory of verbal ideas is given in his *Rhetoric* and his more specific thoughts on poetry in notes in the *Poetics.* Wimsatt and Brooks write that whereas Plato was "mathematical and vigorously abstract" Aristotle was "biological . . . empirical, and concrete." Some of his best known ideas are his concern with the nature of tragedy and comedy; but perhaps most closely related to the theme of this book is his doctrine of *catharsis,* the empathy and pity evoked by tragedy and the pleasure and laughter induced by comedy, both acting as a purgation of the emotions. Modern theories and procedures of bibliotherapy are given in Chapter 9.

[15] Wellek, René. *A History of Modern Criticism 1750–1950.* Vols. 1 and 2 New Haven: Yale University Press, 1955.

[16] Wimsatt, W. K., Jr., and Cleanth Brooks. *Literary Criticism: A Short History.* New York: Knopf, 1957.

The Greeks influenced the Romans in criticism as in other intellectual pursuits although these effects are not notable in one of the Latin passages available to us, Horace's *Ars Poetica.* Horace includes instructions on how to write but does not always follow them in his own verse. Wimsatt and Brooks translate some of Horace's verse with phrases like the following: "Only three speakers at a time," "scenes of butchery off stage," and "the orchestra will be harder to please than the peanut gallery." Other Romans attempted literary criticism. For example, the single work of the unknown Longinus is still included in anthologies of critical writing.

Later writers such as Augustine and Thomas Aquinas were concerned with theories of beauty more than with the effects of literature. Only a few names stand out in classical and medieval criticism but the numbers begin to multiply from the Elizabethan Age onward. Critical writing flourished when other writing flourished, probably not for the reason there was more material to evaluate so much as the existence of a stimulating climate encouraging various kinds of literary endeavor. Accordingly, in English criticism appeared such men as Ben Jonson, Dryden, Addison, and Samuel Johnson. In other places Voltaire and Diderot, Lessing, Goethe and Schiller, Italians, and some Russians, contributed to literary theory. In England a bit later Shelley, Wordsworth, Coleridge, Arnold, and others were concerned with theories of poetry, with broad relationships to naturalism, idealism, or humanism, with such divergent topics as *imagination* and *classicism.* Since the concern of this book is not literary theory so much as the effects of reading, much critical writing can be summarized by saying that most of the critics named were concerned with poetic diction rather than poetic impact, with the writer not his audience. An exception is the last named figure of the mid-Victorian era, Matthew Arnold. Wimsatt and Brooks find a "didacticism" in much he writes. They quote his complaint:

> We have poems which seem to exist merely for the sake of single lines and passages; not for the sake of producing any total impression. We have critics who seem to direct their attention merely to detached expressions, to the language about the action, not to the action itself.[17]

Because he was concerned with a "high seriousness" in poetry, Arnold necessarily considered the effects of reading it. In his essay *The Study of Poetry,* he implies effects in his aims for the poet:

> More and more mankind will discover that we have to turn to poetry to interpret life for us, to console, to sustain us.[18]

[17] Arnold Matthew. "The Study of Poetry," First published in introduction T. H. Ward (ed.). *The English Poets.* New York: Macmillan, 1880. Included in Arnold's *Essays in Criticism, Second Series.* London: Macmillan, 1888.

[18] *Ibid.*

But Arnold does not develop his theme of effects and like many other critics is concerned with "'the very highest poetical quality."

Instead of analyzing Arnold or others, we may look for clues to possible impact in terms of certain modern movements in criticism, the intentions of a group rather than the specifics of one man's ideas. Wimsatt and Brooks, for example, have chapters on art as social propaganda, art for art's sake, expressionism, psychological interpretations, implications of semantics, and psychoanalytical concepts. Each of these movements, explicitly or implicitly, is concerned in part with effects on the reader – but many writers in each school would be surprised at such a claim. Their central concern has been elsewhere. Most critical writing of the last seventy-five years focuses on other literary topics (*Seven Types of Ambiguity, The Rhetoric of Fiction*), but the critical theory usually includes some reference to the reactions of the reader.

A few examples illustrate the point. Novels of social protest, or propaganda, from Zola through Steinbeck, have stimulated critics to discuss the social responsibilities of writers, and authors have attempted, explictly or implicitly, to influence the reader's social attitudes. Such literature may be especially important to parents or teachers of adolescents at a time when youth achieve some grasp of and identify with broader social problems. To the teacher the question is not usually a choice among approaches such as the genius of the writer, the work of art itself, or the social background against which the work was composed. Rather, the work itself helps determine the critical approach or the method of study. Protest against social conditions in Victorian England or in early twentieth century America add meaning to Dickens or to Dos Passos. In the United States of the thirties, the depression years are an unknown setting to the adolescent of the affluent sixties, unless he studies these years directly. In those days Hunt[19] wrote, "An economic dogma as a basis for literary criticism is no worse, I suppose, than a theological or psychological one." He did not mean that literature had to be interpreted in terms of some narrow Marxian formula, but rather that there may be a point to "arousing public indignation over the injustices of our economic order" of a particular era. Tolstoy stated that the great writers have been contemporary, and Hicks[20] wrote, also in the thirties, "What we demand of a writer is that he honestly confront the central issues of his own age." A theme of social reform runs through many of the novels of H. G. Wells and the plays of G. B. Shaw. Shelley was part of a democratic revolution, Tennyson lived in an era of Victorian progress, Whitman was concerned with the worker and the "American dream," and Mailer was

[19] Hunt, Everett L. "The Social Interpretation of Literature," *English Journal, 24:* 214–19, 1935.

[20] Hicks, Granville. "Literature and Revolution," *English Journal 24:*219–39, March 1935.

influenced by war and postwar conditions. The counter argument is that social forces are only partly understood by the contemporary writer, and the "values of art" may transcend barriers of time, space, economic strife, and the immediate social context. The social setting in which a writer worked on the social message contained in his writing may be negligible, apparent, or dominant. The work itself should be studied in these terms and in relation to possible influence on the reader's social philosophy or specific interpersonal ideas.

Other movements or schools show less concern for the effect on the individual. The movement "art for art's sake" stressed an aestheticism associated in England with such men as Swinburne, Wilde, Pater, and Ruskin, and provides a negative example of interest in the influence of literature. Benedetto Croce's expressionism is conceived in semipsychological terms not unlike some of the labels for cognitive processes of current interest to many psychologists. He explains both the mental organization of the poet and the structure of the poem in terms of aesthetic intuition. It is more difficult to reconcile his first step of intuition-expression as parts of the same thing than to include his other two factors of conceptualization and volition in the creative process. Croce is concerned, not with genre or critical paraphernalia, but with the nature of art expression and impression. He is not interested in analysis of literary works as complexes of meaning or as literal or symbolic structures.

Psychological interpretations run through earlier criticism but achieve more substance in the twentieth century with the developing science of psychology. The connected use of psychological analysis and the discipline of semantics is best illustrated in the work of I. A. Richards. As described in Chapter 3, Richards made one of the first empirical studies of students' responses to poems. He is concerned with errors and misinterpretations, not only in reactions to poems but in responses to words, in attaching referents to the verbal symbol. Some recent studies,[21] discussed in Chapter 7, suggest that there is a connection between the two phenomena. From the semanticists' point of view, Richards distinguishes between the emotional and referential uses of language, between the emotional effect produced in the reader and the measures by which it is produced. Not all critics support this "separatism." Finally, the influence of Freud (and also of Jung and Adler) on literary criticism has been great in the present century; indeed, the experimental psychologists regard Freud as more of a literary man than a psychologist. Some further elucidation of the psychoanalytic point of view appears below. Critics currently writing can usually be assigned to one or more of these critical movements

[21] Hinze, Helen A. K. *The Individual's Word Associations and His Interpretation of Prose Paragraphs.* Unpublished doctoral dissertation (University of California, Berkeley, 1956).

(Eliot's neoclassicism, Brooks's formalism, Fiedler's psychoanalytic approach, etc.) or to the New Criticism devoted to intensive reading of the text and the relation of form and structure to meaning. The current emphasis on the study of symbol and myth had some roots in Freud's writing but has gone beyond him. The present stress on literature as literature for its own sake is not unrelated to "art for art's sake." Intensive textual analysis places less emphasis on biography and history, more on formal and structural qualities of the work itself, but does not completely ignore psychological and historical factors. There is a continuity in the ways men have theorized about and reacted to various forms of literature.

## *Psychoanalytical Influences in Literary Study*

Psychoanalytic approaches to literary analysis have been so persuasive, artful, and subtle in the last generation that a special note on them is in order. Sometimes extreme enough to border on the ridiculous, at other times they have been penetrating and insightful, but unlabeled "courtesy of Freud (or Jung)." They have added some possible insights about the character of Hamlet but they have also attempted to explain the nursery rhyme, "Jack and Jill," in terms of the birth trauma, including the dream symbol of birth as falling down hill. Freud himself wrote of the values of literature, history, and mythology in the study of human nature. One of Fromm's books is *The Forgotten Language: An Introduction to the Understanding of Dreams, Fairy Tales and Myths.*[22] More recently Lesser has written on *Fiction and the Unconscious.*[23] Many writers were especially influenced by psychoanalytic concepts in the 1920's and 1930's; some critics have been using the concepts ever since Freud burst on the literary scene. Whether acceptable or unacceptable to the reader, the viewpoints in these works should be understood and their applications in relation to specific writing recognized and then evaluated. Can effects be interpreted in terms of such concepts as the subconscious or id or dream symbols?

Literary criticism influenced by psychoanalytic concepts has appeared in at least three categories: (a) studies of common themes running through different kinds of writing, (b) analysis of literary symbols in psychological terms, and (c) deductions about the author's personality and life from evidence found in his writings. Conversely, psychoanalytic writing bristles with literary references. Thus the psychoanalytic approach to human behavior is used to explain some of the "inner meanings" of a

[22] Fromm, Erich. *The Forgotten Language. An Introduction to the Understanding of Dreams, Fairy Tales and Myths.* New York: Rinehart, 1951.

[23] Lesser, Simon O. *Fiction and the Unconscious.* Boston: Beacon Press, 1957.

work of art or of the personality of the artist and literature is often used to illustrate psychoanalytic beliefs.

In the first category, great literature has always been concerned with the universal themes of birth, identity, marriage, alienation, and death. The *Electra* of Euripides and the *Electra* of O'Neill are quite different plays in depicting different worlds but not in certain underlying themes. Myths and folktales illustrate similarities in different cultures as they deal with basic patterns of human problems and conflicts. Gaylin[24] points out that the transient popular art of different eras, the *East Lynnes* or the *Ben Hurs* of a previous day, the hack literature of a period reveals not only common problems but common needs of a particular time and group. Such popular writing deserves more careful analysis than it has so far received. It illustrates changing needs in a shifting environment while great writing is called great as it emphasizes "profound emotions and conflicts common to all ages and cultures." Many writers with psychoanalytical views put fairy tales in the "universal" category. They contain parallels to dream symbols and reveal fantasies, especially those originating in the Oedipus situation. In the words of Schwartz, "The fairy tale . . . like psychoanalysis, views human behavior as conflict. . . . [It] exhorts the child through the stages of childhood to a satisfactory heterosexual adaptation, and, in fantasy, helps him resolve some of the significant conflicts he might have."[25] Similarly, in popular children's literature, Stevenson's *Child's Garden of Verses* reveals the games and fantasies of a child up to seven or eight years. *The Prince and the Pauper* illustrates the fact that most children at some time long to change their lives. In other books, a child replaces a deceased parent and in many stories he "tames" a parent. A book like *Alice in Wonderland* can be a mine for psychoanalytic interpretations[26] of phenomena or hypotheses running through much of our literature.

The second movement, the study of symbol, has been an important part of modern criticism. In psychoanalytic terms symbols as expressions of instinctual needs were first studied in dreams. Such phenomena and their symbols can be regarded first of all at the explicit level — they are what they seem to be. But dream components and literary symbols may also be interpreted on deeper, less accessible levels where things are not what they seem. It is perhaps in this area of interpretation that the psychoanalytically oriented writer has gone to extremes, has committed literary excesses which serve to discredit an approach which has many virtues.

[24] Gaylin, Willard M. "Psychoanaliterature: the Hazards of a Hybrid," *Columbia University Forum, 6:*11–16, Spring 1963.

[25] Schwartz, Emmanuel K. "A Psychoanalytic Study of the Fairy Tale," *American Journal of Psychotherapy,* October 1956, pp. 740–62.

[26] Schilder, Paul. "Psychoanalytic Remarks on Alice in Wonderland and Lewis Carroll," *Journal of Nervous and Mental Disease, 87:*159–68, 1938.

Most psychologists would question birth trauma in "Jack and Jill" and castration fears in "Little Bo-Peep." They would reject Mott's[27] contention that Christmas customs are full of birth trauma symbolism – that St. Nick's "little round belly" is symbolic of a pregnant woman, that his bag represents the human uterus, that going down the chimney symbolizes the child's birth struggle, and that the Christmas tree suggests the Oedipus struggle. Such reaching for metaphor and gratuitous interpolation may border on the absurd but should not be confused with the deliberate use of tokens by the thoughtful writer, consciously or unconsciously employing symbolism.

The third area of deduction about an author's life or personality must similarly be judged as containing both insights and excesses. Many critics accept the working hypothesis that a novel or play is a direct expression of the author's personality even though they may not espouse the term "substitute gratification." This raises the question of the extent to which a writer is in command of his fantasy. For example, Virginia Woolf claimed she did not know psychoanalysis (although a brother was an analyst) and therefore could not use symbols intentionally. Poe does not usually seem to be in control of his symbols, but Updike in his novel *The Centaur* appears to be in full charge. Baldwin's writing is impregnated by childhood influences plus a powerful drive for social justice for his people.[28] In many cases, a combination of motives, deduced biographically as well as psychoanalytically, may explain much writing. Louisa May Alcott may have used *Little Women* to make money as well as for catharsis. In his plays, notably *Long Day's Journey Into Night,* O'Neill may have found psychological release, but he also worked toward a unique contribution to American drama. It is no news that writers write for the market as well as for analyzing themselves and the psychoanalytic habit of looking for a single influence or cause is suspect.

Trilling has said that the effects of Freud on literature were no greater than the reciprocal effects of literature on Freud. The father of psychoanalysis, however, clearly stated the point that the writer's personality is affected by unconscious influences:

> A powerful actual experience arouses in the writer the remembrance of an earlier experience, belonging mostly to childhood, out of which the wish now proceeds which achieves its fulfillment in the literary production; in the production itself elements from the new occasion and from the old memory both may be recognized.[29]

Most critics would accept Freud's view, perhaps with certain limitations.

[27] Mott, F. J. "Drama and the Evocation of Unconscious Images," *Journal of Clinical Psychotherapy,* 7:783–93, 1946.

[28] Baldwin, James. *The Fire Next Time.* New York: Dial, 1963.

[29] McCurdy, Harold G. "Literature and Personality," *Character and Personality,* 7:300–308, 1939.

For example, in interpretation of the writer's personality from a novel McCurdy states safeguards: (a) the novel must be considered as a whole, not in isolated incidents, (b) caution should be used in making symbolic interpretations, and (c) if possible, it is valuable to study chronologically several novels by the same author to note changes running through them.

Sharper criticisms of the use of psychoanalytic concepts in the three areas have been made by such critics as Cowley[30] and Trilling.[31] These writers believe that it is impossible to explain a work of literature involving language by the behavior of infants at the preverbal stage of development. In informal correspondence in the bulletin *Literature and Psychology,* Cowley wrote, "Freudians are wrong in believing that maladjustments due to birth trauma or feeding difficulties or weaning difficulties are the sole explanation of neuroses." More recently he has expanded his criticism of the single point of view – the "specialized and partial standard for judging works of art"[32] whether historical, biographical, expressionist, moral, or psychoanalytical. He criticizes psychoanalytically oriented critics in the person of Leslie A. Fiedler:

> In a work almost as long as Parrington's "Main Currents in American Thought" he has proclaimed that all our great novelists are sexually immature, that their work represented an escape from a female-dominated world into male companionship, and that "The Last of the Mohicans," "Moby Dick," and "Huckleberry Finn," are almost identical fables of homosexual miscegenation. Mr. Fiedler's book is a final exploit of criticism cut loose from its moorings and sailing across the moon like a Halloween witch on her broomstick.

Trilling finds both advantages and disadvantages in Freudian and neo-Freudian approaches to literature. He believes that psychoanalysis is the only system of psychology which attempts to get at the subtlety and complexity of the human mind. The analytical method tries to explain the "inner meanings" of a work of art (such as Ernest Jones on *Hamlet*) and to explain the personality of the artist. Trilling finds something akin to Aristotle's notion of catharsis for both writer and reader. Understanding the pain and tragedy of literature can be a help in facing the greater pain and tragedy of life. However, Trilling questions Freud's theory of dream and states "we can accept neither Freud's conception of the place of art in life nor his application of the analytical method," although the Freudian view may open and complicate human behavior:

[30] Cowley, Malcolm. "Psychoanalysis and Writers," *Harper's, 209:*87–93, 1954.

[31] Trilling, Lionel. "Freud and Literature," *Criticism: The Foundation of Modern Literary Judgment* (Mark Schorer, Josephine Miles, and Gordon McKensie, eds.). New York: Harcourt, Brace, 1948.

[32] Cowley, Malcolm. "Criticism: A Many-Windowed House," *An English Teacher's Reader* (M. Jerry Weiss, ed.). New York: Odyssey Press, 1962.

Despite popular belief to the contrary, man, as Freud conceives him, is not to be understood by a simple formula (such as sex) but is rather an inextricable tangle of culture and biology.[33]

Despite its immoderate claims and extravagant interpretations, the person interested in the effects of literature must be aware of possible psychoanalytic influences in each of the writer, the content, and the reader. Fact and fancy, time and space, may blur as in Proust's *Remembrance of Things Past* and some of Virginia Woolf's novels. The stream-of-consciousness approach may be found in literature written by Conrad or Joyce, and studied by able high school students. Daydreams or secret thoughts may be the center of such books as Faulkner's *The Sound and the Fury* or the teen-age novel. Writers contrast primitive and civilized behavior and deliberately or unconsciously borrow from the ancient myths, the hero stories, the archetypes of birth, conflict, and death. Some of the ideas of psychoanalysis, used in moderation, can give hypotheses about the writer, his material, and its effects on the reader.

## *Some Other Critical Viewpoints*

A brief historical account of literary criticism and of psychoanalytic concepts applied to literature can be supplemented for the reader, teacher, and embryo critic by examples of the types of approaches or methods found in critical writing. It is difficult to say that one of these methods is better than any other or that it makes accessible whole truth. Rather the reader or the interpreter can be aware that he is utilizing a special approach or combination of approaches to the short story, novel, poem, or drama under consideration. The biographical critic is concerned with the author's life and its relation to his writing. The moral critic may be looking for philosophical truths and lessons in ethics. The social and political critic relates the material to the causes concurrent with the writing—from displaced agricultural workers to international revolutions. The expressionist critic may follow the dictates of Croce in looking for honesty and spontaneity in expression. The historical critic sees a work of literature as an event like the battle of Marathon or the fall of the Bastille. He is concerned with the effect of a series of events on a particular event. As suggested above, the psychoanalytical critic reveals how the author sublimated his antisocial drives or used imagery and symbol to depict such Freudian concepts as birth trauma, parental rejection, or the death wish. The "new" or "textual" or "integral" critic avoids such "extraneous" elements or "fallacies" and concentrates on the work itself. The student of

[33] Trilling, Lionel. "Freud and Literature," *Criticism: The Foundation of Modern Literary Judgment* (Mark Schorer, Josephine Miles, and Gordon McKensie, eds.). New York: Harcourt, Brace, 1948, p. 182.

literature, and of criticism, must be conscious of these and other approaches if he is consulting evaluations made by others – or building his own competences.

In the midsixties the teacher or student of literature must be aware, for example, of some critics' intense preoccupation with myth, symbol, and allegory. Melville in 1852 wrote that he was astonished at the awesome allegorical significances people were finding in his novel, *Moby Dick*. Charles Poore[34] wrote in the *New York Times* in 1963, "Well, Melville should be living at this hour. The whaling industry is fading but there is tremendous critical vitality in the high and arcane exegetic art of Moby-dickery."

As a corrective to excessive concern with allegory and symbol, the casual reader, the student, the book reviewer, and the teacher can sometimes apply the idea of reading at various levels or depths. In person or in class, one can read *Tom Sawyer* as an account of boyhood adventures, as a picture of life on the Mississippi in a by-gone age, or as an exploration of some of "the infinitely shadowed humors of Mark Twain" in contrasting respectability (through Aunt Polly) with the raffish life (represented by Huck Finn). The more complex novel *The Adventures of Huckleberry Finn* can be read as a journey down the Mississippi, a journey down the "river of life," or as a study of conflict in a boy who vacillates between a traditional loyalty to a slave-holding society and a deeply felt commitment to the humanity of "Nigger Jim." Similarly, with *The Catcher in the Rye, Lord of the Flies,* and other books popular with young people, several levels of response are possible – and different readers will respond in different ways.

Sometimes this response may be enhanced and deepened by some grasp of the basic tools of literary study such as awareness of point of view, semantic examination of meaning and tone, and analysis of structure. The latter may include consideration of words and syntax, use of image, metaphor and symbol, progression of ideas or plot, and literary conventions. Meaning may be both explicit and implicit. Mode, as attitude to or view of the world, may be romantic, comic, tragic, ironic, or some combination of these. For most readers, analysis is not an end in itself. Rather, an awareness of the complex ways in which the piece of literature embodies its meanings may add to understanding of the whole. In a hackneyed but succinct phrase, the reader moves from the question, "What does the poem mean?" to "How does a poem mean?"

One example of an answer to this question is found in the sound of a poem – how the poet has used sound to convey meaning. Alexander Pope did not carry the ideas far enough when he wrote, "The sound must seem an echo to the sense." A modern view is that the sound is its own

[34] Poore, Charles. "Books of the Times: On the Old Frontiers of American Literature," *New York Times,* August 18, 1963, p. 7

sense. Perrine[35] makes use of the idea in his college text *Sound and Sense: An Introduction to Poetry,* although his book contains examples of much more than sound. The poet uses sound by his choice and arrangement of words and by his use of accent. He may employ alliteration, assonance, consonance, and onomatopeia. Young children can identify rhyme, repetition, and refrain. They can learn that much of the world's poetry does not employ rhyme, but when used rhyme may be terminal (at the end of lines) or internal (within lines). MacLeish has written that "A poem should be wordless/ As the flight of birds." The poet employs words in many ways, somehow developing a meaning that goes beyond the meaning of individual words.

One example of analysis used in modern criticism is the emphasis on symbol, archetype, myth, and fable. Events and objects in the short story or novel are examined in relation to patterned explanations of the universe, of the classical gods, or of nature. *David Copperfield* and *Treasure Island* suggest possible solutions to the Oedipus conflict, and the mast carried by the main character in Hemingway's *The Old Man and the Sea* is likened to a cross. The theme of the "double" (close resemblance) runs from primitive folktales to the dualistic or schizophrenic personalities of *Dr. Jekyll and Mr. Hyde* and *The Picture of Dorian Gray.* Such emphasis goes back to primitive man's use of symbols, shaped by his needs and purposes. This sometimes resulted in his confusion of words and things. In the minds of primitive man the "momentary gods" are stabilized, however, through the medium of words and, in turn, through stories that may become myths or fables. Langer[36] believes that myth is the "primitive phase of metaphysical thought, the first embodiment of *general ideas.*" This symbolist view of art has been espoused by many critics, in some cases to the extent that they impose their preconceptions on a work of art. Langer views legend, myth, and fairy tale, not so much as literature, but as fantasies, as the "natural materials" of art. This distinction has not been accepted by certain modern critics who have been influenced by the findings of anthropological studies that myth and ritual are to be found in all primitive cultures. Freud's interest in dreams and mythology also add fuel to the flame of speculation. Frye[37] has written that "literature follows after a mythology" and "all themes and characters and stories that you encounter in literature belong to one big interlocking family." He argues, therefore, for the necessity of teaching the Bible as literature and for developing knowledge of the classical myths. Some critics go beyond

[35] Perrine, Lawrence. *Sound and Sense: An Introduction to Poetry.* New York: Harcourt, Brace, 1963.

[36] Langer, Suzanne K. *Philosophy in a New Key* (3d ed.). Cambridge, Mass.: Harvard University Press, 1942, p. 201.

[37] Frye, Northop. *The Educated Imagination.* Toronto: Canadian Broadcasting Corporation, 1963, p. 18.

established mythologies to show how a writer like Faulkner creates some original myths, in his case about southern United States. Others look to material down through the generations to show similarities in theme.

Such criticisms can have some of the joys of detective work. As Frye and others point out, the story of the mysterious birth of a hero was told long before the account of the finding of Moses in the bulrushes. It was also told of Perseus in Greek legend, passed into literature in Euripides' play *Ion*, and was used by Plautus and Terence and other Roman writers of comedies. Then it got into fiction in *Tom Jones* and *Oliver Twist* and may reappear in modern science fiction. Cinderella appears in women's magazines in many guises, and the latest mystery story may contain a Bluebeard.

This sampling of a few types and current movements in criticism – social interpretations, historical approaches, linguistic analysis, psychoanalytic concepts, and intensive reading of the text – are not placed in competitive position. Where the emphasis is upon the reader's response, not too much weight can be given to any one school of criticism. A fixed response may become a substitute for the freer and more difficult task of reading closely and describing one's own reactions. The point of view may vary not only with the reader but with the material read. As Brower and Poirier[38] have remarked, "The moral question is no more 'right' than the historical question or the linguistic question or the psychological question." The reader can sharpen his apperception by knowledge of the writer's tools and by a clear purpose for reading, but these do not need to interfere with his first, original reactions to factual article or elaborate fantasy. No parent or teacher can really dictate a youth's perception of a story, play, or character. The teacher should never be guilty of a trivial hunt for biographical deviations, unconscious aggressions and literary ambiguities, images or symbols. He can, however, read some of the literary analyses of an individual critic reacting to a particular writer or an individual work of art. We sharpen our own perceptions, intensify our own reactions by a study of the specific example.

## *Criticism and the Typical Reader's Responses*

The sections above illuminate rather than explain the responses of the "ordinary" or "average" reader. Literary criticism as here described is a specialized, technical, intellectual skill approached by some students of English literature but achieved regularly by a comparatively small group of scholars. It develops through years of study in a circumscribed field and is therefore far removed from the responses of a child to a poem, the ef-

[38] Browser, Reuben A., and Richard Poirier (eds.). *In Defense of Reading.* New York: Dutton, 1962.

fects on an adolescent of a short story, or the reactions of a subscriber to a lending library when he reads the latest novel. The literary scholar is concerned with the grammar of criticism – with theme, structure, metaphor, symbol, ambiguity, irony, and the like. He is concerned with a theory of literature rather than pragmatic problems of understanding, appreciation, and interaction of teacher, student, author, and a piece of writing. Despite this considerable gulf between specialist and typical reader, the skilled responses of the scholar may throw light on the more commonplace responses of youth and of the more casual adult reader. An analysis of the craft of criticism indicates approaches for the teacher of English and his group, and the writings of the expert may suggest categories and modes of response which can be studied empirically by the researcher.

The wide variety of schools of criticism, here noted rather than discussed, give some support to the teacher of English who believes that responses to a piece of literature may exist in many forms. The romanticist may explain it mystically as a product of genius, the pragmatist sees it as a moral or social message, the Freudian interprets it as an example of aggressive or substitute reaction. Historically, fashions in criticism have changed, but the discipline usually retains certain basic characteristics. There are times when the teacher of literature must use some of the historical or biographical background of a work of art, relate it to a myth or legend, or read closely to gain meanings partly hidden. Some knowledge of the development of literary criticism, accordingly, can add depth to consideration of a work by a teacher and his group. Similarly, the above discussion of the work of the critic also gives hints for the teaching-learning process whether in the classroom or in the book review column. The critic is considered, not as faultfinder or even as judge, but as one who communicates part of his experience of a work of art and encourages others to react in diverse ways, form their own opinions, and defend their positions. The critic may at times supply some background information about a writer or his work. He is familiar with literary devices and conventions, an understanding of which may add meaning to the poem or play. He may point the way toward informed judgment in a day of uncertainties or in the minds of youth who are in the process of acquiring skills in literary interpretations or knowledge of ethical values.

Similarly, the analysis of a literary work may suggest categories for studying the reactions to literature or the psychological impact of a work on emotions, attitudes, or ethical values of the reader. This is not to say that a poem, story, or play must be considered only as vicarious experience for the reader or as a moral weapon for producing better citizens. If a literary work produces responses, the responses are a form of behavior which can be studied. The teacher sometimes wants to know not only the quick, overt response of a group but whether more deep-seated changes in thinking and behavior are taking place. He may suspect that the most usual response to *Look Homeward, Angel* and *Of Human Bondage* is some sort of identification with the principal character and *The Ugly American* or *Cry, the Beloved Country* shapes the reader's attitudes to other peoples. Some of the categories used in the studies by Russell and Whitman, and the results of studies by Squire, Wilson, and Skelton discussed in Chapter 7, were described by critics before they were validated empirically.

The current mode of *explication de texte* offers both expediting and obstructing measures for empirical study. It encourages teacher and reader to go beyond the "clear, dictionary region of meaning" to the hidden meanings, from external description to internal structures. It encourages the reader to move from explicit meaning to implicit meaning. There is time even in a crowded school term for the intensive textual analysis of the form and content of a few literary works when pupils have developed some background for it. Conversely, modern criticism often discourages biographical or social data which may add to the youthful reader's understanding. It emphasizes intellectual response to the exclusion of an emotional response which may contribute greatly to impact on a ten- or fifteen-year-old or even an adult. It may neglect some of what Auden called the "play" or "game" element in literature which can be so attractive to the younger reader. As suggested in the last section of the book, some combination of the different types of response provides the best opportunity for developing appreciation of and permanent interest in literary works. The reactions of the beginner and the sophisticated scholar differ at least in degree; however, there is some fundamental likeness in the reactions of the "ordinary" reader and the skilled critic. The intuitive response of the critic, bolstered by years of study, may produce the more fundamental truths, which may be a beacon to the younger or the less sophisticated reader and a guide to the experimentalist.

*Part Two*

# Research Backgrounds

# CHAPTER 5 | The Reader and His Environment

The reiterated theme of this book is that the act of reading always concerns both an individual and some printed or written material. What happens to the individual as his eye searches the page is our special concern. Such effects are a product, not only of the content of the material, but also of the person doing the reading and the setting in which it is done. To understand the situation thoroughly we must comprehend what is intended by the writer and also the fact that the reader's experience, or the conditions under which the reading is done, may cause him to derive ideas congruent with or completely opposite from those intended by the writer. The kind of person he is, his needs and dreams, his purposes and experiences, his approaches to the page, will all determine the end result, the climax to the process of reading. In the words of Emerson, "'Tis the good reader that makes the good book."

Personal factors which affect the impact of an article, story, or poem are often included under the rubric individual differences and relate to such items as stage of development, sex, mental ability, and background of experience. Environmental factors relate to such items as character of home, socioeconomic status, group pressures, and community mores. All of these varied but interrelated forces are possible determinants of the individual's personality. A number of writers and researchers have attempted to explore rather specifically the interrelationships of personality and reading effects. The present chapter reviews some of these attempts and indicates some of the difficulties in arriving at clear-cut or final conclusions. We know that personality and reading are related but are unsure of the extent and nature of the relationships. First, this uncertainty may be caused by doubts about the nature of the effects of reading or even because of questions still unanswered about more specific responses during reading. Second, controversy may be related to different theories on how learning, including learning to read, takes place and especially the role of personal adjustment in the learning. Third, personality is an elusive term. Different theories of personality propose varying parameters, described and interpreted in various ways. If we were more sure of what responses to reading are, the role of adjustment or mental health in learning, and our theory of personality, we could be much more exact in describing interrelationships between reading and personality.

Despite this negative introduction stressing difficulties, all is not lost. Fortunately, although a wide range of personal factors is found in any school class or adult group, many common factors are also at work. Even if individuals reach developmental levels at different times, children go through the same general stages of development. Certain patterns of interest and personality and certain behavior distinguish the sexes. Large groups of people are of comparable mental ability. They come from one of rural, small town, or big city backgrounds. Homes usually have certain elements in common and people of a particular socioeconomic and educational class often read the same newspapers, watch the same television programs, and avoid the same lecturers. Accordingly, it seems worthwhile to explore some of the possible relationships between the reading process, the person doing the reading, and the milieu of the activity.

## *Personality and Learning: General Considerations*

A number of psychologists have testified to the close relationships among personality factors, learning, and achievement. For example, McCarthy[1] summarized years of experience in child psychology by stating, "The type of personality adjustment a child makes and the quality of his interpersonal relations in early childhood are important determiners of *what* he learns, of *how* quickly he learns, and how effectively he *retains*." McCarthy believed that emotional insecurity is the basic cause of most learning difficulties which are not caused by mental defect. In a study of about 400 first-graders in Sweden, Malmquist[2] found that reading success was positively associated with factors of self-confidence and stability as judged by teachers' ratings of these characteristics. In a study of 112 college readers' reactions to fine fictional selections, Thayer and Pronko[3] found agreements on character interpretation and believed it was possible to predict responses by knowing certain of the reader's affective predispositions. Such sample results are far from complete as evidence, but they give a tantalizing glimpse of possible relationships among personality factors, learning, and reading behavior.

Despite such specific bits of information the weight of the evidence is

[1] McCarthy, Dorothea. "Personality and Learning," *American Council on Educational Studies, 13*:93–96, 1949.

[2] Malmquist, Eve. *Factors Related to Reading Disabilities in the First Grade in the Elementary School.* Stockholm, Sweden: Almquist and Wiksell, 1958.

[3] Thayer, L. O., and N. H. Pronko. "Some Psychological Factors in the Reading of Fiction," *Journal of Genetic Psychology, 93*:113–17, 1958.

against any clear-cut, one-to-one relationship between personality traits and reading achievement and responses. In a review of 250 studies of interrelationships of language and personality Russell[4] concluded that "the dearth of specific evidence about interrelationships of language behaviors and personality is due, not to lack of knowledge about language development, but to lack of success in defining and measuring personality." Sometimes personality is related to physical characteristics, as in Sheldon's work. Especially with school students, personality may be measured in terms of sociometric ratings by one's peers. Counsellors like to include standardized intelligence and aptitude tests in appraising personality. Some tests of interests, such as those of Strong and Kuder, seem to give clues to personality. Projective measures such as the Rorschach and Murray's Thematic Apperception Test require skilled analysis to draw inferences about personality. Psychoanalytic theories date back to Freud and certain analytic theories to Jung. Gordon Allport developed his psychology of the individual, and Carl Rogers' theory of the self has evolved from his work in nondirective therapy. Perhaps the most common attempt to get at personality is in self-report measures, such as the California Test of Personality for school children and Gough's California Psychological Inventory for adults. Although many psychologists defend the thesis that "having some data is better than having no data," the results of studies using these instruments discourage heavy reliance on personality measures, especially by themselves.

Gross's[5] *The Brain Watchers* gave some of the facts against personality tests in journalistic style, deploring the "pseudo-scientific hucksters" who sell the tests in quantity to school people and businessmen. Some fifteen years earlier Ellis[6] reviewed more objectively over 350 studies and concluded that personality questionnaires available up to that time were of questionable value in group diagnosis and guidance and of even less value in delineation of individual adjustment or personality traits. He stated that "no real endeavors have been made to show that, when used according to their standard directions, these instruments will do the clinical jobs they are supposed to do; meaning, that they will adequately differentiate neurotics from non-neurotics, introverts from extroverts, dominant from submissive persons, and so on." The studies quoted toward the end of this chapter are valuable, accordingly, not because they illustrate some definite relationship between reading and broad, well-established personality traits, but because they suggest clues to the influence of

[4] Russell, David H. "Interrelationships of the Language Arts and Personality," *Child Development and the Language Arts,* Bulletin of the National Conference on Research in English. Champaign, Ill.: National Council of Teachers of English, 1953.

[5] Gross, Martin L. *The Brain Watchers.* New York: Random House, 1962.

[6] Ellis, A. "The Validity of Personality Questionnaires," *Psychological Bulletin, 43:* 385–440, September 1946.

specific factors of personality or environment on reading responses. Such specific clues may be taken up by a parent or instructor to move toward desirable goals for the child or the high school and the college student.

Recent research has been concerned less with the relationships of general personality scores and emotions to learning behavior and more with the effects of specific personality measures and somewhat more clearly defined emotional factors. For example, some investigators have employed concepts such as tension, stress, and anxiety defined in terms of specific situations or components. Freud himself identified three types of anxiety: *reality* anxiety, *neurotic* anxiety, and *moral* anxiety or feelings of guilt. Modern test makers sometimes speak of "test anxiety" or "manifest anxiety."[7] Sarason and his coauthors[8] used such items as: "When you are home and you are thinking about your reading lesson for the next day, do you worry that you will do poorly on the lesson?" On the basis of replies to such questions Sarason divided elementary school children of similar scores on general mental tests into two groups of "high anxiety" and "low anxiety" children. He found that the high anxiety group did better on rather specific mental tasks where alertness to errors improved the score. On tasks requiring more flexibility and creativity, such as drawing a person, the less anxious children were superior. The latter tended to do better critical thinking and to be more spontaneous and productive. Other studies have shown that students at all levels up through college who can be labeled as anxious tend to be rigid in their responses and to do better on specific tasks calling for straight recall of material read. Low anxiety students excel in tasks requiring them to reorganize ideas creatively. Anxiety, whether experimentally induced or built up by a series of past failures, inhibits interpretation in reading situations.

Studies of other emotional states tend to confirm the findings about anxiety that there is no simple answer to the influence of emotions but that they affect behavior and achievement differently in different situations with different persons. Emotional appeals by a parent, teacher, or advertiser may be effective with "low anxiety" students although their effects tend to be transitory rather than permanent. A certain amount of tension may be desirable for the majority of people in problem-solving situations which do not threaten the individual. Sometimes tensions are specific to a single situation, such as oral reading in a group, but they may build into generalized feelings of guilt, fear, and hostility. Highly anxious children are likely to respond best to goals which can be reached by hard work and are set by authority; low anxiety children do better where originality and independent judgment are desired outcomes. It may be that in

[7] Taylor, J. A. "Drive Theory and Manifest Anxiety," *Psychological Bulletin, 53:* 303–320, 1956.

[8] Sarason, Seymour B., and others. *Anxiety in Elementary School Children.* New York: Wiley, 1960.

reading of a work type and in other learning tasks there is an optimal amount of tension or emotion, but that this optimum varies with the characteristics of the individual and the nature of the task.

## *Personality and Learning: Overt Behavior*

The general relationship of emotion, personality, and learning can be translated into specific behavior of the individual. In such manifestations as attitudes and interests there are overt behaviors which lend themselves to psychological study. School or college achievement is another area where manifest, even public behavior, may be related to personality or emotion. For example, in a survey of research on personality adjustments in the 1940's, Tuddenham[9] concluded that the best personality adjustment is associated with "high average" achievement in school and college and that the extremes of low achievement and the highest achievement were likely to contain more students with maladjustments. Tuddenham further suggested the influence of environment when he found some evidence that delinquency was commonest in deteriorated districts of cities but that personality problems were most common in desirable socioeconomic areas.

Although "life adjustment" is not one of the central goals of education as it once was, there seems no good reason for discarding the concept of *adjustment* or *mental health* as one of the desirable outcomes of education. In a country where one out of eight of the pupils in school will spend some time in a mental hospital it may be well for the school to combine with some other community agencies in promoting positive mental health for all. From the 1930's to 1950's many American schools had an aroused concern for children's and adolescents' social relations, personal problems, and adjustments to their peers. The difficulty of a teacher in elementary school looking after thirty youngsters or one in high school assuming responsibility for as many as 125 adolescents caused doubts about the school's ability to assume this role. A changing philosophy of education which discarded "fads and frills" in favor of academic fundamentals further caused teachers, parents, and school patrons to question any emphasis on mental health. However, changing concepts of mental health such as those described by Smith[10] have added clarity and cruciality to the role of mental health in human behavior and learning.

Modern concepts of mental health include the overt functioning of the individual, which is the concern of this section and is considered further

[9] Tuddenham, R. D. "Adjustment in School and College," *Review of Educational Research, 13*:429–31, 1943.

[10] Smith, M. Brewster. "Research Strategies Toward a Conception of Positive Mental Health," *American Psychologist, 14*:673–81, November 1959.

in Chapter 9. For example, Jahoda[11] conceptualized mental health as a matter of degree and consisting of six components, one of which was "environmental mastery" and related to adequacy in work, play, love, interpersonal relations, and problem-solving behavior. Persons who espouse such a point of view deplore an emphasis on academic achievement which requires much memorization and drill on facts, which prizes the glib use of words over genuine understanding. They say it is important to know the facts but also to use and apply the facts, and this functioning may involve emotion and personality, not as something to be ignored, but to be included as part of the total process. As Almy[12] has put it, "The crucial test of any school's contribution to mental health lies not so much in the skills and knowledge it purports to teach as in its effectiveness in helping youngsters to incorporate these into their day-to-day living." The intimate relationships between emotion, personality, and daily functioning, even in academic learnings, make it impossible to discard the concept of *mental health* in relation to much behavior, including reading.

There is considerable evidence that emotional and personality factors may be just as important as purely cognitive factors in accounting for educational achievement and other kinds of valued overt behavior.[13] Some of the factors which produce the effectively functioning person, as compared with the ineffective person, undoubtedly lie in cultural backgrounds of home, of social class, and of community influences. McGuire and others write of academic difficulties in relation to the "alienation syndrome of anxiety, mistrust, pessimism, self-centeredness and resentment" all barriers to adequate learning. In an unpublished study of about five hundred college women, for example, Prouty[14] found clear differences between over- and under-achievers in specific items of a group of personality tests. The high achievement group were characterized by

1. Greater freedom from worries.
2. More confidence in their own ability.
3. Increase in religious skepticism.
4. Higher ethical principles.
5. Increase in introversion.
6. Lower social skills.

[11] Jahoda, Marie. *Current Concepts of Positive Mental Health.* New York: Basic Books, 1958.

[12] Almy, Millie. "Intellectual Mastery and Mental Health," *Teachers College Record, 63:*468–78, March 1962.

[13] McGuire, Carson. "Cultural and Social Factors in Mental Health," *Review of Educational Research, 32:*455–63, December 1962.

[14] Prouty, Helen L. *Personality Factors Related to Over- and Under-achievement of College Students.* Unpublished doctoral dissertation (University of California, Berkeley, 1951).

7. Less ability to accept criticism.
8. Greater enjoyment of reading and broader interests.

Other specific studies described below also include reference to overt functioning in relation to personality factors or specific test items.

In addition to relating specific items on personality tests to effective functioning as an individual, some research reports reveal data in relation to overt behavior in the form of reading choices and interests. Standard summaries of reading research suggest that there are available at least three hundred reports of careful studies of preferences and choices, but many of these do not involve the characteristics of the readers beyond age, sex, and grade in school. As early as 1940 Gray[15] gave a theoretical basis for investigating both reading preferences and personality. He stated:

> It seems that for the adult, reading is a method of attack, a form of adjustment, and almost, if not entirely, a way of living. For the child, it gradually becomes part and parcel of many phases of his development, and as such it slowly builds unity and coherence in his life.

Two unpublished studies by Reed[16,17] involved close study of items on various personality tests, teacher observation, and actual reading of two sixth-grade classes. Although the groups were small, Reed used what amounted to a case study approach involving many records combined with some small group statistical analysis. He found that children in the top quarter of scores on the *Mental Health Analysis* were about three times as accurate as children in the bottom quarter when they stated their reading preferences, and these were checked against their actual reading over a period of a year. Both high and low groups alike preferred animal and adventure stories, but the low group read more family life and sports stories — which could be related to needs for security and achievement. Stimulated by the school program, nearly all children read many books besides tests and the low quarter read about three-fourths as many as the top group. At this sixth-grade level the comics were respectable; Reed obtained a correlation of 0.80 between number of comics read and popularity measured by sociometric choices.

In a second study which was partly a follow-up of the same group twelve years later and which also involved a total of 859 sixth-grade children, Reed used analysis by computer of as many as 32 variables to study

[15] Gray, C. T. "Reading Ability and Personality Development," *Educational Forum, 4*:133–38, January 1940.

[16] Reed, Charles H. *Interrelations of Various Measures of Personality and Reading in Two Sixth-Grade Classes.* Unpublished master's thesis (University of California, Berkeley, 1948).

[17] Reed, Charles H. *Relationships of Personality and Reading Choices of Sixth-Grade Children.* Unpublished doctoral dissertation (University of California, Berkeley, 1962).

relationships between personality and reading choices. Like other investigators he found significant differences between the choices of boys and girls of this age. Boys chose more books classified as "adventure" and "sports," girls chose more "fanciful fiction." Generally boys chose more "science," girls more on "family life," "mysteries," and "poetry." There were no significant differences on "animal stories" and "humor and nonsense." Correlation data led Reed to conclude, as suggested above, that the grouping of personality scores into subtotals and totals tends to decrease or cancel out relationships; correlations between definite reading preferences and specific personality traits are variable and may be positive and high, approximately zero, or negative. In relation to achievement, Reed found a correlation of 0.48 for boys and 0.52 for girls between "Reading Achievement" and "Adequate Outlook and Goals." In another analysis he found that personality scores in this category contributed 36 to 40 per cent of the variance in Reading Achievement for boys and 25 to 41 per cent for girls, although this was markedly less when mental age was included. In his longitudinal study, college students' reactions to their sixth grade activities and comments suggested that the earlier reading had had some effects in the ensuing years.

Two other studies involving overt behavior were carefully planned and executed. Ladd[18] analyzed relationships among various measures of 315 children in grades three to five who came from middle and low socioeconomic backgrounds and from schools with traditional teaching methods. She found good achievement in reading positively associated with favorable scores on attitudes to school, amount of time spent in reading for recreation, pleasure in oral reading before the class, number of books owned by the child, and by teachers' ratings of self-confidence, persistence, and concentration of attention. In a study described more fully in the chapter dealing with effects of reading, Wollner[19] reported that 25 per cent of her subjects were engaged in excessive reading because of emotional problems and that another 16 per cent were avoiding reading for a similar reason.

Taba[20] recorded and classified the discussion of books and stories by 25 students in an eighth-grade class. She found that projections (attempts to understand and evaluate behavior) accounted for 51 per cent to 87 per cent of the statements made by individuals. Less frequent were general-

[18] Ladd, Margaret R. *The Relation of Social, Economic and Personal Characteristics to Reading Ability.* Contributions to Education No. 582. New York: Bureau of Publications, Teachers College, Columbia University, 1933.

[19] Wollner, Mary H. *Children's Voluntary Reading as an Expression of Individuality.* No. 944 New York: Bureau of Publications, Teachers College, Columbia University, 1949.

[20] Taba, Hilda. *With Perspective on Human Relations: A Study of Peer Group Dynamics in an Eighth Grade.* Washington, D.C.: American Council on Education, 1955.

izations, self-references, and irrelevancies. Taba believed that her classification of responses showed four types of readers:

1. Those who enter into a story freely and fully without generalizing about it.
2. Egocentric readers who find meaning only in light of their own experience.
3. Egocentric readers who make prescriptive judgments about story characters.
4. Readers who project or generalize and thus find new experiences in their reading.

Another attempt to link reading and overt behavior has been made by some writers who see the reading of horror and crime comic books as a cause of juvenile delinquency. Wertham[21] stated that comic books indoctrinate children with stereotyped images and prejudices against certain races and minority groups. Particularly insidious is the harmful influence of comic books on the sexual development of children in the direction of sadism, masochism, homosexuality, frigidity, and sexual hypochondriasis. Such scare words attract attention to a problem but fail to establish a scientific basis for a causal relationship between reading comics and delinquency. Rather, the doctrine of multiple causation mentioned elsewhere suggests that personality factors, living conditions, home influences, and the reading of undesirable literature may combine to produce antisocial behavior. Jahoda[22] gave a more moderate summation of Wertham's views as follows:

1. Anti-social impulses, which may be caused by a variety of factors, are reinforced and stimulated by reading.
2. Constant exposure to tales of violence and horror will destroy sensitivity in the "good and normal" child.

The perplexing problem of relating personal, cultural, and social variables to intellectual and dynamic aspects of behavior and achievement has not been solved. A purely cognitive view of any intellectual activity, including reading, is likely to give only one part of the picture. Research has not demonstrated any one-to-one relationship between personality variables and behavior manifestations but bits of evidence about the relationships are accumulating. This is particularly true of the next section which considers relationships between personality variables and reading difficulties.

[21] Wertham, Frederick. "What Are Comic Books?" *National Parent-Teacher, 43:*16–18, March 1949.

[22] Jahoda, Marie. *The Impact of Literature: A Psychological Discussion of Some Assumptions in the Censorship Debate.* New York: American Book Publishers Council, 1954. (Mimeographed).

## *Reading Difficulties and the Characteristics of the Reader*

The personality of the reader in relation to reading difficulties or retardation has long been a subject of concern to clinicians and teachers who deal with people having reading problems. In 1941 Gates[23] summarized the research to that date and gave results from some of his own studies. These have been explored and amplified in succeeding years but still provide a good summary of knowledge in this area. Slightly modified,[24] these conclusions were:

1. Personality difficulties are frequently but not universally associated with reading difficulties.
2. In cases where they occur together personality difficulties may be causes, concomitants, or results of reading difficulties.
3. Emotional difficulties usually appear as part of a constellation of difficulties causing reading retardation.
4. There is no single personality pattern characteristic of reading failure and there is no proved one-to-one relationship between type of adjustment difficulties and type of reading disabilities. For example, feeling of insecurity resulting from undue home pressure for achievement may result in low reading achievement marked by withdrawal; compulsive, anxious reading marked by frequent errors; or it may result in higher achievement in reading than would be expected from mental level.
5. Symptoms associated with reading difficulties are commonly aggressive reactions, withdrawing tendencies, or general insecurity and apprehension.
6. If emotional, adjustment disturbances are one of a group of primary causes of reading difficulties, retardation in other academic learnings often occurs.
7. If reading difficulties are a cause of emotional difficulties, skilled remedial work in reading may clear up rather easily a considerable number of difficulties. If deep-seated personality difficulties are a cause of reading difficulties, ordinary remedial work is likely to be ineffective and more intensive therapy is required.
8. Diagnosis and remediation in reading are often more acceptable to children and to parents than [is diagnosis and therapy] in fundamental personality maladjustments. Accordingly, the reading aspects of a problem may be emphasized in the beginning stages of treatment.
9. The above generalizations probably apply to the other language arts as much as to reading. They should all be regarded as hypotheses for further scientific study.

[23] Gates, Arthur I. "The Role of Personality Maladjustment in Reading Disability," *Journal of Genetic Psychology*, 59:77–83, September 1941.

[24] Russell, David H. "Reading Disabilities and Mental Health: A Review of Research," *Understanding the Child*, 16:24–32, January 1947.

A number of investigations since the Gates summary have added further insight into relationships of reading difficulties and personality difficulties. From a sample of some two hundred studies a few that add further insights may be mentioned. Robinson's[25] work was noteworthy as a study continuing over five years and involving experts in different fields, including psychiatric judgments of emotional problems. In 22 cases of extreme difficulty in reading she found nine cases with emotional difficulties. She believed that "emotional reactions of children may be created by family problems or attitudes within the home." Robinson supported the conclusion that a group or syndrome of causes usually lies at the root of reading difficulties but ranks social, visual, and emotional difficulties in the first order of causal importance. She stated that

> Correcting a visual difficulty does not teach a child to read but enables him to learn with greater ease when he is given remedial instruction. Likewise, psychiatric treatment for an emotional problem results in no reading growth without teaching, but it may remove an emotional block so that the child is able to direct his attention toward learning.

In a study of children at the fourth, fifth, and sixth grade levels Baker[26] compared two groups of superior and retarded readers, defined in terms of superiority or inferiority of reading scores in relation to mental test results. Comparisons were made in various tests of mental and verbal abilities, on reading activities, and on the California Test of Personality. There was no significant difference in total personality adjustment scores between the two groups, but there were more superior readers with high ratings in self-adjustment and more retarded readers with high ratings in social adjustment. In a similar study of good and poor readers at the seventh grade level Bouse[27] found about twice as many maladjusted poor readers as maladjusted good readers. The retarded readers felt insecure both at home and at school. Most of them were fully aware of both their reading difficulties and some of the factors in their maladjustments.

In another study comparing 264 retarded and 264 proficient readers in grades four to seven, Sister Vera[28] concluded that the extent of retardation was not related to scores on the California Test of Personality. Gann[29]

[25] Robinson, Helen M. *Why Pupils Fail in Reading*. Chicago: University of Chicago Press, 1946.

[26] Baker, Norma. *Characteristics of Superior and Retarded Readers in the Intermediate Grades of the Elementary School.* Unpublished doctoral dissertation (University of California, Berkeley, 1953).

[27] Bouse, Louise. "Emotional and Personality Problems of a Group of Retarded Readers," *Elementary English, 46:*544–48, December 1955.

[28] Vera, Sister Mary. "A Critical Study of Certain Personality Factors as Determining Elements in a Remedial Reading Program," *Catholic Education Review, 40:*145–61, March 1942.

[29] Gann, Edith. *Reading Difficulty and Personality Organization.* New York: King's Crown Press, 1945.

used more comprehensive measures of personality, including three tests, one inventory, and a questionnaire to get at personality factors. She found little relationship between personality measures and reading scores in three groups of elementary school children (superior, average, and poor readers) although she had some evidence that retarded readers are "emotionally less well-adjusted and less stable." She concluded that reading disabilities are part of the "total personality" and should be studied as such. Holmes[30] made a multiple correlation analysis of factors underlying reading disabilities in college students. He studied the effect of 37 variables in students' power and speed of reading and concluded that "a differential analysis of the personality traits fails to reveal any distinctions peculiar to the non-powerful group of readers."

Other studies could be quoted, some giving positive relationships between personality and reading difficulties, others suggesting insignificant or zero relationships. In the early investigation by Ladd[18] mentioned above, of 315 children in New York City, he found a correlation of only .11 between reading scores and total personality score and higher relationships between reading and attitude, and reading and overt activities such as amount of time spent in reading for pleasure. In 1940 Wilking[31] reviewed a number of investigations and cautioned against an easy assumption of positive relationships. He concluded, "Much more study of the problem is necessary before definite conclusions can be drawn concerning the role played by personality as a causative factor, or even as an accompanying factor, in reading disability." A little later Stauffer[32] supported the theory of multiple causation rather than emotional disturbances as a sole cause of reading difficulties. In contrast, Wynne[33] found only a slight relationship between reading and general personality scores of elementary school children on an adaptation for children of three tests of personality (with intelligence partialled out, coefficients of correlation were in the 0.20 to 0.25 range). Some clusters of test items, however, showed a high selective ability to discriminate between good readers and poor readers. These could be described by such terms as confidence, conformity to accepted standards, assurance in social relations with peers and adults, and need for activity.

[30] Holmes, Jack A. "Factors Underlying Major Reading Disabilities at the College Level," *Genetic Psychology Monographs, 49:*3–95, February 1954.

[31] Wilking, S. Vincent. "Personality Maladjustment as a Causative Factor in Reading Disability," *Elementary School Journal, 42:*268–79, December 1941.

[32] Stauffer, Russell G. "A Clinical Approach to Personality and the Disabled Reader," *Education, 67:*427–35, March 1947.

[33] Wynne, Robert L. *The Relationship between Reading Ability and Personality Inventory Responses in Elementary School Children.* Unpublished master's thesis (University of California, Berkeley, 1955).

Spache[34] found evidence of relationships between reading retardation and scores on the children's form of the Rosenzweig Picture-Frustration Study. He found that the test can be used to identify five major personality patterns related to the child's failure in reading:

1. An aggressive or hostile group in conflict with authority figures.
2. An adjustive group who seek only to be inoffensive.
3. A defensive group which is oversensitive and resentful.
4. A solution-seeking group which attempts the role of peacemaker.
5. An autistic group characterized by blocking or withdrawal.

The puzzling and contradictory nature of the results about personality and reading retardation and indeed, the more general relationship of emotions, personality and reading, is evident from these summaries of careful studies. Some causes of lack of clear relationship have been mentioned above; others can be added:

1. The complex nature of reading and of personality, and the superficial nature of many of the tests used to measure them.
2. The widespread influence of emotion on learning and behavior, and more particularly on perception which is a basis for all reading.
3. The lack of sophistication in experimental design of research, with especial reference to differences in results of case studies and of treatments of mass data.
4. The need for further clarification of personality as a form of motivation for all learning, including learning to read and lifetime reading habits.

Despite this lack of agreement in fact, and the four theoretical reasons for it, there is little question about the application of the theory of multiple causation to the problem. Most investigators, whether working with single cases or with large groups of school children, agree that causes of reading difficulties are seldom single and alone. Instead they exist as a syndrome. Total personality scores as such will not show great differences, but specific personality traits joined to factors in home and in school, to physical factors, to language and background of experience, and to group and community mores, may account for the etiology of reading difficulties. The moral for parents and teachers seems clear. Children with reading difficulties cannot usually be helped by much tutoring on single reading skills. Multiple causes demand multiple remedies.

This implication has been influential in current programs in clinics and in special school classes helping retarded readers. Although one part of diagnosis is to isolate specific educational difficulties and practice intensely on improving them, another part of the treatment may include play or other individual or group therapy along with the practice on

[34] Spache, George. "Personality Patterns of Retarded Readers," *Journal of Educational Research, 50*:488–93, February 1957.

skills. In 1955 Smith[35] mentioned seven studies in which therapy had been used successfully as part of remedial work in reading. Both Bills[36] and Seeman[37] used play therapy successfully in conjunction with other remedial activities. Their work, and that of a related nature, is reported more fully in the next chapter. Another study by Donald Smith and his associates[38] was an attempt to break down generalized categories of personality into specifics which might guide instruction, to establish a relationship between the student's personality and the teacher's method. Eighty college students representing two definite personality syndromes were assigned to sections of corrective reading classes (for which they had volunteered) on the basis of personality inventory scores. Group A students were high in anxiety but low in permeability or openness to outside influence. Group B students were also high in anxiety but also high in permeability. Type A students were relatively uninfluenced by either directive and structured or by permissive teaching methods. Type B students made optimum progress with directive methods of instruction characterized by compulsory attendance, fixed schedule of activities, careful instructions, lectures, and dominance by the instructor. Carried to its logical conclusion, the Smith study may mean that there is no one best method of teaching, that students of different personality may respond optimally to quite different class procedures.

Finally, Holmes has suggested another intriguing theory to explain these conflicting results.[39] Not all of the studies described above fit into his theoretical concept, but he explains many of the results in terms of two main ideas. He states that between 1953 and 1959 approximately one hundred experimental studies were made in the area of personality and reading and that conflicting results can be explained, at least in part, in terms of "gradient shift" or developmental analysis involving different stages of child and adolescent functioning. He believes that the positive relationships found between reading and personality in primary grades become inconsistent in intermediate grades and junior high school and seem to disappear in senior high school and college. There is, accordingly, a shift in relationships as individuals advance through the grades. Second, Holmes relates results to his own theory of substrata factors in reading. He believes that discrepancies between parental attitudes and

[35] Smith, Nila B. "Research on Reading and the Emotions," *School and Society, 81:* 8–10, January 1955.

[36] Bills, Robert E. "Nondirective Play Therapy With Retarded Readers," *Journal of Consulting Psychology, 14:*140–49, April 1950.

[37] Seeman, Julius, and Benner Edwards. "A Therapeutic Approach to Reading Difficulties," *Journal of Consulting Psychology, 18:*451–53, December 1954.

[38] Smith, Donald, and others. "Reading Improvement as a Function of Student Personality and Teaching Method," *The Journal of Educational Psychology, 47:*47–59, January 1956.

[39] Holmes, Jack A. "Personality Characteristics of the Disabled Reader," *Journal of Developmental Reading, 4:*111–22, Winter 1961.

children's self attitudes may be more important for school learning than the child's attitudes to himself as expressed on a paper-and-pencil personality test. He sees such differences in personality dimensions as *mobilizers* — deep-seated value systems which help focus and organize a complex ability. The mobilizers are not interests and they concern concept integration rather than concept formation. They are not accessible to superficial personality test items. In other words, Holmes is concerned not only with skills but also the way the student marshals his skills, not only with item responses but with evidential background relationships.

## *The Environment*

There seems to be little question that the home and community environment affects the amount and kind of reading done by child or adult. Some children grow up in a home, perhaps of college-educated parents with books around them from birth and reading taken for granted as an activity in which everyone engages. Others spend their early lives where print, except perhaps for an occasional tabloid, is unknown and books are something remote from life which a teacher makes you use. Periodical surveys by the American Institute of Public Opinion (the Gallup Poll) suggest that only about half the total of American adults can remember a book, other than the Bible, which they have read during the previous year but that heavy newspaper reading, book buying, and use of other communication media are typical of approximately 10 per cent of the adult population, mainly near the upper end of the educational and socioeconomic scale. Other surveys have shown that, as the educational level of the population rises, people read more difficult material, and they read a greater amount. The flourishing condition of the book clubs, the rise of paperbacks, and newspaper reading which increases more rapidly than the general population, all indicate changes in the sociology of reading. Writers and lecturers may deplore the low level of American taste in television and print, but there is some evidence of upgrading of taste in the content of such magazines as *Look* and *Saturday Evening Post.* Even the picture magazines may be more sophisticated if one can believe *Variety's* famous headline, "Stix Nix Hix Pix." People may not be reading the best things, but they do read. As one writer has put it, "More people are reading without moving their lips."

The place of reading habits in our national life has been analyzed in studies which involve reading of all kinds of materials.[40,41,42] Except for a

[40] National Society for the Study of Education, *Adult Reading*, 55th Yearbook, Part II, Chicago: University of Chicago Press, 1956.

[41] Russell, David H. *Children Learn to Read* (rev. ed.). Boston: Ginn, 1961, Chap. I.

[42] Squire, James R. "Literacy and Literature," *English Journal, 49*:154–60, March 1960.

few historical studies, little evidence is available about reading habits of literature ranked as good or great. In general, the great dramatists and novelists of the past have been read by a small minority. In a series of essays on the sociology of literature, Lowenthal[43] expressed the belief that "the most telling truths about society and the individual are contained in a literature that is not read by the broadest strata." Lowenthal stated that the literature of social impact lies somewhere between the history which must "depersonalize social relationships in favor of an emphasis on larger events" and "at the other extreme, memoirs, autobiographies and letters [which] provide us with more personal data." Furthermore, "The fictional work . . . combines the advantages of these two extremes." In other parts of his book Lowenthal illustrates that content analysis of the materials and close textual criticism of literary works can both be used to isolate specific ideas which may influence the social thinking of reader or spectator.

Such information and essays on the sociology of reading deal in large-group behavior, providing clues to the wide variety of situations in which children and adults are reading from day to day – or not reading. The scientific evidence about the effects of specific environments on reading behavior and response is almost nonexistent, except in relation to broader socioeconomic or class differences which affect personality, amount of leisure time, availability of books, and other factors. The literature on socioeconomic differences is too extensive to be summarized here. We know that children in a home in which parents and other adults share their own delights in worthwhile children's books tend to grow up with a habit of reading. We know that if an urban adolescent gang values other things, or if the climate of a high school stresses the importance of athletics and school dances, an adolescent in the gang or the high school is not likely to read much unless he is a nonconformist, perhaps, and does it surreptitiously. In some groups the interaction among the individuals facilitates reading; in other groups it inhibits it. The studies of reading habits in relation to specific environmental situations are, however, sparse and limited.

There is considerable evidence that child-care practices influence the child's adjustment and specifically may facilitate or inhibit the oral language which is the basis for later reading.[44] Experiences in listening to stories and using language in many ways in the preschool years may develop readiness for reading in first grade or even earlier. Success in beginning reading has an emotional concomitant which may affect not only

[43] Lowenthal, Leo. *Literature, Popular Culture and Society.* Englewood Cliffs, New Jersey: Prentice-Hall, 1961.

[44] McCarthy, Dorothea (ed.). *Factors that Influence Language Growth.* Bulletin of the National Conference on Research in English. Champaign, Ill.: National Council of Teachers of English, 1953.

later reading skills but the reading habits of childhood and adolescence. Before the child comes to school he has probably caught some of the attitudes toward reading of the people in his apartment or block and of the older children whose conduct he emulates. The personal relations in the classroom may be the next important factor. Strang[45] quotes one bright fourteen-year-old boy who had not learned to read in elementary school. The boy explained, "In the first grade, I didn't like the teacher – I mean, she didn't like me. And I had the same teacher for two years." In the primary and later grades, the pupil first learns perception of signs – adding meaning to the visual impression of a word, word-part, or words. Once he has acquired some facility in recognition and some ways of getting at the author's meaning such as the words themselves and using the context, he begins to experience feelings in the act of reading and begins to translate into his own words and emotions and to read "between the lines." His feelings may be of enjoyment, interest, and satisfaction or of dislike, embarrassment, resistance, and hostility. These feelings in turn influence the way he looks at the next reading situation coming up in the school day or week and the way he approaches the newsstand and the library when he has some time on his hands.

Specific studies of the effects of environmental and personal settings on responses to reading are hard to discover. Wolfenstein[46] found differences in mothers' and children's reactions to the fantasy in a story dealing with the experiences of the first child during the time a second child is expected and ending with the birth and homecoming of the new baby. The fantasy life of ten four-year-olds was first studied in individual play sessions with family dolls and doll furniture. The ten mothers then read the story to their children and reported their own and their children's reactions within a few hours of reading. The story was also read later to the children in a group. The fantasy consisted of the child in the story creating a strange new animal combining the characteristics of various animals when he heard about the new baby. Wolfenstein found that the mothers tended to dissociate the fantasy from the rest of the story; their attitude was that the fantasy was superfluous. She believed that the mothers preferred repression to sublimation and that they displayed feelings of "maternal omnipotence." The children's reactions were in marked contrast to the mothers' in the acceptance of the fantasy of the strange animal as part of the story. However, the mothers' preferences for repression created conflicts and "in some of these four-year-old children the enjoyment of fantasy was considerably interfered with." Wolfenstein believed that the story as the child receives it "has been subjected to the

[45] Strang, Ruth. "A Dynamic Theory of the Reading Process," *Merrill-Palmer Quarterly of Behavior and Development,* 7:239–45, 1961.

[46] Wolfenstein, Martha. "The Impact of a Children's Story on Mothers and Children," *Monographs of Society for Research in Child Development,* 9:1–54, 1946.

continual commentary of the reactions of the mother as expressed in her tone of voice, her tenseness at certain points, her relaxedness at others." She concluded that a child's story must be adapted not only to the needs of the child but also to those of the adult who will do the reading.

Another study dealing with the influence of the home on readiness for reading rather than specific reading effects is that of Milner,[47] who found that children in the lowest third of their first-grade class in language abilities lacked opportunities for communication with their parents. They did not have breakfast with them and there were few household routines which gave rise to give-and-take conversation and linguistic stimulation in the family circle. Children in the upper third of the group had these language experiences and enjoyed more displays of affection by parents. Similarly, Almy[48] found positive relationships between reading success and such home experiences as looking at books and magazines, being read to, and development of interest in words, letters, and numbers.

Other studies relating environment to reading may be mentioned briefly. In a 1937 investigation of opportunities for bright, average, and dull children in New York City, Lazar[49] noted a positive relationship between intelligence scores of the children, socioeconomic status, and the number of books and magazines in the home. Bright children from poor homes had inferior tastes in reading. In later studies Sheldon[50] found that one-half of the children from superior homes had reading as a hobby compared with one-fourth of the pupils from average homes and only one-tenth of those from below average homes. There was no relationship between liking for reading and extracurricular activities; contrary to expectation, an interest in sports was higher with the good readers than with the poor readers. On the other hand, several studies of reading interests have shown that children of similar sex and age living in different parts of the country have similar tastes in reading. For example, Rudman[51] concluded, "There appears to be little difference in the reading interests of children from rural, urban and metropolitan centers." Evidently factors in the home and immediate environment are of greater importance in affecting reading than are factors in the wider environment.

[47] Milner, Esther. "A Study of the Relationships between Reading Readiness in Grade One and Patterns of Parent-Child Interaction," *Monographs of Society for Research in Child Development,* 22:95–112, 1951.

[48] Almy, Millie C. *Children's Experiences Prior to First Grade and Success in Beginning Reading.* Contributions to Education No. 954. New York: Bureau of Publications, Teachers College, Columbia University, 1949.

[49] Lazar, May. *Reading Interests, Activities, and Opportunities of Bright, Average and Dull Children.* Contributions to Education No. 707. New York: Bureau of Publications, Teachers College, Columbia University, 1937.

[50] Sheldon, W. D., and W. G. Cutts. "Relation of Parents, Home, and Certain Developmental Characteristics to Children's Reading Ability," *Elementary School Journal,* 53:517–21, May 1953.

[51] Rudman, H. C. "The Informational Needs and Reading Interests of Children in Grades IV through VIII," *Elementary School Journal,* 52:444–51, April 1952.

This observation is underscored by a number of other studies of the role of parents in developing reading interests and tastes. The parent is usually the dominant factor in the environment of the young child, and he will usually adopt some ready-made parental attitudes through imitation. As the child grows older, it is the parent who determines socioeconomic conditions, cultural traditions, and the amount and kind of reading material in the home. It is the parent who reads to the child an hour a day, an hour a month, or not at all. It is the parent who loves to read or who uses only the pictorial media. In a study involving 250 parents and 305 children aged seven through thirteen years Jefferson[52,53] used a fictitious list of annotated titles and had some of the children and parents examine copies of different children's books. He found that most of the parents estimated their children's choices accurately in terms of like and dislike. The children showed more interest, however, than their parents estimated they would in stories labeled "Mystery and Detective" and "Human and Whimsy," and the parents overrated their interest in books labeled "Travel Stories." Parents of girls underestimated their interest in stories of "Love and Romance." The parents, largely a middle-class group, showed an awareness of differences of reading interests among boys and girls. There was, however, evidence that individual parents' abilities to estimate their children's reading interests varied widely from negative to positive significant correlations and that it was harder for parents to estimate the appeal of books they examined than their children's interest in a list of annotated titles.

In comparison with studies of home background, considerable research has been done on the classroom environment or "climate," especially in elementary schools. These studies, however, tend to be descriptive of the environment or the teacher rather than relating climate to such specific pupil behavior as reading activities. There is agreement among observers that the social climate of the classroom is heavily influenced by the teacher but personality tests have not been productive of much knowledge of what teacher characteristics are important. Leiderman[54] and his associates have presented a summary of eight studies showing that productive behavior of pupils is related to the behavior of teachers. For example, children undertake more self-initiated work when teachers are warmest and friendliest. Teachers who tend to reject students had little influence on self-initiated or required work. Leiderman concluded with

[52] Jefferson, Benjamin F. *Some Relationships between Parents' and Children's Preferences in Juvenile Literature.* Unpublished doctoral dissertation (University of California, Berkeley, 1956).

[53] Jefferson, Benjamin F. "Some Relationships between Parents' and Children's Preferences in Juvenile Literature," *Elementary School Journal,* 58:212–18, January 1958.

[54] Leiderman, G., T. Hilton, and H. Levin. "Studies of Teachers' Behavior: A Summary Report," *Journal of Teacher Education,* 8:33–37, December 1957.

other investigators, however, that the prediction of the effects of teacher behavior and personality is a complex task.

A number of studies have shown some positive relationships between teaching competence and specific personality traits, but these differ with the investigator and the tests used. MacKinnon[55] summarized some of the studies and his own researches on the creative personality by hypothesizing ten psychological dimensions of superior teaching performance. They included health and vitality, intellectual competence, social presence, good judgment, identification with the teacher's role, social and emotional maturity, originality, fairmindedness, and personal courage. A specific study involving certain personality traits as determined by some parts of Gough's *California Psychological Inventory*[56] was made by Hoihjelle[57] of 61 able teachers in a California county. The six traits selected for study were related to Guilford's ideas of creativity and were dominance, self-acceptance, capacity for status, self-control, sociability, and social presence (spontaneity). Hoihjelle found that three groups of teachers using basal, individualized, and language experience approaches to beginning reading could not be differentiated with respect to the six personality traits. There were differences in their classrooms, however, relative to scores on the Wrightstone Pupil-Teacher Rapport Scale,[58] which is a rating scale for such classroom matters as "degree of social interaction," "quality of social integration," "interest," and "role structure." In other words, the methods of reading instruction used by the teacher were related to classroom climate, with classrooms of teachers using the language experience approach being scored significantly higher in social climate than classrooms of teachers using the other two methods. This method was characterized by greater self-expression in writing and discussion than was true of the other methods. Specific personality traits of teachers were not significantly related to classroom climate scores.

The evidence about environmental influences suggests that, next to the home and school, the immediate community is the most important determiner of young children's attitudes, values, and behavior. A number of studies have shown that attitude toward other ethnic or religious groups may be well established by the time a child is in first grade. For example,

[55] MacKinnon, D. M. "Identifying the Effective Teacher, Implications of Personality Assessment," *California Journal for Improvement of Instruction, 1*:8–13, October 1958.

[56] Gough, H. G. *California Psychological Inventory.* Palo Alto: Consulting Psychologists Press, 1957.

[57] Hoihjelle, Anna L. *Social Climate and Personality Traits of Able Teachers in Relation to Reading Instruction.* Unpublished doctoral dissertation (University of California, Berkeley, 1961).

[58] Wrightstone, J. W. *Pupil-Teacher Rapport Scale.* New York: Board of Education, City of New York, Bureau of Educational Research, Division of Tests and Measurements, 1951.

a study by Radke and co-workers[59] of children in kindergarten and the first two grades found "Not only are races and religious groups differentiated . . . but varying shades of hostility and friendliness are expressed about each. . . . The nature of the aggressions . . . follows the peculiar patterns of the immediate neighborhoods." The differences in community pattern of Suburbia and Urbania have been dramatically outlined by Conant,[60] including the values attached to formal education.

In the favored socioeconomic community much stress may be placed on doing well in school and on the "book learning" necessary to get into college. In the urban slum school "book learning" has little meaning, except perhaps for some minimum essentials, largely unrelated to other activities and something to be evaded as much as possible and dropped as soon as possible. School books in which everyone is clean and scrubbed and in which parents and children politely say "Please" and "Thank you" may contribute to a growing sense of frustration, a feeling of difference from much of the world, and a rejection of books which are unrelated to everything else the pupil knows. After six or seven years of practice in aggression and counteraggression, with a high premium on one's ability to protect oneself, with practice in immediate gratification of needs rather than planning ahead, "book culture" may be not only irrelevant but also dangerous.

In contrast, the child in the favored home and neighborhood has probably had stories read to him from an early age, sees his parents and other older persons reading newspapers, magazines, and books, may have books in his home, sees a newsstand or bookshop as he walks familiar streets, and lives not far from a public library. Such a setting will not make avid book readers of all children but it will create an attitude which perceives reading at least as normal and recurrent behavior and sometimes as a very rewarding activity. The child in such an environment will look for long hours at the same television shows as the child in the lower socioeconomic area, but there is some evidence that he will begin to cut down his televiewing in favor of other activities at a younger age. In addition a school with a well-stocked library and some teachers who love books help create interest in, and the habit of reading. Specific experimental evidence of this phenomenon is hard to find; illustrations and empirical data exist in every community.

One example of the importance of socioeconomic influences was given by Curry,[61] who studied reading achievements of three I.Q. groups of

[59] Radke, M., H. G. Trager, and H. Davis. "Social Perceptions and Attitudes of Children," *Genetic Psychology Monographs, 40:*437, November 1949.

[60] Conant, James B. *Slums and Suburbs.* New York: McGraw-Hill, 1961.

[61] Curry, Robert L. "The Effect of Socio-Economic Status on the Scholastic Achievement of Sixth Grade Children," *British Journal of Educational Psychology, 32:*46–49, February 1962.

sixth-graders. He found that the effect of socioeconomic status of family on scholastic achievement increases greatly as intellectual ability of pupils decreases. Another study[62] reported some of the usual class differences in reading and other leisure-time activities in different socioeconomic groups in a California city. Distinct differences were found among white, Negro, and Chinese-American children. The Oriental children exceeded the others, and the white children exceeded the Negro children, all of the same socioeconomic class, in preferences for reading activities and in library card ownership. However, the Oriental children seemed to have less time for reading. Negro children exceeded the other two groups in church attendance and in outdoor play activities in playgrounds.

The few studies quoted above of the influence of home, school, and community environments suggest the wide range of circumstances which may affect a person's reading and his responses to it. As pointed out by writers and lecturers, there may be dangers of conformity in our culture with the same houses, appliances, furniture, and cars in many streets and the same television programs watched by millions. However, in relation to reading, and probably other intellectual activities, the chief fact of life is probably not conformity but diversity. Children grow up in very different home environments, adolescents find themselves in very different neighborhoods, and adults live in very different communities with widely varying customs and mores, including those concerned with the printed page.

## *Conclusion*

The evidence about reading and the personality of the reader summarized in this chapter is a reminder of Voltaire's statement that "Doubt is not a very agreeable state, but certainty is a ridiculous one." The certainties of conclusive evidence still evade us despite hundreds of attempts to relate reading and personality but the explorations of possible relationships are of some interest in themselves and point the way to further experimental analysis. The above materials have suggested some reasons why clear-cut relationships are difficult, perhaps impossible to establish. The complex nature of the reading act and of personality, the lack of adequate measures of the two phenomena, the necessity of moving away from vague, general descriptions to specific items on tests or overt behavior, and the need for considering different relationships at different developmental stages of the individual's growth all contribute to the present lack of established fact.

[62] Jung, Raymond. *Leisure Activities and Preferences of Children of Different Socio-Economic Status and from Different Ethnic Groups.* Unpublished doctoral dissertation (University of California, Berkeley, 1963).

Despite these difficulties and uncertainties there is considerable positive evidence supporting the relationship between personality (and emotion) and general learning behavior and the overt communication activities of children and adults. The concept of mental health and its importance for learning may be currently neglected in discussions of school programs but has many applications to achievement and to conduct, including reading habits. Measures of mental health and personality are most reliable and valid as total scores but may have to be pinpointed in particular items or clusters of items to show strong relationships to reading habits or success. For example, in several studies mentioned in the chapter, such as those of Malmquist, Wynne, and Spache, the factor of *confidence* seems to be related to reading competence and habit. In addition, the evidence of relationships between personality and certain kinds of overt reading behavior, as in the Reed study, is fairly clear. Persons select particular types of reading materials and other types of communication in terms of personality factors or needs, whether it is reading newspapers or using other media to reinforce one's own attitudes and values[63] or persons with high anxiety levels reading predominantly about their own problems.[64]

Reading difficulties provide further evidence of the close relationship between reading and personality maladjustments. Not all children or adolescents experiencing reading difficulties have personality problems but the chances are good that a quarter to one-third of them will show such symptoms. The problem of causation is much less clear; one can only state, as Gates did twenty years ago, that emotional difficulties may be causes, concomitants, or results of reading difficulties. In individual cases, the skilled clinician can sometimes get at primary causes and vary remediation accordingly. In cases where emotional difficulties seem to be causes of reading difficulties some form of therapy should usually accompany practice in specific reading skills. The function of reading materials themselves as means of therapy is explored more fully in the discussion of bibliotherapy in Chapter 9.

Finally, the reader's personality is largely a product of home and environmental influences, and these factors are therefore intimately related to reading attitudes, achievements, and habits. Again, the evidence is not of the order that a specific type of home or neighborhood will produce a specific set of reading activities or responses; instead social influences may greatly influence the place of reading in a person's total pattern of living. Evidence in psychological literature suggests that direct experiences have

[63] Cooper, Eunice and Marie Jahoda. "The Evasion of Propaganda: How Prejudiced People Respond to Anti-Prejudice Propaganda," *Journal of Psychology*, 23:15–25, 1947.

[64] Kay, Herbert. "Toward an Understanding of News-Reading Behavior," *Journalism Quarterly*, 31:15–32, Winter 1954.

a greater influence on human behavior than do vicarious experiences. In its broadest terms Kurt Lewin formulated the psychological law: Behavior is always a function of both personality and environment. The wide variations in the cultural settings in which youth grow up today pose tremendous problems for schools, libraries, and welfare agencies as well as those concerned with the "higher literacy" of our nation. But reading is also always an individual matter and many skeins of relationship between reading and personality must still be unravelled. In a paradoxical way, television and the other mass media give children a common background of experience which erases some differences and therefore give greater influence to personal characteristics as determiners of reading ability and habit. As never before, reading involves personal interests, needs, habits, frustrations, anxieties, and expectations.

# CHAPTER 6 | The Content of the Material

The effects of reading normally depend not only upon the reader himself but also upon the ideas to which he is exposed. The ideas may be stated directly and clearly as in a well-written newspaper story or hortatory message, or they may be presented more indirectly and subtly in a newspaper story, poem, piece of fiction, or any other writing.

One hypothesis of communications experts, English teachers, and some critics is that the indirect method is likely to be more effective in influencing ideas or conduct. On the television screen the "hard sell" directing people to go out and buy a certain brand of soap flakes or automobile may not prove so effective as a more indirect presentation of the virtues of the particular soap or car. We need some more empirical evidence to determine not only these results but also the more academic problem of what kind of material to include in the curriculum. Most teachers today shy away from the approach of the Aesop's fable or the early McGuffey readers with the lesson clearly stated (sometimes in heavy type) at the end of the selection. The implication is more likely to be grasped, the moral learned, the ethical value understood if the reader has an opportunity to contribute his own interpretation of the ideas contained in the printed material. On the other hand, transfer of learning is difficult and children, especially young children, may fail to see any implication for themselves in a good story or other selection. How directly shall the advertiser or author present his ideas?

Although the answers to the query are still partly unknown, there is no question about the importance of the content of the message. If *Uncle Tom's Cabin* influenced a whole nation so did Hitler's *Mein Kampf*. What is in the communication determines its effects, if any. The *Lady Chatterley* debate in the Old Bailey and various efforts to ban books from the libraries of the United States are based on the assumption that the content of the books is harmful in some way. Knowing why certain material is dangerous or salutary is a difficult and complex task, but ways of determining just what the content of a passage is have been worked out with some certitude by different social scientists.

## *Content Analysis*

The careful study of documents has long contributed to the results of historical research. More recently analysis of radio programs and other types of verbal communication has been conducted by social psychologists. Some of the techniques of both fields can be applied to the materials of reading in what is usually called "documentary analysis" or "content analysis." For example, in a preliminary edition of his standard work *Content Analysis in Communication Research,* Berelson describes content analysis as "a research technique for the objective systematic and quantitative description of the manifest content of communication." It is based on such assumptions as the following:

That inferences about the relationship of intent and content or between content and effect can be made.

That study of manifest content is meaningful – a common meeting ground for communicator, audience, and the analyst.

It is a common universe of discourse among the relevant parties.

Quantitative description is meaningful in terms of competence.

Categories analyzed may include subject matter, direction, standards, values, methods, authorities, targets, and devices. Berelson was modest in his claims for the technique. "Content analysis, as a method, has no magical qualities – you rarely get out of it more than you put in, and sometimes you get less. In the last analysis, there is no substitute for good ideas."[1]

Some more recent studies of content analysis have gone beyond the problems of codification of ideas with which Berelson was largely concerned. Pool[2] in 1959 spoke of "a sophisticated concern with the problems of inference from verbal material to its antecedent conditions and . . . counting internal contingencies between symbols instead of the simple frequencies of symbols." Other writers in the same volume distinguish between "representational" and "instrumental" communications or approaches, the first concerned with the content of the lexical items present in the passage, the second, not with what the message says at face value, but with what it conveys, given its context and circumstance. Thus content analysis can be concerned with both quantitative and qualitative matters, with external as well as internal factors and relationships, and with both descriptive and inferential procedures.

There are many problems to be considered in analysis of even simple materials. Obviously, quantitative descriptions are often on firmer foundations than inferences which may depend on the individual perceptions

[1] Berelson, Bernard. *Content Analysis in Communication Research.* Glencoe, Ill.: The Free Press, 1952.

[2] Pool, Ithiel de S. (ed.). *Trends in Content Analysis.* Urbana: University of Illinois Press, 1959.

of the analyst. Although quantification is more verifiable scientifically, the findings may also be more pedestrian than the intuitive insights of the skilled biographer or critic. Frequency and importance are not necessarily equated although it may be assumed that frequency of statements provides a good index of intensity of attitude expressed in the text. As well as frequency, the coder may well be concerned with contingency – not only how often the symbol or idea occurs but also how often it appears in conjunction with other symbolic units. For example, in his classic analysis of Richard Wright's autobiography *Black Boy*, White[3] frequently found a relationship between personality characteristics and mention of physical safety. White's analysis illustrated, as well, the problem faced in all content analysis – that of deriving the categories to be counted. Such categories may be determined a priori, but they usually grow out of preliminary analyses of the data themselves. For example, White first read *Black Boy* carefully and wrote out his impressions of the personality of the subject. The categories indicated were then checked for frequency of occurrence and similar categories added when found in a second reading of the book. Similarly, McConnell[4] listed elements of success found in a group of biographies written for children and then used these and additional topics in an analysis of factors related to success as recounted by writers of biographies for juveniles. Only after a thorough listing of all possible related categories does a frequency count of their occurrence have significance.

## *School Texts*

Because in earlier times school texts were a child's first books, and sometimes his only books, great power has been attributed to the influence of these texts on ideas and ideals. Mosier's[5] book about the McGuffey Readers was entitled *Making the American Mind.* Superpatriot groups sometimes view with alarm what they regard as a trend toward socialism or a lack of patriotism in more recent social studies texts. (The term *social studies* is itself disapproved as being somewhat like socialism instead of being the history and the geography of an earlier era.) Although clear proof of the influence of readers and other texts is still lacking, the importance of content is generally accepted and therefore should be described.

Robinson,[6] for example, compared the content of children's readers

[3] White, R. K. "Black Boy: A Value Analysis," *Journal of Abnormal and Social Psychology, 42*:440–61, 1947.

[4] McConnell, Gaither A. *An Analysis of Biographical Literature for Children.* Unpublished doctoral dissertation (University of California, Berkeley, 1952).

[5] Mosier, Richard D. *Making the American Mind.* New York: King's Crown Press, 1947.

[6] Robinson, Helen M. "Personality and Reading," *Modern Educational Problems.* Report of 17th Conference. New York: Educational Records Bureau, October 1952.

during five different periods of American history and found them related to major objectives of the school and its public. Before 1775 content and objectives were primarily religious. From 1775 to 1825 religious and secular motives received about equal emphases. From 1825 to 1875 secular motives and practical affairs dominated the content. From 1875 to 1915 the literary emphasis prevailed; since 1915 a wide variety of objectives have determined the content of readers.

The famous McGuffey Readers, still proposed ever so often, do not come off so well under careful analysis as a few die-hard proponents would suggest. For example, Mosier found the books solidly on the side of a conservative philosophy in the conflict between Jeffersonian and Hamiltonian brands of government. Despite the fact they were often the books of children on the frontier, Mosier found that the books "adopted Blackstone's explanations for the origin of private property and found with him that property was bestowed on the few in order that a leisure and ruling class be created, and that time . . . might be devoted by society's ruling groups to the cultivation of the arts." The successive editions of McGuffey changed with the times but never quite accepted the democracy of the Western Movement.

Anderson's[7] recent analysis suggested that despite their reputation, the McGuffey Readers actually did not contain as much material on "moral and spiritual values" as are found in two different sets of modern readers. Such values as human personality, moral responsibility, common consent, and devotion to truth received proportionally more space in the recent books. In another analysis, Estenson[8] found that the McGuffey's contained about the same amounts as modern readers of economic, nationalistic, and military materials but about twice as much religious material.

The content of recent series of children's readers has, however, been criticized on several grounds. In a study published in 1946 Child[9] and others examined the content of the materials in a group of third-grade readers. They found that the treatment of various categories of behavior was such as to encourage certain motives and activities and discourage others, with a dominance of middle-class values which might be foreign to children of a different background. Their study gives a list of possible effects of the books which should be verified by further research on the overt influences of reading.

[7] Anderson, Paul S. "McGuffey *vs.* the Moderns in Character Training," *Phi Delta Kappan, 38:*53–58, November 1956.

[8] Estenson, E. V. "McGuffey — A Statistical Analysis," *Journal of Educational Research, 39:*445–57, February 1946.

[9] Child, Irvin L., Elmer H. Potter, and Estelle Levine. "Children's Textbooks and Personality Development: An Exploration in the Social Psychology of Education," *Psychological Monographs 60,* No. 3, American Psychological Association, 1946.

The charge of "middle class bias" has been made frequently against modern readers, especially in the primary grades. The children are always too clean and well dressed, have too many possessions, and live in a too beautiful single family dwelling. It is doubtful, however, if a reading text would be accepted by lower class children themselves if it represented slum background and the father of the family sitting in the kitchen in his undershirt, drinking out of a beer can. In his brisk, journalistic survey of a wide selection of schools, Mayer[10] reacted to this problem, "American schools are always going to promote middle-class values, because the national community they serve is over-whelmingly middle-class in orientation and even in 'self-image'. . . . the damage done to the child by insisting on a middle-class common core is easily overstated."

Numerous studies have also been made of the difficulty of readers and other school texts. Such investigations are usually concerned with features such as vocabulary, sentence length, and sentence structure and are usually subsumed under the "readability" of the materials. Chall[11] made a comprehensive survey of such studies up to 1955, but they are not the primary concern of this chapter. The difficulty of the material influences the effect it may have on a particular reader, but the typical measures of difficulty so far developed use mechanical counts such as the number of hard words. The concept load, abstraction level, and idea type are not thereby measured.

An example of a study comparing American and Soviet textbooks capitalizes on interest in contrasting the two educational systems, but the author's method of content analysis was unsophisticated. Trace[12] reported only the estimated vocabulary of Soviet texts and, in the case of readers, listed the authors and titles of selections in the textbooks of the two countries but did not analyze ideas or attitudes involved. He believed that Soviet readers were better because they contained at the fourth-grade level for example, some 10,000 different words instead of a typical 1,500 to 1,800 words in American texts. In other words he assumed that because a text is harder it is better. He also assumed that American children's recognition vocabulary is influenced by their reading of texts in social studies, science, health, and other content areas. He failed to apply content analysis at the concept level and told little about the kinds of ideas found in selections by Pushkin, Turgenev, Chekhov, and other writers. In so doing he made the assumption that well-known literary figures are better writers for nine-year-olds (fourth graders in the U.S.) than are less well-known authors who write specifically for children. This assumption

[10] Mayer, Martin. *The Schools*. New York: Harper, 1961, p. 117.

[11] Chall, Jeanne. *Readability: An Appraisal of Research and Application*. Columbus: Ohio State University, Bureau of Educational Research, 1957.

[12] Trace, Arthur S., Jr. *What Ivan Knows That Johnny Doesn't*. New York: Random House, 1961.

is indeed a surprising one in a country where literature for children has always flourished and which has a rich storehouse of children's books ranging at least from Louisa May Alcott's *Little Women* to the modern classic, E. B. White's *Charlotte's Web.*

## *Children's Literature*

Attempts to analyze juvenile literature have not been commensurate with the size of the publishing enterprise which produces books for children and adolescents. In the United States in the early 1960's about 18,000 titles were published annually and approximately 10 per cent of them could be classed as juvenile books. Juvenile literature too had its best sellers, some of them grouped with unrelated titles as in the Little Golden Books or the Landmark Books, and some of them in series by the same author such as Farley's *Black Stallion* series or Boylston's *Sue Barton* books about nursing. Many new titles were added to the list every year, and old favorites such as the tales of Hans Christian Andersen or *Tom Sawyer* or *Heidi* were republished many times. The question whether these books could be classed as "literature" was a moot one. It was true that despite television and other distractions children were reading, but what were they reading?

The superficial answer to what children and adolescents read or view has been precisely investigated half a hundred times. Educational literature contains many studies of children's reading interests going back to before 1900 and continuing through to the 1960's. A notable example was Terman and Lima's[13] book *Children's Reading* (1935), and more recent examples are two books by Norvell[14] (1950 and 1958). Witty[15] has made several thorough studies of children's interests in various areas and has over a dozen annual reports of their choices of television programs (to give "literature" an even broader connotation). But most of these investigations of reading and televiewing have simply listed favorites as chosen by a large number of children, and give few or no hints about why children make the choices or what are the actual contents of books or programs. In comparisons to lists, the number of studies of the concepts or assumptions children meet in books, magazines, television, and elsewhere are scanty.

[13] Terman, Lewis M., and Margaret Lima. *Children's Reading: A Guide for Parents and Teachers.* (2d ed.) New York: Appleton-Century, 1935.

[14] Norvell, George W. *The Reading Interests of Young People.* Boston: Heath, 1950; Norvell, George W. *What Boys and Girls Like to Read.* New York: Silver Burdett, 1958.

[15] Witty, Paul A. See annual reports on choices of television programs in issues of *Elementary English.* Champaign, Ill.: National Council of Teachers of English.

As might be expected, children, and especially young children, are attracted to books by their physical format. As early as 1922 Bamberger[16] studied the effects of size of book and format on children's choices. More recent studies[17,18] have shown children's preferences in color and illustrations which may be said to relate to ideas because pictures are important in determining what concepts the very young child gains from a story.

The subtler problem of concepts presented, of ideas approved or disapproved, of writer's attitude or reader's inferences, has not been as thoroughly investigated. In a number of general articles, librarians and others have supported the content of modern juvenile books. In 1951 Blair[19] suggested that in current children's books "the paths of independence and integrity are pointed out without the ever-present moralizing of the nineteenth century or cloying sentimentality of ten or twenty years ago." From such books she believes the child learns new attitudes, acquires knowledge of how to attack problems, and may find release from the emotional tension the problem has created. Jacobs[20] similarly stated that literature can be a way of exploring both the social scene and problems of personal development. He said, "The characters in American children's fiction experience and adjust to their cultural inheritance: a world of things, of natural resources, of events, of values, of groups, of customs, of institutions, all co-mingled." He warns, however, that from his books the child may get the idea that the typical American is white, Protestant, comfortably middle-class in socioeconomic status, and of northern European extraction.

Jacobs's general article is based in part on a careful analysis[21] of thirty-nine books of historical fiction in terms of material and nonmaterial aspects of culture. He was especially concerned with the concepts of democracy to which the child reader is exposed in these books.

One of the branches of juvenile literature related to historical fiction and supposed to be both interesting and effective in influencing values is biography. The confidence in the inherent worth of biography is a matter of belief rather than empirical evidence, but the content of biographies

[16] Bamberger, Florence E. *The Effect of the Physical Make-up of a Book Upon Children's Selection.* Johns Hopkins University Studies in Education No. 4. Baltimore: Johns Hopkins University, 1922.

[17] Rudisill, Mabel. "Children's Preferences for Color versus Other Qualities in Illustrations," *Elementary School Journal, 52:*444–45, April 1952.

[18] Whipple, Gertrude. "Appraisal of the Interest Appeal of Illustrations," *Elementary School Journal, 53:*262–69, January 1953.

[19] Blair, Virginia A. "Recognizing Problems Through Fiction," *Childhood Education, 28:*169–72, December 1951.

[20] Jacobs, Leland B. "Cultural Patterns in Children's Fiction," *Childhood Education, 23:*431–34, May 1947.

[21] Jacobs, Leland B. *Democratic Acculturation in American Children's Historical Fiction.* Unpublished doctoral dissertation (Ohio State University, Columbus, 1945).

for juvenile readers is of interest. Mumford[22] believed that the task of the biographer is not to praise or blame the life he is presenting, but to reconstruct the geographical and social environment in which the subject moved. In the 1930's Jones[23] found that, except for a changed vocabulary, there were few differences between modern writing and biography of antiquity. He identified eight main types of the "new" biography in terms of the assumptions contained in them. He categorized the factual or semi-factual approaches as Freudian, medicopathological, psychological, and psychographic. Others were purely fictional, the informal, the debunking, and the archeological. "Life and time" studies make derivative biographies possible.

McConnell[24] analyzed 24 biographies written for children which appeared on several lists of recommended books. These included such titles as James Daugherty's *Daniel Boone,* Cornelia Meigs' *Invincible Louisa,* Sandburg's *Abe Lincoln Grows Up,* and Graham and Lipscomb's *Dr. George Washington Carver, Scientist.* The personal traits most frequently related to work activities and to successful achievement were persistence, effort, and intelligence. Personality characteristics most frequently displayed by the subjects in their relations with people were friendliness, kindness, and agreeableness. The subjects of the biographies were also frequently characterized by a constellation of simplicity, humility, modesty, and idealism. In general, nonconformity in relation to ideas and circumstances and conformity in relations with people were emphasized and approved.

## *Fiction for Adolescents*

Just as some children read stories written for teen-agers or for adults, so some adolescents read a number of the stories for children analyzed above. In addition, however, a large group of books and stories aimed expressly at the teen-ager is called by some variation of the title "books for teen-agers."

Such books have a difficult time with most critics who call them puerile and inane and suggest that adolescents would be better off reading good adult books. Donald Adams once remarked in the *New York Times* that all books written for readers beyond the age of twelve were "a phenomenon which belong properly only to a society of morons." One wonders,

[22] Mumford, Lewis. "The Task of Modern Biography," *English Journal, 23:*1–9, January 1934.

[23] Jones, Howard M. "Methods in Contemporary Biography," *English Journal, 21:* 113–22, February 1932.

[24] McConnell, Gaither A. *An Analysis of Biographical Literature for Children.* Unpublished doctoral dissertation (University of California, Berkeley, 1952).

however, if Mr. Adams had read Esther Forbes' *Johnny Tremain*, Maureen Daly's *Seventeenth Summer*, or some of the other books written for adolescents which may be way stations to more adult books. The genetic or developmental point of view suggests that a book for children or adolescents may have considerable impact on the reader if he reads it at the psychological moment. Two or three years later it may be scorned as "baby stuff," but for a few months, or a year or two, it may be "just right" or "the best book I ever read" – until the next one comes along. For example, the boy who reads *Johnny Tremain* may be inspired to dig into more adult historical works, and the girl who enjoys Daly may move on to Charlotte Brontë, Willa Cather, or Jane Austen.

Some writers have defended teen-age books in other ways. Burton[25] devotes several chapters to the way they may be used in school. Other writers explain their value in terms of the characteristics or needs of their readers. For example, Emery[26] suggested that the modern adolescent is not characterized by revolt, nor conformity, nor a drive for success. Rather he is engaged in a "search for something to believe in, something to make life worthwhile" like heroism or rejection of false values. Similarly Carlsen[27] has suggested that the adolescent has at least three basic needs which may be fulfilled, at least in part, by his reading. These are (1) "assurance of status as human beings," (2) "assurance of his own normality," and (3) "a need for role-playing." Different types of content such as animal and adventure stories, stories of adolescent life, and stories involving vocations may contribute to these three needs. Just how books contribute to such needs has been enthusiastically assumed rather than carefully investigated by some proponents of adolescent literature.

One of the more plausible assumptions has been that stories of careers will help adolescents explore the demands of various occupations and professions. Splaver[28] suggested that "career novels are book-size fictional tales of the 'girl meets boy – girl loses boy – girl wins boy again' variety with information regarding the occupation of the hero or heroine interwoven into the tales." Examples were such books as Cora Kasius' *Nancy Clark, Social Worker*, and Helen Hayes and Mary Kennedy's *Star on Her Forehead*. Splaver made the modest claim that if the occupational information is accurate and up to date "this form of literature may play a significant role in stimulating these readers to search for further information in the non-fiction career books." A perusal of titles of such books suggests

[25] Burton, Dwight L. *Literature Study in the High Schools*. New York: Holt, 1959.

[26] Emery, Anne. "Values in Adolescent Fiction," *Library Journal, 83:*1565–67, May 15, 1958.

[27] Carlsen, G. Robert. "Behind Reading Interests," *English Journal, 43:*7–12, January 1954.

[28] Splaver, Sarah. "The Career Novel," *Personnel and Guidance Journal, 31:*371–72, 1953.

that there are more of them for girls than for boys and that they describe the "glamor" careers more frequently than the workaday occupations.

Both critics of the books and adolescents themselves can be aware of some of the assumptions underlying fiction for adolescents. In a study of the four-year literature curriculum of one high school Sherwin[29] located no less than 2,300 assumptions. These he put into two main categories (1) social – "man and man," and (2) psychological – "man as man." The assumptions were grouped under such headings as marriage, religion, economics, education, and personality. The literature program thus gave a wide range of assumptions stated implicitly and explicitly, with considerable emphasis on a romantic approach, and with approval of moral virtues such as fidelity, chastity, and truthfulness, not always logically consistent. Sherwin warned that the assumptions "may either fail to be perceived by students or, what is worse, may be accepted by them uncritically and perhaps unconsciously . . . we as teachers do not wish to slip ideological 'mickies' to our students."

Novels of adolescence may be described in two main categories which may or may not overlap, (1) stories written for adolescents and (2) novels about adolescence. The second category has been analyzed in Kiell's[30] book *The Adolescent Through Fiction* in terms of nine developmental problems characteristic of adolescence. Kiell quotes extensively to illustrate writers' accounts of such problems as physical development, social acceptance, family relations, cultural conflicts, and choosing a career. Some of the writers typically read by adolescents include Alcott, Twain, Kipling, Dickens, Hardy, Wolfe, and Crane. Other descriptions of adolescence by such writers as Goethe, Tolstoy, Dostoevsky, and Stendahl may be somewhat beyond the reach of most teen-agers but may help the adult reader explore in depth. The problem of guiding the adolescent from the easy and superficial to the complex and penetrating has been tackled by Taba[31] and others in book lists such as *Reading Ladders for Human Relations* which group books in terms of progressive insight and power and are considered further in Chapter 11.

Carpenter[32] inquired why some adolescent novels remained childish and amusing, such as Booth Tarkington's *Seventeen,* while others became genuinely mature and wise, as Jessamyn West's *Cress Delehanty.* He believes that stories about adolescence which have not been accepted as of

[29] Sherwin, J. Stephen. "Patterns of Assumptions in a High School Literature Curriculum," *Journal of Educational Sociology, 29*:321–29, April 1956.

[30] Kiell, Norman. *The Adolescent Through Fiction.* New York: International Universities Press, 1959.

[31] Taba, Hilda (ed.). *Reading Ladders for Human Relations.* Washington, D.C.: American Council on Education, 1949.

[32] Carpenter, Frederic I. "The Adolescent in American Fiction," *English Journal,* 313–19, September 1957.

permanent worth have been those "which described their heroes from the superior point of view of the adult, condescendingly." In contrast, the novels which have sometimes achieved greatness "have entered into the confusions of their adolescents at first hand, and have described them through the eyes of their protagonists, as in *Huck Finn* and *Catcher in the Rye*." He finds the central theme of these novels to be the individual's search for genuine values. Huck and Holden Caulfield have a common hatred of hypocrisy and both engage in a search for integrity – both developed by the boys themselves and reflecting the problems of their parents and elders.

## *Adult Literature*

Both children and adolescents view the so-called adult television program, scan the adult magazine, and occasionally read the adult book. The content analysis of the mass media and writing for adults could occupy many books and is only sampled here. For example, the comics, although declining from publication peaks in the early 1950's, are widely read by children and adults, with an apparent peak in their use by children around eleven or twelve years. Comic books and strips vary widely from the informative and amusing to the fantastic and vicious. The writer has summarized some analyses of the comics in a book on reading instruction.[33] These suggest that most comics are about "100 per cent Americans" and seldom mention minority groups. Animals are important, especially if humor is intended. Adventure is serious business. Such stereotypes as the following appear frequently:

People in authority are often stupid.
People are either good or bad and you can usually tell by appearance.
The end justifies the means.
Scientists are usually sinister people.
Romantic love and money are at the heart of life's problems.

A content analysis of Sunday comic strips made in 1961[34] indicated an increase in the total number of strips, greater continuity in stories from week to week, and an increase in romance, action, and adventure. Although the domestic humorous situation still predominated, there were more short-time cycles dealing with current problems such as war or science and technology.

Television programs are often more than "the modern comic" label sometimes attached to them, but many of them also represent a medium

[33] Russell, D. H. *Children Learn to Read.* Boston: Ginn, 1961, pp. 14–15, 387–91.

[34] Barcus, Francis E. "A Content Analysis of Trends in Sunday Comics, 1900–1959," *Journalism Quarterly,* 38:171–80, Spring 1961.

shared by children and adults. Like the comics, the range of programs is so wide that no generalization can apply to them all. Westerns are stereotyped and crime programs are often full of violence and sadism, but other shows are amusing and informative. Documentary and live news programs may have an impact and immediacy which no magazine article or book can match. A study by Schramm[35] of televiewing habits and effects verified the fact that school-age children viewed television on an average of over twenty hours a week, with a peak of three or four hours a day around the sixth and seventh grades followed by a gradual decline in the amount of use. After the age of three or four, patterns of viewing change quickly from children's programs to Westerns, adventure programs, crime shows, situation comedies, popular music and variety shows, and other adult types of program. "Most of it is fantasy and entertainment." Schramm is inclined to rate the physical effects of television as unimportant, the emotional as much less innocuous, and the cognitive effects as largely nonexistent except for the very young.

Similar studies have been made of the content of the mass magazines. Kerrick[36] found, in college groups, that the pictorial caption will tend to cause "a significant general modification of judgments regarding the picture it accompanies." The picture magazines too can editorialize. In a study of the content of three adult magazines most popular with Indiana high school students, Taylor[37] found that 86 per cent of the stories were set in the United States and 87 per cent were contemporary. The social classes most frequently portrayed were upper middle, indeterminate, and lower middle. Characters were typically Americans of Anglo-Saxon or Nordic origin seeking romance, power, justice, and wealth – and nearly all reached their goals. Taylor concluded that magazine fictional short stories may lead to the development of undesirable attitudes toward certain American social classes. This was corroborated in part by another study by Berelson and Salter[38] who stated that "minorities as defined make up 40 per cent of the population of the United States but make up only 10 per cent of the population of short stories" in magazines. However, magazines also differ widely. Albrecht[39] found different con-

[35] Schramm, Wilbur, Jack Lyle, and Edwin B. Parker. *Television in the Lives of Our Children.* Stanford: Stanford University Press, 1961.

[36] Kerrick, Jean S. "The Influence of Captions on Picture Interpretation," *Journalism Quarterly, 32:*177–82, Spring 1955.

[37] Taylor, Velma L. *An Analysis of Fictional Short Stories Found in Current Magazines Read Most Often by Indiana High School Students with Reference to Treatment of American Social Classes.* Unpublished doctoral dissertation (University of Indiana, Bloomington, Indiana, 1953).

[38] Berelson, Bernard, and P. J. Salter. "Majority and Minority Americans – An Analysis of Magazine Fiction," *Public Opinion Quarterly, 10:*168–90, Summer 1946.

[39] Albrecht, Milton C. "Does Literature Reflect Common Values?" *American Sociological Review, 21:*722–29, December 1956.

tent on family life in magazines he described as lower class, such as *True Story* and *True Confessions*, middle class such as the *Saturday Evening Post*, and upper class such as *Atlantic* and *The New Yorker*. He found a greater difference from the total in the content of the last category than in either of the other two. Familistic trends were more distinct at the upper and the lower than at the middle level. The upper level showed more concern for status, the lower more concern for family unity. In another study Ginglinger[40] tested the criticism of digest magazines as supplying pseudoculture and emphasizing mainly material welfare and group conformity.

Scores of studies of the content of newspapers have been made by people in schools of journalism and others. For example, an analysis made by Deutschmann[41] in 1959 categorized the news page content of seven New York City, three Cleveland, and two Cincinnati dailies over a month's time. There was considerable similarity in the items chronicled in the various papers. Newspapers read by more readers who had college educations contained less pictorial material than other newspapers. Similarity in content is also increased by the exact use of wire service material from the Associated Press and United Press and by the printing of the same columnists in widely scattered parts of the country. As Alistair Cooke put it, the steelworker in Gary, Indiana, and the date farmer in Indio, California, get their news in the same packages.

Analysis of popular taste in novels has been provided in such books as Hart's[42] *The Popular Book* and Hackett's[43] *Sixty Years of Best Sellers*. In another study Harvey[44] matched 22 best selling novels published between 1930 and 1946 with 22 "poor selling" novels of the same period. After using content analysis and combining discriminating factors into a prediction equation, he found that the best forecast of sales came from the ingredients of readability, affectionate attitude, and moderate emotion on the part of the central male character, and a sentimental theme. The titles listed by Hart and by Hackett and such characteristics as Harvey found to be discriminatory indicate neither the quality nor the staying power of a book, nor do they indicate importance beyond the category of popular choice. Quality cannot be confused with quantity, and the

[40] Ginglinger, Genevieve. "Basic Values in 'Reader's Digest,' 'Selection' and 'Constellation,'" *Journalism Quarterly*, 32:56–61, Winter 1955.

[41] Deutschmann, Paul J. *News-page Content of Twelve Metropolitan Dailies*. E. W. Scripps Company and Michigan State University Communications Research Center, 1959.

[42] Hart, James D. *The Popular Book: A History of America's Literary Taste*. New York: Oxford, 1950.

[43] Hackett, Alice P. *Sixty Years of Best Sellers*. New York: Bowker, 1955.

[44] Harvey, John. "The Content Characteristics of Best-Selling Novels," *Public Opinion Quarterly*, 17:91–114, 1953.

method of content analysis described in this chapter is probably most successful in getting at quantity or frequency. However, constant repetition of an idea or theme, implicit or explicit, in television shows, magazines, or books may result in a cumulative and therefore greater impact on the viewer or reader. The sample results given in this chapter, therefore, are a complement to the analysis of literature made by the perceptive critic and described, in part, in Chapters 3 and 4.

# CHAPTER 7 | Comprehension: Literal and Interpretive

Someone has remarked that "A man must be an inventor to read well." Invention varies from a slight adaptation of another man's ideas to a startling new discovery, and reading may be said to have a similar range of creativity. In the most pedestrian effort the reader must take the black and white symbol and transform it into corresponding sound or meaning; he must spell out or say the word *horse*, and he must be able to associate the symbol with some kind of four-legged quadruped that works on a farm, runs races, or pulls a cart. In a more thoughtful approach to his reading, the reader may summarize a long article in two or three sentences, disagree with his newspaper editorial, or find some insight into human behavior only partly suggested by the author of a novel. Reading may range from simple association to subtle interpretation.

Logical analysis of the activity of reading also suggests that there are at least four different levels of comprehension on which we may function as we read. The primary child reading his first story or the semiliterate puzzling out a newspaper story in which he knows only a few words may both be reading at the first level of comprehension. This is at the word identification level with most of the effort going into sounding or spelling out words. Here the reader is concerned with getting the word or phrase and is seldom able to follow the whole story or argument.

At the second level of comprehension the child or adult goes beyond word recognition to a general impression of the paragraph, page, or passage. Perhaps the child reads the comic book with considerable attention to the pictures and races through the text to find how the hero was rescued from the cliff. The semiliterate person may go through the newspaper account getting enough of it to understand the drift of the happenings. The more able reader may skim the story quickly for the main idea.

The third level of comprehension is more demanding. It means reading for the exact literal meanings of the sentence or the article or the book.

When we do this we must be sure to get it right. We must get the facts in a history book, or we must follow the directions accurately.

The fourth level of comprehension goes beyond literal details to some sort of selection, interpretation, and fresh understanding of the materials. The reader puts himself and his thinking abilities into the reading. The written materials at this level may be only a stimulus to help the reader feel excitement, enjoy beauty, or gain insight into his own or others' problems. At the fourth level of comprehension reading is sometimes close to what we call critical thinking. The reader sifts, accepts, and rejects depending upon his experience and his purposes. Sometimes the reading is creative in terms of enjoyment or appreciation. Sometimes it involves understanding implied or inferred meanings. In reading a literary work the reader will understand the images used and will recognize some of the symbols that the author is employing to make his message dramatic. The third grader or the business executive who is reading creatively keeps adding something of his own to what the author has written.

The four levels of comprehension are usually overlapping and are dependent upon the reader's purpose, especially at the third and fourth levels. In both literal and interpretive reading there are varied kinds of comprehensions. Reading for details is not the same as reading to get the main idea of a story. Reading to follow directions is not the same as outlining the author's main idea and supporting details. Some adults who have read much fiction may be good at reading quickly for a general impression but may be poor in obtaining the exact details of a chapter on science. In the primary grades of school the comprehension of many pupils is limited to recognizing words, grasping sentence meaning, and reading short paragraphs for general impression or for some details. Usually at the intermediate grade level the children expand these abilities and may read for as many as ten or fifteen different purposes. In the first grade he may know how to read to follow the events of a short story, but it may not be until the fifth or sixth grade that he can organize the ideas in a longer chapter. Fairly early he may learn to recognize emotional reactions and motives of characters in the story. Perhaps more experience is needed before he can distinguish between statements of fact and opinion. Much practice under teacher guidance may be necessary before a pupil can draw inferences from a passage; many adults have never learned to do it. This listing of various comprehensions in reading suggests that one of the most important reading heights we can gain is that of flexibility of reading in different ways for different purposes.

The different levels of comprehension, and the varied kinds of comprehension most of us have to apply in school and out, suggest that reading is a complex process. The complexity of reading may lie partly in perceptual aspects of what we see and in functional aspects of how we use it, but it would seem to lie most of all in the field of comprehension. Even young children seem to use reading in different ways for different purposes.

There is further evidence against a simple, unitary concept of reading comprehension. In addition to the analytical approach suggesting levels of comprehension, both experience and empirical studies indicate that comprehension is not an "all or none" affair but rather a matter of degree. "We see though a glass darkly." "We know in part and we prophesy in part." All of us, eight-year-olds or forty-eight-year-olds, have had the experience of reading something and knowing all about it, reading something else and only grasping part of the message, and reading another passage and being completely baffled by it. When children or adolescents take reading tests, they get some answers to questions on a paragraph right and some wrong. Other studies of children's knowledge of concepts have revealed that, at a particular age level, some concepts are known, some unknown, some partly known.[1]

The third fact which complicates the meaning of comprehension, especially for teachers, is that children and adolescents seem to respond to meanings in different ways at different age or grade levels, and that they differ widely at any one stage, including the time they reach an adult level of approach to meaning. For example, Reichard and others[2] believed that they identified three sequential levels in the meanings children attached to concepts: (a) the concrete, (b) the functional, and (c) the abstract. Some support for the idea of children's definitions was found in a study by Feifel and Lorge.[3] Gerstein,[4] constructed a multiple choice test based on the vocabulary test of the Bellevue–Wechsler intelligence tests. For each stimulus word she provided an alternative definition representing each of the three levels of response (concrete, functional, and abstract) and asked the subjects to select the best definition of each term. Her results indicated a trend in the hypothesized direction of three levels, but the utility of the method was not completely demonstrated. In a similar study of children in the third, sixth, and ninth grades Russell and Saadeh[5] found fairly clear-cut differences between choice of concrete and functional definitions, especially between the third and sixth grades, but a

[1] Russell, D. H. "Concepts," *Encyclopedia of Educational Research* (rev. ed.) (Chester W. Harris, ed.). New York: Macmillan, 1960, pp. 323–33.

[2] Reichard, S., M. Schneider, and D. Rappaport. "The Development of Concept Formation in Children," *American Journal of Orthopsychiatry, 14:*156–61, January 1944.

[3] Feifel, Herman, and I. Lorge. "Qualitative Differences in the Vocabulary Responses of Children," *Journal of Educational Psychology, 41:*1–18, January 1950.

[4] Gerstein, Rena A. "A Suggested Method for Analyzing and Extending the Use of Bellevue–Wechsler Vocabulary Responses," *Journal of Consulting Psychology, 13:* 366–70, October 1949.

[5] Russell, D. H., and I. Q. Saadeh. "Qualitative Levels in Children's Vocabularies," *Journal of Educational Psychology, 53:*170–74, August 1962.

blurring between functional and abstract choices at all levels. However, older children definitely chose fewer concrete definitions as "best."

The concept of levels of comprehension, the evidence suggesting it is a matter of degree, and the empirical studies of qualitative differences in responses to words all suggest that comprehension of a word, passage, poem, or book is not a simple affair. Indeed the words we use in discussing the phenomenon – words like "comprehension," "understanding," and "meaning" – are difficult, subtle, and twistable. Different writers and critics use the words in different ways, and psychologists, anthropologists, linguists, and others who study language have difficulty in agreeing on the terms. The scientific study of any form of behavior, including verbal behavior, demands precise definitions, but these have not yet been completely determined in the area of language. For example, should we say a college student reads and "understands" an article if he gets correct 80 per cent of the questions asked on it? Or is a 50 per cent correct score enough for some articles? Most of us would not be content with the latter if a nurse were reading directions for giving us medicine but might accept it after reading a newspaper account of a boxing match.

In Australia a few years ago I heard the anecdote in which the young apprentice fitter was asked by his foreman, "How many thousandths are there in an inch, Bill?" The reply was, "I dunno, Boss, but there must be millions of 'em." Back in the United States I read the results of a poll conducted by the Public Opinion Research Center of Princeton University. It found that of 90 million adults in the United States, 33 million of us do not know what a *tariff* is. Fifty-four million do not know what causes *inflation,* and over 70 million do not know what is meant by a *subsidy* – some farmers regard it as a sort of cover crop. And 85 million of the 90 million adults don't know what a *reciprocal trade treaty* is. It is not only the school boy who makes the mistakes. The problem of *meaning* is not just something for the primary grades, it runs through all reading and languages.

## *The Nature of Meaning and Understanding*

Discussions of the nature of meaning go back at least to Plato's *Theaetetus* and have continued to occupy philosophers and teachers ever since. There are at least two broad areas of meaning included in such discussions, the one aesthetic and the other scientific. These may be distinguished in De Quincey's words as the literature of power and the literature of knowledge. This section is largely concerned with the latter but the chapter later suggests that writing to give knowledge often overlaps with the writing which has the power to change men's minds. Because of a title which every subsequent writer must have envied, the best known work on meaning is probably Ogden and Richards'[6] *The Meaning of Meaning*, but it represents only one approach to the problem. As a stimulating introduction to semantics, the book is concerned with the varied meanings of words or the relationships between verbal symbols and their referents, but it and similar works do not answer nearly all the questions about meaningful verbal behavior. Students of philosophy and linguistics may be interested in the signification or semantic rule for a term, but study of language behavior involves many more specific responses of sign users.

Semanticists are inclined to stress language in relation to behavior and they therefore distinguish carefully the kind of meanings the receiver of the message gets in two kinds of language, one referential or report language, and the second emotive or affective language. No moral tones are attached to these labels – report language may pass on false information and affective language may be found in such poems as *Paradise Lost*. The semanticists further agree that the mood, attitude, and purpose of both speaker and writer or the listener and reader all may affect the meanings gained from the message. They emphasize, accordingly, the context in which a particular word or statement is set – the verbal context, the experiential context, and the physical or situational. For example, in relation to verbal context, metaphor should be taught as "a basic aspect of language, not as a mere ornament of poetry." Furthermore, the semanticist believes that "Students should learn to recognize that definitions are nearly always partial and tentative."[7]

The approaches of psychologists to the problem of meaning vary widely from those of semanticists and from one another. For example, Bousfield[8] suggests that meaning may be "not only an unnecessary concept for verbal learning but a concept bound to lead to confusion. Like the concept of emotion it is ambiguous, and it is tied up with philosophical considerations going beyond the domain of psychology." Near the end of his book *Verbal Behavior* Skinner[9] suggests that there may be such things as nonobservable, symbolic responses to signs which are a part of total verbal behavior, but they are not a part of his concern with the topic. In an intermediate position Osgood[10] uses associative methods to support hypotheses about mediation and semantic differential. At the

[6] Ogden, C. K., and I. A. Richards. *The Meaning of Meaning*. New York: Harcourt, Brace (also Harvest Books HB29), 1936.

[7] Thomas, Cleveland A. "Semantic Concepts for Secondary School English," *English Journal, 49*:186–91, March, 1960.

[8] Bousfield, W. A. "The Problem of Meaning in Verbal Learning," *Verbal Learning and Verbal Behavior* (Charles N. Cofer, ed.). New York: McGraw-Hill, 1961.

[9] Skinner, B. F. *Verbal Behavior*. New York: Appleton-Century, 1957.

[10] Osgood, Charles E., G. J. Suci, and P. H. Tannenbaum. *The Measurement of Meaning*. Urbana: University of Illinois Press, 1958.

other end of the scale is Piaget, who, with his collaborators, has published at least fifteen books which deal wholly or partly with children's concepts. Most of his results have been obtained by the use of what he terms the "clinical" method, a combination of observation and interview.

There is at present no generally accepted, standardized method for measuring meaning. Logical definitions may refer to signification, denotation, connotation, equivalence, or implication. Meaning may refer to a relation between terms, a habit, or frequency of usage. From the point of view of introspection, Titchener taught that meaning is the conscious context which, under certain conditions, accrues to a "core" of sensory or imaginal content. Noble[11] used experimentally an index of stimulus meaning *m* defined in terms of mean frequency of continued written associations made by subjects in a one-minute interval and gave indexes of meaningfulness for 96 words. More recently, Osgood[12] has used associative techniques and factor analysis to determine components in entering into semantic description and judgment. By asking subjects to associate freely he obtained constellations of words surrounding the stimulus words and on analysis, found these could be identified in such terms as "evaluative," "strength," and "activity" factors. These peripheral "meanings" varied widely with different individuals. Other studies such as that of Wesman[13] have shown a close relationship between the subject's knowledge of words and their frequency on some standard word count. Underwood and Schulz[14] have summarized the literature on frequency and meaningfulness. From their research they concluded that frequency will accurately predict the difficulty of learning materials which are of low meaningfulness, but that the factor of pronounceability is the best predictor for more meaningful materials. In general, the psychological literature on the topic of meaning has changed from speculative and verbalistic approaches to operational definitions useful in quantitative and experimental discussions. The approaches to meaning have been characterized by diversity rather than unanimity.

Reports of attempts to get at meaning in school settings have included such topics as some thirty ways of testing vocabulary, the use of word lists, and various concepts of "vocabulary ability."[15] The more recent of

[11] Noble, C. E. "An Analysis of Meaning," *Psychological Review, 59:*421–30, November 1952.

[12] Osgood, C. E. *The Measurement of Meaning.* Urbana: University of Illinois Press, 1958.

[13] Wesman, A. G., and H. G. Seashore. "Frequency Vs. Complexity of Words in Verbal Measurement," *Journal of Educational Psychology, 40:*395–404, November 1949.

[14] Underwood, Benton J., and Rudolph W. Schulz. *Meaningfulness and Verbal Learning.* Philadelphia: Lippincott, 1960.

[15] Russell, D. H. *The Dimensions of Children's Meaning Vocabularies in Grades Four through Twelve.* University of California Series in Education No. 5. Berkeley: University of California Press, 1954.

these studies has grappled with such problems as precision in the use of words (*bold* versus *reckless*), breadth of meaning, as in knowledge of multiple-meaning words, depth of meaning, as in a thorough understanding of *democracy,* and the ability to produce and use one's vocabulary in speaking, writing, reading, and listening. Every primary teacher knows that even young children bring different referents to such words as *parlor* ("The queen was in the parlor") and that meanings are uncertain until words or other symbols have been put into sentences or other context. (By itself a *skate* may be a piece of sports equipment, a fish, or an old horse.) Words or other symbols become informative as they are embedded along with other signs which mutually modify their potential ambiguities in some context. Both psychological experiment and school practice utilize an operational definition of mastery of a concept in terms of the speed and accuracy with which a subject is able to classify new instances correctly.

From the research point of view, and even from careful observations in classrooms, this operational approach is not completely satisfactory. Broudy[16] points out that mastery of subject matter may refer to "(1) the efficiency of response, (2) the area over which control is exercised, or (3) the level of control employed." In the analysis of meaning or of concepts in the teaching–learning situation the idea of level of response may be especially fruitful. Some of these overlapping levels of response may be distinguished as follows:

1. The student repeats verbatim a textbook's or the teacher's definition.
2. The student gives a delayed response of textbook or teacher definition, as in a subsequent examination.
3. The student paraphrases the textbook's or the teacher's definition.
4. The student supplies examples of the concept.
5. When presented with an example, the student categorizes the phenomenon correctly.
6. The student shows a wide variety of knowledge about the concept, derived from observation, discussion, reading, experimentation, and other activities.
7. The student generalizes effectively about the concept, relating it to other concepts and to broad ideas and issues.

Some empirical support for such a hierarchy of meaning or of levels of understanding concepts is found in an unpublished doctoral study by McNaughton.[17] By varying the questions asked on some historical case

[16] Broudy, Harry S. "Mastery," *Language and Concepts in Education* (B. O. Smith and R. H. Ennis, eds.). Chicago: Rand McNally, 1961, pp. 72–85.

[17] McNaughton, A. H. *Ability of Seventh Grade Children to Infer Meaning and to Generalize from Two Selections of Written History Material.* Unpublished doctoral dissertation. (University of California, Berkeley, 1961).

materials he found that seventh-graders could respond on at least five levels. These he described as (1) copied facts, (2) qualified facts, (3) concrete concepts, (4) abstract concepts, and (5) generalizations. In many cases the type of response depended upon the type of question asked by teacher or interviewer, but responses at these levels were the result of reading the same material. It seems probable that readers who are not in school may respond similarly at some five or seven levels. The McNaughton study suggests that a brief examination of the research on comprehension in reading may be of value.

## *Empirical Studies of Comprehension in Reading*

A typical way of examining an idea like comprehension in reading is to review historically the attacks on the problem. As suggested above, the psychological study of meaning and meaningfulness began under the parental roof of philosophy and then moved out to establish a home of its own.

More recently, psychologists have attempted to study word meaning in terms of discrimination between items, ability to generalize or conceptualize, and more specifically in terms of denotative and connotative associations. The knowledge of the meanings of the single words contained in it is probably the most potent influence on grasp of meaning of a sentence, paragraph, or longer passage.[18] Because the study of word meanings is a whole field in itself, the studies mentioned below are limited to ones of comprehension in the reading of sentences, paragraphs, and passages; investigations involving wordparts and words only are omitted.

The classic investigation of children's comprehension of meaningful material is one published by Thorndike[19] in 1917. He presented to 200 pupils from grade six copies of the following paragraph with questions to be answered by them.

In Franklin, attendance upon school is required of every school child between the ages of seven and fourteen on every day when school is in session unless the child is so ill as to be unable to go to school, or some person in his house is ill with a contagious disease, or the roads are impassable.

The first question asked "What is the general topic of this paragraph?" Here are some typical answers of the sixth-grade pupils:

| | |
|---|---|
| Franklin | Subject and predicate |
| In Franklin | Subject |

[18] Ayer, Adelaide M. *Some Difficulties in Elementary School History.* Contributions to Education, No. 212. New York: Bureau of Publications, Teachers College, Columbia University, 1926.

[19] Thorndike, Edward L. "Reading as Reasoning: A Study of Mistakes in Paragraph Reading," *Journal of Educational Psychology,* 8:323–32, June 1917.

| | |
|---|---|
| Franklin attendance | The sentence |
| Franklin School | A letter |
| Franklin attending school | Capital |
| School days of Franklin | A capital letter |
| Doings of Franklin | To begin with a capital |
| Franklin attends to his school | The first word |
| It is about a boy going to Franklin | A general topic |

This discouraging partial list of the answers may have been due in part to a system of teaching reading which in 1917 emphasized sounds of words more than meanings of sentences or paragraphs. The two columns suggest that the children may have been associating answers with two important words in the paragraph, one of them *Franklin* and the other the word *paragraph*. Thorndike believed that some words are more potent than others in determining the meaning the readers obtained from the paragraph. He believed that, in reading,

> The mind is assailed as it were by every word in the paragraph. It must select, repress, soften, emphasize, correlate and organize, all under the influence of the right mental set or purpose or demand.

Thorndike also believed that reading a paragraph with comprehension was a bit like solving a problem. It involves understanding of organization and analysis of ideas such as occur in problem solving.

Following the fresh impetus given by Thorndike and the studies of children's eye movements in reading different kinds of material, school people began further study of reading comprehension largely through analysis of test results. After the introduction of tests in World War I the movement for intelligence and achievement testing spread rapidly to schools. During the 1920's and 1930's many reading tests were developed and many articles written which reported the relationships between comprehension and other factors in the reading process. Many of the investigators found that intelligence and knowledge of word meaning are more closely related to comprehension than any other factors they studied. In the 1940's some investigators carried the relationships of test results further by doing a factor analysis of them to determine what kinds of abilities in comprehension seem to cluster together. For example, in 1944 Davis[20] identified the following factors which go to make up comprehension: knowledge of word meanings; ability to reason; ability to identify the writer's intent, purpose, or point of view; ability to grasp detailed statements in the passage; and knowledge of literary devices and techniques. A different system of factor analysis suggested that these different abilities could be combined into some unitary factor which could be called verbal ability. Other statistical analyses have produced a similar

[20] Davis, F. B. "Fundamental Factors of Comprehension in Reading," *Psychometrika*, 9:185–97, September 1944.

factor of verbal ability plus some knowledge of meaning vocabulary as two important components of comprehension.

During the 1950's a number of investigators avoided the test approach in favor of introspective and retrospective techniques for getting at the reader's thinking while reading. Gray[21] reported a study by Swain among college students in which he attempted to find out whether during reading they focussed primarily on the analysis of language or on the reconstruction of meaning. Swain found that the reader's reaction depended upon his level of competence. The poor readers focussed most of their attention on word perception, better readers on the analysis of language in identifying the author's meaning and on the restructuring of meanings in the light of background or purpose. Another study reported by Gray was based on interviews with sixth-grade pupils. Piekarz[22] found that the poorer readers limited their responses to literal meanings and gave only a little attention to implied meanings or to critical reactions. Competent readers, on the other hand, made a greater variety of response in the three areas of literal meanings, implied meanings, and evaluations. They were more objective and critical in dealing with certain passages. Such findings substantiate the ones of McNaughton mentioned above.

The results of studies largely involving the test approach have been summarized by Lennon[23] in a way that encourages further study of comprehension. He reviewed some thirty studies of reading comprehension and concluded that the following components of reading ability can be measured reliably.

1. A general verbal factor closely related to vocabulary knowledge and scores on a verbal intelligence test.
2. Comprehension of explicitly stated material, understanding literal meanings, and ability to follow directions.
3. Comprehension of implicit or latent meaning such as the ability to draw inference, to predict outcomes, and to perceive a hierarchical arrangement of ideas within a selection; may be labelled "reasoning in reading."
4. Appreciation – "seeing the intent or purpose of an author; judging the mood or tone of a selection; perceiving the literary devices by means of which the author accomplishes his purposes."

Another example of the introspective or retrospective type of study

[21] Gray, W. S. "New Approaches to the Study of Interpretation in Reading," *Journal of Educational Research, 52:*65–67, October 1958.

[22] Piekarz, Josephine A. "Getting Meaning from Reading," *Elementary School Journal, 56:*303–309, March 1956.

[23] Lennon, Roger T. "What Can Be Measured," *The Role of Tests in Reading*. Vol. 9 of Proceedings of Annual Education Conferences (Russell Stauffer, ed.). Newark: University of Delaware, March 1960, pp. 67–80.

mentioned above, is Pickford's[24] analysis of the reports of eighteen "educated adults" (not otherwise described) who had read twelve short and nine longer extracts of prose and poetry. In trying to analyze their behavior during reading, these adults reported:

1. Imagery – usually as an obstruction to meaning and giving an incomplete setting.
2. Puzzlement – with curiosity as a motive for further interpretation.
3. Elementary critical functions such as reconciling two different points of view.
4. Some involvement of feelings and emotions, as in rationalization and self criticism, with the self-concept influencing the interpretations made.

Because the evidence from both test results and introspective reports indicates some forms of emotional response and appreciation in much reading, some further analysis of the term *appreciation* is of interest.

## *Appreciation*

Lennon's encouraging conclusion that even in the drudgery of responding to tests, there may be an element of appreciation in reading seems to have a firm foundation in fact. Lord David Cecil's[25] intuitive statement that "The artist's first aim is not truth but delight" has been validated in a number of empirical British studies. In a factor analysis of scores made in terms of aesthetic judgments Eysenck[26] found a general factor of good taste (which he labeled "T") in judging art and a bipolar factor contrasting "formal" and "representative" art products. Such a T factor was related to response to form and design and to emotional expression plus some technical factors such as rhythm, color, and appropriateness of expression. Furthermore, Eysenck believed that "capacity for literary appreciation correlates [positively] with pictorial and musical appreciation." Gunn[27] had secondary school and university students rate nineteen poems of varied content and excellence. He included poems by Coleridge, Browning, Keats and other poets, and some verse "devoid of literary merit." Like Eysenck, Gunn[27] found a general aesthetic factor related to liking, emotional effect, mode of expression, and appeal of subject, and a

[24] Pickford, R. W. "Some Mental Functions Illustrated by an Experiment in Reading," *British Journal of Psychology, 26:*49–58, July 1935.

[25] Cecil, Lord David. *The Fine Art of Reading.* New York: Bobbs-Merrill, 1957.

[26] Eysenck, H. J. "The General Factor in Aesthetic Judgments," *British Journal of Psychology, 31:*94–102, July 1940.

[27] Gunn, Douglas G. "Factors in the Appreciation of Poetry," *British Journal of Educational Psychology, 21:*96–104, June 1951.

bipolar factor related to rhyme, mental imagery, and other elements which he labeled "Technical." Williams, Winter, and Woods[28] tested 200 British boys and girls with five measures of literary appreciation such as scaled, ranking, and triple comparison tests. They found some evidence of a sense of "literary quality" – structure, aptness of simile, ingenuity in metaphor – appearing at about twelve years of age. Although there is always the question of how validly appreciation can be tested by paper-and-pencil or by interview, and although they are incomplete at this stage, such studies suggest an appreciation factor, involving some reaction to literary quality, which is somewhat separate from literal comprehension of a piece of literature. It should be noted, however, that literary appreciation is probably not typical of young children depending on their own resources, and it may be that response to literary forms is a more abstract ability than the capacity to appreciate more concrete art forms. Such a finding suggests a distinction between appreciation and the enjoyment which children may experience as a parent reads *Winnie-the-Pooh* or a teacher reads *The Wind in the Willows*. It also raises the question of whether or not appreciation has developmental characteristics and can be taught.

From her experience in teaching English, Early[29] has identified three stages in which she feels appreciation develops. The first of these she labels "unconscious enjoyment" in which "the reader knows what he likes but doesn't know why." This stage is possible even for people who have little or no reading skill. For example, children can listen to poems and stories to enjoy the rhythm, the alliteration, the simple, satisfying subject. Adolescents or adults respond to a definite plot with realistic conclusion, characters that may be stereotypes, humor that may be obvious, and content somewhat related to the individual's experience. The question may be raised as to whether this is "unconscious" enjoyment, but some components of literary appreciation are present. In the second stage which Early labels as "self-conscious appreciation" the reader continues to enjoy reading on the level of easy acceptance but puts more of himself into the reading. "He asks why. In fiction and drama he looks for logical development of character – he becomes less interested in simple themes, more willing to probe for literature's answers to the questions that beset mankind." Thus the reader may move over into questions of allusions and symbolism, of the evaluation of the "rightness" of a metaphor, of judgments on the values implicit in the narrative. Early calls her third stage "conscious delight." In it "the reader responds with delight, knows why, and relies on his own judgment." He takes pleasure in imaginative litera-

[23] Williams, E. D., L. Winter, and J. M. Woods. "Tests of Literary Appreciation," *British Journal of Educational Psychology, 8:*265–84, November 1938.

[29] Early, Margaret. "Stages of Growth in Literary Appreciation," *English Journal, 49:*161–67, March 1960.

ture as an end in itself; "his main purpose is neither sociological, nor psychological, but aesthetic." Early believes that not many high school students or even many university students achieve this final stage.

An intuitive and logical analysis of the process of appreciation such as Early has given should be checked empirically to further illumine the process and to give hints to teachers of literature on what they can expect and how they may go about developing appreciation. Attempts have been made, not always successfully, to get empirical evidence about abilities in literary appreciation and judgment through some form of measure of them. Some literary scholars may be horrified by the idea, but the tests may also be viewed as attempts at greater understanding of an elusive response. For example, as early as 1921, Abbott and Trabue[30] constructed a test, not of choosing between authors, but of variants of the original poem. In two sets of thirteen poems each, ranging from Mother Goose to Shakespeare, the reader was asked to choose the best among the original, "sentimental," "prosaic" and "metrical" (awkward movement) versions. For example, the following versions of Amy Lowell's "To A Sea Shell" were used:

Set 3. *To A Sea Shell*

A(. . . . . . .)
Sea Shell, please sing me a song
Of ships and sailor-men;
Of strange kinds of birds and trees
On the Spanish Main:
Of fish and seaweed in the sea,
And whatever creature there may be, –
Sea Shell, please sing me a song!

B(. . . . . . .)
Sea Shell, Sea Shell,
Sing me a song, Oh please!
A song of ships and sailor men,
Of parrots and tropical trees.
Of islands lost in the Spanish Main
Which no man ever may find again,
Of fishes and coral under the waves,
And sea-horses stabled in great green caves –
Sea Shell, Sea Shell
Sing me a song, O please!

C(. . . . . . .)
Tender, tender Sea Shell,
Wilt thou sing me, please,
Of thy happy, happy home
'Neath the tropic trees?

[30] Abbott, Allan, and M. R. Trabue. "A Measure of Ability to Judge Poetry," *Teachers College Record,* 22:101–26, March 1921.

Ah, the coral islands!
Ah, the wondrous fish!
For such a song I'd give thee, dear,
Whate'er a Shell could wish.

D(.......)
Sea Shell, I ask you will
You sing a song, please.
All about the ships and sailors
And the parrots in their tropical trees.
The islands I have read about on the Spanish Main
That no one will see again,
The fish and coral under the wave,
Sea Horses that have their stables in caves;
Sea Shell, I ask you will
You sing a song, please.

Abbott and Trabue found no discrimination ability in the fifth and sixth grades, some ability in terms of Mother Goose, Scott's "Marmion," and Tennyson's "Bugle Song" by the seventh and eighth grades, but no consistent scores until the upper high school grades on the variants quoted of "To A Sea Shell." They concluded, "Vigorously expressed feeling is the demand of the middle years – upper grades, high school, and early college. Restraint, understatement are not for them, nor the delicate adjustment of intensity of expression to the validity of its occasion."

In a similar type of study, Carroll[31] measured appreciation by asking the student to distinguish "the good from the less good, and the less good from the very bad." In the sets of four prose passages the first was obtained from a book regarded as of excellent quality, the second from books usually rated as of poor quality, the third from the "less literary" magazines, and the fourth by mutilation of other passages. Unfortunately the passages are too short to be representative of such sources as a good novel, and the reliability estimates given by the author are too low to assure consistency in the scores made by individuals. The test is perhaps most useful as a stimulus to a discussion of good style or literary merit in a group of high school students.

In another study Hartley[32] confined her test to the understanding of the poet's intent by having college students choose one of four interpretations of a "unit of poetry." In a group of 28 college students the correlation of scores on the Hartley test and the Abbott-Trabue test was 0.79, which was higher than the correlations of the Hartley test, with scores on a prose

[31] Carroll, Herbert A. "A Method of Measuring Prose Appreciation," *English Journal*, 22:184–89, March 1933.

[32] Hartley, Helene W. *Tests of the Interpretative Reading of Poetry for Teachers of English*. Contributions to Education, No. 433. New York: Bureau of Publications, Teachers College, Columbia University, 1930.

reading test, a test of literary vocabulary, and a test of literary content. An example follows:

> 8. Like a volley of shot your flocks alight,
> Scattering gracefully over the sedge,
> Palled in spume from the cauldron's edge.
> Surer than furrow's is breaker's pledge:
> Whom the welter of sea and sky invite
> On the lands of men show sudden fright.
>
> The birds prefer the water (1) for food, (2) for safety, (3) to be near the cauldron's edge, (4) because of the sedge.

Such a test assumes that the poet has had one principal message and that differing interpretations are wrong. The "best" interpretation was established by Hartley using an experienced jury technique, but only after several revisions was the test in such form that there were almost complete agreements on the items. Where the writer is being intentionally ambiguous, measures of appreciation or interpretation are more difficult to apply.

In fact, the measures proposed by Abbott, Carroll, Hartley, and others may raise more questions than they answer. Most English scholars are wary of such "mechanical methods" of getting at appreciation or critical ability, and some test makers would add that the tests themselves are not good tests in terms of reliability, validity, and other criteria applied to measuring instruments. It seems to the writer, however, that such "quality scales" may have some virtue in that the reader is asked to evaluate the whole, to give his first response to the total unit rather than an analysis of virtues and defects word by word or line by line. This kind of analysis may come later in a critique.

One of the problems is that of agreeing on a definition of *appreciation.* Sometimes it is defined in terms of specified reactions to literature, sometimes in terms of skills or abilities basic to appreciation, such as determining author's meaning or judging literary worth. After reviewing available research, Harris[33] analyzed comprehension of literature into four operations: (1) translating, (2) summarizing, (3) inferring the tone, mood, and intent, and (4) relating technique and meaning. Harris found by factor analysis of intercorrelations of tests of these abilities that a general function of comprehension was adequate to account for the correlations. Despite difficulties of defining clearly, a listing in *Tests in Print*[34] mentioned some thirty-five attempts, as wholes or as parts of batteries of tests, to get at the factor of comprehension or appreciation of literature, usually at the secondary school level.

[33] Harris, Chester W. "Measurement of Comprehension of Literature." *School Review, 56*:280–89, 332–43, May, June 1948.

[34] Buros, Oscar K. *Tests in Print.* Highland Park, New Jersey: Gryphon Press, 1961.

The test approach may not be as illuminating as introspective techniques or as the content analysis studies of both literal and interpretive understandings described below in the section "Other Studies of Interpretation." Perhaps a combination of methods is needed. Although he was referring to visual art forms, French's[35] conclusion still applies, "I realize that the wide, exciting area of children's [and adolescents'] aesthetic development is almost unexplored. I realize that we must devise new research methods to get at the elusive, intuitive, emotional response that we call aesthetic." One hypothesis about appreciation needing further investigation is that it may occur in three stages. First, it has a considerable emotional component based on past experience of the reader and on response to such characteristics as rhythm or beauty of language. The second stage comes in the realization of the fuller meaning of the material – its application to one's own life, its functional value. The third stage comes in terms of relationships – how it may lead to new ideas or generate new discoveries. Such proposals need checking in a series of observational and experimental studies.

## *Factors Affecting Comprehension and Interpretation*

Some of the empirical studies of comprehension and appreciation discussed above give clues to factors in the reader, in the materials, and in the total situation while one is reading which may affect comprehension. In the words of Proust, "Every reader reads himself"; his experiences, his hopes, and fears may influence what he finds on the page. But the material may affect how much the reader puts himself into his reading. It may be a factual report or it may include emotive language. It may be delightful in content or so difficult in ideas that frustration results. Finally, as suggested in Chapter 5, the situation of enjoying a well-written tale in a congenial peer group may stimulate comprehension which differs from plugging along on a chapter for next day's crucial test in school; reading a mystery story in bed engenders comprehension different from preparation for an appearance before a purchasing committee in business or a tax official. Such everyday observations have been confirmed, rather than new causes discovered, in studies of factors that affect comprehension. The empirical approaches, however, have given weight to the view that there are many different comprehensions and that the factors affecting literal comprehension may be different from those relating to inferential, intuitive reading and to appreciation.

A number of studies have verified the noncontroversial hypothesis that literal comprehension is related to the general intelligence of the reader,

[35] French, John E. "The Perils of Research," *Art Education*, 9, No. 4, 8–11, May 1956.

the knowledge and previous experience of the reader, and his interest in the material. Correlations between general intelligence scores and reading comprehension scores typically run in the 0.40's to 0.60's, depending upon the tests used, and explainable in part because so many measures of so-called general intelligence have a high verbal content. The factor of knowledge was verified by Chall[36] using a reading test based on knowledge of health and disease in the fifth and sixth grades. Children who knew more about tuberculosis, for example, got more from paragraphs on the topic, suggesting that reading is a circle; we read to gain experience and we get more out of reading if we have some related experience. The third factor of the relation of interest to comprehensions is not so clear. Bernstein[37] has demonstrated with junior high school students that interest improves comprehension but the possible causal connection needs further study. Most parents and teachers know some boy classed as a poor reader who may have difficulty with third-grade stories but who reads eighth-grade or adult materials if they are about model airplanes. Interest comes close to emotional factors which may affect interpretive as well as literal comprehension.

At least a score of careful researches have demonstrated that individuals vary widely in their emotional responses to words. In a study involving twenty undergraduate college women, Bruner and Postman[38,39] analyzed the effect of symbolic value in perceptual organizations of positive, negative, and neutral symbols and concluded that "What is perceived reflects the predispositions, goals and strivings at the moment of perceiving." Both recognition and recall are easier for positively and negatively toned words than for neutral words. What might be called "high value" words or words which have emotional significance for the reader are identified and remembered better than "low value" words and lead to more autistic responses. Autistic responses to words are found in both children and adults at all levels of development. They seem closely related to the experience and the mental set of the reader. Some so-called errors of interpretation of literature should probably be labeled autistic or idiosyncratic responses.

Perhaps the most important result of the personal reaction to words is that this response affects comprehension of passages with value-loaded words. After a careful review of studies of individual interpretation

[36] Chall, Jeanne S. "Influence of Previous Knowledge on Reading Ability," *Educational Research Bulletin 26*:225–30, December 1947.

[37] Bernstein, Margery R. "Improved Reading through Interest," *School Review, 62*: 40–44, January 1954.

[38] Bruner, Jerome S., and Leo Postman. "Symbolic Value as an Organizing Factor in Perception," *Journal of Social Psychology, 27*:203–208, May 1948.

[39] Bruner, Jerome S., and Leo Postman. "Perception, Cognition and Behavior," *Journal of Personality, 18*:14–31, September 1949.

and word association, Hinze[40] reported a study in which college students were asked to associate freely with words taken from each of two prose paragraphs, one an "emotional" passage from Kafka, the other an "objective" or intellectual report relating to science and liberal education. They labeled these associations (often scores of them) as positive or negative with different words having largely positive, largely negative, or mixed responses. Some time after in a second interview, Hinze had the subjects read the two paragraphs and checked their comprehension or interpretation of them. On analyzing the two sets of data she found a consistency with which the subjects attached meanings to words in associative response and in context. She found also that predominantly positive or negative associations were subsequently reflected in interpretation and gave some clues to the "cognitive style" of the individual. Furthermore, when the responses to words were "unidirectional" (more than 80 per cent either positive or negative), interpretation of the paragraphs was much more consistent and related to expert objective estimates of meaning than when the subject had many "conflict words" (mixed positive and negative associations). If the predominant associational content of the word for the individual coincided with the direction in which the writer used the word, then adequate interpretation occurred. If, however, the predominant associational content opposed the direction of its use in the paragraph, then misinterpretation occurred. For example, the student for whom *obedience* in one paragraph was a unidirectional, positive concept had difficulty in understanding *disobedience* when he encountered it in the paragraph. Misinterpretations occur when key words in the paragraph are "conflict words" and when associations are consistently opposed to the direction suggested by the author. Finally, and not unexpectedly, the paragraph by Kafka on parent–child relationships had more "conflict words" and yielded more misinterpretations than did the paragraph dealing with science and education. The ability to interpret affective materials adequately may be a better measure of skill in reading comprehension than the ability to interpret nonaffective materials adequately.

The Hinze study combines an examination of both materials and personal factors in relation to comprehension and interpretation. Another set of studies has investigated personal characteristics in terms of the attitude with which the reader approaches the printed page. McCaul[41] found that the attitudes of intellectually superior children in grades seven to ten tended to affect their interpretation of materials read in regard to the motives they ascribed to the persons about whom they read. Students

[40] Hinze, Helen A. K. *The Individual's Word Associations and His Interpretation of Prose Paragraphs.* Unpublished doctoral dissertation (University of California, Berkeley, 1959).

[41] McCaul, Robert L. "The Effect of Attitudes upon Reading Interpretation," *Journal of Educational Research,* 37:451–56, February 1944.

with initially favorable attitudes tended to ascribe favorable motives more than students with neutral or unfavorable attitudes. McCaul believes the reader may be influenced by previously held attitudes as much as the listener or the arguer. In a study of eleventh grade students McKillop[42] found that the relationship between attitude toward a topic and ability to answer questions on the topic after reading depended in part on the kind of questions asked. When the comprehension questions dealt with specific fact and detail, little relationship to attitude was found. "On questions of judgment, evaluation and prediction it [relationship to attitude] is regularly obtained." In a group of younger children (fifth and sixth grades) Groff[43] found that the relationship between attitudes expressed toward four types of content material (related to boys' interests, girls' interests, airplanes, and manners) and critical reading scores on samples of such material ranged in the 0.30's depending upon the content of the material and the attitudes expressed. Groff believed that relationships to critical reading scores, in descending order of magnitude, were true of general reading ability, general intelligence, attitudes toward different content types of material, attitude toward reading as a school activity, chronological age, socioeconomic status, and attitudes toward school and teacher.

Although the studies quoted suggest that personal factors and type of material affect comprehension in an interchangeable, even reciprocal way, there is another approach to content in relation to comprehension. In school or out of it many people use reading to accomplish a specific goal, whether it be directions for getting to the next bus, or finding the sequence of events leading up to the French Revolution, or suggestions for building a compost heap on a suburban acre. Such activity may be labeled functional reading. In school it may be associated with science, geography, mathematics, and any of the fields of the curriculum; all require highly developed reading abilities. Furthermore, what is good reading in one area does not necessarily apply to another. For example, in a study of ninth-grade pupils Bond[44] found negative relationships between scores on tests of reading comprehension in history and in science. An effective way of reading a novel may not be a good way of handling a magazine article or some aspect of chemistry or of following the development of character in a play. Different disciplines require varied reading skills

[42] McKillop, Ann S. *The Relationship between the Reader's Attitude and Certain Types of Reading Responses.* Studies in Educaton. New York: Bureau of Publications, Teachers College, Columbia University, 1952.

[43] Groff, Patrick J. *Children's Attitudes Toward Reading and Their Critical Reading Abilities in Four Content-Type Materials.* Unpublished doctoral dissertation (University of California, Berkeley, 1955).

[44] Bond, Eva. *Reading and Ninth Grade Achievement.* Contributions to Education No. 756. New York: Bureau of Publications, Teachers College, Columbia University, 1938.

because they differ in technical vocabulary, in thought patterns used, and in specialized devices for presenting information such as graphs, symbols, and equations. A good library contains different kinds of reference books for different subjects. In functional reading in any technical field, however, certain abilities are required, such as ability to focus on some purpose for reading, ability to locate information in books and libraries, ability to select and evaluate information, ability to organize what is read, and ability to use and remember what is read.

Probably the crucial factor here is not so much the content as the purpose of the reader. One may read a weekly news magazine for recreation, for specific facts, or to find arguments for and against a point of view. The purpose rather than the material dictates the kind of reading one does. As suggested in Chapter 8, reading may be an anodyne, a pursuit of factual knowledge, or an emotional response to beauty of words or ideas depending upon the set purpose of the reader. Kipling's *Jungle Book* may give a child considerable factual knowledge about animals, provide escape from an intolerable home or classroom situation, or give practice in following a sequence of events. The dominant factor in comprehension, accordingly, is the purpose of the reader, stated or unstated. What he understands is guided largely by the dynamic of why he reads.

## *Other Studies of Interpretation*

The previous chapter has indicated how content analysis may be applied to various types of literature; the same method of analysis may be applied to students' responses to reading materials. The coding and analysis present difficulties, but there is considerable advantage to working with free responses rather than the circumscribed replies demanded by most reading tests. This section presents some studies which might have been included in Chapter 8 on reactions to reading, but are given here because they seem closer to comprehension and interpretation of literary works than to overt reactions to reading. They are investigations of the understanding of prose and poetry rather than examples of the many studies of interest in, or liking for, various types of literature. If in the words of Jackson,[45] "Literature contains seeds which can develop only in the mind of the reader," some of the possible tender plants of development need to be studied. We are not yet at the stage where we can suggest a full-fledged theory of interpretation for we do not know the principles and criteria which students or adults use in making such judgments. However, we have some empirical evidence on what students say in judging a poem or a short story, or novel. Such evidence gives leads to

[45] Jackson, Holbrook. *The Reading of Books.* London: Faber and Faber, 1946, p. 22.

better measures of the ability and eventually to some generalizations about the process.

Two early and influential studies were those of Richards,[46,47] mentioned in Chapter 3. The first involved free responses to thirteen poems by Cambridge undergraduates. The second was a study of student and adult responses to various prose passages such as part of a sermon from *Elmer Gantry* and a statement about the Oxford Movement employing much metaphor. In both reports Richards stressed the errors made in interpretation. "I shall offer evidence, in plenty, that passages of ordinary everyday prose of no unusual difficulty – were wildly and inexplicably misread." Although he calls them inexplicable, he goes on to explain some of the errors or difficulties. He lists them as follows:

1. Difficulty of making out the plain sense of poetry.
2. Difficulties of "sensuous apprehension" or reaction to form, sound, and rhythm.
3. Difficulties with imagery, especially visual imagery.
4. Influence of mnemonic irrelevances "the misleading effects of the reader's being reminded of some personal scene or adventure, erratic associations, and the interference of emotional reverberations.
5. Critical traps of stock responses.
6. Sentimentality.
7. Inhibition or the reverse of sentimentality.
8. Doctrinal adhesions such as religious beliefs.
9. Technical presuppositions.
10. General critical preconceptions such as a theory of the nature and value of poetry.

Richards' reports stimulated much interest in empirical studies in criticism but unfortunately gave no solid quantitative data on the frequency of "correct" responses or of the ten difficulties here listed. One other English writer later claimed that Richards "quoted such of their answers as suited his purpose" rather than summarizing all answers.

Such criticisms of method do not negate the fact that Richards influenced a considerable number of critical empirical studies in both England and the United States. Like Richards, an English investigator, Black[48] found "disappointingly low levels of attainment" among teachers' college students in understanding more ordinary prose than Richards used. Black discussed:

[46] Richards, I. A. *Interpretations in Teaching.* London: Kegan Paul, Trench, Trubner, 1937.

[47] Richards, I. A. *Practical Criticism: A Study in Literary Judgment.* New York: Harcourt, Brace, 1929.

[48] Black, E. L. "The Difficulties of Training College Students in Understanding What They Read," *British Journal of Educational Psychology,* 24:17–31, February 1954.

1. Failure to understand the writer's intention.
2. Failure to detect subtle irony (but not obvious irony).
3. Difficulty with new, ambiguous, obsolete, and technical words, and abstract concepts.
4. Difficulty in understanding allusions.
5. Failure to understand metaphors.
6. Failure to use context.
7. The reader's preconceptions.

A study in the United States was Loban's[49] investigation of responses to short stories. He compared reactions of adolescents who were rated as socially sensitive and as socially nonsensitive. Loban found that all the adolescents missed important implications of the stories and accordingly needed experience in discussing the significance of the literary texts. Many readers expressed artificial and superficial concepts which did not come to grips with the stories. The least sensitive individuals wanted to attach blame to someone and often had little to say. Both groups did not welcome new values or concepts in stories and did not relate literary and religious values. They favored stories within their own range of emotional and intellectual maturity.

Three other studies which suggested that high levels of interpretation were not possible for elementary school children involved the use of fables. Barlow[50] used paired experimental and control groups in the seventh and eighth grades. The children were asked to write the lessons conveyed by fifteen of Aesop's Fables. Then the experimental group was given twelve lessons of twenty minutes each, treating simple analysis, abstraction, and generalization. Both groups were retested one year later on the fables. The experimental group gained 64 per cent; the control group lost 9 per cent. The Barlow study suggests that some skills close to reasoning abilities are important in interpretation of literary materials. With a younger group of 400 children in grades two to four, Goldman[51] found that the young children could not draw inferences and, accordingly, that their use in character education at this level may be limited. Even simple fables were not understood in these grades. This finding was verified in an unpublished study by Kravitz[52] in which about twice as many pupils in

[49] Loban, Walter. "Adolescents of Varying Sensitivity and Their Responses to Literature Intended to Invoke Sympathy." Unpublished doctoral dissertation (University of Miami, Coral Gables, Fla., 1949). See also Loban's *Literature and Social Sensitivity*. Champaign, Ill.: National Council of Teachers of English, 1954.

[50] Barlow, M. C. "Transfer of Training in Reasoning," *Journal of Educational Psychology, 28* (2):122–28, February 1937.

[51] Goldman, Sadie. "The Fable as a Medium for Character Education," *Elementary English Review, 16*:223–25, 228, October 1939.

[52] Kravitz, Bernard. "How Children in Grades IV, VI and VII Are Able to Generalize about the Moral of a Fable They Have Read." Unpublished term paper (University of California, Berkeley, 1960).

grades six and eight as pupils in grade four could give an acceptable interpretation of the "lesson" in "The Milkmaid and Her Pail." Of the 60 per cent in the fourth grade who did not interpret correctly one group thought that the story did not teach a lesson and the others wrote something like "she should not carry the pail of milk on her head." Fifteen per cent of the eighth graders failed to interpret this simple fable correctly.

In another unpublished content-analysis study Skelton[53] analyzed the responses of 270 fourth, fifth, and sixth grade children to their listening to and reading of four poems fairly typical of the ones studied in elementary and junior high school. They were *Bird Talk* by Aileen Fisher, *If Once You Have Slept on an Island* by Rachel Field, *The Fairies Have Never a Penny to Spend* by Rose Tyleman, and *Richard Cory* by Edwin Arlington Robinson. Skelton's categorization of the free responses to the poems and the percentage of responses in each category were as follows:

1. Non-interpretive (irrelevant; admission of inability to understand) 1 per cent.
2. Critical interpretation (general feeling of like or dislike) 5.7 per cent.
3. Denotative-interpretive (giving literal translation or meanings) 49.4 per cent.
4. Author-connotative (dealing with the author's purpose or theme) 8.1 per cent.
5. Reader-connotative (not suggested by author but "read into" the poem; a reader's personal reaction) 35.7 per cent.

The differences among the three grades were negligible, but girls tended to give a larger number of responses than boys. The brighter pupils and better readers tended to give more responses in the reader-connotative and author-connotative categories. The group averaged between four and five "response units" or ideas for each poem with little difference between the easiest and the hardest poem. Fourth graders gave almost equal numbers of subjective and literal (denotative) responses, but sixth graders made only about one-half as many subjective as denotative interpretations.

Squire[54] made an investigation of the responses of high school students to four short stories with themes of personal development. In over 14,000 response statements coded by content analysis Squire found that the fourteen-, fifteen- and sixteen-year-old students' most frequent response was an interpretational reaction (42 per cent); the others in decreasing

[53] Skelton, Glenn. *Children's Responses to Selected Poems in the Fourth, Fifth and Sixth Grades.* Unpublished doctoral dissertation (University of California, Berkeley, 1963).

[54] Squire, James R. *The Responses of Adolescents to Literature Involving Selected Experiences of Personal Development.* Unpublished doctoral dissertation (University of California, Berkeley, 1956).

order of frequency were narrational, associational, and self-involvement comments, as well as literary and prescriptive judgments. Self-involvement and literary judgment responses varied inversely in the interpretations of the stories. The sources of difficulty in reacting to the stories seemed to be:

1. Inadequate comprehension of words and implications of words.
2. Reliance on stock responses.
3. "Happiness binding" – insisting on a happy ending (Hollywood version?).
4. Predetermination of viewpoint because of critical predisposition.
5. Misleading effects of erratic associations motivated by the desire to achieve certainty in interpretation.

The wide variety of responses and possible causes of them was stressed, and some parallel to Richards' findings is evident.

Wilson[55] used Squire's categories of response in analyzing the reactions of college freshmen to three novels, Salinger's *The Catcher in the Rye*, Steinbeck's *The Grapes of Wrath*, and Hemingway's *A Farewell to Arms*. He found that these students, on the average three or four years older than Squire's group, made fewer narrational responses and self-involvement statements and more interpretational responses (65 per cent as compared to 43 per cent) than the younger group. Other findings of the Wilson study were as follows:

1. Literary judgment responses (direct or implied judgments of the story as a story) decreased from a mean of 19 per cent before the study to a mean of 9 per cent after the study, a statistically significant change.
2. Interpretational responses (generalizations attempting to discover the meaning of the story, motivational forces, or the nature of the characters) increased from a mean of 54 per cent before the study to a mean of 78 per cent after the study. The differences were statistically significant for two works, but not for *The Catcher in the Rye* (64 per cent to 80 per cent).
3. Narrational responses (a factual repeating of details or incidents without attempting to generalize or interpret) decreased from 13 per cent before the study to 3.6 per cent after the study.

Except possibly in the category of self-involvement, these findings give evidence of what many English teachers hope – that study and class discussion of literature do change response to it.

In addition to numerical analysis, Wilson made a descriptive analysis of the responses, some typical and some atypical, of nine individuals to each

[55] Wilson, James R. *Responses of Students in Freshman English to Three Novels*. Unpublished doctoral dissertation (University of California, Berkeley, 1963).

book. In general the results were congruent with the numerical coding, but they also illuminated the intensity of feeling of certain subjects, gave clues to "maturity" of response, and captured some of "the uniquely patterned responses and individual interpretations" of the different subjects. For example, for two types of response Wilson had some evidence for the following:

> Relationships between self-involvement and interpretational adequacy were complex. Interpretational adequacy increased as the intensity of involvement decreased (Flora); [it] decreased as involvement decreased (Wilma); [it] increased while self-involvement did not change (Ann and Laura). . . . A sudden increase in involvement released more adequate interpretations (Nan); but too intense an involvement blocked out interpretation (Sally and Grace).

A final example of the content analysis approach to interpretation is a study by Scribner[56] comparing the reactions of junior-college freshmen, English teachers, and well-known literary critics to the four poems, Blake's *The Tiger*, Frost's *The Road Not Taken*, Milton's *On His Blindness* and Robinson's *Richard Cory*. Scribner asked students and teachers to respond in terms of the main idea or theme, other important ideas, the author's intention or purpose, the tone or mood of the poem, and personal reactions. Responses of 330 students, 23 teachers of other students, and the writings of some seven or eight critics (Ciardi, Daiches, Eliot, Frye, Schorer, and so on) about each poem were analyzed. Scribner concluded that the students tended to be concrete and literal in many of their comments, while both the teachers and critics were more abstract and symbolic in their statements. The highest percentage of students concurring on any one question was 72 per cent on the theme of Frost's *The Road Not Taken*. The highest percentage of agreement among the teachers was 96 per cent on the theme of *Richard Cory*. More teachers than students concurred on the themes of *The Tiger* and *On His Blindness*, and agreed with the critics' analyses of themes. Student responses about "form, sound and rhythm" were vague and general. The critics' responses were not directly comparable. They were naturally fuller than those of the other two groups since the critics had months, perhaps years, to prepare their statements, and gave interpretations in breadth and depth which only indicated possible directions for study of the poems. Scribner stressed the variety and uniqueness of all responses and found greater differences in the "more difficult" poems of Milton and Blake. She believed that greater capacity for abstraction and generalization, and greater insight into symbolism, characterized the more experienced groups. Although not asked for directly, the most frequent comment of the students on causes of difficulty was "lack of exposure to poetry."

[56] Scribner, Marion I. *The Responses of Students, Teachers and Critics to Selected Poetry*. Unpublished doctoral dissertation (University of California, Berkeley, 1960).

## *Conclusion*

This chapter is an illustration of the belief that empirical studies of reading comprehension, even when they move over into the less tangible areas of appreciation and interpretation, yield many valuable insights. Older studies involving reading tests have perhaps not proved so fruitful as later explorations involving introspection, although the "scientific" validity of such later studies is more difficult to establish. Some recent improvements in methods of using content analysis[57] have enhanced the values of self-report. The Gray and Lennon summaries have indicated research accomplishments up to the 1950's through a variety of approaches. They have suggested that the labels on reading tests are sometimes poor indicators of the functions performed by the test but that tests can have considerable value in measuring limited types of comprehension. Richards' pioneer investigations explored the problem of response, made some beginning suggestions for method, and revealed student difficulties in the interpretation of poetry and prose. Later studies have refined his methods, at least in the quantitative sense, and given data for wider age ranges and different types of reading material. As suggested in Chapter 1, writing may be studied by many means other than the psychological, but at least a beginning has been made in the psychological interpretation of the reader's responses.

To illustrate the point, such studies summarized above as those of Black, Harris, Groff, Pickford, and Williams have illustrated the variety and complexity of response and factors associated with it. Some of these relate to the reading skill and personality of the reader, some to the characteristics of the material read, and some to the environmental setting in which the reading is done. The Hinze, Loban, Scribner, Squire, and Wilson studies probe more deeply into aspects of response to literary materials. They support the view that readers respond to literature in unique and selective ways and give some clues as to why this is so. If a student or citizen is reading an arithmetic problem or an income tax regulation, there is usually only one response that is desired and considered to be correct. To must other reading, especially of literary materials, one brings his total experience, interests, and understandings and therefore his response is necessarily and desirably a unique and personal one. Most of the studies mentioned here analyzed responses in the form of written data sometimes supplemented by oral interview. While there is agreement on the worth of free response methods, some other ways of getting at interpretative reactions should be devised. Probably the responses will always be idiosyncratic, for life and literature are both too dynamic to produce a static research paradise.

[57] Pool, Ithiel de S. (ed.). *Trends in Content Analysis*. Urbana: University of Illinois Press, 1959.

Although responses to literature will always be largely individual, some interpretations are better than others. Perrine[58] makes this point, illustrating it with two examples of the poetry of Emily Dickinson and Walt Whitman. This takes us into the question of teaching interpretation of poetry, which has been a thread running through many of the investigations cited in this chapter and which is considered more fully in Chapters 10 and 11. If comprehension may occur on several different levels, should the teacher or critic attempt to raise the level of the reader's response, or does this result in mere parroting of ideas? If several different kinds of response are desirable, how does the teacher or writer encourage flexibility in comprehension? If a matter of taste is involved, how does a student move from a liking for stories of raw adventure, to stories of character development or of mood, or to Milton's *On His Blindness*? The chapters mentioned give some clues, not recipes.

[58] Perrine, Laurence. "The Nature of Proof in the Interpretation of Poetry," *English Journal 51*:393–98, September 1962.

# CHAPTER 8 | The Effects of Reading

Literature sometimes affects people. When Keats first saw Chapman's *Homer* he testified:

> Then felt I like some watcher of the skies
> When a new planet swims into his ken;
> Or like stout Cortez when with eagle eyes
> He star'd at the Pacific.

In the *Tatler* Richard Steele wrote of his godson:

> He would tell you the mismanagements of John Hickerthrift, find fault with the passionate temper of Bevis of Southampton and loved St. George for being the champion of England; and by this means had his thoughts insensibly moulded into the notions of discretion, virtue and honour.

The claim that literature may not only fill us with "wild surmise" but also affect our fundamental beliefs and values has been stated in terms of the teacher by Hicks:[1]

> Literature does affect the lives of its readers. How and why, we do not know, and the effect certainly cannot be measured. But it is there, and even the blank-faced boy or girl in the aisles in front of us may be touched in ways that baffle definition. We cannot control the effect of literature, cannot be sure that it is what the author wanted or what we think he wanted. . . . We bring the student and the book together and let the thing happen – rejoicing most of the time if anything at all happens that is perceptible.

What does happen when boy (or girl or adult) meets book? Besides the comprehension of its literal meaning, what may ensue? What by-products or even central consequences? The previous chapter has dealt with cognitive responses to reading, with the intellectual activities subsumed under terms such as *comprehension* and *interpretation*. This chapter explores the broader and more hazardous terrain of the overt effects of reading. Beyond the intellectual responses is the more elusive area of comprehension plus attitude and resulting behavior. In interpreting a

[1] Hicks, Granville. "Assumptions in Literature," *English Journal, 25:*709–17, November 1936.

speech or story the listener's or reader's activities and beliefs may possibly be affected by the message. Are one's deeply-held values affected by the word?

The chief difficulty in recording such effects comes not so much from lack of affirmation as from an overwhelming amount of personal testimony to the values of literature – declarations that range through all kinds of writing and that bear witness to all kinds of effects but which are more often characterized by enthusiasm than objectivity. Perhaps the search for objective evidence is a vain one and we should be content with the personal examples of Keats and Steele or the more modern ones of George Bernard Shaw and Winston Churchill. The testimony of such great men may give greater insight into the glories of literature than any verifiable evidence unearthed in a psychological study, but the bias of this volume is that empirical evidence be stated wherever possible. Accordingly, the chapter deals not with occasional personal testimony but with research evidence, often rather elusive, of the possible effects of reading on the reader.

The statements of hope for the effects of literature are not hard to find. In a book on the teaching of literature which was published in 1902 but which still has many good things to say, Chubb[2] wrote:

> The supreme aim of literary and linguistic training is the formation of character. This includes and transcends all other aims. . . . The springs of a man's character are in his loves and hates, his tastes and desires, his ideals and aspirations; and the life of these depends much upon the light and the perspective with which they have been invested by the imagination. This imaginative exaltation of life, of noble longings and ideals, it is the province of art, and especially of literature as the highest art, to achieve, and, in turn, foster and communicate.

A careful study which falls between the way of insight and the method of experimental evidence is a good introduction to discussions of effects which follow. In 1940 Waples, Berelson, and Bradshaw[3] in a little book *What Reading Does to People* identified five effects:

1. Instrumental – gaining greater competence in solving practical problems.
2. Prestige – relieving feelings of inferiority by choosing materials which increase self-approval.
3. Reinforcement – strengthening one's attitude or developing new, related attitudes.
4. Respite – escape reading for relaxation from tension.
5. Esthetic – responding to beautifully written materials.

[2] Chubb, Percival. *The Teaching of English in the Elementary and the Secondary School.* New York, London: Macmillan, 1903.

[3] Waples, Douglas, B. R. Berelson, and F. R. Bradshaw. *What Reading Does to People.* Chicago: University of Chicago Press, 1940.

Unfortunately the authors give no quantitative data to show which of these occur most frequently in different age or socioeconomic groups or with various kinds of materials. The list, however, constitutes a good hypothesis about possible types of effect.

The more fundamental question is whether we have any hard evidence that reading affects attitudes and behavior or whether we must be content with subjective testimony. The question stimulates the hypothesis that a piece of literature may or may not affect an individual, scarcely a world-shaking conclusion. This might be put more positively that literature may affect some people under certain circumstances such as the reader being able to identify with a character or idea and the reading being reinforced by other classroom, home, or community activities. Toward the end of this chapter some research evidence is given about these and related hypotheses. Because a group of miscellaneous investigations is not the most convincing evidence, some other indications of possible effects are first considered.

## *Related Phenomena*

The closest parallel to the effects of print or writing probably occurs in studies of the effects of other mass media. This realm of the social psychologist or of the "communications expert" has been explored in a number of ways. For example, Schramm[4] has edited a book entitled *The Process and Effects of Mass Communication,* and Hovland[5] has written a summary of research entitled "Effects of the Mass Media of Communication," listing 150 references. Hovland reported that "there is at present no adequate conceptual framework within which to classify the diverse types of effects reported." He found some distinction between long-term and short-term effects. Other authors speak of effects as "manifest" or as "latent." One study of effects on political beliefs distinguished three types of response: activation, reinforcement, and conversion. Hovland adopts the psychological point of view that one cannot talk about *the* effects, but only about "particular sets of responses selected for study." His section on major factors influencing effects includes studies of:

1. The communicator – *who* says something is usually as important as *what* is said.
2. The communication – the content transmitted.
3. The medium – as in comparisons of the results of print, movies, lectures, radio, and television.

[4] Schramm, Wilbur (ed.). *The Process and Effects of Mass Communication.* Urbana: University of Illinois Press, 1954.

[5] Hovland, Carl J. "Effects of the Mass Media of Communication," *Handbook of Social Psychology, II* (Gardner Lindzey, ed.). Reading, Mass.: Addison-Wesley Publishing Co., 1954, pp. 1062–1103.

4. The audience – personality factors both in individuals and in groups.

His discussion of overt behavior resulting from communications is concerned with areas of interest to the social psychologist such as purchasing, voting, and the retention of information.

Another psychological area which makes use of interpretation of various types of imaginative productions is that usually labeled "projective tests." These involve study of the individual's responses to different materials, not as reactions per se but in terms of what they reveal about the respondent's personality. The best known tests such as the Rorschach and the Thematic Apperception test do not involve verbal materials, nor do attempted analyses of drawing or play, the latter by such authorities as Anna Freud, Eric Erikson, and Louise Despert. However, the experimentation with verbal materials has included the use of both incomplete sentences and incomplete stories. In a summary of the research on projective tests, White[6] believed that incomplete stories may work best between the ages of five and ten years for revealing conflicts. Difficulties in these tests arise in the tester's interpretation of the responses but indicate the wide range of the responses studied for their own sake.

Related in theory to projective tests is the belief in the power of verbal materials to help the individual identify and solve his problems. This belief has been illustrated in such book lists as *Reading Ladders for Human Relations*[7] and *Character Formation through Books*,[8] which group titles for elementary and secondary school students and indicate some of the characteristics they may illustrate or problems they attack. In *Literature for Individual Education* Raushenbush[9] discusses work with college students in such sections as "Modern Problems through the Novel" and "The Individual and the Family." Examples of anthologies for college students based upon the theory of interaction between reader and text are *Psychology through Literature*[10] and *Patterns for Living.*[11] Some of the theory and practice of bibliotherapy suggested by these books is included more fully in the following chapter. Proponents of the theory and of the broader utilitarian place of literature do not confine their study to literary techniques or the facts of their composition but try for an "experiential

[6] White, R. W. "Interpretation of Imaginative Productions," *Personality and the Behavior Disorders* (J. M. Hunt, ed.). New York: Ronald, 1945.

[7] Crosby, Muriel (ed.). *Reading Ladders for Human Relations.* Washington, D.C.: American Council on Education, 1963.

[8] Kirchen, Clara J. (comp.). *Character Formation Through Books: A Bibliography.* Washington, D.C.: Catholic University of America Press, 1945.

[9] Raushenbush, Esther. *Literature for Individual Education.* New York: Columbia University Press, 1942.

[10] Shrodes, Caroline, Justine Van Gundy, and Richard Husband (eds.). *Psychology Through Literature.* New York: Oxford University Press, 1943.

[11] Campbell, Oscar J., Justine Van Gundy, and Caroline Shrodes (eds.). *Patterns for Living.* New York: Macmillan, 1947.

involvement" culminating in fundamental understandings of oneself and of human relationships. Here are effects indeed – if they can be obtained and validated.

Some of the writing in social psychology dealing with effects goes back at least thirty years to such books as Blumer's[12] *Movies and Conduct* and Cantril and Allport's[13] *The Psychology of Radio.* These and other studies did not involve careful control of experimental conditions in terms of modern research design but they testified to the power of the media to influence ideas, attitudes, and conduct. Before television became dominant in the recreational lives of most children, many articles were written and a few studies made of the effects of the comics. At their peak in the early 1950's nearly one billion comic books a year were published in the United States and, as one speaker put it, "The children read almost as many of them as the adults do." Opinions of their effects ranged from Wertham's[14] case for comics as the cause of juvenile delinquency to statements that the desirable ones stimulated imagination, gave reading practice, and offered a sort of catharsis for feelings of insecurity or aggression. One of the better studies of the comics is that by Wolf and Fiske[15] based on detailed interviews with a sample of 104 children, carefully stratified with respect to age, sex, and economic status. Each subject was asked about his comic-reading habits and social adjustment, and was also observed while reading a Superman story.

Three clear stages in comic reading were found. The first was the "funny animal" stage, such as Walt Disney comics, in which animals have human characteristics and do homey, realistic things. The second was the "fantastic adventure" in which the characters look like humans but have supernormal powers, such as Superman or Captain Marvel. The third was the "true or classic" comic, that is, a book adaptation or other factual material put in comic-strip form. In the "normal" child these coincided with developmental stages – the youngest children preferred "funny animals," the eleven- to twelve-year-olds preferred "fantastic adventure," and those over twelve years the "true or classic" comics.

Three types of comic readers were found: the moderate readers (46 per cent of the children) who enjoyed comics as a pastime, the indifferent or hostile readers (17 per cent) who found comics "unreasonable or trite," and the fans (37 per cent) who preferred by far the "fantastic adventure" comics with an invincible hero. The fans were found to be "neurotic" in that comic reading engulfed their whole life. They were interested only in the general aura of the story (especially its triumphant end), and lifted

[12] Blumer, H. *Movies and Conduct.* New York: Macmillan, 1933.

[13] Cantril, H. and Allport, G. W. *The Psychology of Radio.* New York: Harper, 1935.

[14] Wertham, Frederick. *Seduction of the Innocent.* New York: Rinehart, 1954.

[15] Wolf, Katherine M., and Marjorie Fiske. "The Children Talk About Comics," *Communications Research 1948–49*. New York: Harper, 1949, pp. 3–50.

comic reading to a position superior to other activities, including eating. The children were classified as to their social adjustment and it was found that 50 per cent of the "neurotic" children were comic fans. The authors concluded that the child's problems were there before the comics came along to relieve him. For "normal" children the comics functioned as an adaptation mechanism and satisfied real developmental needs.

## *Television*

By the early 1960's there were more television sets than bathtubs in use in the United States. Studies by Witty indicated that elementary-school children in the Chicago area spent over twenty hours a week watching television but that this dropped to about twelve hours per week for high-school youth, who gave about an equal time to radio. From its beginning parents and teacher groups have been concerned about the effects of television, with criticisms increasing in volume in the late 1950's because of the heavy programming of westerns and crime pictures. Many of the fears of adults about the effects of television have not been documented, but sufficient evidence has been produced to warrant concern about the content of programs, especially some of those intended for adults but viewed by children. For example, in 1962 during one week in August a station in Los Angeles was on the air for 127 hours. Of these hours 82.5 per cent were filled with films, many over twenty years old, and 60 per cent of the daytime and evening programs up to nine o'clock (allegedly for children's viewing) were devoted to programs featuring crime activities.[16] A couple of years earlier a team of 300 students from Pepperdine College in the same city monitored television programs for a week from 7 A.M. to 1 A.M. daily. They recorded 258 instances of property destruction, 3,696 acts of violence, and 7,887 commercials.[17] There is no question about the undesirable content of many programs, judged by ordinary standards of decency. There is little evidence, however, of what the specific effects of them are on children, adolescents, and adults.

Meyersohn[18] gave an objective account of television as entertainment and television's purported taste-debasing effects. He reminds us that most critics of television and research people "are more educated and sophisticated than the general TV viewer." In relation to the first problem he points out that early purchasers of television sets were likely to be those whose educational level was relatively lower than their income level and

[16] Shayon, Robert L. "Memo to a Foundation," *Saturday Review*, December 8, 1962, p. 31.

[17] O'Flaherty, Terrence. *San Francisco Chronicle*, May 26, 1960.

[18] Meyersohn, Rolf B. "Social Research in Television," *Mass Culture: The Popular Arts in America*. (Bernard Rosenberg and David M. White, eds.). Glencoe, Ill.: The Free Press, 1957, pp. 345–57.

who were in families with children. Because television has been directed toward entertainment it has displaced the entertainment features of other media. In relation to low taste levels of television programs, Meyersohn points out that every mass medium has resigned itself to giving up some of its potential audience but attracts as many people as it can by providing a wide range of content and activities. General magazines contain dozens of different sections or departments, and newspapers carry "women's pages, comics, astrological forecasts, bridge games and crossword puzzles." Radio and television similarly provide "drama, comedy, sports, news, movies, music – everything." Because of the high percentage of the total audience needed for a good rating or to "break even" in an expensive production, television attempts to keep as low as possible the number of people who will be antagonized by or uninterested in any particular program. In this process it reduces the number who can be truly enthusiastic or interested. This, says Meyersohn, is "the meaning of the low taste levels of TV." But all this is not specific evidence about the ways television affects its viewers. "No systematic confirmation or denial can yet be made of the charges against [television]."

In a book intended for teachers of English, Postman[19] accepts that television is "only one voice and one influence [on children] and . . . not necessarily a malignant or an overwhelming [one]." He points out that most of the available studies are those of short-term effects (partly because mass television is only about fifteen years old) and that tracing changes in the deepest attitudes involves years. He believes, however, that there is clear evidence that television may affect consumption in other media, that facts may be learned in incredibly large numbers, and that good television may expose the viewer to "high culture" such as the plays of Euripides, Shakespeare, and Shaw.

Postman's summary suggests indirectly that research on the impact of television has reached two out of three possible levels – or depths. As in research on other social phenomena, first studies were of the type labeled "surveys" or careful observations of current conditions. These were followed by correlational studies to determine, for example, what characteristics or other activities were associated with televiewing. The third research stage, not yet reached, comprises carefully controlled experimental studies which give evidence about some specific facts in televiewing. In the first area of the survey study, we know from Witty[20] and others that elementary school children watch television on an average of over twenty hours a week. High school students spend much less time on television, less than the average adult. Furthermore, all age groups spend as much time

[19] Postman, Neil. *Television and the Teaching of English.* Champaign, Ill.: National Council of the Teachers of English, 1961.

[20] Witty, P. A. "Effective Utilization of Mass Media: Effects on Children," *Childhood Education, 33:*104–108, November 1956.

on television now as when it was new. From a second group of studies of factors related to televiewing we know that children who watch television go to bed later (Himmelweit[21]), that a moderate amount of televiewing does not seem to affect school grades although excessive amounts may (Scott[22]), and that watching television may even be associated with increased book reading (Himmelweit). A careful study of the televiewing habits of over six hundred boys and girls in the fifth and sixth grades led Bailyn[23] to the conclusion that the order of frequency of exposure to various media, from most to least frequent, was television, comic strips, books, comic books, radio, and movies. Correlations among amounts of time spent in leisure activities led Bailyn to conclude that users of mass media can be described best in two categories. One consists of consumers of the pictorial media – television, movies, and comics; the other consists of users of books and radio. Factors associated with high exposure to the pictorial media were lack of parental supervision, low I.Q., fathers in worker or service occupations, and type of religious affiliation. Such correlational studies add to our information about the television audience without indicating causes or effects.

Experimental evidence on cause and effect is still lacking although researchers at the first two levels have speculated about the third. For example, Klapper[24] believes that the primary determinants of attitude are home, school, religion, and peer groups and that television tends to reinforce rather than change these attitudes. Schramm also states that television is "only one voice and one influence" in people's lives, and believes that the effects of television on the child depend upon the personality and needs of the child himself. Bailyn extended her findings from relationships to possible causes when she found that boys of the fifth and sixth grades with high exposure to television tend to classify people in stereotyped categories of good or bad, show little concern for motivation of characters, and seem to gain some of their self-image in the aggressive-hero types found in television drama. Girls of this age group do not show these relationships. In another careful study, based on interviews with mothers and children, Maccoby[25] related televiewing to the fantasy life of children, frustration-aggression, and vicarious habit formation. She believed that "TV probably plays a role similar to that of the

[21] Himmelweit, Hilda, and others. *Television and the Child.* New York: Oxford University Press, 1958.

[22] Scott, Lloyd F. "Television and School Achievement," *Phi Delta Kappan, 38:*25–28, October 1956.

[23] Bailyn, Lotte, "Mass Media and Children: A Study of Exposure Habits and Cognitive Effects," *Psychological Monographs, 73,* No. 1, 1959.

[24] Klapper, Joseph. *The Effects of Mass Communication.* Glencoe, Ill.: The Free Press, 1960.

[25] Maccoby, Eleanor E. "Television: Its Impact on School Children," *Public Opinion Quarterly, 15:*421–44, 1951.

fairy tales and fantasy play which have been part of children's lives since our earliest records of man."

The possible effects of television on the viewer have been traced in some detail in the paragraphs above because the parallels between watching television and reading a story are apparent and numerous. There are differences in these activities since silent reading is done by oneself whereas television may be watched in a group. Furthermore, reading is likely to make more demands on the reader for imagery and interpretation than the half hour of entertainment in a typical television story. As one gifted adolescent put it, "Well, in television you're just passive; you just sit there and a picture flashes on the screen; it takes no effort – you just watch it. In a book, if you really want to enjoy it, you try to visualize things. To read a book takes much more effort than just to watch a show. In a book you really have to be participating."[26] Such differences do not negate the fact that the activities have many parallels, and a review of research on television and other media not only illuminates the problem of effects but suggests at least two hypotheses about the impact of reading. First, in a scientific sense effects is a slippery word. The problem of the existence and amount of effects is difficult to demonstrate directly. The evidence about the effects of books must be obtained deductively from surveys and studies of relationships rather than inductively in experimental situations. Second, the experimental studies of the effects of reading are, at present, scattered and fragmentary. Some of them, such as the Waples report quoted at the beginning of this chapter, give some excellent leads to further study. Others deal with specific subjects, usually children, in specific situations. The next two sections report survey studies of reading interests which give clues to possible effects and present a summary of scattered, experimental investigations.

## *Studies of Reading Interests with Implications Regarding Effects*

Since the first published study of children's reading interests by True,[27] made in 1889, there have been at least 150 careful studies of reading interests of children, adolescents, and adults. Most of these have been of the survey type mentioned above, and their authors have been content to record such items as favorite titles, kinds of books enjoyed, and parts of the newspaper read regularly. We know from these, for example, that among their enduring favorites, girls list such classics as *Little Women, Heidi,* and *Black Beauty,* whereas boys are more likely to put down *Treasure Island, Tom Sawyer, Call of the Wild,* and *Robinson Crusoe.* We

[26] Strang, Ruth. "Reading and Study as Viewed by Adolescents," *High School Journal, 41:*326–31, May 1958.

[27] True, M. B. "What Do Children Read?" *Education, 10:*42–45, 1889.

know, too, that children of all ages like animal stories, and folk and fairy tales. Titles and themes may supply some clues to the effects of books, but the following summary of interest studies includes only those which give some direct evidence as to why they are read frequently and enjoyed. As before, much of this evidence is at the correlational level rather than showing cause and effect.

Reading interests are affected by the characteristics of the reader, as well as the content of the material. Many studies have established that interests change with age. One of the first studies showing developmental trends was that of Terman and Lima[28] sampling from preschool to fifteen years. The principal interests at various age levels were:

*Before five years:* Mother Goose rhymes, other jingles, simple fairy tales, and little nature stories.

*Six and seven years:* Animal talking stories, Mother Goose, some of the shorter fairy tales.

*Eight years:* Fairy tales, beginning interest in stories of real life.

*Nine years:* Realistic stories, continued but less interest in fairy tales, reading used to satisfy curiosity.

*Ten years:* Adventure, stories of other lands, travel, beginning of interest in biography, boys beginning to read books on mechanics and invention, some myths and legends.

*Eleven years:* Series repeating same characters in adventure and mystery, boys' increasing interest in science, interest in animal and nature stories declining.

*Twelve years:* Reading interest at its highest, biography, stories of home and school life, boys' interest in more sensational adventure, girls beginning to read so-called adult fiction.

*Thirteen, fourteen years:* New reading interests of more specialized type, often related hobbies, boys' mechanical and scientific interests intensified, girls reading more romantic fiction and perhaps reading boys' adventure stories.

*Fifteen years:* Noticeable decline in amount of reading, continued specialization of interests.

Because the Terman and Lima study was first published in 1935, it does not necessarily reflect choices today; it shows that they change with the years. For example, the summary above may not give enough place to animal stories, and the choice of fairy tales around eight years may have been superseded by the large number of modern children's books with factual backgrounds about trains, airplanes, and space travel. There is also evidence that modern children read more magazines and newspapers than mentioned in this study, illustrating the importance of accessibility in choice of reading materials.

[28] Terman, L. W., and Margaret Lima. *Children's Reading.* New York: Appleton-Century, 1935.

Other factors in the reader besides age which affect enjoyment are sex and I.Q. As suggested by Terman and Lima, at about ten years boys and girls begin to diverge in their reading tastes: after that boys want to read books about boys, and girls want to read books about girls although they occasionally dip into boys' books. Modern American culture may influence older boys to read more factual books, especially those dealing with science, mechanics, and how-to-do-it books. By twelve years most girls are interested in romance, even the so-called adult romantic novel, but these are usually scorned by boys of this age. The findings about intelligence of the reader are less clear-cut. Both Thorndike[29] and Norvell[30] have found that the bright child's choice is superior in quality to that of the dull child of the same chronological age, but that the older dull child may choose much the same books as the younger bright one. Since amount of reading depends upon accessibility of material, the bright child with the higher socioeconomic level home is likely to read more books, newspapers, and magazines. Wollner[31] found great differences in the number of books available to different socioeconomic groups.

The attempts to relate reading to the personality of the reader have been considered more fully in Chapter 6. Popular girls and boys may read as much as or more than the individuals in the rest of the class but, especially among boys, the omnivorous reader is sometimes the "lonesome reader." As suggested in the earlier chapter, Mitchell[32] found a small but positive correlation between readership and social acceptability in the sixth grade.

The evidence about how much teachers affect reading interests is sparse. Perhaps most children have enjoyed some book read to them by their teacher or caught some of the enthusiasm of a good teacher of literature, but empirical data are scanty. Norvell[33] reported that superior teachers did not improve children's stated preferences for books but that inferior teachers did lessen their liking for books. Jefferson[34] found considerable correspondence between children and their parents in choices of

[29] Thorndike, Robert L. *Children's Reading Interests.* New York: Bureau of Publications, Teachers College, Columbia University, 1941.

[30] Norvell, George W. *What Boys and Girls Like to Read.* New York: Silver Burdett, 1958.

[31] Wollner, Mary H. *Children's Voluntary Reading as an Expression of Individuality.* Contributions to Education No. 944. New York: Bureau of Publications, Teachers College, Columbia University, 1949.

[32] Mitchell, Mary Alice. *The Relationship of Reading to the Social Acceptability of Sixth Grade Children.* Contributions to Education No. 953. New York: Bureau of Publications, Teachers College, Columbia University, 1949.

[33] Norvell, George W. *What Boys and Girls Like to Read.* New York: Silver Burdett, 1958.

[34] Jefferson, Benjamin. *Some Relationships Between Parents' and Children's Preferences in Juvenile Literature.* Unpublished doctoral dissertation (University of California, Berkeley, 1956). Also *Elementary School Journal,* 58:212–18, January 1958.

books. Children in grades three to six showed more interest in "mystery," "humor," and "love and romance" but less interest in "travel" books than their parents expected. Parents varied greatly in their understanding of their own children's favorite type of stories, and their influence tends to favor or disapprove, not specific titles or types of material, so much as a general climate of interest in books.

One of the more comprehensive studies of interests which goes beyond a listing of titles or types is that of Rudman,[35] who distinguished between children's "read-about" and "ask-about" interests or between what they read and what they really want to know. In their reading, over 6,000 pupils in grades four through eight showed strong interests in literature, animals, sports, and science. In their "ask about" interests the children showed concern for questions relating to ethics, values, and religion and, especially with the older children, personal problems and relations with peers. Parents of some of the children wanted them to read more reference books and ask more about vocations than they seem to do.

In another somewhat specific topic regarding interests, Vandament and Thalman[36] investigated reactions of over a thousand children to various types of fantasy. Youth in the sixth and tenth grades preferred materials, from most to least, classed as books, comic books, and magazines. The achievement type of fantasy was found most frequently in story books, and the social and aggressive types most in comic books. No differences in aggression were found in the preferences of children and adolescents from different socioeconomic backgrounds.

Wollner's study[37] of twelve- and thirteen-year-olds mentioned in Chapter 6 explored the question of why children read. She thought that these children found intellectual satisfactions in forward style, plot, suspense, using reading skills, finding facts, and developing the beginnings of taste. She also believed the group found psychological satisfactions in refuge from unpleasant conditions and escape from disappointment or boredom. She thought they found substitute satisfactions in companionships and in forbidden experiences. These children read for "identification with, and projection of, their own growing and experimental selves. An individual's reading tended to reflect the assumption on his part of some role which he desired to play."

An unpublished study by Lynch[38] attempted to determine why children

[35] Rudman, Herbert C. "Informational Needs and Reading Interests of Children in Grades IV through VIII," *Elementary School Journal*, 55:502–12, May 1955.

[36] Vandament, William E., and W. A. Thalman. "An Investigation into the Reading Interests of Children," *Journal of Educational Research*, 49:467–70, February 1956.

[37] Wollner, Mary H. *Children's Voluntary Reading as an Expression of Individuality*. Contributions to Education No. 944. New York: Bureau of Publications, Teachers College, Columbia University, 1949.

[38] Lynch, Margaret. *Children's Ideas About Their Favorite Books*. Unpublished master's thesis (University of California, Berkeley, 1958).

chose what they did as their best-liked reading. She first ascertained the usual patterns of reading interests for a group of suburban children who had many books accessible in libraries, and then interviewed children who typified and who deviated from these accepted patterns. As other investigators had discovered, Lynch found that girls read more than boys but believed this favored group reached a peak of reading activity around ten years instead of the twelve or thirteen years of earlier investigations. This suggests the possibility that the suburban child in a "good" family and environment not only reads considerably but begins other activities, perhaps social in nature, at a comparatively early age. Lynch also found possibilities of the existence of the "lonesome" reader, but the "friendly" and "popular" reader occurs three times as frequently. After giving the usual results such as favorite titles and authors, Lynch comments on the interviews. She believes that this favored group used books "to explore life rather than to escape it." Some of them "used books to help them sort fact from fancy," some as a "means of finding ways to utilize their environment," or of doing things. "Many children used books to understand how adults think, to help them realize that life is a mixture of the good and the bad." The reliance on authors in series of books may have indicated that style is important. "Many of the children's comments in the interviews confirmed this interest in style, although the children seldom had a conscious understanding of what they were characterizing." Some of the children's criteria came from their value systems in which they viewed "goodness" in social rather than individual terms and in which the girls valued kindness and obedience, the boys helpfulness to others and bravery. Both boys and girls liked a "sad part" in a book, not because of a desire to express emotions but in recognition of the fact that a good plot requires variety and a change of pace. "An all happy story would be boring." Lynch finally warned that many of the authors and titles listed by these children are unknown to most teachers and librarians because they have been published in the last seven or eight years and are not the established juvenile classics.

Two studies of the reading interests of large samples of English children also went beyond a listing of favorite types and titles. Jenkinson's study[39] gave results for almost three thousand youth from twelve to fifteen years. She found the students' tastes different from those of adults and therefore questioned the school syllabus. Jenkinson believed that at this age books are read not so much for imbibing knowledge, even when the reader wants facts, as for their emotional content. In such books as *The Prince and the Pauper* there is a concern for identifying with social role rather than the social history which is a background to the tale. In a number of popular books such as *Heidi* one or both parents are dead,

[39] Jenkinson, A. J. *What Do Boys and Girls Read?* (2d ed.) London: Mettiner, 1946.

there is some taming of grown-ups, and the moral virtues of the hero or heroine are more evident than the most conscientious teacher could hope to improve upon. Jenkinson points out that analytical studies of fairy tales reveal some of the same universal fantasies and defense mechanisms as found in the favorite titles of this group of older children. She believes that fantasy is related to the child's stage of development, that the reader who gets something from *Heidi* may not be ready for *Emil and the Detectives* or *The Scarlet Pimpernel.*

In a second English study, Whitehead[40] used attitude-scale responses of nearly two thousand students in secondary schools between the ages of eleven and sixteen. For books commonly read in school the students agreed or disagreed with such statements as, "It was a waste of time to read this book," and "This book is all right to pass the time when you have nothing better to do." Preferred books included *Treasure Island, Prester John, Christmas Carol,* and *Kidnapped.* Unfavorable ratings were given to *A Tale of Two Cities, Gulliver's Travels,* and *The Pilgrim's Progress.* Whitehead presents evidence that in this age range, differences in sex, age, teacher, and school are "unimportant in determining attitude as compared with the qualities inherent in the novel itself." The characteristics of the preferred books, rated by adult judges, were easy language, dealing with themes "that are relatively immature emotionally," easy identification with the hero or heroine, and the "element of wish-fulfillment is comparatively open" and undisguised. The quality of "imaginative coherence" was of little influence on attitudes to the novels.

In conclusion, these and a few other studies of interests go beyond a surface list of favorite titles or themes in an attempt to get at the thorny problem of why different books are read by children of different ages. Studies of adult reading interests such as those of Hackett[41] have been confined largely to titles of best sellers. Hart[42] has indicated changes in content in the popular book in America. Tests of the Waples' hypotheses about reasons for adults' reading are still needed as well as a more systematic attack on some of the problems raised by Terman and Lima, Lynch, and the other investigators. As ordinarily planned, such studies of reading preferences can give only indirect evidence, can only suggest possible effects of reading. The investigations quoted, however, illustrate that it is possible to go below surface choices to get at reasons why children or adults read what they do. These reasons change with such factors as age, family circumstances, and the personality of the reader, but

[40] Whitehead, Frank. "The Attitudes of Grammar School Pupils Towards Some Novels Commonly Read in School," *British Journal of Educational Psychology, 26:* 104–111, 1956.

[41] Hackett, Alice. *Sixty Years of Best Sellers.* New York: Bowker, 1955.

[42] Hart, James D. *The Popular Book: A History of America's Literary Taste.* New York: Oxford University Press, 1950.

the most important factor is probably the interactive one of the qualities of the printed material. Somehow psychologists, teachers, and librarians must attempt to build bridges between the needs of the reader and the ideas or emotional tones of the printed page. When people find in reading some of the answers to their deepest needs, cognitive and affective, they are not only likely to become habitual readers but better persons because they are able to attack some of their problems through reading. Passing interest becomes permanent interest if reading supplies wants. Reading interests are both a product of previous experiences and a springboard to future activities. They give no direct evidence of the effects of reading, but they indicate circumstances in which there may be effects and give clues to what the effects may be in relation to the reader's needs.

## *Two Summaries of Studies on the Effects of Reading*

Gray[43] summarized some thirty reports related to possible social effects of reading in a general way which did not include direct evidence from the earlier studies. He believed that reading *may* influence (1) beliefs, (2) attitudes and morale, (3) public opinion, (4) voting, and (5) crime and anti-social behavior. He also agreed that comprehension and critical interpretation are influenced by the experience and personality of the reader.

Russell[44] summarized some seventy studies concerned with the personal impact of reading. He indicated the need for teachers and librarians to study the effects of reading and suggested that the empirical studies in this area may be categorized into four overlapping areas: (1) the characteristics of the material read, (2) the content of ideas communicated, (3) the traits of the reader, and (4) the overt responses made. Most of the studies on characteristics and content of materials are reported in Chapter 6 of this volume, on the traits or personality of the reader in Chapter 5, and some of the studies of overt responses in specific situations are described below. The writer believed that the researches cited in this area "give some clues to the complexity and subtlety of the impact of reading as measured by responses to printed materials. Most reading tests do not get at these deep-laid and wide-ranging responses . . . the effects are often personal and original and [that] the same passage may produce different effects on different students."

[43] Gray, William S. "The Social Effects of Reading," *School Review, 55*:269–77, May 1947.

[44] Russell, David H. "Some Research on the Impact of Reading," *English Journal, 47*:398–413, October 1958.

## *Memories of Children's Literature*

The psychology of memory is a relatively undeveloped field. The classic studies of Ebbinghaus dating back to 1885 stimulated interest in the process of forgetting but directed attention away from memory as a retrieval system. As commonly used, *memory* is a generic term implying previous experiences and including percepts, images, facts, and concepts. There is experimental evidence that children make use of memory as early as the first year of life. The content of older children's memories has been studied by the Dudychas.[45] Some of the influences of personality and emotions on memory were explored in Bartlett's *Remembering.*[46] On the basis of nearly twenty years' study of perceiving, learning, and remembering, Bartlett concluded that cognitive functioning, including memory, is influenced by the subject's interests, attitudes, emotions, and goals. In this approach recall is not mere reproduction but may be an active construction in which the attitude of the subject is the major determinant of the recall of the original situation. Bartlett was not concerned with the rote, veridical response of specific details, but his work applies to memories of literature not read for specific facts. For example, in a study of high school seniors' reactions to Hugh Walpole's novel *Fortitude,* Meckel[47] concluded that the vividness with which situations in this novel of family life are remembered appears to be related to the predispositions of the reader.

Paul[48] used one of Bartlett's stories and checked some of his theories in studies of the responses of female secretaries to elliptical and to explicated versions of a North American Indian folktale. He found that factors of familiarity, explication, and coherence all facilitated learning and remembering and supported Bartlett's theory of the concept of *schema* or internal organizations of past experiences which function as a unified whole. Paul further believed that such *schema* are reorganized by importations (additions of material), substitutions, and fragmentations. Most subjects showed importations and distortions when the stimulus material was gappy, ambiguous, and too long to be memorized in a rote fashion. Paul also hypothesized a difference in cognitive style of nonimporters

[45] Dudycha, G. J., and W. M. Dudycha. "Childhood Memories: A Review of the Literature," *Psychological Bulletin,* 38:668–82, 1941.

[46] Bartlett, Frederick C. *Remembering: A Study in Experimental and Social Psychology.* New York: Macmillan, 1932.

[47] Meckel, Henry C. *An Exploratory Study of the Responses of Adolescent Pupils to Situations in a Novel.* Unpublished doctoral dissertation (University of California, Berkeley, 1946).

[48] Paul, Irving H. "Studies in Remembering: The Reproduction of Connected and Extended Verbal Material," *Psychological Issues, 1,* No. 2, pp. 1–152, 1959.

and importers – the former was "leaner in structure" and more continuous and coherent. Such ideals give no direct effects of reading but clues to possible effects.

More direct claims for effects have been made in half a dozen other studies of the memories of adults for the literature of their childhood. An early study by Lind[49] of the beliefs of college students about the causes and effects of their childhood reading listed four main categories:

1. Reading as escape, including fantasy.
2. Reading as temporary diversion, including identification with a character.
3. Reading as an organizing influence on personality, including biography and clues to vocation.
4. Reading in relation to objective interests or instrumental values of reading.

Russell[50] studied beginning teachers' memories of childhood literature. Their written responses suggested five effects: (1) identification with characters; (2) emotional responses beyond identification as in humor, the thrill of adventure and fear; (3) contribution to overt activities as in dramatic play; (4) escapism, and (5) specific reactions to details. The memories were classified roughly as pleasant (50 per cent), unpleasant (30 per cent), and neutral (20 per cent). In a second study,[51] Russell asked elementary, secondary, and college level teachers to list books which had affected them most in childhood, in adolescence, and in adulthood. Approximately one hundred responses were obtained for each of the teacher groups. The most frequently listed effects of reading were "as a contribution to values, a philosophy of life, or religious convictions," and provision for "an increased understanding of human behavior and problems." The responses listed most rarely were exemplified by "reading for escape and relaxation," and "enjoyment of illustrations."

The respondents demonstrated considerable variation for childhood and adolescence influences with the "enjoyment of humor, adventure, or romance" mentioned most frequently. Responses related to adulthood concentrated more upon reading as contributing to "values, philosophy of life, and religious convictions." The patterns of response were found not to differ greatly for elementary, secondary, and college teachers.

[49] Lind, Katherine N. "Social Psychology of Children's Reading," *American Journal of Sociology, 41:*454–69, January 1936.

[50] Russell, David H. "Teachers' Memories and Opinions of Children's Literature," *Elementary English, 26:*475–82, December 1949.

[51] Russell, David H. "A Second Study of Teachers' Memories of Children's Literature," Paper given at American Educational Research Association, Chicago, Ill., February 1963.

Similarly, Collier and Gaier[52] asked students in classes in educational psychology to summarize their favorite childhood story, report the circumstances of first encountering it, and to compare present and past impressions of it. The women reported folk and fairy tales, fiction, and animal stories as their most frequent categories; for the men, the most frequent were fiction, folk and fairy tales, and animal stories, with religious stories, poetry, and biography well down the list. The fiction mentioned was labeled largely realistic – *Tom Sawyer* and *Robinson Crusoe* by the men and *Heidi* and *Little Women* by the women. Factors in the choices were a happy ending, the pictures, and the story heard before the age of six for the women and between seven and ten years for the men. About two-thirds of the group considered their old favorite to be their present preferred story for children.

Reports from a large number of respondents are found in a study by Weingarten[53] of 1,256 older students and adults to two questionnaires on the personal benefits of their voluntary reading. The average student checked four values, but the only one checked by more than half the group was the contribution of reading to a "philosophy of life." The benefits of reading in descending order of frequency were as follows: helped understanding of the meaning of life, 61 per cent; changed attitudes, 39 per cent; stimulated imitation in behavior of a character, 34 per cent; helped in finding the ideal self, 33 per cent; read about a problem similar to their own, 33 per cent; tried to develop personal qualities read about, 30 per cent; increased self-understanding through identification, 29 per cent; helped in the solution of their own problems, 20 per cent; and helped in the selection of a vocation, 11 per cent. The books reported most useful were the Bible, *Seventeen, The Robe, Seventeenth Summer, Of Human Bondage, The Prophet,* and the *Autobiography of Benjamin Franklin.* Despite these considerable percentages, Weingarten believed that only a small part of the reading of the group revealed developmental values to the reader.

Another study of high school students gave more optimistic results about the effects of reading than many others. One weakness of the study was the use of a questionnaire which may have invited favorable answers. One leading question was, "What books or magazines have had a good effect on you; bad effect on you?" Lorang[54] got lists of favorite books and magazines from 2,000 high school students and the statement from 75 per

[52] Collier, Mary J., and Eugene L. Gaier. "Adult Reactions to Preferred Childhood Stories," *Child Development, 29*:97–103, 1958.

[53] Weingarten, Samuel. "Developmental Values in Voluntary Reading," *The School Review, 62*:222–30, April 1954.

[54] Lorang, M. C. "The Effect of Reading on Moral Conduct and Emotional Experience," *Studies in Psychology and Psychiatry,* 6, No. 5, 1945.

cent of them that they had been influenced by such reading in either "moral conduct" or "emotional experience." These books and magazines were classified as desirable or undesirable by a jury of librarians and other professional persons, and the type of conduct and values represented in them were analyzed. In view of the individual nature of perception and response such an analysis may be questioned in relation to a wide range of students. Lorang believed, however, that she found some evidence of emotional response, imitation of behavior, identification tendencies, and other reactions.

Another study of memory plus testimony involved children in grades four to eight. Smith[55] used a "free response" technique in which they were asked to write about any reading material that had changed their thinking or attitudes; 60.7 per cent of them told of changes in attitudes which had taken place as a result of reading. Stories about people and about animals had this effect more often than any other type of content; 37.4 per cent of the attitude responses were concerned with people, and 33.3 per cent with animals; 30.1 per cent reported changes in concepts, ideas, and understandings in such areas as social studies, sports, science, animals, people. Only 9.2 per cent of the total responses indicated changes in behavior from reading. "In some of the cases changed thinking came as a result of information which corrected or clarified concepts, or yielded new concepts entirely; in other cases the change apparently took the form of modified attitudes; and in still other cases reading seemed to have resulted in changed behavior." Smith gave no details on how she categorized the responses.

This and the other investigations of memory plus free response illustrate a number of weaknesses in terms of methods of research. Because we know so little about the psychology of memory, its distortions and "importations," we cannot list specific effects for certain books or certain kinds of stories in a one-to-one relationship. Furthermore, when individual reactions are related to personality and needs, sometimes the most dramatic or vital data are lost in a general summary. In the tabulation of reactions not all the studies quoted used the safeguards needed in content analysis of responses. But perhaps the greatest weakness of this method is the source of the data – the subject's desire to give some congenial answers. This tendency may not be as great among adults as among children, but it seems probable that even among the adults, effects of reading are written down with greater frequency than they appeared, or influenced the subject, in actuality. With this reservation, it is still possible, however, to get some impression from memory studies of the kinds of effects reading may have. These impressions may be factually oriented or

[55] Smith, Nila. "Some Effects of Reading on Children," *Elementary English*, 25:271–78, May 1948.

emotionally toned; they may be concerned with literary qualities or answers to personal problems; they probably relate more often to attitude than to behavior.

## *Immediate Responses in Specific Reading Situations*

In addition to memory studies of possible long-term effects of reading, a number of empirical studies of more immediate reactions to verbal materials are available. These vary widely in the thoroughness with which the situational and response variables have been controlled and analyzed. They are probably as valuable in illustrating what future research workers might attempt as in contributing any final results to our present state of knowledge about effects. Because they are specific observations they suggest a number of interesting hypotheses. The studies are miscellaneous in character, so are summarized in order from young children to older children to adolescents to adults.

Cappa[56] studied the responses of 2,500 California kindergarten children to storybooks read by their teachers. These children showed enjoyment of familiar stories in a relaxed and secure situation. Their responses were categorized into eight types, the two most frequent of which were the desire to look at the book which had been read (38 per cent) and the request that the story be read or told by the teacher (27 per cent). Other responses were drawing pictures, dramatic play, and retelling of the story by children to other children. These responses were categorized as overt actions 68 per cent and verbalized activities 32 per cent.

Martin[57] tape-recorded the reactions of first graders to 26 "story hour" books. He found that the stories provided many opportunities for extending experiences such as in the acquisition of new words. The children enjoyed participation with rhyming words and motor activities. Probably the most frequent functions of the stories were stimulating the search for new experiences to discover what the world is like and providing opportunities to identify with persons, animals, and things in order to understand their own problems. The stories also gave chances to clarify what is meant by "right" and "wrong" and to learn cultural expectations for the children. In Alice Dolgleish's *Bears on Hemlock Mountain* the children identified with Jonathon's fears all the way over the mountain, and they enjoyed the tugboat's carefree disregard of elders in Gramatky's story *Little Toot.* The stories which brought the least response were the folktales *Puss in Boots* and *Stone Soup.*

[56] Cappa, Dante. *Reactions of Kindergarten Children to Story Books by Teachers.* Unpublished doctoral dissertation (University of California, Berkeley, 1953).

[57] Martin, Clyde. "But HOW Do Books Help Children?" *Library Journal,* October 15, 1955, pp. 2333–337.

Grace and Lohmann[58] studied the responses of boys and girls in the second grade to nine short stories depicting parent–child conflict situations. After hearing each story in an individual interview situation the child was asked to pretend he was a story character and to tell what he wanted to do and how he felt "inside." In order of frequency, the commonest responses were active opposition (42 per cent), simple compliance (28 per cent), constructive behavior (22 per cent), and emotional reactions (13 per cent). "The pattern of response of a child seems to be similar whether the mother or the father is the frustrating agent. Sex does not appear to be a determining factor in the development of the response pattern of a child."

Boyd and Mandler[59] studied the reponses of 96 third-grade children (eight- and nine-year-olds) to stimulus stories and pictures with either human or animal main characters. Their findings included the following:

1. Stories with human characters elicit more personal identification and involvement than animal stories.
2. Animal pictures tend to elicit more original material than human pictures.
3. Socially disapproved behavior in the stories elicits expressions of punishment and socially approved behavior more projection of the self.
4. Socially disapproved behavior by human characters may arouse more anxiety than such behavior by animal characters.

Foulds[60] analyzed responses of 28 Scottish children from nine to twelve years to poems, books, films, reading preferences, things to think about, a similes test, story completion, a play questionnaire, and a dramatic production. The children's choices of a character they most resembled corresponded closely to predictions of independent raters. In other words, a child's fictional choices are predictable because they cohere with other observable aspects of his personality. However, the child-fictional character relationship is secondary because it is dependent upon other factors which caused his original and customary daydreams, such as "instinctual drives" and home environment. Foulds suggests, therefore, that fiction can only reinforce existing tendencies.

Bone's[61] case report of extending children's experiences is somewhat more optimistic but based on more general observations. In guided read-

[58] Grace, H. A., and J. Lohmann. "Children's Reactions to Stories Depicting Parent-Child Conflict Situations," *Child Development, 23:*61–74, March 1952.

[59] Boyd, Nancy A., G. Mandler. "Children's Responses to Human and Animal Stories and Pictures," *Journal of Consulting Psychology, 19:*367–71, 1955.

[60] Foulds, Graham. "The Child's Response to Fictional Characters and Its Relationship to Personality Traits," *Character and Personality, 11:*64–75, September 1942.

[61] Bone, Robert. "Using Literature to Extend Children's Experiences," *Elementary English, 36:*314–18, May 1959.

ing around a theme some children appear to pick up new techniques of behavior and the majority appear to be influenced somewhat. A picture-discussion technique which included the use of Brink's *Caddie Woodlawn* gave evidence of new insights into different problems and traits of behavior.

An unpublished study by Regan[62] of the reaction of superior sixth graders to Mark Twain's *The Prince and the Pauper* showed that a study of several of Twain's writings enabled the more perceptive members of the group to "become accustomed to thinking of Mark Twain as a social 'critic,' although their notions of social criticism are naturally immaturely formed." Asked the main idea of the story the most frequent response (54 per cent) was categorized as "You should be yourself." Other interpretations of about equal frequency were "You must work hard to make your dreams come true," "Everyone is equal and should have an equal chance," and "It's harder to be a pauper than a prince." Asked why they thought Twain wrote the book, the majority replied in the category, "He didn't like English royalty; he preferred the American form of government." Such responses illustrate the distortions of habit and stereotyped thinking. ("You must work hard to make your dreams come true" has no relation to the story because Tom Cantry's dream was fulfilled accidentally, not as a result of hard work.) They also illustrate that with careful preparation and collateral reading some superior twelve-year-olds are ready to begin to generalize about an author's purpose – half of the children suggested that the book was a political or social satire. In the total number of responses, however, a majority of the children were still inclined to seek a personal maxim in their reading of the "Be yourself" variety.

In a completely different category a number of studies have shown the functional or instrumental values of reading for children in the upper elementary or high school grades. As only one example of a considerable number of studies, Rudolf[63] showed that, at the eighth grade level, improved skills in various kinds of reading paid off in terms of more general academic achievements.

Another group of studies relates to attitudes. Investigations such as those of Jackson[64] and of Carlsen[65] give fairly clear evidence that the reading of materials that is favorable to Negroes or other ethnic groups will influence elementary and secondary students toward more favorable

[62] Regan, Carole. "Response of Fourteen Sixth Grade Students to *The Prince and the Pauper*," Unpublished term paper (University of California, Berkeley, 1962).

[63] Rudolf, Kathleen B. *Effective Reading Instruction on Achievement in Eighth Grade Social Studies.* Contributions to Education No. 945. New York: Bureau of Publications, Teachers College, Columbia University, 1949.

[64] Jackson, Evalene P. "Effects of Reading Upon Attitudes Towards the Negro Race," *Library Quarterly, 14*:47–54, January 1944.

[65] Carlsen, George Robert. "A Study of the Effects of Reading Literature About the Negro on the Racial Attitudes of Eleventh Grade Students in Northern Schools," Unpublished doctoral dissertation (University of Minnesota, Minneapolis, 1948).

attitudes to members of such groups. There is, however, no basis for believing in a one-to-one relationship of cause and effect. For example, Carlsen found that results for eleventh grade students depended upon previous attitudes. When students in Northern schools were favorable or neutral in attitude toward Negroes before they read books about them, their attitudes became more favorable; those who were previously unfavorable became more unfavorable. Material containing propaganda contrary to the reader's views may result in confusion and irritation, not a change of attitude. The positive results are clear, furthermore, for only rather immediate, not permanent, attitudes. It seems reasonable to hypothesize that attitudes created by reading can be nullified by other influences or that, if they are to be sustained, they must be strengthened by other experiences in the home, on the playground, in school, and in other community activities.

Still another group of investigations, often involving adults and mass media other than books, rather consistently shows positive effects in limited areas for a short time. As suggested above, some of these studies have been summarized by Hovland[66] and are the work of social psychologists or "communications experts." A few examples from newspaper reading illustrate typical findings. During World War II Seward and Silvers[67] tested beliefs in the accuracy of newspaper reports. They believed that they found evidence of the familiar phenomenon that people select reading to support their predispositions. They also found evidence of: (1) "a tendency to believe one's own government rather than the enemy," (2) "a tendency to believe good news rather than bad," and (3) "a tendency to believe news adverse to its source rather than favorable to its source." In a later study Kay[68] stated, on the basis of intensive interviews, that anxiety determines news reading behavior. He found that persons with high anxiety levels read considerably about themselves and their problems; individuals with both high anxiety and low anxiety read for information which might reduce their anxiety. Tannenbaum[69] found that different newspaper headlines introducing the same news story exerted a significant influence on the opinions of college students. Another study[70] found that newspaper subscribers differed from non-subscribers in their knowledge and attitudes concerning fluoridation of public water supplies.

[66] Hovland, Carl J. "Effects of the Mass Media of Communication," *Handbook of Social Psychology, II* (Gardner Lindzey, ed.). Reading, Mass.: Addison-Wesley Publishing Co., 1954; pp. 1062–1103.

[67] Seward, John P., and Evely E. Silvers. "A Study of Belief of Accuracy in Newspaper Reports," *Journal of Psychology, 12:*209–18, October 1943.

[68] Kay, Herbert. "Toward an Understanding of News-Reading Behavior," *Journalism Quarterly, 31:*15–32, Winter 1954.

[69] Tannenbaum, Percy H. "The Effects of Headlines on the Interpretation of New Stories," *Journalism Quarterly, 30:*189–97, Spring 1953.

[70] Brinton, James E., and L. Norman McKown. "Effects of Newspaper Reading on Knowledge and Attitude," *Journalism Quarterly, 38:*187–95, Spring 1961.

In the miscellaneous researches summarized above there is a common thread of positive evidence of specific influence upon information and attitude and sometimes even behavior, at least for a limited time. Although the weight of the evidence is on this side, some studies give less grounds for optimism. For example, Havighurst[71] had children and adolescents write about "The Person I Would Like to Be Like." Only about 10 per cent of the characteristics listed could be classed as historical personages or fictional heroes about which the students had read. The "ideal self" was determined much more frequently by older persons known to the writers. Banks[72] also found that American historical biography had little influence on the behavior patterns or judgments of reputation of eleventh-grade students. Reactions to 28 well-known Americans were not changed by the acquisition of further information about them during a semester's study. Negative results were also obtained in another investigation of the effects of the reading and discussion of biographical literature in Lodge's[73] investigation involving eighth-grade pupils in two small California schools. The children wrote on the topic "The Person I Would Like to be Like" before and after work on an eight-weeks' biography unit which included such books as *Abe Lincoln Grows Up, Young Hickory, Invincible Louisa, Narcissa Whitman,* and *The Story of Clara Barton.* Data were also collected from other writing and by interviews. Both direct and indirect measurements indicated that "the influence of biography on the moral ideology of the [young] adolescent is slight." Traits prized by this age group were being friendly and easy to get along with, being happy and cheerful, and being honest. Changes in identification with favorite characters or persons were also infrequent.

Perhaps one reason for the lack of positive results in these studies is that they are less concerned with the specific facts, attitudes, or aspects of behavior studied in the investigations described earlier and involve broader beliefs and values. The term *value* here refers to that which is desirable or worthy of esteem for its own sake. It relates to what we hold "to be good and true and right, or the reverse." Values are involved in important ideas like honesty, charity, loyalty, and justice. These are meanings related to the self. As Allport[74] has put it, they are "matters of importance" as distinct from mere matters of fact and are therefore less likely to be affected by a single article, poem, or book than are more

[71] Havighurst, Robert J., M. Z. Robinson, and M. Dorr. "The Development of the Ideal Self in Childhood and Adolescence," *Journal of Educational Research, 40:*241–57, 1946.

[72] Banks, T. and others. "We Tested Some Beliefs About the Biographical Method," *School Review, 59:*157–63, March 1951.

[73] Lodge, Helen C. *The Influence of the Study of Biography on the Moral Ideology of the Adolescent at the Eighth Grade Level.* Unpublished doctoral dissertation (University of California, Berkeley, 1953).

[74] Allport, Gordon W. "Values and Our Youth," *Teachers College Record, 63:*211–19, December 1961.

superficial phenomena. Snapper[75] explored the reactions of 55 high school juniors to "value-laden generalizations" in the form of statements and as embedded in anecdotes and incomplete plots and arguments. An example was "Helping the poor at great personal sacrifice is better than acquiring wealth." His analysis showed that 46 per cent of patterns of response were logically inconsistent and that strong expressions of agreement or disagreement with the statements or assumptions or "value-laden generalizations" had little predictive power in relation to the verbally described social situations. Explanations of positions were focused on details to an almost complete neglect of the broader assumptions on values. Snapper concluded that "It is presumptuous to assume that a specific story will contribute to a specific value for a particular student. Selection [of material] is not so important as what is done with a story in a classroom." He further believes that continued attention should be given to the recognition and challenging of "value-laden" assumptions but that logical analysis is "a fallible technique" for evaluating characters and people.

Thayer and Pronko[76] investigated a possible cause of difficulty with character values contained in fiction. They administered a test of attitudes toward controversial moral issues and a measure of desirable and undesirable personality traits to a group of college sophomores and then checked their reactions to characters in fiction of an ambiguous type. They found that without description or with ambiguous description the students tended to ascribe desirable traits to a character they liked and undesirable characteristics to someone disliked. When the stories contained complex or somewhat undesirable moral issues, they tended to color the reader's imagery and conceptualization. "Functional cues may take precedence over structural cues in an ambiguous reading situation." One theory in regard to values suggested by Bratton[77] is that it is possible to combine studies of classical writers such as Emerson and Thoreau and Hawthorne with fiction more directly related to youth's problems and values.

## *Conclusion*

The empirical studies quoted in this chapter leave little room for doubt that the act of reading has effects on the reader. While there is still no evidence that the effects are as independent and profound as some philos-

[75] Snapper, J. Marion. *A Study of High School Juniors' Reaction to and Use of Literary Assumptions.* Unpublished doctoral dissertation (University of California, Berkeley, 1958).

[76] Thayer, Leo O., and N. H. Pronko. "Factors Affecting Conceptual Perception in Reading," *Journal of General Psychology. 61*:51–59, July 1959.

[77] Bratton, Dorothy. "Reading for Therapy," *English Journal, 46*:339–46, September 1957.

ophers, English teachers, or librarians have posited, this lack of documentation may be a result of inadequate methods and materials of research rather than the meagerness or superficiality of the effects themselves. We have evidence which goes beyond enthusiastic but subjective testimony. Reasoning by analogy, parallels in psychology, and the stronger conclusions from specific studies focused on specific behavior resulting from use of the mass media and inferences from studies of reading interests all help to add weight to a positive conclusion. Some of the more detailed (if unvalidated) evidence suggesting effects has been found in the careful analysis of adults' memories of the effects of poems and stories and books during their childhood. A group of experimental studies with subjects ranging from kindergartners to adults gives evidence of specific effects under controlled conditions. These and the other reports add up to concrete proof. They suggest, however, that it is unwise to talk about the general effects of reading. We can only discuss the responses of certain individuals to particular materials under clearly defined conditions. This usual scientific caution, however, need not be perceived as a limiting factor. There are many more kinds of material to be tried out under various experimental conditions before we have a complete catalogue of possible effects of the literary experience. In Chapters 10 and 11 are suggestions for what parents of young children and teachers of older children can do to encourage lively responses and more than temporary effects.

The evidence seems equally clear that if we are to use its influence on ideas and behavior as one of the aims of literature study, we must discard the vague, sentimental approach that "books are good for children." The evidence here adduced suggests that we must at least be at the stage of saying "Some reading is good for some children at certain times." In elementary school, but more particularly at secondary and college levels, the aims of literature study may also be affected. Literature can be studied as types and as techniques and perhaps in terms of the facts surrounding its composition. But in addition to these intellectual goals, and especially perhaps with younger children, it can also be taught as experimental involvement culminating in fundamental concepts of the self, of the motivations of others, and of human relationships. If the creative and disciplined writer can organize the chaotic stuff of experience his writing may be of considerable help to his reader. The chief aim of teaching some literature in the fourth grade may be emotional response; in the sophomore college class it may be intellectual grasp of the style or subtle thought, but at neither level are the effects completely one or the other.

*Part Three*

# Applications

# CHAPTER 9 | Reading and Mental Health: Clinical Approaches[1]

When asked to write about any book that had been significant to him during his high school years, a college freshman who was a superior student in English stated, "I found I was able to see myself and some of my problems in the character and difficulties of the main character of the book. After a few pages I found I was not merely reading the book, I was also living it."[1] The book was Salinger's *Catcher in the Rye*.

In reply to the same question another student said of *Portrait of the Artist as a Young Man*, "In reading Joyce's novel I *was* the 'young man.' I had had no such feeling of empathy before this experience."[2] Commenting on the book that "affected you most" in childhood an English teacher wrote of Kate Seredy's *The Good Master* as follows: "The father of the Hungarian family became my idol because I had no father." Asked the same question about reading in adolescence that had most impact another teacher named Hugo's *Les Miserables*, and added "[This book] awakened an interest in social injustice . . . and made me aware [probably for the first time fully aware] of the insecurity and heartaches caused by poverty."

These and other introspective reports suggest that the act of reading may sometimes give the reader greater self-insight and better understanding of others. Such desirable outcomes are often equated with mental health. The study of imaginative literature needs no justification as a worthy pursuit in its own right, but sometimes parents and teachers (and literary scholars) become interested in the uses of literature. For example, can reading be used to foster the social and self-adjustments of

[1] Russell, D. H., and Caroline Shrodes. "Contributions of Research in Bibliotherapy to the Language Arts Program," *School Review*, 58:335–42, 411–20, September, October, 1950.

[2] Whitman, Robert S. "Significant Books and Their Impact on Superior English Students," Unpublished term paper (University of Illinois, Urbana, 1963).

children, or youth, or even adults? Can reading about one's problems in fiction help one to solve them in fact?

The process of using books for psychotherapy has been specified in the label bibliotherapy. As suggested below, the idea has been put into practice in many hospitals and by a few teachers of English. The label and the process have not been widely accepted by psychologists, and particularly by experimental psychologists, who want some harder evidence than present case studies can give. However, some clinical psychologists have been willing to try out the process with individual patients and have reported occasional successes in using books to improve adjustment to self or to others. The case against bibliotherapy has been summarized by Jahoda[3] in a review of research on possible effects of reading in relation to censorship. She concluded, "The examination of psychological assumptions about the impact of books made by nonpsychologists yields a somewhat confused picture, in which definitions are absent or tautological, and assertions about impact range over a wide area. . . . There is a large overlap in content matter between all media of mass communication. . . . It is virtually impossible to isolate the impact of one of these media on a population that is exposed to all of them."

Nevertheless, some of the possible uses of bibliotherapy have been reviewed by Russell and Shrodes,[4] and Shrodes[5] has developed a theory of bibliotherapy which states a number of useful hypotheses in psychological terms. As suggested in a section below, the case for bibliotherapy has not been established in terms of clear-cut research evidence, but the present state of knowledge provides some serviceable working hypotheses for teachers, librarians, and clinical workers. These must be considered in the larger context of what is meant by mental health.

## *Mental Health*

In the United States the phrase *mental hygiene* came into use in the early 1900's, influenced by Clifford Beers'[6] book, *A Mind That Found Itself*, an account of his incarceration in "lunatic asylums" and his courageous struggle to achieve a more normal existence. In subsequent years the term

[3] Jahoda, Marie. *The Impact of Literature: A Psychological Discussion of Some Assumptions in the Censorship Debate*. New York: American Book Publishers Council, 1954. (Mimeographed).

[4] Russell, D. H., and Caroline Shrodes. "Contributions of Research in Bibliotherapy to the Language Arts Program," *School Review*, 58:335–42, 411–20, September, October, 1950.

[5] Shrodes, Caroline. *Bibliotherapy: A Theoretical and Clinical Experimental Study*. Unpublished doctoral dissertation (University of California, Berkeley, 1949).

[6] Beers, Clifford W. *A Mind That Found Itself*. New York: Longmans, Green, 1907.

*mental health* brought to the reader's or listener's mind a picture of mental illness or severe personality disturbance. The notion that mental health concerns "crazy people" in "lunatic asylums" has been gradually supplanted by the idea of positive characteristics related to one's functioning as an individual or as a member of a group. Most descriptions of mental health have consisted of lists of desirable traits characterizing the well-adjusted person. For example, one list[7] contained the following items:

1. *Objective judgment:* the ability to look at all kinds of facts squarely and accurately.
2. *Autonomy:* the ability to deal with daily events in a self-starting, self-directing manner.
3. *Emotional maturity:* the ability to react to events with emotions appropriate in degree and kind to the nature of the situation.
4. *Self-realizing drive:* the habit of working purposefully to one's full capacity.
5. *Self-acceptance:* a positive, self-respecting attitude toward one's self.
6. *Respect for others:* the same attitude toward others.

The authors of this formidable list suggested that mental health consists in striving for a balance among these various objectives, but more rigorous psychologists who insist on experimental backing find the evidence for such concepts vague and elusive.

Smith,[8,9] for example, has pointed out that "mental health is inherently an *evaluative* concept and that science has not yet learned how to deal surefootedly with values." He further states that "greater concern with positive mental health has not been accompanied by proportionate gain in research and scientific understanding." Such words as *normality* and *adjustment* are value-laden words. Does normality mean averageness? Adjustment to what? Smith recognizes that "research is not going to solve our value problems for us, to absolve us from having to make responsible decisions," but he suggests that research can contribute to the identification and clarification of human values which will give a "toehold on positive mental health." Although research has not so far provided any complete answers, it still seems possible to speak with some assurance about the historical development of the idea of mental health and some of its possible components.

At different times the mental hygienist, the teacher, and the clinical psychologist have stressed three concepts of mental health:

[7] Peck, R. F., and J. V. Mitchell, Jr. *Mental Health.* What Research Says to the Teacher, No. 24. Washington, D.C.: National Education Association, 1962.

[8] Smith, M. Brewster. "Mental Health Reconsidered: A Special Case of the Problem of Values in Psychology," *American Psychologist, 16:*299–306, June 1961.

[9] Smith, M. Brewster. "Research Strategies Toward a Conception of Positive Mental Health," *American Psychologist, 14:*673–81, 1959.

1. *The mentally healthy person is adjusted to his group.* He gets along well with his peers; he is a social success; he participates in many community activities.
2. *The mentally healthy person understands and accepts himself and others.* This concept emphasizes the individual's unique development. He is ordinarily self-sufficient. He may be more solitary than the somewhat extrovert person of the first definition. He has developed "a sense of self" as advocated by Jersild[10] and others.
3. The mentally healthy person is *"aware, identified, skeptical, responsible, employed and tense."*[11] This definition of the well-adjusted person suggests that he is prepared for living in the modern world. He must be ready for changes. He must be aware of different sides. He must be able to attack and to solve his problems.

These three aims or philosophies of mental health all have meaning for those who work with groups of children, adolescents, or adults, but one of them may be more important than the others for a certain person. Probably no one of the concepts is more important than the other in considering all children, but one of them may apply much more than the other two to the personality of any one child or adolescent. There are different desirable forms of adjustment for different individuals. One child's group skills, for example, may easily excel those of another, but each may be making an adequate adjustment. One adolescent may be more sensitive than another to his own and the world's problems but both achieve a reasonably happy, purposeful, and productive life.

The varied nature of mental health in different individuals is underlined by other attempts to describe some of the components of this goal. As suggested above, some of these may be vague or slippery concepts, but such writers as Jahoda have produced lists with some scientific backing. For example, she suggested multiple criteria for mental health in one article[12] and later analyzed six major themes or categories reflected in clinical reports rather than experimental evidence.[13] In what Smith called "her insightful commentary or distinctions and convergences of the writings of significant theorists of different schools" Jahoda included the following components of mental health:

[10] Jersild, A. T. *In Search of Self.* New York: Bureau of Publications, Teachers College, Columbia University, 1952.

[11] Barclay, Dorothy. "Roots and Branches of Personality," *New York Times Magazine,* August 9, 1953.

[12] Jahoda, Marie. "Toward a Social Psychology of Mental Health," *Symposium on the Healthy Personality* (M. J. E. Senn, ed.). New York: Josiah Macy, Jr., Foundation, 1950, pp. 211–30.

[13] Jahoda, Marie. *Current Concepts of Positive Mental Health.* New York: Basic Books, 1958.

1. *Attitudes toward the self,* including validity of the self-concept, self-acceptance, and sense of identity.
2. *Growth, development, and self-actualization.*
3. *Integration,* including balance of psychic forces, a unifying view of life, and resistance to stress.
4. *Autonomy,* including development toward independence.
5. *Clear perception of reality,* including freedom from ego-involvement and empathy or social sympathy.
6. *Environmental mastery* – a miscellaneous group related to adequacy in love, work, and play; efficiency in meeting environmental demands; and capacity for adaptation and adjustment.

The redundancy in the list is evident. Systematic study of correlation and overlap of scores on various measures of these traits may, in time, enable students of mental health to simplify the list or indicate the relative importance of individual traits for specific individuals. A multiple basis for mental health will probably always be a congenial theory for many psychologists and sociologists and, depending on their value systems, individuals will differ in the emphasis they wish to give to each characteristic.

In concluding his critique of mental health concepts Smith suggests that research along two main lines is desirable, some dealing with what he calls "internal system properties" (such as self-attitudes and integration), and properties of the external system (such as perception of reality, environmental mastery). These two categories are related to the historical development of the idea of mental health which for a time emphasized social adjustment but which later turned to self-understanding.

Even in these broad categories, however, there may be disagreement about relative importance. For example Ciardi[14] speaks of the

> peer-group that has become the fetish of the religion of "social adjustment", a religion which, in an earlier development of the tribe, was called "conformity". . . . There can, of course, be dangers, both real and imagined, in letting a child lose touch with others of his own age. The left-out child may have an unhappy childhood and such a childhood can damage both the child and the person the child grows into. On the other hand, a manageable amount of social maladjustment can be just the blessing that drives a child to introspection and even to ideas.

In one sense, Ciardi is arguing, not for the elimination of all difficulties, but for some balance between social and personal maladjustments. He might also agree that the mentally healthy person is aware of problems, identified with ideas, employed in working on disturbing situations, and a bit tense rather than complacent. This chapter is concerned, then, not

[14] Ciardi, John. "Manner of Speaking," *Saturday Review, 46:*16, May 11, 1963.

only with the role of printed and literary materials in one's social adjustment and self-adjustment, but also as an aid in working on one's problems. It is the writer's opinion that the study of literature has many facets and purposes but that one of these (perhaps a minor one except for a few parents, teachers, and clinical workers) is the use of literature to help the individual understand himself and his associates and to grapple with some of his problems. Reading may occasionally be a form of psychotherapy.

## *Identification*

The process called identification, exemplified in the first two examples at the beginning of this chapter, is usually regarded as a fundamental part of bibliotherapy. Because of its importance, the concept is here described before consideration of the more inclusive term bibliotherapy.

Identification is classified as one of the so-called defense mechanisms or mechanisms of adjustment, the part of Freudian theory first domesticated within American academic psychology. Freud began to write about the mechanisms in the 1890's and by 1900 he had named repression, projection, identification, and condensation. Later he added fixation and regression, and Ernest Jones in 1908 added what was to become perhaps the best-known mechanism – what he called rationalization. Although many American psychologists of the time and later did not accept all psychoanalytic theory, they found the concepts useful in explaining human motivation and behavior. In American psychology since 1910 there has not been a systematic study of the mechanisms, and so there is a consequent lack of experimental evidence about their nature. Many writers relate mechanisms to the self-concept. As Hilgard[15] pointed out in 1949 "all the mechanisms imply a self-reference, and [that] the mechanisms are not understandable unless we adopt a concept of the self." He bolstered his point by some experimental evidence of the mechanisms as "defenses against anxiety" and as "self-deceptive." The latter characteristic occurs in the "*denial* of impulses or of traits, or of memories" and in *disguise* of them, such as occurs in projection and identification. The need for such self-deception arises from the more fundamental need to maintain or to restore self-esteem. Hilgard concluded that the mechanisms may be integrated with other aspects of motivation and learning provided that this self-reference is accepted.

Stimulated by Hilgard's paper, students of the self-concept made many empirical studies in succeeding years; but these have been neither world-shaking nor very illuminating. In a review of over five hundred studies of

[15] Hilgard, E. R. "Human Motives and the Concept of the Self," *American Psychologist, 4*:374–82, 1949.

the self-concept up to 1958 Wylie[16] found many explorations of the topic, few solid data about the nature and connections of the self-concept, and little further evidence about the relationship of the self-concept and identification.

Similarly, the experimental study of identification as such has been somewhat unsatisfactory. This may be partly due to lack of agreement on what identification is. As Bronfenbrenner[17] has suggested, the term has had three loose conceptions: "(1) *behavioral* (acting like one's parent), (2) *motivational* (wanting to be like one's parent), and (3) *emotional* (being effectively involved, positively or negatively, with one's parent)." Elsewhere Bronfenbrenner[18] describes these as conscious or unconscious identity in overt behavior, motivation or disposition to act like another, and psychological forces compelling a child to emulate a model.

In an introduction to a series of articles on identification and learning theory, Mowrer[19] concludes that "identification is a concept of extraordinary scope and significance. But it is also evident that the phenomenon needs to be more sharply defined logically and more fully investigated empirically." In the same series Martin[20] suggested some developmental applications of identification and concluded that "identification is not just conscious imitation of behavior . . . Johnny does not behave *like* his father; he *is* his father." Parsons[21] also has suggested that shifts in meaning or kind of identification are typical and are a function of the developmental characteristics of a child. Identifications in early stages are diffuse and related to concrete behavior. In later stages they are more differentiated and organized around symbolic role-entities. Furthermore, what the child strives to internalize will vary with the content and clarity of his reciprocal relationships with older people. He will learn, for example, to seek a different type of solution to needs from his mother and from a friend as he learns that these two are different. Havighurst and colleagues[22] believe that the importance of family figures to the child older than ten

[16] Wylie, Ruth C. *The Self-Concept: A Critical Survey of Pertinent Research Literature.* Lincoln: University of Nebraska Press, 1961.

[17] Bronfenbrenner, W. "Family Structure and Development," *Newsletter,* Division of Development Psychology, American Psychological Association, Fall, 1958, pp. 1–4.

[18] Bronfenbrenner, W. "Freudian Theories of Identification and Their Derivatives," *Child Development, 31:*15–40, March 1960.

[19] Mowrer, O. H. "Learning Theory and Identification: I. Introduction," *Journal of Genetic Psychology, 84:*197–99, 1954.

[20] Martin, William E. "Learning Theory and Identification: III. The Development of Values in Children," *Journal of Genetic Psychology, 84:*211–17, 1954.

[21] Parsons, T., and R. F. Bales. *Family Socialization and Interaction Process.* Glencoe, Illinois: Free Press, 1955.

[22] Havighurst, R. J., Myra Robinson, and Mildred Dorr. "The Development of the Ideal Self in Children and Adolescents," *Journal of Educational Research, 40:*241–57, 1946.

shows a decrease with increasing age. Around six to eight years identification is with parents. Then it radiates from the family circle to other attractive adults and finally becomes stabilized in later adolescence around a nonexistent, composite self.

Other studies and observations suggest that identification through literature is easy and common in preschool years and the primary grades.[23] Only gradually are distinct barriers between reality and fantasy established. In the story-listening situation, with some of the barriers down, the child often identifies himself with a character in the story. As soon as he hears that Peter Rabbit is a naughty little rabbit, he feels sympathy for him, and the good little rabbits being temporarily disposed of in the blackberry patch, he becomes Peter in his adventures in Mr. McGregor's garden. Before ten or eleven years the comics are an incitement to dramatic play or the actual imitation and working out of situations and events depicted, but from eleven or twelve years onward there is evidence of a different impact, more in accord with the Aristotelian hypothesis that reading can be a substitute gratification for wants and impulses which need not be acted out. The susceptible adolescent and the vulnerable adult, however, may continue to find gratifications in reading, some at the level of simple escape; others arrive at completely unrealistic satisfactions which widen the gulf between the real world and the world of fantasy. As suggested in the discussion of mental health, the involvement in fantasy by children, adolescents, and adults is a matter of degree not of black and white, and may range from desirable to undesirable, from productive stimulation of imagination to unhealthy absorption in an unreal world. Because of a certain connotation that identification is undesirable beyond childhood it may be pointed out that older adolescents and young adults, through identification or projection, sometimes perceive accurately the motivations of parents or older friends. Such insight may be productive of tolerance of frailties and more realistic attitudes toward their limitations and strengths, including the reduction of guilt feelings which may have resulted from earlier rejection of parental standards.

A number of such reasons for encouraging identification have been stated, often without empirical evidence, but there may be values in fostering it occasionally in home, school, and library through story hours, selected television, recordings, drama, and other devices. Through identification with people and ideas children may learn to accept their culture and find their places in it. Through play they may develop insights into their own anxieties and other emotional difficulties. "Through play a child liquidates some of his problems and relieves himself of worry and anxiety by talking about and dramatizing the things that disturb him."[24]

[23] Russell, D. H. "Identification Through Literature," *Childhood Education, 25:* 397–401, May 1949.

[24] Lambert, Clara. "Identification Through Play," *Childhood Education, 25:*402–405, 1949.

This suggests the therapeutic values of play which can be extended to other imaginative activities, including listening to and reading stories. The theory of catharsis through literature goes back to Aristotle and relates to the purging of emotions through the uncensored and spontaneous release of feelings. Identification involves catharsis because the feeling that one is a certain character implies that one participates in his motivations and conflicts, lives his life, and shares his emotions. The problem of the emotions may be resolved by release of tension through substitute or symbolic gratification. If emotions are being repressed, identification may permit the emergence of latent affect. The concept of identification, accordingly, takes us into an examination of what happens during response to literature and in the process we label bibliotherapy. Lack of firm empirical data beyond a considerable range of clinical reports dictates that the discussion be labeled a theory of bibliotherapy.

## *A Theory of Bibliotherapy*

In a theoretical-clinical study Shrodes[25] described bibliotherapy as "grounded on the theory that there is an integral relationship between the dynamics of the personality and the dynamics of the aesthetic experience." With such relationship the experience "may be utilized for personality assessment, adjustment and growth." She believes as follows:

> Response to imaginative literature parallels closely the dynamic processes that occur in psychotherapy; namely, identification, projection, catharsis, transference, insight, and growth. The last is made possible through the reader's exposure to comparative value systems which may provide a stimulus and foundation for building a philosophy of life.

Shrodes and other writers believe that bibliotherapy may be used as an adjunct to other therapy. Especially when the individual's problems are not deep-seated or overwhelming it may be used with considerable economy of time compared to psychoanalysis. It may also be used with considerable variety of available material. Once a student's or patient's difficulties have been diagnosed, it is not difficult to find short stories, novels, or other literature which parallel the individual's experience. The individual may reject these materials or may find in them at least some partial solution to his own problems. Parents and teachers should undoubtedly beware of playing amateur psychiatrist, but when difficulties are fairly accessible the reading of selected material related to the individual's problem may help.

Shrodes[26] states some of the assumptions and theory of bibliotherapy:

[25] Shrodes, Caroline. *Bibliotherapy: A Theoretical and Clinical Experimental Study.* Unpublished doctoral dissertation (University of California, Berkeley, 1949).

[26] Shrodes, Caroline. "The Dynamics of Reading: Implications for Bibliotherapy," *ETC.*, *18:*21–33, April 1961.

> Reading, like all other human behavior, is a function of the total personality. When we read fiction, poetry, or drama, we perceive selectively in accordance with our needs, goals, defenses, and values. Parallel in substance and function to the primary phases of psychotherapy, the vicarious experience induced by reading includes identification, projection, and introjection; transference of emotion from early experience to current symbols of it; catharsis; and insight. However, the reader will abstract from the work of art only what he is able to perceive and organize; what he experiences and feels will determine the nature of his perceptions and the meaning he attaches to them. He may make an identification that will enhance his self regard; he may project onto a character feelings that have been repressed. He may introject meaning that will satisfy his needs and reject implications that are threatening to his ego.

The summary suggests that the process of bibliotherapy is engendered, usually not by didactic writing, but by imaginative literature in the form of fiction, drama, poetry, and nondidactic biography. Didactic writing with express directions about how to achieve positive thinking or peace of mind may contribute to intellectual awareness of a problem but will seldom elicit the emotional experience which makes therapy possible. It is the artist who has created a character in a context of human experience who has the power to stimulate the reader to see himself and others, to be the person depicted, and thus to grow in self or social awareness.

In exposition of the above summary, bibliotherapy may be explained theoretically in terms of *identification, catharsis,* and *insight,* terms originating in psychoanalytic literature and viewed with some suspicion by many American psychologists. In such terms, bibliotherapy becomes a process of identifying with another character or group so that feelings are released and the individual develops a greater awareness of his own motivations and rationalizations for his behavior. *Identification* is the real or imagined affiliation of oneself (or sometimes a parent or a friend) with a person or group in the story, poem, or drama. Identification may be facilitated by familiarity of persons or situations depicted. It may augment self-esteem if the character is admired or increase feelings of belonging by reducing the sense of difference from others. It may increase understanding of the parent or friend, be productive of a more realistic attitude toward their limitations or strengths, and even reduce a sense of guilt which was a product of earlier difficulties with that parent or friend.

Such a description suggests that identification usually involves *catharsis.* The fact that the reader feels he is the character read about means that he shares the character's motivations and conflicts, and expresses vicariously his emotions. As the reader puts himself in the place of others he comes to understand the needs and aspirations of these others — and of himself. The reading may therefore provide for a release of tension through symbolic gratification of socially unacceptable urges or substitute gratification of socially approved motives.

As a third stage, if the self-recognition in identification is borne out in reality, the identification represents *insight,* seeing oneself in the behavior of the character, achieving an awareness of one's own motivations and needs. If his adjustments to life situations are maladaptive, the individual's recognition of himself in the character may help in breaking certain habits. On the other hand, if the character appears to work out a satisfactory solution to his problem, there is an opportunity for the reader to incorporate some of the character's behavior in his own solutions to a problem.

Identification does not always lead to insight for it may consist simply in imputing one's own motives to others, in reading one's own interpretation into the behavior of the fictional character. One form of such identification comes in seeking a scapegoat or venting upon the character a strong emotion felt in an earlier affective experience. In general, however, the close interrelationships and interaction of identification, catharsis, and insight are apparent. Other descriptions of the possible therapeutic effects of reading, notably that of Lesser,[27] also employ psychoanalytic concepts.

Lesser believes that three unconscious processes can be distinguished in response to the reading of imaginative literature. They are, of course, intermingled with one another and also with all the conscious processes involved in reading.

*Unconscious Perception and Understanding:* The unconscious can immediately and intuitively understand some things which our conscious intelligence finds puzzling and even inexplicable. This unconscious perception and understanding of literature is basically "spectatorial"; it requires that one part of us remain aware of the fictional, or make-believe, character of the reading experience.

*Unconscious Acting Out:* When we read imaginative literature, we are not only spectators, we are also actors. We unconsciously participate in the action of the works we read. This process is similar to identification but goes much further: "When we are engrossed, a great deal of evidence indicates, we imaginatively experience the entire action," acting out every role ourselves.

*Unconscious Analogizing:* As we participate vicariously in the imaginative literature in which we are absorbed, we often create stories structured upon the literature we are reading. We analogize. These stories we create are highly elliptical; they may involve nothing more than the recognition of a similarity between a fictional event and something which has happened to us – a rapid reliving of the experience.

Lesser believes that the response to tragedy differs only in degree from the response to other literature. All literature involves a cathartic process (or abreaction) that is based on the unconscious perception, acting out, and analogizing of the literary experience. The dynamism of tragedy arises from an enforced, drastic, and sudden shifting of roles – a shift from participant to spectator. It is this abrupt reversal (peripetsia)

[27] Lesser, Simon O. *Fiction and the Unconscious.* Boston: Beacon Press, 1957.

which causes the catharsis, the intense abreaction which is the response to tragedy.

Some other claims for the values of bibliotherapy give additional ideas for the development of a theory of bibliotherapy. From the medical point of view, Oliver[28] in his book *Fear* says, "The right kind of book may be applied to a mental illness just as a definite drug is applied to some bodily need." Menninger[29] stated:

> . . . the whole matter of bibliotherapy of the relief of suffering by the psychological processes induced by reading, is a field in which we have little scientific knowledge. But our intuition and our experience tell us that books may indeed "minister to a mind diseased" and come to the aid of the doctor and even precede him.

Other writers have suggested more specific values of bibliotherapy. Appel[30] believes bibliotherapy can help the individual as follows:

1. To acquire information and knowledge about the psychology and physiology of human behavior.
2. To live up to the injunction "know thyself."
3. To "extrovert" the patient and arouse interest in something outside the self.
4. To effect a controlled release of unconscious difficulties.
5. To offer opportunity for identification and compensation.
6. To help clarify difficulties and give insight into one's own behavior.

Bryan[31] believes that bibliotherapy can help develop maturity and nourish and sustain mental health. She states such specific values as:

1. Giving the person the feeling that he is not the first to encounter the problem he is facing.
2. Permitting the reader to see that there is more than one solution to his problem or more than one choice to be made.
3. Helping the reader see the basic motivation of people involved in such a situation, including his own.
4. Helping the reader to see values in experience in human rather than material terms.
5. Providing facts needed in solving a problem.
6. Encouraging the reader to plan and execute a constructive course of action.

[28] Oliver, John R. *Fear.* New York: Macmillan, 1928.

[29] Menninger, Karl A. *Human Mind.* New York: Knopf, 1937.

[30] Appel, Kenneth E. "Psychiatric Therapy," *Personality and Behavior Disorders* II (J. M. Hunt, ed.). New York: Ronald, 1944, pp. 1107–63.

[31] Bryan, Alice I. "Personality Adjustment through Reading," *Library Journal, 64:* 573–76, August 1939.

In addition to some of the points made above, Gottschalk[32] believes that reading may have therapeutic values:

1. By stimulating the patient to discuss problems which he ordinarily avoids because of fear, shame, or guilt.
2. By helping the patient to analyze and synthesize further his attitudes and behavior patterns.
3. By providing vicarious life experiences without exposing the person to the real dangers of actual experience.
4. By reinforcing, by precept and example, acceptable social behavior and inhibiting infantile patterns of behavior.
5. By stimulating the imagination.
6. By enlarging the sphere of interests.

Rosenblatt[33,34] has analyzed the contributions of imaginative literature less in medical terms and more in relation to the work of the teacher. She believes that prolonged contact with personalities in books may have such social effects as:

1. Leading to increased social sensitivity, enabling the reader to put himself in another's place.
2. Developing the habit of interpreting the interactions of temperament upon temperament.
3. Enabling one to feel the needs, sufferings, and aspirations of other people.
4. Helping an individual to assimilate the cultural pattern by acquainting him with the attitudes and expectations of his group.
5. Releasing the adolescent from provincialism by extending awareness beyond his own family, community, and national background.

Rosenblatt further recognizes the preventive values of literature. It may prevent the growth of neurotic tendencies through vicarious participation in other lives. The guilt-possessed or rebellious adolescent may understand himself better even if his conduct is not prized in his environment. "Frequently literature is the only means by which he can see he is 'normal' and allay guilt and fear thereby."[35]

These possible values of bibliotherapy help to extend the concept of the process. They indicate some of the newer possible uses of literature

[32] Gottschalk, Louis B. "Bibliotherapy as an Adjuvant in Psychotherapy," *American Journal of Psychiatry, 104*:632–37, April 1948.

[33] Rosenblatt, Louise M. "The Enriching Values of Reading," *Reading in an Age of Mass Communication* (S. S. Gray, ed.), New York: Appleton-Century, 1949, pp. 19–38.

[34] Rosenblatt, Louise M. *Literature as Exploration.* New York: Appleton-Century, 1938.

[35] Rosenblatt, Louise M. *Ibid.*

in the clinic or classroom with a group or the individual. It should be clear, however, that many of the statements above are assumptions rather than established facts. Many of them are based on a psychoanalytic psychology which is not widely accepted (see Chapter 3), and suggestions for individual case studies and classroom procedures have not been verified in controlled, experimental situations.

As suggested above, some doubts about bibliotherapy have been expressed by Jahoda[36] in her review of possible effects of literature in relation to censorship. Just as people select programs which include content with which they are reasonably familiar in radio and television, some self-selection probably exists in regard to fiction. "People start to read a book and drop it because they are 'not interested' . . . they cannot establish a link of familiarity between the vicariously presented matter and the reality of their own lives." Jahoda believes that young readers find it especially hard to establish some sense of identity with mere descriptions or with a searching analysis of human motives. What grips the imagination of children is a sequence of events – a story. Because personality factors influence selection, "what a reader gets out of a book is largely determined by what he brings to it." Furthermore, there is some evidence to indicate that the absorption of information from print occurs more easily than the assimilation of attitudes, values, and standards, especially if these run counter to the individual's established ways of seeing the world. Preexisting attitudes may be confirmed, but the chances are fairly good that the reader will not be unduly influenced by the attitudes and values he meets in fiction unless there is no alternative in the environment. Some studies in social psychology suggest that personal contacts have psychological advantages over reading. Personal contact is more pervasive than reading matter, permits greater flexibility if resistance is offered, offers immediate rewards from compliance, and may be built on the trust or respect given a well-known source. In other words, direct experience may have greater influence than the printed word in changing attitudes. It may be argued that reading a good story often becomes a direct, as well as a vicarious experience, but Jahoda's point is that direct contact is the more powerful influence on behavior and feelings.

A specific example of questions about identification occurred to Meckel[37] as a result of his study of high school seniors' responses to Walpole's novel *Fortitude*. He found that vividness of memory for incidents in the book was associated with reading ability and with personality pre-

[36] Jahoda, Marie. *The Impact of Literature: A Psychological Discussion of Some Assumptions in the Censorship Debate.* New York: American Book Publishers Council, 1954. (Mimeographed).

[37] Meckel, Henry C. *An Exploratory Study of the Responses of Adolescent Pupils to Situations in a Novel.* Unpublished doctoral dissertation (University of Chicago, Chicago) 1946.

dispositions. Furthermore, identification does not necessarily follow from familiarity:

> Identification between the reader and a character may be repressed and the reading content criticized or rejected (a) by unacceptable behavior of the central character or characters closely associated with him, (b) unacceptable changes in the behavior of the character or unacceptable traits which develop as the character is delineated, and (c) by unpleasant experiences which happen to the character and which are uncongenial to the reader. Fear of emotion or the desire to avoid emotion may result in repression of identification with a character who gives way to his emotions.

Jahoda's summary and Meckel's findings for a specific group illustrate the point that there is nothing automatic about bibliotherapy. Even when the story deals with a problem which is the individual's true problem, and the situation described is related to his past experiences, it does not follow that the act of reading will help clear up the problem, increase social or self-insight, or contribute to the mental health of the reader. It becomes necessary, therefore, to turn to the clinical and research literature on the topic to see what is being done about bibliotherapy and to look for evidence about when it does or does not help the individual.

## *Studies in Bibliotherapy*

Studies in bibliotherapy are of three main types: (1) surveys of practice, especially in hospitals, (2) clinical studies, and (3) examples of its use in teaching, especially with retarded readers.

In a pioneer volume in 1923, Jones[38] included discussions of the uses of books in hospital libraries and gave classified reading lists. Bryan later wrote a series of three articles[39,40,41] which developed a theory of bibliotherapy and stated steps needed in making it a more exact science. While most writers use the term with reference to mental hygiene literature, to books of a didactic nature concerned with adjustment, personality, child rearing, and similar topics, Bryan included the whole range of literature – novels, plays, poetry, religion, art, and science – in the materials to be used in bibliotherapy. Schneck[42] gave one of the most complete

[38] Jones, E. Kathleen (ed.). *The Hospital Library.* Chicago: American Library Association, 1923.

[39] Bryan, Alice I. "Personality Adjustment through Reading," *Library Journal, 64:* 573–76, August 1939.

[40] Bryan, Alice I. "The Psychology of the Reader," *Library Journal, 64:*7–12, January 1939.

[41] Bryan, Alice I. "Can There Be a Science of Bibliotherapy?" *Library Journal, 64:* 773–76, October 1939.

[42] Schneck, Jerome M. "Bibliotherapy and Hospital Library Activities for Neuropsychiatric Patients," *Psychiatry, 8:*207–28, February 1945.

lists of bibliographies for use in bibliotherapy, but he confined his account largely to materials for use in general hospitals and with neuropsychiatric patients. Tyson[43] reviewed some of the writing on bibliotherapy before analyzing the content of mental hygiene texts, popular books, and a popular journal on personal adjustment.

Medical explorations (rather than experiments) in bibliotherapy seem to be the most numerous group described in the literature. Schneck[44] described the bibliotherapy project which has been operating at the Menninger Foundation in Topeka, Kansas, for several years. Earlier, Menninger[45] described briefly a few cases of the use of books such as Pearl Buck's *Exile* and Hale's *Man Without a Country.* An early report on the use of bibliotherapy in the United States Veterans Hospitals was written by Creglow[46] and a later account was a survey by Keneally.[47] A bibliography of twenty years of writing which totalled 264 references, most of which were concerned with practice in hospitals, was assembled by Dolan, Donnelly, and Mitchell.[48] Unfortunately the section labeled "Research and Case Studies" was largely confined to anecdotal notes and abbreviated case histories. "How a Doctor Uses Books" was a typical title of an article erroneously labeled "research."

Reports of clinical uses and case studies of bibliotherapy are also numerous. In the study in which she developed a theory of bibliotherapy Shrodes[49] illustrated its applications in a group of five college students with an intensive documentation of one case. Elsa, a twenty-seven-year-old college senior, spent four weeks reading short stories, essays, and single chapters from novels dealing with family relationships and social pressures. The authors included Virginia Woolf, Joseph Wood Krutch, Pearl Buck, Sally Benson, Louis Bromfield, and others. On the basis of reactions to this material, five other novels were chosen and a few individual interviews used to obtain records of responses to them. These responses and the changes in them were analyzed carefully, correlated with other data, and the relations to theory established.

Moore[50] described some of his pioneer clinical work in relating mental

[43] Tyson, Robert. "Content of Mental Hygiene Literature," *Journal of Clinical Psychology,* 5:109–14, April 1949.

[44] Schneck, Jerome M. "Studies in Bibliotherapy in a Neuropsychiatric Hospital," *Occupational Therapy and Rehabilitation,* 23:316–23, December 1944.

[45] Menninger, Karl A. *Human Mind.* New York: Knopf, 1937.

[46] Creglow, Elizabeth. "Therapeutic Value of Properly Selected Reading Matter," *U.S. Veterans Administration Medical Bulletin,* 7:1086–89, November 1931.

[47] Keneally, Katherine G. "Therapeutic Value of Books," *Youth Communication and Libraries* (Frances Henne, ed.). American Library Association, 1949, pp. 69–77.

[48] Dolan, Rosemary, June Donnelly, and June Mitchell. *Bibliotherapy in Hospitals.* Washington, D.C.: U. S. Veterans Administration, 1958.

[49] Shrodes, Caroline. *Bibliotherapy: A Theoretical and Clinical Experimental Study.* Unpublished doctoral dissertation (University of California, Berkeley, 1949).

health to the role of books in the Child Guidance Center of Catholic University. He[51] also gave case examples of the use of specific titles with children to improve their social adjustment. Blanchard[52] reviewed her clinical experiences with children who had learning difficulties which were aided by psychotherapy. Lazarsfeld[53] discussed some ways of using books, based on twenty years' experience in psychotherapy. While she believed that there is not necessarily an exact parallel between fiction and real life, there may be a close relationship between a story and problems as the client imagines them. Of importance to teachers and hospital workers is her conclusion that "Response to fiction can be generated only after the ground has been prepared by the usual methods of psychotherapy or counseling." Lazarsfeld made the cautious conclusion that "people who like to read can make strides toward the discovery of their real selves by accompanying one trained in psychological techniques upon a few conducted literary tours."

A number of other clinical reports are listed in the bibliographies mentioned above. Ryan[54] for example, suggested what she labeled a "new concept" — that today the psychiatrist is "captain of a treatment team" and that members of it, including a librarian who knows about bibliotherapy, have definite responsibilities in treatment.

Research on the use of bibliotherapy in schools, like that in hospitals, is not satisfactory from the point of view of research design but is sometimes of interest as preventive as well as corrective measures. An article by Sister Mary Agnes[55] and the investigation by Sister Lorang[56] developed some hypotheses which require further investigation. Sister Mary Agnes found some improvement in the adjustments of four out of five children in the upper elementary grades after the reading of four or five books, although only one of the five children saw any connection between their own problems and those of the book characters. Sister Lorang used a questionnaire to get opinions of 2,308 high school students, in eight

---

[50] Moore, Thomas V. *Personal Mental Hygiene.* New York: Grune and Stratton, 1944.

[51] Moore, Thomas V. "Bibliotherapy," *Catholic Library World,* pp. 11–20, October 1943.

[52] Blanchard, Phyllis. "Psychoanalytic Contributions to the Problems of Reading Disabilities," *Psychoanalytic Study of the Child,* Vol. 2. New York: International Universities Press, 1946.

[53] Lazarsfeld, Sofie. "Use of Fiction in Psychotherapy (A Contribution to Bibliotherapy)," *American Journal of Psychotherapy, 3:*26–33, January 1949.

[54] Ryan, N. J. "Bibliotherapy and Psychiatry: Changing Concepts, 1937–1957," *Special Libraries, 48:*197–99, May–June 1957.

[55] Mary Agnes, Sister. "Bibliotherapy for Socially Maladjusted Children," *Catholic Education Review, 44:*8–15, 1946.

[56] Lorang, Sister Mary Corde. *The Effect of Reading upon Moral Conduct and Emotional Experience.* Studies in Psychology and Psychiatry, Vol. 6, No. 5. Washington, D.C.: Catholic University of America Press, 1945.

schools, about specific books and magazines they had read and the effects of this reading on them. Fifty-three per cent of the group said they had tried to act like a character in a book and 21 per cent like a character in a magazine. The effects of books were found to be significantly better than the effects of magazines, but the study needs further validation of these and other questionnaire responses.

The values of literature in inducting the child into his culture have been investigated by the Shaftels[57] who made an exploratory study of the use of problem-stories based upon the developmental tasks of middle childhood. After reading and discussing the stories, the children were given an opportunity to act out their solutions.

Two descriptions of the use of bibliotherapy in school classrooms are given by Newell[58] and by Lindahl and Koch,[59] the first in primary grades, the second in intermediate classes. The accounts illustrate more hope than proof. An attempt to get more specific data was made in a little study by Webster.[60] She interviewed 80 first-grade children and found that 35 indicated fear of the dark and five fear of dogs. The children were then divided into groups of seven (with one group of five), and for a five-week period they heard the investigator read a story about the dark or about dogs. There was nondirected discussion of each story immediately after the reading, with sharing of personal experiences and of reactions to the story. Webster reports, "When the interviews were repeated three months after the reading of the last story it seemed that twenty-nine of the thirty-five had reduced fear of the dark. . . . Three of the five pupils who had reported fear of dogs indicated a change from general fear of dogs to fear of 'some dogs' and 'mean dogs.'" Webster attributes the change at least in part to group discussion which went beyond the "static phase of mere acceptance" of dogs or the dark.

A somewhat more intensive study of equated eighth grade groups was made by Herminghaus.[61] He first wrote a guide for teachers, with three sections: (1) the nature of personality, the role of reading in the formation of personality, and methods of using bibliotherapy, (2) an index of children's problems in relation to book titles, (3) an annotated bibliogra-

[57] Shaftel, George, and Fannie R. Shaftel. "Report on the Use of a 'Practice Action Level' in the Stanford University Project for American Ideals," *Sociatry,* 1:57–65; December 1947, and 2:245–53, March 1948.

[58] Newell, E. "At the North End of Pooh, a study of bibliotherapy," *Elementary English, 34:*22–25, January 1957.

[59] Lindahl, H. M. and Katherine Koch. "Bibliotherapy in the Middle Grades," *Elementary English, 29:*390–96, November 1952.

[60] Webster, W. Jane. *Some Effects of Stories on the Reduction of Fears of First Grade Children.* Unpublished master's thesis (University of California, Berkeley, 1960).

[61] Herminghaus, Earl G. *The Effect of Bibliotherapy on the Attitudes and Personal and Social Adjustment of a Group of Elementary School Children.* Unpublished doctoral dissertation (Washington University, St. Louis, 1954).

phy of books suitable for use in bibliotherapy, with interest level and reading level indicated. The two groups were tested with the California Test of Personality and with the two projective tests, the Rosenzweig Picture-Frustration Study, and the Thematic Apperception Test. As a result, the experimental group using the reading materials made statistically significant better scores on personal and social adjustment as measured by the California test. On the Rosenzweig test there were significant changes in the incidence of feelings of aggression. Herminghaus believed he obtained "some evidence in support of the hypothesis that bibliotherapy can be used in modifying children's attitudes in desirable directions and in producing a higher degree of personal and social adjustment."

## *Therapy and Remedial Reading*

The use of therapy in connection with the correction of reading difficulties offers many examples of clinical and case-study substantiation of the place of bibliotherapy. The incidence of reading retardation in the school (and adult) population is a matter of debate because percentages vary with the standards set for efficient reading. The census accepts as literate anyone with education (and supposed reading ability) above the fourth grade; some writers have suggested that reading ability as high as that of the average tenth grade student is desirable in a world where we all must rely on print. Many estimates of retardation in school cluster around the 10 to 12 per cent figure, with retardation defined as one year or more below grade level in the primary grades and two years or more retardation in the upper grades. Whatever the standard, and however efficient reading instruction may be, some pupils in every school have reading difficulties. There is general agreement from hundreds of reports of diagnostic studies that boys outnumber girls about four to one in the retarded group and that the cause of retardation is complex and multiple, not simple and single. For this reason, no single cure such as more phonics or more speed practice is likely to be effective. Instead, the reading clinician makes a careful study of possible physiological, social, educational, and emotional factors which may be associated with the reading difficulty. Remediation by teacher or clinic worker is thus usually based on multiple findings.

Reading difficulties may or may not be accompanied by emotional difficulties. In a review of eight researches Gates[62] estimated that "among cases of very marked specific reading disability about 75 per cent will show personality maladjustment." In another summary Witty[63] concluded

[62] Gates, Arthur I. "Role of Personality Maladjustment in Reading Disability," *Journal of Genetic Psychology*, 59:77–83, September 1941.

[63] Witty, Paul A. "Reading Success and Emotional Adjustment," *Elementary English*, 27:281–96, May 1950.

that about 50 per cent of children with reading difficulty exhibited personality problems as well as reading problems. The specific role of emotional difficulties in reading retardation has been examined by Blanchard,[64] Ephron[65] and others. Whether the percentage of reading disability cases with emotional disturbances is 20 or 80, there is agreement that the emotional difficulties may be either causes, concomitants, or results of the reading difficulties. Furthermore, in recent years there has been agreement that because of a direct relationship between reading and emotional difficulties, an attempt to modify feelings and attitudes by therapy should also modify reading performance. In other words, remedial reading activities should sometimes include therapeutic treatment.

Smith[66] has given examples of how the following kinds of therapy may be an adjunct to practice in remedial and developmental reading: art therapy, language therapy, psychodrama, play therapy, individual interview, group interview, and tutorial group therapy. Axline[67] was a pioneer in the use of play therapy with retarded readers. In two studies Bills[68,69] found that a group of retarded readers who had emotional difficulties and who were given play therapy improved their reading more than a comparable group who had specific reading practice only. In a second group of retarded but well-adjusted readers there was no advantage to the group who had play therapy. Seeman and Edwards[70] also reported favorable gains in reading ability associated with group therapy but no corresponding change in personality measures. Fisher[71] reported that a group of six delinquent boys who received remedial reading instruction and who met in a group therapy situation at the end of six months made a 39 per cent increase in reading ability over a comparable group which had no group therapy sessions. Lipton and Feiner[72] also re-

[64] Blanchard, Phyllis. "Psychoanalytic Contributions to the Problems of Reading Disabilities," *Psychoanalytic Study of the Child,* Vol. 2. New York: International Universities Press, 1946.

[65] Ephron, Beulah Kanter. *Emotional Difficulties in Reading; a Psychological Approach to Study Problems.* New York: Julian Press, 1953.

[66] Smith, Nila B. *Reading Instruction for Today's Children.* Englewood Cliffs, N.J.; Prentice-Hall, 1963.

[67] Axline, V. M. "Nondirective Therapy for Poor Readers," *Journal of Consulting Psychology, 11:*61–69, 1947.

[68] Bills, R. E. "Nondirective Play Therapy with Retarded Readers," *Journal of Consulting Psychology, 14:*140–49, April 1950.

[69] Bills, R. E. "Play Therapy with Well-adjusted Retarded Readers," *Journal of Consulting Psychology, 14:*246–49, 1950.

[70] Seeman, Julius, and Benner Edwards. "A Therapeutic Approach to Reading Difficulties," *Journal of Consulting Psychology, 18:*451–53, 1954.

[71] Fisher, Bernard. "Group Therapy with Retarded Readers," *Journal of Educational Psychology, 44:*354–61, October 1953.

[72] Lipton, Aaron, and Arthur Feiner. "Group Therapy and Remedial Reading," *The Journal of Educational Psychology, 26:*180–90, June 1956.

ported positive effects for a group approach where the therapy was based in part on the notion that reading is used at times as a weapon in a person's self-defense. In what may be described as a combination of group therapy and psychodrama, McCann[73] found that "dramatic dialogues" were useful in treating both personality and reading difficulties simultaneously.

The examples quoted are not specific illustrations of the use of bibliotherapy directly, but they illustrate once again the dynamic nature of the reading process and the fact that different kinds of therapy may be associated with improved reading ability and interest. Along with the examples of the more specific studies of bibliotherapy described earlier they suggest that the concepts of *therapy* and *reading* often go together and that reading may sometimes be used as an aid to attitude change and personality adjustment.

## *Conclusion*

This chapter explores the possibilities of reading contributing to positive mental health. The term *mental health* is somewhat varied and elusive with consequent difficulty in establishing relationships to it, especially those of cause-and-effect. Any evidence which exists is largely confined to clinical experiences, usually in mental or general hospitals. From the time of Aristotle men have believed that books can affect attitudes and character, but proof of the belief is still not established. The experimental evidence is almost nonexistent; the individual testimony is formidable.

The use of reading and literature to affect self-knowledge and social insight may be categorized into preventive and corrective procedures. The assumption in the first activity is that children and youth can be introduced through books to the developmental tasks which most youth face and can be thereby prepared to meet them in more effective ways. Such a function may be performed by the parent, the teacher, and the librarian who helps the youth select literature which deals with such problems as parent-child relationships or overcoming shyness. Further discussion of these possibilities occurs in Chapters 10 and 11. The corrective function has been described here as bibliotherapy, a process of dynamic interaction between the personality of the reader and literature which may be utilized for assessment of difficulties, adjustment toward mental health, and growth into maturity.

Because the serious study of bibliotherapy is still in beginning stages, some of the chapter is devoted to the development of a theory of bibliotherapy along lines suggested by Bryan, by some medical practitioners, and

[73] McCann, Mary. "Dramatic Dialogues for Simultaneous Treatment of Reading and Personality Problems," *Journal of Educational Psychology*, 38:96–104, February 1947.

especially by Shrodes.[74] The essential parts of the process were described in terms of *identification, catharsis,* and *insight* and the first of these explored in some depth. These concepts originated in psychoanalytic thinking but have been accepted by other psychologists; they are sometimes imprecise and maladapted to exact experimentation and it may be that clinical reports are the best evidence we can get. Furthermore, most people do not seek to change themselves through reading as often as they seem to desire to reinforce their own habits and attitudes. A number of clinicians suggest that the ideas and symbols of literature will not induce a desirable response that is not already latent in the reader. Furthermore, we read selectively. "Not only does the eye find what the mind is seeking, the mind finds what the heart is seeking."[75] With these limitations in mind it is still possible to view literature as a catalyst to isolate and sharpen problems and therefore to provide a basis for fresh, adaptive behavior aimed at solving them. Imaginative literature enables a reader to view his experience in new ways from the perspective of a detached observer. Since literature combines fantasy and reality, the reader can be both spectator and participant. This involvement does not happen automatically whenever a reader opens a book, but may occur in guided reading, usually with the opportunity for discussion. The evidence of individual testimony and widespread hospital usage indicates that this kind of participation does occur and offers an opportunity for further research of both preventive and corrective usage. The positive values claimed for bibliotherapy in certain accounts and the reservations about it raised in others point clearly to the necessity of validating the procedure experimentally.

Besides lack of validation, another limitation which is evident in the above literature is the paucity of work with the average, mildly disturbed person outside the clinic or hospital. Several writers suggest that bibliotherapy is more likely to be successful with younger people, several believe that it is most applicable in cases of only mild disturbance. The implications for schools and colleges, with their facilities for recommending books and discussing them in group guidance situations, would seem to be fairly clear. In such practice, limitations such as reading ability of pupils and home and community influences must also be recognized.

In addition to the necessity of validation of the process and the extension of the work into schools, a third implication for research and practice concerns the values of imaginative versus didactic and factual literature. A number of analysts prescribe factual books for their patients and believe that these are best when the individual needs more contact with reality. Psychiatrists and psychologists admit, however, that great artists

[74] Shrodes, Caroline. *Bibliotherapy: A Theoretical and Clinical Experimental Study.* Unpublished doctoral dissertation (University of California, Berkeley, 1949).

[75] Shrodes, Caroline. "The Dynamics of Reading: Implications for Bibliotherapy," *ETC., 18:*21–33, April 1961.

are penetrating interpreters of the human personality. Since the great writer has the power to understand, describe, and project to the reader some phase of personality, he should be enlisted as an ally in diagnosis and therapy. There are some suggestions that admonitory, prescriptive reading is largely an intellectual exercise whereas the identification, projection, and other mechanisms involved in reading imaginative literature may incorporate into the reading situation the emotional behavior associated with change in most maladjustment. A further possibility is that *both* factual and fictional materials are useful, depending upon the particular needs of the individual, and therefore the teacher's or librarian's task is to find some balance between these types of material.

In addition to the needs for further study, there are a number of suggestions arising out of available literature more directly concerning the work of the librarian and English teachers. One problem is that of what kind of story for what kind of difficulty. Should the adolescent with parent-child problems have a story of family conflict recommended to him, or must he be approached more indirectly? Will the quiet, withdrawn boy profit by reading about a person like himself or about an extroverted, popular adolescent? Some clinicians find it impractical to prescribe books on the basis of one diagnostic category, one set of etiological factors, or one type of personality. Rather the individual's present psychological status, his emotional state, the amount of his withdrawal from reality, and his ability to profit from reading are taken into account. The answer for the clinician, the teacher, or librarian, then, is not a clear-cut one. The recommendation of pleasant, cheerful books instead of stories dealing with emotionally disturbed characters, morbid themes, or unhappy endings may seem to be a good beginning for a child or youth who is himself unhappy and disturbed, but perhaps, at some later time, he will need to read stories which deal more directly with his problem. Perhaps the child or adolescent who has already built fairly satisfactory psychological defenses should not be forced to tear these down because of a more direct discussion of his problems in literature. The teacher or librarian can work at best on an experimental basis, trying different sorts of stories and giving opportunities for discussing and restructuring these in the group situation, with perhaps deeper analysis in individual interview.

Finally, it is doubtful whether the reading of books is a complete substitute for firsthand experience. The timid little girl in fourth grade, the insecure adolescent, the college student wrestling with conflicts in values, or the withdrawn adult settles his problems, not in books but in everyday encounters with others in his world. At best his reading can be the beginning of a change which must be fulfilled in day-by-day conduct. Chapters 10 and 11 give more suggestions for encouraging beginnings and establishing practices associated with acceptable adjustment or mental health.

# CHAPTER 10 | Children and Literature

## Virginia M. Reid

A more exact title for the next two chapters might be "Exploring Literature with Children (and Youth) in Terms of Possible Effects on Attitudes, Appreciations, and Values." This somewhat orotund label has been discarded in favor of the simpler one above, but the two chapters do not cover all the possibilities inherent in the simpler title. There are already a number of useful books designed to help parents introduce their children to good literature by such writers as Annis Duff,[1] Anne Eaton,[2] Josette Frank,[3] Nancy Larrick,[4] Lillian Smith,[5] and Ruth Tooze.[6] Furthermore, several journals and worthwhile books for both elementary and secondary teachers offer help in exploring various types of literature. This help may also be found in anthologies of literature compiled by May Hill Arbuthnot,[7] Lillian Hollowell,[8] Miriam Huber,[9] Edna Johnson,[10] and others, and by books more closely related to teaching methods by Burton,[11] Loban,[12] Whitehead,[13] Huck and Kuhn,[14] and others. Because

[1] Duff, Annis. *Bequest of Wings.* New York: Viking, 1944.

[2] Eaton, Anne. *Treasure for the Taking.* New York: Viking, 1946, 1957.

[3] Frank, Josette. *Your Child's Reading Today.* New York: Doubleday, 1960.

[4] Larrick, Nancy. *A Teacher's Guide to Children's Books.* Columbus, Ohio: Chas. E. Merrill, 1960.

[5] Smith, Lillian. *The Unreluctant Years.* Chicago: American Library Association, 1953.

[6] Tooze, Ruth. *Storytelling,* Englewood Cliffs, N.J.: Prentice-Hall, 1959.

[7] Arbuthnot, May Hill. *Children and Books* (3d ed.). Glenview, Ill.: Scott Foresman, 1964.

[8] Hollowell, Lillian. *A Book of Children's Literature* (3d ed.). New York: Holt, 1966.

[9] Huber, Miriam. *Story and Verse for Children.* New York: Macmillan, 1955.

[10] Johnson, Edna, Carrie Scott, and Evelyn R. Sickela. *Anthology of Children's Literature.* Boston: Houghton Mifflin, 1948.

[11] Burton, Dwight. *Literature Study in the High School.* New York: Holt, 1959, 1964.

two chapters could not possibly encompass all that should be said about sharing and teaching good literature, and because this book is primarily about the reader rather than the literary text, the following sections make suggestions to parents and teachers largely in terms of the effects of reading on children today.

## *Today's Children*

The child of today's mechanized, computerized world is influenced by pressures unknown by children of previous generations. Knowledge is doubling every seven years, we are told. Newspaper headlines and titles in periodicals such as "Kindergarten Is too Late," scream the need for children to learn more and to learn faster. Yet children are distracted and frustrated by being caught up in the social unrest of today, the population explosion, and the ever increasing mobility of that population.

Children are pawns of pressure groups who stage "sit-outs" from school or "march-outs" from academic endeavors. One four-year-old preschooler when asked to give someone else a turn riding a tricycle, threw himself on the ground and announced to an anxious teacher, "I'm demonstrating."

Today children are better informed and exposed to more ideas than the youth of previous generations. Television takes them around the world and into outer space. It transports them backward to prehistoric ages and forward to lunar flight-time. Fortunately, the world of children's books is changing along with the children. There now are new types of books as well as a greater availability for most children.

Despite the social and cultural changes in children, however, the basic human needs remain the same. Children of the space age read for the same reason as did children of pioneer days. No one has stated their drives for reading more directly than Arbuthnot,[15] who says that children read to satisfy these six needs:

1. Need for security – material, emotional, intellectual, and spiritual.
2. Need to belong – to be part of a group.
3. Need to love and be loved.
4. Need to achieve – to do or be something worthy of respect.

---

[12] Loban, Walter, Margaret Ryan, and James R. Squire. *Teaching Language and Literature.* New York: Harcourt, Brace, 1961.

[13] Whitehead, Robert. *Children's Literature: Strategies of Teaching.* Englewood Cliffs, New Jersey: Prentice-Hall, 1968.

[14] Huck, Charlotte S., and Doris Young Kuhn. *Children's Literature in the Elementary School* (2d ed.). New York: Holt, 1968.

[15] Arbuthnot, May Hill. *Children and Books* (3d ed.). Glenview, Ill.: Scott Foresman, 1964.

5. Need for play – the need for change.
6. Need for aesthetic appreciation.

The writer would add the need for time to be a child. Le Shan[16] quotes from a booklet published in 1963 by the Play School Association:

> Being a child isn't what it used to be. Huck Finn is a delinquent, Tom Sawyer isn't working up to capacity, and Heidi is in foster care. Jim Hawkins is too young to be a cabin boy, and whoever would let Alice just sit there doing nothing but dream through a summer afternoon? . . . Today's child often walks a tightrope between neglect and pressure. He gets too much stimulation or none at all. He may have forgotten how to play. . . . Parents worry whether children will excel before they leave Kindergarten.

Dr. James Hymes has often expressed in speeches his concern about adults who are thinking more about what children will someday become than about what they already are; they best learn through firsthand experience and personal exploration.

In increasing numbers children are failing in school. Holt[17] states that "they fail because they are afraid above all else, of failing, of disappointing or displeasing the many anxious adults around them, whose limitless hopes and expectations for them hang over their heads like a cloud."

Another cloud hanging over the heads of many children from minority groups has only recently been recognized by publishers and their patrons. Russell has stressed earlier in this text the need for the reader to identify with someone. Until recently many children had no one with whom to identify. The noted librarian and author Arna Boutemps said that when he was a child the only book for children that he could find was *My Little African Cousin,* with which he certainly didn't identify, and the situation was no better for his children, who were offered *The Pickanniny Twins.* Larrick[18] reported in 1965 on a three-year study of children's books. She found that "only four-fifths of one per cent of children's books from the sixty-three publishers tell a story about American Negroes today," and even these books if they treated critical problems were "usually so gentle as to be unreal."

Today the situation is much better. Not only are more books about multicultural children available, but also there are more good books.

Sutherland[19] says that "one of the most encouraging trends is seen in the story that is about a child's problems, a child who is a Negro among other things, rather than about a child's problems as a Negro. They exist and they are needed, but the other is welcome."

[16] Le Shan, Eda. *Conspiracy Against Childhood.* New York: Athaneum, 1968.

[17] Holt, John. *How Children Fail.* New York: Pitman, 1964.

[18] Larrick, Nancy. *"The All-White World of Children's Books," Saturday Review,* September 11, 1965.

[19] Sutherland, Zena. "A Change for the Better," *Saturday Review,* March 16, 1968.

The objectives of a literature program, as stated by Keating,[20] "should be to make reading emotionally and psychologically rewarding as well as educational at all reading levels. . . . Feelings as well as facts are associated with what we read."

A child's response to people may well be conditioned by his exposure to those he meets in books which stir his emotions. It becomes our task, then, to provide both the literature and the experiences with literature that will satisfy the needs of today's children.

We will need to know:

1. What constitutes children's literature.
2. The natural interests of children and the books which feed these interests.
3. Some criteria for judging quality in children's books.

## *What Is Literature for Children?*

### Content Defined

The recently completed English Teacher Preparation Study[21] defines "Children's literature as that body of literature which has appeal and interest for children and which can be understood by them." It includes that prose and poetry which stimulate curiosity, stretch the imagination, and awaken a sense of wonder. It should extend children's horizons and should deepen their understanding of themselves and others. Literature for children should be works of substance and sincerity, and be told in effective and memorable language. Fenwick[22] states that children's literature must be considered as "a segment of all serious literature, a commentary upon life in dimensions that are meaningful to children."

There is recent evidence that the status of children's literature is being recognized and acknowledged. For the first time this year (1969) the 20th Annual National Book Awards Committee included the category "Juvenile." The winner, Meinert De Jong,[23] won the same award of $1,000 for his *Journey From Peppermint Street* as did the winners from all other categories. In addition the National Book Committee noted that

[20] Keating, Charlotte. *Building Bridges of Understanding*. Tucson, Ariz.: Palo Verde Publishing Co., 1967.

[21] *English Teacher Preparation Study: Guidelines for the Preparation of Teaching English.* A cooperative study by the National Association of State Directors of Teacher Education and Certification, National Council of Teachers of English, and the Modern Language Association of America. Champaign, Ill.: National Council of Teachers of English, 1968.

[22] Fenwick, Sara Innis. *A Critical Approach to Children's Literature.* Chicago: University of Chicago Press, 1967.

[23] De Jong, Meinert. *Journey from Peppermint Street.* New York: Harper, 1968.

children's literature has become an increasingly important category in the total literary endeavor.

Less significant but worthy of note is the appearance of "A Children's Bestiary" in the "Your Literary I.Q." column of *Saturday Review,* March 1968. Readers were asked to identify animal characters such as Aslan, Bambi, and Charlotte, and to "leash them to their creators." Regular readers of this column will readily agree that this is a distinct departure from the usual adult fare.

Some of the literature for children "reflects excellence in writing, in design, and in the essential features that distinguish an art form." Georgio[24] states in the recent publication *Children and Their Literature,* that "children's literature contains a substantial collection of fictional, factual, and poetic works designed specifically for children as well as those drawn from adult literature."

Jacobs[25] defines literature in terms of what it does for the child:

1. Literature is entertainment.
2. Literature refreshes the spirit.
3. Literature helps explore life and living.
4. Literature is a guidance resource.
5. Literature stimulates creative activities.
6. Literature is beautiful language.

## A Balanced Program

If a child is to be given a chance to develop a sense of values to live by, we must provide a planned exposure to a balanced program.

Balance Number 1 – between the old and the new. He is entitled to know those stories and poems that have enthralled generations of children. As Annis Duff said, the book may be old, but the child is always new.

Today's child also needs to know books that are written in the idiom and style of today, a style to which he is attuned. The *San Francisco Chronicle* recently carried an article from the *New York Times* quoting Margaret Mead, "The world the youth are in tune with and take for granted is different from the world of their elders . . . who have simply sat back and read a book while the world was changing."

Balance Number 2 – between realism and fantasy. Realistic stories for children are those stories which show life as it is or was. These stories deal with human understanding. The actions of the characters are con-

[24] Georgio, Constantine. *Children and Their Literature.* Englewood Cliffs, New Jersey: Prentice-Hall, 1969.

[25] Jacobs, Leland. "Give Children Literature," *Readings on Contemporary English in the Elementary School.* (Iris M. Treat and Sidney W. Tiedt, eds.). N.J.: Prentice-Hall, 1967.

vincingly believable. The stories range from contemporary novels and animal stories to historical fiction. Huck and Kuhn[26] use three categories to present books "related to the developmental tasks of childhood": history, fiction, and biography.

Interested as the child is in knowing the real here and now, or the equally real then and far away, most children also want to "dream the impossible dream" and to experience the impossible or improbable world of make-believe.

Balance Number 3 – between fiction and nonfiction. One type of realism not included in the previous section was that of nonfiction. The best books in this field provide specific, authentic information and at the same time kindle the child's sense of wonder. He will want to know "what next?" if the author avoids giving the impression that the subject is closed and that there is nothing left to discover.

The category of fiction cuts across the old and the new and includes folk tales, myths, fables, legends, and tall tales, as well as stories of adventure, mystery, humor, and family life.

## Children's Natural Interests and the Literature to Nourish Them

The four-, five-, and six-year-olds are active, eager to know, and have a keen interest in words. They need to be physically involved as they respond to repetitive phrases, such as: "I'll huff and I'll puff, and I'll blow your house in," or

> The grand old Duke of York
> He had ten thousand men:
> He marched them up a very high hill,
> And he marched them down again!

or

> What can you do.
> What can you do.
> What can you do with a shoe?
> You can put it on your ear,
> Your heary-leary-ear, you can put it on your ear, ha, ha,
> Now what can you really do with a shoe.

or, again

> Millions and millions and millions of cats?

Also, the teacher needs to know appropriate choices for older children.

Current favorites are humorous books, such as *Harriet the Spy,*[27] *The Egypt Game,*[28] and *From the Mixed Up Files of Mrs. Basil E.*

[26] Huck, Charlotte S., and Doris Young Kuhn. *Children's Literature in the Elementary School* (2d. ed.). New York: Holt, 1968.

[27] Fitzhugh, Louise. *Harriet the Spy.* New York: Harper, 1964.

[28] Snyder, Zilpha Keatley. *The Egypt Game.* New York: Antheneum, 1967.

*Frankweiler;*[29] the tender allegory *Single Light;*[30] and excellent historical fiction such as *Marathon Looks on the Sea.*[31]

Not to be overlooked are nonfiction titles, such as *Great American Negroes*[32] and *How Animals Tell Time,*[33] or the distinctive collections of poetry, such as *Tune Beyond Us,*[34] and *I Am the Darker Brother.*[35]

There is a regrettable tendency for some teachers and parents to take pride in the child who is reading books intended for young adults and adults. It is not always the too hasty adult, however, who offers children adult material. Often it is the adult who does not *know* suitable books for children nor the criteria for choosing them. He relies instead on those he remembers that he had read sometime – usually when he was older than a child. Or he may depend on collections, such as The Great Books.

If, as Chukovsky[36] says, "they reach up," for adult literature – fine, but let us not in our rush overlook the wealth of books which, like the little bear's chair is "just right" for a child at a certain age.

> A child is a child wherever he may be.
> But a child is a child only once. . . .
> And some day if he is not a child who is helped to grow then he may not be the adult he could have been.

One of the most helpful guides to adults responsible for guiding children's reading is the outline prepared by Huck and Kuhn[37] in their comprehensive volume *Children's Literature in the Elementary School.* This outline, called "Books for Ages and Stages," charts some of the characteristic growth patterns, offers some implications for selection and use of books, and lists some suggested books for each particular stage of development. Preschool and Kindergarten, Early Elementary, Middle Elementary, and later Elementary are the four stages covered.

Over the past five years, Stanchfield[38] has been engaged in a research study involving 400 first-grade children in an effort to identify and de-

[29] Konigsburg, Elaine. *From the Mixed-Up Files of Mrs. Basil E. Frankweiler.* New York: Atheneum, 1967.

[30] Wojciechowska, Maia. *Single Light.* New York: Harper, 1968.

[31] Coolidge, Olivia. *Marathon Looks at the Sea.* Boston: Houghton Mifflin, 1968.

[32] Richardson, Ben. *Great American Negroes.* New York: Thos. Y. Crowell, 1956.

[33] Selsam, Millicent E. *How Animals Tell Time.* New York: Morrow, 1965.

[34] Livingston, Myra Cohn. *Tune Beyond Us.* New York: Harcourt, Brace, 1968.

[35] Adoff, Arnold. *I am the Darker Brother.* New York: Macmillan, 1968.

[36] Chukovsky, Kornei. *From Two to Five.* Berkeley: University of California Press, 1963.

[37] Huck, Charlotte S., and Doris Young Kuhn. *Children's Literature in the Elementary School* (2d. ed.). New York: Holt, 1968.

[38] Stanchfield, Jo M. *The Effect of High-Interest Materials on Reading Achievement in the First Grade.* Chicago: Century Consultant, 1968.

velop material which captured the interest of both boys and girls. She has been particularly interested in identifying the reading interests of boys. Contrary to many previous interest surveys which state that six-year-olds prefer to read about familiar experiences, the boys check this characteristic as being of least interest.

Stanchfield reports that out of 50 categories the boys preferentially ranked these twelve:

1. Outdoor life.
2. Explorations and expeditions.
3. Sports and games.
4. Science fiction.
5. Sea adventure.
6. Tales of fantasy.
7. Historical fiction.
8. Humor.
9. Every day life adventure of boys their own age.
10. Outer space.
11. Mystery and detective.
12. War.

The least-liked categories included:

1. Music.
2. Plays.
3. Art.
4. Family and home life.
5. Poetry.

Of a total of 20 characteristics of reading interests, the 7 best-liked were:

1. Unusual experiences.
2. Excitement.
3. Suspense.
4. Liveliness and action.
5. Surprise or unexpectedness.
6. Fantastic, fanciful, or weird elements.
7. Funny incidents.

The boys showed a consistent and almost identical pattern of least interest and least liking for four characteristics or literary qualities:

1. Sadness.
2. Family love and closeness.
3. Anger, hatred, cruelty, fighting, brutality.
4. Familiar experiences.

## *Current Literature Programs in Elementary Schools*

"All men do not agree on what they would have children learn." Aristotle's statement applies equally well today. Current programs of literature reflect much divergent thinking.

Program planners of today seem to be disciples either of Bruner or Piaget. Bruner's[39] answer to the question of what shall be taught is: "The curriculum of a subject should be determined by the most fundamental understanding that can be achieved of the underlying principles that give structure to the subject." "We begin," Bruner continues, "with the hypothesis that any subject can be taught effectively in some intellectually honest form to a child at any stage of development."

This last statement has probably been quoted by more speakers and writers in the educational field than any other in recent years. It has also given rise to curriculum studies and projects which have searched to discover the structure of English and then to determine the sequence in which the content would be introduced to children.

### The University of Nebraska Curriculum Center

In Chapter 11, Squire describes the various pilot programs developed by the English Curriculum Centers supported by the U. S. Office of Education. The kindergarten to twelfth grade literature program created by the University of Nebraska[40] seems to have exerted the most influence on elementary programs. The Center has developed a structured English Curriculum for Elementary Schools based on a sequence of literature units including integral work in language and composition. Part of the premises of the program are stated as follows:

> The elementary school program for language, literature and composition should not be confused with a reading program. It is neither such a program nor a substitute for such a program. The development of methods for the teaching of reading is the proper concern of the reading expert and not of this study. Further linguistic research may lead to improvements in methods for the teaching of reading; and, when sufficient research data indicates that these improvements have been made, they should be synthesized in this curriculum. Our concern is with showing such literature as will make reading worth the effort, composition an exercise in the imitation of excellence, and language study more than a bore.

The materials for this program consist of 70 units for the various grade levels plus two ancillary materials: *Poetry for the Elementary Grades*, and

[39] Bruner, Jerome S. *The Process of Education.* Cambridge, Mass.: Harvard University Press, 1960.

[40] Nebraska Curriculum Development Center. *A Curriculum for English: Introduction to the Elementary School Program K–6.* The University of Nebraska, Lincoln, 1965, p. 2. (Mimeographed).

*Language Explorations for the Elementary Grades.* The suggested units endeavor to arrange in spiral fashion literary works in an articulated sequence designed to develop the concepts essential to the literature program. Sixty-nine of the units are divided into groups described by the Center as "pseudogenres," folk tales, fanciful stories, animal stories, adventure stories, myth-fable, other lands and people, historical fiction, and biography. The remaining unit presents to sixth graders the poetry of Frost.

The effect of this curriculum has been widespread. Some cities have purchased the unit outright and have provided training for their teachers in the use of the materials. The writer participated in two such workshops in Honolulu and Hilo to help teachers prepare their own lesson plans using the Nebraska units supplied by the Hawaii State Department of Education. Other cities in developing their own curriculum guides have been influenced by the Nebraska approach.

### City Curriculum Guides

One curriculum guide developed by Pasadena City Schools[41] is entitled *Children's Literature: A Resource Guide for Enriching the Study of Literature Grades 4–6.* Sample lessons are provided in each of the following areas of literature: myths, legends, fairy tales, and fables as well as traditional and contemporary classics.

The foreword of the Philadelphia guide[42] states, "A well balanced instructional program for elementary school children must include systematically-planned and enthusiastically-presented experiences and activities related to excellent children's literature." This guide presents a structured program only insofar as it provides a sequential list of good read-aloud material.

For grades one and two suggested titles are given for folk and fairy tales, fables and myths, fanciful tales, animal stories, stories of real life here and abroad, biography and poetry. For grades three and four the above categories are repeated and the category of historical stories is added. For grades five and six all previous categories are repeated and the category of hero tales is added.

*Roads of Excellence Through Books*[43] developed by the San Leandro Unified School District also reflects the concern for coverage of various genres by defining the area of emphasis for each grade level.

[41] *Children's Literature: A Resource Guide for Enriching the Study of Literature Grades 4–6.* Pasadena City Schools, Pasadena, Calif., 1964.

[42] *A Literature Program; Year One Through Grade Six.* Philadelphia Public Schools, Philadelphia, Penn., 1966.

[43] *Roads of Excellence Through Books.* Prepared by San Leandro Unified School District, and published by Alameda County Board of Education, Alameda, Calif. 1968.

Grade 1 Mother Goose.
Grade 2 Animal and Nature Stories, Friends and Family Life, Fanciful Tales.
Grade 3 Fairy Tales, Caldecott Award Books.
Grade 4 Fables, Folk Tales, Tall Tales.
Grade 5 Fantasy, Biography.
Grade 6 Mythology, Newbery Award Books.
Grade 7 Epics, Historical Fiction.

Children and teachers are not restricted in their reading to the area of emphasis. Also included are suggested time allotments, resource materials and persons, general instructional practices and techniques.

## State Guides and Frameworks

A sequential growth curriculum in experiences with literature from kindergarten through grade twelve has been prepared by Wisconsin teachers under the direction of Robert C. Pooley and Leonard Kosinski.[44] This state project gives the following guiding characteristics of a good literature program:

1. It is sequential. In type of content, in reading difficulty, and in maturity of the concepts involved, it moves progressively from simple to more difficult and challenging materials.
2. It is comprehensive. From kindergarten through grade twelve children and youth should experience every type and form of literature, including children's classics; the great myths and legends; poetry from nursery rhymes to Wordsworth and in some cases Milton; fiction of all types, including the great short stories and some of the great novels; biography and essay; and drama from simple one-act plays to *Julius Caesar, Macbeth,* and *Hamlet.*
3. It is adjusted to levels of ability. This adjustment may take two forms. The curriculum itself should make specific content recommendations for students of high achievement, for those of normal attainment, and for those who learn more slowly. These distinctions should be recognized at all school levels. Second, each teacher in his own room or with each class should be aware of the potential of his own students, and should modify recommended materials and methods to meet as far as possible the individual needs and capacities of each student.
4. It is balanced between instruction and encouragement of individual free reading. The curriculum should indicate what to teach so as to advance the interests, skills, and enjoyments of students. It should also include recommendations of a wide range of collateral reading, viewed as an integral part of the total literature course at each school level. School libraries, public libraries, and the purchase of paperback books are resources for such a program.
5. It makes effective use of supplementary materials. Each teacher should have available for classroom use (easily obtainable from a central point) a three-speed phonograph, a tape recorder, a radio, and a motion picture pro-

[44] *Teaching Literature in Wisconsin.* Wisconsin English Language Arts Curriculum Project. Department of Public Instruction, Madison, Wisconsin.

jector. In some areas a television set will be desirable. Teachers should be familiar with films, recordings, and other devices related to literature, and make regular use of them where appropriate.

6. It recognizes the new as well as the old. Without neglect of the standard classics, teachers should be familiar with contemporary literature from their own reading, suggest to the librarian books to be purchased, and keep abreast of books in the area of literature added to the library. One indication of a good literature program is close coordination between teacher and librarian at all school levels.

7. It measures the success of instruction by students' ability to deal with literature. One evidence of a successful program is the amount and kind of voluntary individual reading done by students. Another evidence is the capability of students to read, understand, and enjoy a poem; to interpret the significance of a short story; and to report intelligently on the reading of a novel, a play, or a biography. A regular reader who finds pleasure and satisfaction in books is the ideal outcome of our instruction.

Another State publication is the *English Language Framework for the California Public Schools, Kindergarten through Grade Twelve.*[45] This framework is a basic statement of principles and a set of general guidelines to be used by districts and faculties of individual schools in developing programs and writing courses of study fitted to their particular situations.

The literature component is divided into the following sections:

The Principles of Instruction.
The Objectives of the Program in Literature.
The Common Literary Heritage.
Criteria for Selecting Literary Materials.
More Suggestions for the Literature Program.

Worthy of being quoted in full is the statement on Objectives:

The ultimate goal of the school program in literature is not accumulation of facts or anecdotes about literature and its creators, not simply passing acquaintance with major figures and literary movements, not skill in formal literary analysis for its own sake. Each of these does play its part in the process of mature literary appreciation, but it is a secondary, an auxiliary, rather than a primary part. The ultimate goal is, rather, development of students' capacities for continuing engagement with literature as a significant and rewarding human activity. The ideal should be to foster meaningful response to and enjoyment of literature, beginning with the child's first exposure to simple rhymes and stories and increasingly expanding the range of his literary experiences throughout his formal schooling and his adult life. Providing him with such opportunities should enable him better to understand himself as a person, as a member of a human community not circumscribed by a narrow extent of time and space, and as the possessor of a continually developing heritage of literature that can help give direction to his aesthetic and moral life.

[45] *English Language Framework for California Public Schools, Kindergarten through Grade Twelve.* California State Department of Education, Sacramento, Calif., 1968.

This primary aim of literary study is sometimes overlooked under the pressure of meeting the many other demands of the English language program in the schools.

### The Textbook Take-Over

Unfortunately this zeal to get on the structure-and-sequence bandwagon has led some districts and even states to adopt basal textbooks, the use of which would "guarantee" the desired sequential, structured program.

One of the best known of the current textbooks is indeed structured and sequential in the language strand, but the structure of the literature strand is limited to the inclusion of a poem or selection of prose in each section. The purpose of the literature selections as stated in the text's preface is as follows: "But the most important purpose of the reading selections is a very simple one: to teach the child to read more accurately and more sensitively." The teacher of grade three is advised in using Stevenson's poem "Block City" to "note that the emphasis is entirely on bringing the children to an understanding of the poem, not in establishing an attitude toward it. Failure resides in not knowing what the meaning is." The meaning implies that there is one right answer. The teacher is told,

> Whenever he [the student] strays from the poem or story and answers not from words but from the illustration or fancy's flight, he must be brought back: Is that what the line says? Who does what to whom?[46]

The last question may cause us to ask what such a literature program is doing to our students. Appreciation and enjoyment may be a private matter between the child and the poem, and the child's enjoyment may not necessarily be based on his thorough understanding or acceptance of the author's interpretation. Smith[47] has stated:

> A child is more easily persuaded to take pleasure in poetry through the tune of words, through his senses. . . . It is even more true of a child than of a grown-up that as Coleridge says, "Poetry gives much pleasure when only generally, and not perfectly, understood."

This writer also questions the sequence of placing Robert Frost's *Stopping by Woods on a Snowy Evening* in grade four and one of Phyllis McGinley's nursery rhymes in grade five. Finally, strict adherence to a textbook – any textbook – as *the* literature program deprives the child of all the intake and outgo activities which in themselves bring pleasure and promote enjoyment in the world of books.

[46] Roberts, Paul. *The Roberts English Series,* Book 3 (Teacher's Edition). New York: Harcourt, Brace, 1966.

[47] Smith, Lillian. *The Unreluctant Years.* Chicago: American Library Association, 1953.

### Basic Ingredients of a Good Literature Program

The chief ingredient of any literature program must be one of enjoyment. Too many children have an unhappy introduction to books and to reading. Holt[48] compares these children with animals fleeing danger, "who go like the wind, don't look back, remember where the danger was and stay away from it."

Shugrue[49] in summarizing the innovations in the teaching of English since 1958 refers the reader to the issues which emerged from The Basic Issues Conferences of 1958. He says, "Even before Jerome Bruner's influential *The Process of Education* (1960) the Basic Issues conferees affirmed their belief in 'an education in English which is sequential and cumulative in nature, practically and socially useful and permanently rewarding to the mind and spirit of those who are fortunate enough to get it.'" No child will want to flee from a literature program which provides such personal, mental, and social rewards.

## *Early Childhood Experiences with Literature*

Another type of structure is proposed by Britton.[50] He speaks of The Structure of Experience; "Doing isn't versus knowing" he says, but doing is a form of knowing. "Experience is itself a period of structure." He also says that the "template of our stored experiences" shapes new experiences combining both affective and cognitive learning. The structure he outlines takes the child from his young ego-centered stage to the objective older one. He calls the following levels the temporary landmarks in a structure of experience.

1. Acceptance of one's own unimportance.
2. The need to explore from a home base – indoors and outdoors.
3. Pressures to conform versus attempt to be oneself.
4. Adolescent fears of the outside world.
5. The need for privacy coupled with the desire to be part of the world of people.
6. The need for love also the need to compete.
7. The need for adult role while rejecting adults.
8. The need for a life pattern meanwhile rejecting the beliefs and values held by the some.

[48] Holt, John. *How Children Fail.* New York: Pitman, 1964.

[49] Shugrue, Michael F. *English in a Decade of Change.* New York: Pegasus, 1968.

[50] Britton, James. Speech presented at the Conference on English Education, Syracuse, N.Y., March 1969.

Children's pleasurable and satisfying experiences with literature will surely help children to advance from one level to another.

### Listening Experiences

Young children first learn literature by hearing it. The teacher must tell and read aloud large quantities of stories and poems to nourish and satisfy children's appetite for literature. Moffett[51] says that reading aloud by the teacher "puts the teacher in a giving position. While receiving this gift the children become possessed of the urge to do themselves what the teacher does." Many children of nonreading parents will begin to associate books with pleasure, and a sense of literary form will begin to grow within.

Children's responses to literature are not always visible or audible. According to Britton,[52] there are "certainly situations where receptive listening and a following silence are more eloquent testimony of satisfaction than any comment could be." There are also many pleasurable experiences for young listeners in sharing their responses to literature.

Harding[53] says that there appear to be four sequential levels of response "to the quality and pattern of (1) sounds, (2) events, (3) roles, and (4) worlds." He then suggests the various dimensions of response:

SOUND: When children bounce on mother's knee to a song or a nursery rhyme, when they join in the chorus, when they chant "maximum capacity" round the room, and maybe when they chuckle at special words, names, and puns, they are responding to the texture and rhythm of sounds. Such overt actions seem to be both elements of their enjoyment and signs of it.

EVENT: Both rhythm and form involve a pattern of expectation, both for the satisfaction and the modification of the expected pattern. Stories for very young children embody a pattern of events within this rhythm or form. When a child corrects the storyteller and wants the story word perfect, he is asking for confirmation to the pattern (in one respect or the other). At a later stage he may make up topsy-turvy stories with reversals of the pattern; finally he will improvise and impose his own.

ROLE: In free play or classroom drama, children take up the roles of characters in their stories, or perhaps continue the role playing that the story involved them in: "I'm Jack and this is the bean-

[51] Moffett, James. *A Student-Centered Language Arts Curriculum K–6:* A Handbook for Teachers. Boston: Houghton Mifflin, 1968.

[52] Britton, James. *Responses to Literature* (James R. Squire, ed.). Champaign, Ill.: National Council of Teachers of English, 1968.

[53] Harding, D. W. "The Report of the Study Group," *Response to Literature.* Champaign, Ill.: National Council of Teachers of English, 1968.

stalk and you be the Giant." Sometimes children will replay the story, some times reshape and improvise on it, perhaps relating the roles and events more nearly to their own wishes.

WORLD: While a story is being read aloud to a group a child may interpose: "He's a funny boy" (about Jan in "The Silver Sword" perhaps), and the group may begin to talk about his background, his relations with the other characters, etc. A new variety of talk develops to relate and organize elements of the world of that story or to relate the world of that story to the child's own world. It will tie in all the four kinds of response, giving some a new articulation.

In addition to listening to the teacher read aloud, children should have an opportunity to listen to one another read aloud to partners or in small groups. They also should have choral reading experiences where they get the thrill of being part of a group production. They may read captions of a film strip, an experience story dictated by a child, pages from a picture book placed in an opaque projector, or a poem projected from a transparency on an overhead projector.

## Learning Through Play

The importance of play in learning cannot be overemphasized. The adult who says, "I visited their class but the children were only playing," reveals his lack of knowledge about the ways by which children learn. Play is recreation, but is is also the child's work. Of the various types of play important for child development, dramatic play is the most prominent.

"It is quite true and a most significant truth," says Isaacs,[54] "that the child's world is essentially a dramatic world." The records of her study show how often the child's most active interests display themselves through playing the roles of mother, father, and child.

The younger the child, the less self-conscious he is, and he is far less guarded in his responses to literature and to poetry in particular. Holbrook[55] quotes Melanie Klein's suggestion that "the connections between conscious and unconscious are closer in young children than in adults and that infantile repressions are less powerful."

## Dramatic Experiences

Thanks to the Dartmouth Conference, drama is once more considered respectable. Drama as used here should not be confused with theatre. The

[54] Isaacs, Susan. *Intellectual Growth in Young Children.* New York: Schocken Books, 1966.

[55] Holbrook, David. *The Exploring World.* New York: Cambridge University Press, 1967.

latter involves an audience. Performance for an audience comes much later. "Drama is the acting out of feeling and takes the point of view of the participant, for whom it exists."[56]

For young children, dramatic activities include dramatic play, creative dramatics, and informal puppet plays. Dramatic play allows children to "try on" the roles of adults in their daily lives. The first dramatic play is usually solitary play with dolls, blocks, or wheel toys, as props. "Dressing up" is important. The wearing of hats in assuming the male role is important to many boys. Familiar stories creep over into this play, and mother becomes Mother Bear as she dishes out the porridge.

The place of creative dramatics in the primary grades is an important part of any individualized reading program because it provides an opportunity for children to learn from one another. "What is more children's imaginations are stretched, their powers of observations are sharpened and their comprehension of the reading materials upon which the dramatics are based is heightened.[57]

> Creative dramatics consists of the children acting out events that follow pretty closely what actually did happen in the story they have read. But since there are no lines to be memorized, each presentation will be somewhat different from the next, and many children will add additional details spontaneously.
>
> Creative dramatizations in primary grades differ from those of older children in that the younger children insist on playing the whole story. They are not content with less.
>
> The traditional nursery tales are usually "sure-fire." Particularly useful are the cumulative stories which are repetitious in plot, sequence, and dialogue. The more familiar the story, the better the children like to "play" it. Perennial favorites remain:
>
> *Three Billy Goats Gruff,*
> *Three Little Pigs,*
> *Goldilocks and The Three Bears,*
> *The Pancake,*
> and
> *Chicken Little.*
>
> There are many modern stories with similar folk-tale structure which children also like to play. A few of these are: *Ask Mr. Bear,* by Margery Flack; *The Camel Who Took a Walk,* by Jack Twerkov; *The Carrot Seed,* by Ruth Krauss; *Where the Wild Things Are,* by Maurice Sendak.

If we look at one story carefully we can discover the elements which make it a natural for dramatization:

1. The simple beginning which moves directly into action.
2. The cumulative quality of the story . . . this one accumulates suspense as well.

[56] Moffett, James. *A Student-Centered Language Arts Curriculum K–6:* A Handbook for Teachers. Boston: Houghton Mifflin, 1968.

[57] Reid, Virginia (ed.). *Participating Teacher's Guide: Individualizing Your Reading Program.* Cambridge, Mass.: Ealing Corp., 1968.

3. The action varies – he walked along, he skipped, he hopped, he galloped, he trotted.
4. The appeal of conversation between a real boy and animals.
5. The "secret" is shared by the players but is unknown to the audience.
6. The repetitive phrase – especially the chance to say No.

***Puppets*** Another meaningful activity in bringing stories to life is the use of puppets. Such puppets should be of the instant variety which can be made quickly and easily. These include simple hand puppets made from socks or gloves; rod or stick puppets which are simple cutouts stapled or glued to sticks. Gertrude Pels[58] provides many simple patterns.

The puppet stages should be of the instant variety also. Primary tables tipped on the side serve as a fine stage. One primary group used four such tables to share the story of *Harry by the Sea.*[59] They needed the long stage, they said, to show the distance Harry traveled. One episode of the story was enacted at each table.

A piece of construction paper stretched across the lower half of an open door also makes a fine stage. If children feel that scenery is necessary it can be held up on sticks or fastened by clothespins to a wire stretched across the door. Shadow puppets can be shown on an overhead projector as well as by the more traditional method of backlighting a tightly stretched sheet.

### Storytelling

Not only should the teacher tell stories, but also the child should be encouraged to retell stories he has heard and read. Often a child enjoys this experience more if he has something to show at the same time. He may show the original illustrations in a picture book, or his own illustration inspired by the story or book. Picture story boxes and roller movies are more elaborate methods of combining children's art with storytelling. Children also enjoy telling stories with flannel board figures. Simple cutout figures of paper or cardboard can be backed by flannel or sandpaper and can be arranged on the board by the storyteller. The same effect can be gained by using on a magnetic board paper cutouts attached to small magnets.

### Common Literary Heritage

Preschool and kindergarten teachers are alerted in this excerpt from a teachers resource guide.[60]

[58] Pels, Gertrude. *Easy Puppets.* New York: Thos. Y. Crowell, 1951.

[59] Zion, Eugene. *Harry by the Sea.* New York: Harper, 1965.

[60] Reid, Virginia, Helen McDonald, and Tonja Rader. *The World of Language K–2.* Chicago: Follett, in press.

When the Headstart Programs began, one heard such comments as, these disadvantaged children come to school with no background of literature. No one has bounced them on the knee to the rhythm of This is the way the gentlemen ride or "Ride a cock horse to Banbury Cross." No one has read or told them *The Three Billy Goats Gruff*.

We teachers have been deluding ourselves for some time that most children bring with them a common literary heritage. The truth is that almost all children, despite social and economic backgrounds, have been or are disadvantaged in respect to their literary background. To compensate for this educational void we should plan to share with children in many ways those stories and poems which will stretch each child's imagination, develop his vocabulary, increase his sense of personal worth, and maintain his sense of wonder. We believe that the reading aloud of literature is the most important single thing a parent or teacher can do to help a child be successful in school and beyond.

## *Later Childhood Experience with Literature*

Many of the experiences enjoyed by young children continue to be enjoyed by children in the middle and upper elementary grades. They still respond to their literature as individuals and as members of a group, informally as well as in activities which are more structured than in the primary grades.

### Listening Experiences – Reading Aloud by the Teacher

Even though many children can read to themselves and many prefer to do so, it is essential for the teacher and/or librarian to have children hear the language of fine literature. Stories such as *Wind in the Willows, Winnie-the-Pooh,* or *Just So Stories,* as well as poetry, can be more fully experienced if heard.

Schmitt and Sister Mary Nora[61] have supplied the following criteria for choosing books worthy of being read aloud:

> Reading aloud is the most simple and obvious method of introducing to children the best in literature, for only the best deserves to be read aloud and it is only the best that can stand the test. The teacher has an opportunity to acquaint children with books and/or stories which they could not or perhaps would not read for themselves. The teacher chooses materials which he knows well and genuinely likes. The children in their enjoyment of the story learn to appreciate the language of fine literature. Imagination is stimulated, horizons broadened, and something of a permanent impression gained. Such books as *Wind In the Willows, Winnie-the-Pooh, The Just So Stories* seem to have been intended for reading aloud. The same is true of poetry and folk tales. These stories take on new and deeper meaning for the children as they share the

[61] Schmitt, Yvette, and Sister Mary Nora. "What are Some Meaningful Experiences with Literature?" *Children's Literature Old and New*. Champaign, Ill.: National Council of Teachers of English, May 1963.

humor, the adventures, the real problems with which they can identify. It follows that books read aloud in the classroom can be used to promote thinking, discussing, writing, drawing, and many other activities.

Some of the Newbery Medal books are considered dull by the standards of modern youth, but read aloud, *And Now Miguel, The Wheel on the School, The White Stag,* and others become interesting and exciting and children will have gained new insights which they well might not have discovered alone.

In choosing books to read aloud, the teacher might want to consider the following criteria:

1. Books which children could not or would not be likely to read for themselves. Obviously, easy-to-read books are ruled out. This does not mean selections should necessarily always consist of books too difficult for the children to read. Reading *Huckleberry Finn* to the third grade or *King Henry IV* to the sixth is not the recommended course. Conversely, entering kindergartners who have not been introduced to Mother Goose should make her acquaintance without delay.
2. Books which possess those qualities found in all great literature:

   a. Characters who are "round and whole," true to life, with the complexities, motives, actions, and reactions of human beings.
   b. Plot development which is logical and believable.
   c. Narrative which is vivid, meaningful, and rich in vocabulary.
   d. Some underlying significance and/or symbolism (as apart from a moral lesson).

3. Books which broaden horizons, stimulate the imagination, deepen and enrich the reader's understanding of his world and fellowman.
4. Books which gain something in being read aloud and shared:

   a. Because of the humor.
   b. Because they point up some great truth.
   c. Because they stimulate thought and discussion.
   d. Because the language is worthy of being shared and savored.

***Reading Aloud by Children.*** Thanks to the advent of the tape recorders, children not only have the opportunity to read to an unseen audience but also to hear themselves. One child could record by himself, or he could be a member of a small group recording the oral reading of a story, the script for a puppet play, a poem, or a play.

Lack of a recorder does not exclude partner reading, where the children take turns reading to one another. Small groups or the whole class should experience choral reading of rhythmic prose as well as poetry. Recently a fifth grade was caught up in the lore of Americana adapted for choral reading with an amusing rhythmic folk poem from the Appalachian Mountains, entitled *Mama Buy Me a China Doll.*[62] In sharing with other classes, they accompanied this choice verse with transparent puppets laid on two overhead projectors.

[62] Zemack, Harve, and Margot Zemack. *Mama Buy Me a China Doll.* Chicago: Follett, 1966.

### Learning Through Play

The element of play continues to be a significant factor in prompting children's responses to literature even in upper elementary grades.

Such play takes the form of making up and playing guessing games involving characters, events, and plots of stories the children have read. Such games may or not involve pantomime or verbal drama.

### Drama

Children in the upper elementary grades should continue to create their own dialogues and plays based on their reading of poems and stories.

Such plays could be that of role playing or straight story playing.

1. Role playing consists of a child's choosing a character in a story he has read and acting out what he imagines he would have done himself in a similar or different situation. For example, a girl might ask herself what she would have done if she had been Wanda in *The Hundred Dresses,* by Eleanor Estes (Harcourt, 1944).

   Since this is supposed to be the child's own interpretation, he does not have to follow what the character actually did in the story. It's much more fun to think up an entirely new alternative.
2. Story playing. In addition to the role-playing situations, the older children enjoy equally well the actual portrayal of characters and scenes as given by the author. As with the primary children, some traditional stories are played with delight by generation after generation. These stories include *Aladdin, Ali Baba and the Forty Thieves, Pinocchio, Dick Whittington, Wind in the Willows, Alice in Wonderland,* and many more.

   Many contemporary books are equally popular for dramatization. Some of the scenes which have been chosen by various sixth grade classes follow:

   *The Phantom Tollbooth,* by Norton Juster.

   Theme: Happiness

   Milo asked by King to entertain and tells what his courtiers can do. Milo shocks them by mentioning numbers.

   *Tituba of Salem Village,* by Ann Petra.

   Two colonial girls look at the sinful playing cards that the bound boy was given, and they get the beautiful slave girl, Tituba, to tell their fortunes.

   *A Wrinkle in Time,* by Madeline L'Engle.

   Three children searching for "it" are reported to the man with the red eyes.

   *Alvin Steadfast on Vernacular Island,* by Frank Jacobs.

   As Dr. Cranshaw returns home he is met by "Appropriate Gesture."

He explains her title and also those of "Standing Ovation," "The Common Good," "Ultimate Aim," and "Conditioned Reflex" who are all going to help him on his journey to look for "The Doubt."

*Shadow of a Bull,* by Maia Wojciechowska.

Manola is taken to a friend's home to meet Juan and confides his fear of bullfighting.

*The Melendy Family,* by Elizabeth Enright.

By pooling their allowances each of the four children can afford a special adventure. Randy's adventure is to an art festival where he meets Miss Oliphant, who explains the source of the picture he covets.

*The Egypt Game,* by Zylpha Snyder.

The natural interests of children cross all racial barriers as April, Melanie, and Marshall decide on an Egyptian ceremony to bury Elizabeth's cat.

3. Readers Theatre. In addition to having the experience of creating original lines, children should also have pleasurable experiences with language which is more elaborate than that which they are able to produce. For this experience Readers Theatre offers exciting possibilities in developing both an appreciation of literature and personal development of the readers.

   This form of drama has been called, among other things, Concert Reading and Auditorium Reading. Thousands of adult theatre-goers thrilled to *Don Juan in Hell* as it was read to them by Agnes Moorhead, Charles Laughton, Vincent Price, and Tyrone Power.

Children also have responded enthusiastically to staged readings of *Amelia Bedelia, Wicked John and the Devil,* and *Winnie-the-Pooh.* In staging *Winnie-the-Pooh* one sixth grade placed all readers on stools; they read from scripts on music stands, Kanga on a high stool, of course, and Baby Roo on a low stool.

Some examples of Readers Theatre involve the use of costumes and props. Coger and White[63] include *Mary Poppins* and *The Reluctant Dragon* to be performed by college students, but they could be performed by children just as well.

Barnes[64] reported on the four kinds of dramatic work which develop side by side in schools in the United Kingdom:

1. Movement, sometimes with music.
2. Free play, with clothes for dressing-up, and other adaptable "properties."

[63] Coger, Leslie Irene, and Melvin R. White. *Readers Theatre Handbook.* Chicago: Scott Foresman Co., 1967.

[64] Barnes, Douglas. *Drama in the Classroom.* Champaign, Ill.: National Council of Teachers of English, 1968.

3. Enactment of familiar stories.
4. Exploration of the life around them.

This work in drama develops in indefinable sequences existing on two levels. "They are inescapable sequences of development which continue over years, but as the children become older, they become short-term sequences through which a class may pass in coming closer to a particular experience. Or put another way, the earlier stages should never be left behind, but should co-exist with new procedures which the children's development has made possible. These sequences are:

1. Individual – pair – group – whole class.
2. Movement-in-space – pantomime – verbal – improvisation.
3. Free play – selection of dialogue and action.
4. Unpatterned spontaneity – planned performance for peers.
5. Unscripted – children's own scripts – adult scripts."

### TALKING

Mr. James Britton of the University of London Institute in Education has been an invited participant in every outstanding conference on English education in the past two years. At one of these he described the junior school classroom in England:[65]

A junior school classroom is likely to be a room full of things, things to look at and to read and talk about, and most of those would have been produced by the children in the school. And also things to do, things to play with, things to work with, things to work on. In most cases the children will be working individually, or in pairs or in threes or fours, and in most cases they will have chosen what it is they are doing. It will be noticeable that they are talking about it all the time they're doing it, to each other or to the teacher. Now, I know one primary school class in London where there are two items on the class time table. One is called "Your time" and the other is called "My time." What I have been describing to you goes on in "Your time." In "My time" the teacher will be explaining and discussing something with the class as a whole, or watching a dramatic improvisation that some group of children is putting on to show to the others, or reading stories or poems to the whole class, or possibly listening to a child telling the rest of the class something that he's done or read or discovered.

1. Large and Small Group Discussion. Often overlooked in upper elementary grades are illustrations. Picture books are "not only for the very young."[66] An examination of Caldecott award winning books by sixth grade youngsters resulted in several related language learning

[65] Britton, James. "The Role of Language in Learning in the Elementary School," *Reason and Change in Elementary Education.* New Orleans: Second National Conference Project in Elementary Education, USOE Tri-University, February, 1968.

[66] Hopkins, Lee Bennett, and Grace Alloca. "Not Only for the Very Young." *Classroom Practices in Teaching English.* Champaign, Ill.: National Council of Teachers of English, 1968.

experiences. First was a brainstorming session resulting in these questions:

Who is Caldecott?
Why is this Award named after him?
What does the picture on the medal show?
When did the Award begin?
Who were other winners?

Children were allowed to choose two books to compare. Also they used a rating scale on which they rated the books from 1938 to 1967. As a result of this activity they became aware of the great variety in illustrations and of the progress made in publishing books for children.

Moffett offers some valuable ideas for extending pupils' responses to literature.[67]

What I will recommend here has little to do with what is generally called 'class discussion,' which is rarely a real discussion. Although class-wide talk is often helpful or necessary, it cannot teach discussion; it can only benefit from discussion's having been learned some other way. So far as I can tell, the only way is pupil-to-pupil talk in small groups of no more than six. The sheer size of 'class discussion' precludes a high enough degree of attention, participation, and interaction – essential qualities of discussion. The teacher has to talk too much to maintain continuity, and invariably does talk too much. He resorts to prompting by questions, and except for occasional solos by a loquacious few, the children play the very restricted role of answering these questions. As vocal exchange, such a process is severely limited. The heart of discussing is expatiation, picking up ideas and developing them; corroborating, qualifying, and challenging; building on and varying each other's sentences, statements, and images. Questioning is a very important part, but only a part, and should arise out of exchanges among students themselves, so that they learn to pose as well as answer questions. For his part, the teacher should be relieved from the exhausting, semi-hysterical business of emceeing.

In another publication Moffett[68] says that "the teacher's job is to establish the forms of discussion that, when internalized by individuals, will most enhance the growth of thought and speech.

2. Panel Discussions. When three or more children have read a book they would like to discuss, they meet together to plan an agenda of points about the book warranting discussion. Beginners are helped to work within a framework of questions posed by the group, each question answered by one or more members. Shea[69] gives some of the

[67] Reid, Virginia (ed.). *Participating Teacher's Guide: Individualizing Your Reading Program.* Cambridge, Mass.: Ealing Corp., 1968.

[68] Moffett, James. *Teaching the Universe of Discourse.* Boston: Houghton Mifflin, 1968.

[69] Shea, Martha. "What the Gifted Child Reads," *Finding the Right Book.* Library supplement, *The Instructor,* November 1966.

typical panel questions prepared for discussion of *The Ark*[70] and *The Silver Sword:*[71]

Time and setting of each book had been established before questions were discussed.

1. What kinds of courage are shown in these books? Try to give examples.
2. Have you ever been called upon to show real courage?
3. Would you like to be the friend of the characters in either of the books? Why?
4. What do you think of the title The Ark?
5. Do you think either of the authors has a distinctive or individual style? Explain.
6. Do you think either of these books will be of lasting interest or could become classics?
7. In conclusion, let's summarize by discussing the themes of each book. Are they similar? How would you state each theme?

And for *The Return of the Twelves*[72] Reasoner[73] has developed a Teachers Guide about which he says "It is my fondest hope that you will use this Guide as it is intended to release the resources within you the teacher." It is hoped that the many good suggestions included will actually release children through literature as well as "to literature" and that children will discuss not only the questions posed by Reasoner for 32 Yearling Books but will also create their own.

3. Storytelling. "The magic of 'Once Upon a Time' or 'Once there was and was not' is immeasurable", says Durham.[74]

This magic makes it possible for upper grade children to tell stories to younger children and thus recreate the magic.

One highly recommended practice is the forming of storytelling clubs. The initiation fee is the telling of a story acceptable to the listeners. Once accepted as a member of the Storytelling Club the child is ready to be called by the principal or a teacher to tell stories to other classes.

## Writing Experiences

Writing has humorously been referred to as "talk wrote down." Skillful indeed is the teacher who can stimulate in students the same desire to write as he does to talk. This teacher has removed many of the conventional hurdles which prevent a child from communicating freely.

Literature can and does serve as a springboard to creative writing.

[70] Benary, Isbert, M. *The Ark.* New York: Harcourt, Brace, 1953.

[71] Serraillier, I. *The Silver Sword.* New York: Criterion Books, 1959.

[72] Clark, Pauline. *The Return of the Twelves.* New York: Coward, 1964.

[73] Reasoner, Charles. *Releasing Children to Literature.* New York: Dell, 1968.

[74] Durham, Mae. "Books for Storytelling" *Finding the Right Book,* Library Supplement, *The Instructor,* November 1966.

Unfortunately, many assignments repel children rather than attract them to literature. Such assignments include the writing of the usual book reports, essays on the life of an author, or exercises in literary criticism such as the sample given by Moffett:[75]

> Some fifth-grade children were asked to compare, in a single paragraph, a poem and a short story that handled the same theme in somewhat different ways. To the teacher this probably seemed like a sophisticated assignment that would prepare for many similar assignments to come in later years. But sensing, correctly, that the task would be cognitively difficult and would require guidance, she directed them to cover, in this one paragraph, eight points of comparison. This in effect furnished the organization and dictated what virtually every sentence should be about.
>
> First of all, the over-structuring was a give-away that the assignment was too advanced. If children have to have that much guidance they should not be asked to do such a thing. Second, since she had previously emphasized that a paragraph was about one thing, she confused the children by asking them to put eight things in one paragraph, the problem here being both in the original attempt to define a paragraph, like a sentence, as 'one idea', and in the unnecessary injunction to make one paragraph contain all they had to say. Third, for children such an assignment has no point or purpose. They have already appreciated and responded to the poem and story. However the teacher may conceive the task, the children can only see the paper as a kind of test. Far from increasing appreciation, such unpleasant after-chores drive children away from literature. Fourth, it is not the mission of schools to teach for its own sake literary criticism and analysis, which is a college specialty. No evidence supports the strong current belief that direct and explicit critical analysis aids comprehension and appreciation. Much more likely is that it interferes with response, which is the main goal of schools. Response can be deepened and sharpened by small-group discussion based on native reactions and touching on literary technique as it becomes a natural issue (and it will, because content is partly a factor of form). What schools should do is develop intuitions, through authentic writing and through discussion, so that children do not need vivisections and postmortems in order to understand and respond to literature.

A few of the writing experiences which have heightened rather than diminished children's responses to literature are the following:

1. The author or book character you would most like to meet.
2. Ronald asked Zilpha Snyder why she had Robin wear false eyelashes. If you could, what author would you like to interview? What questions would you ask?
3. Recap in written dialogue an improvisation of a story which has been played in class.
4. Adapt a story for Readers Theatre.
5. Bring a book character from the past to the present or the reverse. Discussion of such books at *The Children of Green Knowe,*[76] *Time*

[75] Moffett, James. *Teaching the Universe of Discourse.* Boston: Houghton Mifflin, 1968.

[76] Boston, Lucy M. *The Children of Green Knowe.* New York: Harcourt, Brace, 1955.

*at the Top*,[77] and *Wicked Pigeon Ladies in the Garden*[78] will all help children to know how it feels to be an outsider.
6. Tell what would happen if Caddie Woodlawn met Jo in *Little Women* or Alice in Wonderland met Pooh Bear. Are there others you think would be fun to compare?
7. Compare factual and fictionalized books such as *Tiger of the Snows*[79] and *Banner in the Skies*.[80]
8. Write a story patterned on some story or book you have enjoyed. One nine-year-old boy who had fallen completely under the spell of the Narnia books, wrote his own version. He called it *The Land of Nar*. It was complete with original maps and a newly minted language.

Stemming from individual reading, group reading, and discussions, some groups have produced their own Junior Book of Authors.

In one sixth grade the children felt that inasmuch as each one of them had been an author they would write autobiographical sketches of themselves for the book. They made their own awards, for which they had set standards. They selected what they felt was their outstanding creative writing and presented awards for best story, best illustrations, originality, and so on.

Numerous suggestions for helping youngsters create and write their own books are offered by Wright.[81]

## *Summary*

A literature program for elementary children would be incomplete if it did not do the following:

1. Provide children with books that reveal ethical values to the reader as he identifies with another child faced with similar problems and evaluates his solutions.
2. Discover or uncover first sparks of interest and fan them into lasting flames as readers develop into insatiable readers of science, biography, fantasy, poetry, or drama.
3. Remember that illustrations are important in any program of literature

[77] Ormondroyd, Edward. *Time at the Top*. Berkeley, Calif.: Parnassus, 1963.

[78] Chase, Mary. *Wicked Pigeon Ladies in the Garden*. New York: Knopf, 1968.

[79] Ullman, James, and Norgay Tensing. *Tiger of the Snows*. New York: Putnam, 1955.

[80] Ullman, James. *Banner in the Skies*. New York: Lippincott, 1954.

[81] Wright, Betty Atwell. *Books for Children by Children: Teaching Tips*, unpublished manuscript, 1966.

– "Illustrations are to words what jelly is to bread – increases the nourishment, makes it more delicious and adds a flavor of its own."[82]

4. Include the contributions of ethnic groups with which all children can identify and feel accepted and respected.
5. Set our standards high, and talk up to children, not down.

One of the favorite authors of juvenile literature is Gates,[83] who sets these standards for herself and for all who would write for children:

1. That the author be sincere, that he write straight from his heart to the heart of the child.
2. That the stories be interesting to the child told in a style which is both direct and suited to the story, varying from the swaggery style of the tall tale to the quiet lyrical telling of a fairy tale or myth.
3. That the realistic stories attempt within proper limits to face children with the stern realities of living that as leaders of tomorrow they may be able to cope with the tasks ahead. That the stories show it is the likenesses not the differences between men which is the important thing to remember.

Loban[84] speaks of balancing the literature program with respect not only to the content elements of literature but also to the artistic elements. He builds a bridge from juvenile to adult books as he uses examples from each to demonstrate the important elements of literature.

1. The ability to draw the reader in and make him an imaginative participant.
2. The use of indirection.
3. The elements of symbolism.
4. The awareness of structural form.
5. The presence of irony.
6. The conscious awareness of many other important artistic understandings; the hypnotic power of words arranged in certain orders; the basic myths on which literature draws; the importance of point of view or setting; the development of plot and suspense; the signals by which characterization is accomplished.

In Chapter 9, Russell explored the possibilities of reading contributing to positive mental health; this corrective function he described as "bibliotherapy, a process of dynamic interaction between the personality of

[82] Mosier, Rosalind. "Illustrations are Important," *Finding the Right Book.* Library Supplement, *The Instructor,* November 1966.

[83] Gates, Doris. "The Literary Aspect of a Basic Reading Series," *Contributions In Reading,* No. 2. Boston: Ginn, 1961.

[84] Loban, Walter. "Balancing the Literature Program," *Elementary English,* 43:746–751, November 1966.

the reader and literature which may be utilized for assessment of difficulties, adjustment toward mental health, and growth into maturity." He further stated that imaginative literature enables a reader to be both spectator and participant but that this does not happen automatically whenever a reader opens a book.

And what about the child who never opens a book? Since Russell first began his exploration of bibliotherapy, we have learned much more about the needs of deprived children, particularly those in poverty-stricken areas of the city. Fader[85] calls his program one to "wake up teachers to get the most reluctant reader to read, read, read." He begins with an honest look at children in their English classes and says, "Children are rarely indirect or misleading about what they feel. Unlike adults, children seldom learn to mask, postpone or abrogate the effect of any cause that moves them. Just as the living language is never wrong, so are children always accurate in reflecting things as they really are for them. Therefore I knew there was no use identifying the children as causes of what was wrong in the English class. They may be all that they shouldn't be, but they are, and must be met where they are before they can be led to where they should be (that is, where we are)." Having recognized "where they are" the teacher may then supply books which help children in the areas suggested by Cianciola.[86]

1. Acquire information and knowledge about the psychology and physiology of human behavior.
2. Learn what it means to know thyself.
3. Find an interest outside himself.
4. Relieve conscious problems in a controlled manner.
5. Utilize an opportunity for identification and compensation.
6. Illuminate difficulties and acquire insight into his own behavior.

In the firm belief that books are a significant force in developing personal and social sensitivity, four editions of *Reading Ladders for Human Relations* have been produced.[87] The fifth edition is under way. The forthcoming volume, like its predecessors, is concerned with books which help children to relate to their peers and with the adults in their world.

Fader defines a poverty-stricken child as one who has "a poverty of experience — a poverty which can afflict lives lived at $100,000 a year just as readily as it curses the $1,000 a year existence. The poorest man in the

[85] Fader, Daniel N., and Elton B. McNeil. *Hooked on Books.* New York: Berkeley Publishing Corp., 1968.

[86] Cianciola, Patricia. "Children's Literature can Affect Coping Behavior," *Personnel & Guidance Journal, 43:*897–901, May 1965.

[87] Crosby, Muriel (ed.). *Reading Ladders for Human Relations.* Washington, D.C.: American Council on Education, 1963.

world is the man limited to his own experience, the man who does not read." He directs his book to "every child who may become such a man."

It has been the purpose of this chapter to explore some of the many avenues open to the teacher of young children for taking the child beyond the mere opening of a book, and provide active, meaningful involvement of student readers with the best of literature available today.

## *Aids in Selecting Literature*

To involve children fully in their personal reading and to become fully involved with them in their responses to literature there is no real substitute for the actual reading of the books by the teacher. But the output of children's books has become so voluminous that the teacher is forced to resort to some book-reviewing services. Such aids can be divided into three general categories: 1. Books about children's books, 2. Book lists, and 3. Book-reviewing services to keep one informed on current favorites.

1. Books about children's books:

Arbuthnot, May Hill. *Children and Books.* New York: Scott, Foresman & Co., 1964.

Huck, Charlotte S., and Doris Young Kuhn. *Children's Literature in the Elementary School.* Holt, Rinehart & Winston, 1968.

Smith, Lillian, *Unreluctant Years.* Chicago: American Library Association, 1953.

The above three books were designed as college textbooks for classes in children's literature, but they serve equally well as teacher references on books of lasting interest. As has been said, "the books are old but the children are new."

Larrick, Nancy, *A Teacher's Guide to Children's Books.* Columbus, Ohio: Charles E. Merrill Books, Inc., 1963.

Part I describes children's interests at various levels and books to match. Part II suggests ways teachers relate books to children's personal and social groups, and feed reading appetites. Part III suggests ways to evaluate reading activities.

Fenner, Phyllis, *Proof of the Pudding: What Children Read.* New York: John Day Co., 1957.

This consists of a comprehensive list of the best children's books ever published, as well as a description of the books, why they are so well liked, and their interest level.

Duff, Annis. *Bequest of Wings.* New York: Viking Press, 1944, and *Longer Flight.* New York: Viking Press, 1956.

These two books written by a sensitive librarian and mother offer a provocative account of the way that children and books came together in her family.

From the teacher's point of view, these books recount the endless opportunities to integrate books into the everyday affairs and activities of children. And most important of all, Annis Duff demonstrates the wide variety of books that fill the special needs of children in various stages of their growth into adults.

2. Book lists (revised frequently)

Arbuthnot, May Hill, *Children's Books Too Good to Miss.* Cleveland: Western Reserve University Press, 1959.

A group of specialists suggest which of the old books should be kept alive and which of the new measure up to earlier classics.

*Children's Books.* about $1.25. Washington, D.C.: Association for Childhood Education, International, 1961.

Eaken, M. K., *Good Books for Children.* (3d ed.) Chicago: University of Chicago Press, 1959.

Brief annotations on the most outstanding books reviewed for 15 years (1950–1965) in the Bulletin of the Center for Children's Books.

National Council of Teachers of English, *Adventuring with Books.*

Published about every 5 years. Materials classified by subject and age levels, 3 to 4.

Sragow, Joan (ed.). *Best Books for Children.* New York: R. R. Bowker, 1968.

3. Book reviewing services available to classroom teachers:

Teachers who join certain professional organizations receive monthly journals which devote one section to reviews of children's books. Here are three such journals:

*Childhood Education.* Published by the Association for Childhood Education, International. "Books for Children" is edited by Richard L. Darling.

*Elementary English.* Published by the National Council of Teachers of English. "Books for Children" is edited by Shelton L. Root, Jr.

*The Reading Teacher.* Published by the International Reading Association. "Literature for Children" is edited by Dorothy Kendall Bracken.

Other publications which contain timely reviews of current books are:

*Bulletin for the Center of Children's Books.* Published monthly by the University of Chicago Press. Reviews books for students, preschool through ninth grade. Rates books as recommended, additional, marginal, not recommended.

*Horn Book Magazine.* Published bimonthly by Horn Books, Inc., 585 Boylston St., Boston 16, Mass.

*Saturday Review.* Published weekly. Carries a column about once a month, "Books for Young People," edited by Zena Sutherland.

*Scholastic Teacher.* Published weekly during the school year by Scholastic Magazine, 50 West 44th St., New York 36, N.Y. Published annually. Reviews briefly about 4,000 best juveniles in print. Coded to indicate recommendations.

*Young Readers' Review.* Published monthly, September to June, by Young Readers' Review, Box 137, Wall Street Station, New York. This contains very simple reviews of books approved for grades kindergarten through high school.

Schools which have professional librarians will have these book review sources:

*The Booklist.* Subscription Books Bulletin, published semimonthly, and *Top of the News,* published quarterly, by the Children's Young Adult Services Division, 50 East Huron St., Chicago, Ill.

*A Basic Book Collection for Elementary Grades.* American Library Association, Chicago, Ill.

*Notable Children's Books.* Children's Services Division, American Library Association, Chicago, Ill.

*School Library Journal.* R. R. Bowker, 1180 Avenue of the Americas, New York, N.Y. Published monthly from September to May.

An important additional source is *The Calendar,* a quarterly bulletin published by the Children's Book Council. The publication not only highlights books published for prekindergarten through high school since 1966, but it also keeps the teacher up to date on current happenings in the book world, such as awards and prizes, and reminds the teacher of special books related to special days throughout the year.

*The Calendar.* Published by the Children's Book Council, 175 Fifth Avenue, New York, N.Y. 10010.

A new publication is *Appraisal,* published three times a year by the Children's Science Book Review Committee, Harvard Graduate School of Education, 207 Beverly Hall, Appian Way, Cambridge, Mass. 02138.

# CHAPTER 11 | Teaching Literature: High School and College

## JAMES SQUIRE

As individuals mature, their responses to literature tend to sharpen and become more fully integrated with their personal experience. Wilson,[1] utilizing methods of analyzing the reading responses of college freshmen which had earlier been applied to the responses of adolescents, reported this phenomenon and suggested that the more sophisticated reactions reflected both the maturity of the reader and his literary education. The critic Norman Holland sees the response of mature readers as consisting of both intellection and interjection, as the process of relating the reader's unconsciousness to the central fantasy of the literary work.[2] Many factors, of course, influence even the most sophisticated responses. The content and form of the literary selection, the skill of the reader in comprehending the meanings of the work, the predispositions of the reader and his literary and personal experience – all interact to create a more fully orchestrated response. School and ultimately college programs also become more organized than those at earlier levels, reflecting in part the changing interests of the maturing reader, in part the necessity for providing instruction in critical interpretation, and in part the importance of introducing young people to rich and varied literary experiences of many kinds. The literary and research backgrounds traced earlier in this volume have influenced in various ways the programs in literature as they exist in high schools and colleges today.

Any survey of practices in teaching literature in high school and college

[1] Wilson, James R. *Responses of College Freshmen to Three Novels.* Champaign, Ill.: National Council of Teachers of English, 1966.

[2] Holland, Norman N. *The Dynamics of Literary Response.* New York: Oxford University Press, 1968.

in relation to the impact of reading on the student reader must begin with some review of historical antecedents, if only because the traditions of yesteryear so influence instruction today. A review of the changing aims and organization of contemporary programs will demonstrate how teachers today attempt to relate the demands of content to the reactions of readers. Present knowledge about the responses of high school and college readers seems best summarized separately, followed by a review of teaching approaches conducive to eliciting desirable responses, and a consideration of some of the book lists which assist teachers and parents in identifying literary selections of unique interest to adolescents and young adults.

## *Changing Aims in Literary Study*

Few early programs organized for teaching literature in our schools were concerned with the effects of literature on student readers. Mersand[3] reports that during the last half of the nineteenth century, instruction was characterized by three trends: the development of annotated textbooks for student study, an emphasis on the prescribed reading of a small number of selected texts, and the gradual establishment of uniform college entrance requirements which prescribed both a common body of literary materials and common aims and standards. During this period, according to Purves, literature was used for "literacy, oratory, and moral training.[4] The student read the text for practice in reading and declamation and he read only texts that were uplifting." Only in the selection of literature did teachers concern themselves with effects. This approach, in turn, yielded to concern with literature as history, or the use of literature to implant the cultural heritage, a tendency that remains widespread today. The rigorous, highly selective literature program remained the standard in the schools until 1917 when James Hosic, preparing a statement for a joint committee of the Commission on Reorganization of Secondary Education of the National Education Association and the National Council of Teachers of English, reacted against college domination of the secondary literature curriculum.[5] Hosic attempted to free the high school from prescribed lists and emphasized the function of literature in broadening and deepening imaginative life, in providing materials out of which may

[3] Mersand, Joseph. "The Teaching of Literature in American High Schools, 1865–1900," *Perspectives on English.* (Robert C. Pooley, ed.). New York: Appleton-Century, 1960, pp. 269–302.

[4] Purves, Alan C. "Testing in Literature," *Summative and Formative Evaluation of Student Learning.* (Benjamin Bloom, J. Thomas Hastings, and George Madaus, eds.). New York: McGraw-Hill, 1969.

[5] Hosic, James F. *Reorganization of English in Secondary Schools.* U. S. Bureau of Education Bulletin No. 2, Washington, D.C.: Government Printing Office, 1917.

emerge worthy ideals, in enhancing appreciation and enjoyment, and in stimulating sensitivity. In essence, his was the first major statement of purpose to concern itself with the response of the reader.

The Hosic report encouraged teachers to seek new freedom for programs in literature, and for the next several decades prescribed reading lists yielded to suggested lists and intensive reading yielded to extensive reading. In a national survey conducted in 1933, Smith reported the purpose of literary instruction in a majority of schools was to extend the range of students' interests and understandings; that an increasing number of programs feature extensive, supplementary, or free reading; and that the study of magazines and newspapers was replacing the study of some traditional literature.[6] Two influential curriculum reports published in the 1930's further emphasized the selection of stories within the emotional and intellectual range of pupils: *An Experience Curriculum in English*, edited by Hatfield,[7] and *A Correlated Curriculum in English*, prepared by Weeks.[8] During this period, teachers frequently distinguished between experiences *in* literature and experiences *through* literature. Further impetus to the movement came in a study prepared by Rosenblatt for the Commission on Human Relations of the Progressive Education Association, emphasizing the dynamic relationship between the book and reader and the human experience provided through reading.[9] Thus emerged the conflict between traditionalists concerned with teaching literature to young people through a selected number of standard titles and those who sought freedom to introduce adolescents to literature to which they might respond. Smith[10] reported schools of New York State clinging to traditional approaches as late as 1941, and Berberi's[11] study of literary anthologies revealed that not until the fifties did school anthologies reflect the more progressive views. By the midfifties, strong support for providing diversified reading for young people was expressed in the recommendations of the Commission on the English Curriculum, which stressed the

[6] Smith, Dora V. *Instruction in English*. U. S. Office of Education Bulletin No. 17, Washington, D.C.: Government Printing Office, 1933.

[7] Hatfield, W. Wilbur (ed.). *An Experience Curriculum in English*. New York: Appleton-Century, 1935.

[8] Weeks, Ruth Mary (ed.). *A Correlated Curriculum*. New York: Appleton-Century, 1936.

[9] Rosenblatt, Louise M. *Literature as Exploration* (rev. ed.). New York: Noble and Noble, 1968.

[10] Smith, Dora V. *Evaluating Instruction in Secondary School English*. New York: Appleton-Century, 1941.

[11] Berberi, Edel Ann. *A Descriptive Analysis of Anthologies for the Tenth Grade as the Texts are Related to the Objectives for the Study of Literature as Expressed by National Professional Groups*. Unpublished doctoral dissertation (Indiana University, Bloomington, 1964).

importance of personal values in reading and the relationship of books to individual experience.[12]

Toward the end of the fifties such attitudes toward literature instruction were again challenged, this time by new formulations of purpose placing greater stress on the content and discipline of literary study. A substitution in college instruction of analytical approaches to literature for historical, moral, sociological, and psychological approaches had resulted from the impact of the new criticism and particularly from two influential textbooks, *Understanding Poetry* by Brooks and Warren[13] and *Theory of Literature* by Wellek and Warren,[14] which in institutionalizing the new critical approaches also came to symbolize them. According to these views, extrinsic concerns, such as the reader's reaction, were not admitted as a legitimate aspect of literary study which in its purest sense must concentrate on intrinsic concerns, matters pertaining to the literary work itself. In the schools, a more narrow, selective program, reflecting such intensive study, seemed to be the inevitable result. The report of the Conferences on Basic Issues in The Teaching of English[15] sounded the first public concern in 1958. Critic Northrop Frye[16] even admonished that literature itself could not be taught. What can be taught is criticism, an ordered mode of discourse and of knowledge about literature. But for the schools the point of view was perhaps most fully explicated by the Commission on English of the College Entrance Examination Board in its 1965 report on *Freedom and Discipline in English.*[17] Although admitting that the timing and sequence of study would vary with the competence and maturity of students, the Commission saw the purpose of literary education as teaching students to understand and to evaluate literature, a goal to be achieved by teaching them the art of criticism. Carefully planned, intensive study of selected major works, read in their entirety, was seen as the best way of achieving such a goal, with the actual choice of books made by teachers who should weigh the excellence of each work against

[12] Commission on the English Curriculum. *The English Language Arts in the Secondary School.* New York: Appleton-Century, 1966.

[13] Brooks, Cleanth and Robert Penn Warren. *Understanding Poetry.* New York: Holt, 1960.

[14] Wellek, René and Austin Warren. *Theory of Literature.* New York: Harcourt, Brace, 1956.

[15] *The Basic Issues in the Teaching of English.* A report by the American Studies Association, College English Association, Modern Language Association of America, and the National Council of Teachers of English, 1959.

[16] Frye, Northrop. "Literary Criticism." *The Aims and Methods of Scholarship in Modern Languages and Literatures.* (James Thorpe, ed.). New York: Modern Language Association, 1963.

[17] Commission on English. *Freedom and Discipline in English.* New York: College Entrance Examination Board, 1965.

its suitability for particular students. Instruction would be organized in three ways: by historical pattern, by literary themes, and by genre or type. While rejecting the concept of a prescribed reading list, the Commission emphasized the reading of selected major works of continuing value and called for schools to encourage familiarity with legend and myth, the "literature beyond literature."

Issued about the same time and supporting the Commission's views was Lynch and Evans'[18] critical analysis of 72 high school literary anthologies. Their analysis expressed dissatisfaction with the quality of most literary selections, the alteration of the selection, the dismissal of the past found in most textbooks, the dominance of organization, and the editorial tone of the books.

Reviewing the previous half century of progress in literary instruction, Rosewell[19] in 1965 could comment that instruction seemed to have come full circle: from a rigorous, disciplined content with emphasis on the classics to a broader, general survey of classical and modern literature and back to an intensive scheme calling for a narrow range. Yet Rosewell reported also a growing freedom in use of selections in the schools. Of 934 titles proposed for college entrance lists, only 123 appeared in 1935 and continued to be used thereafter. Anthologies still continued in wide use and selections from British literature still outnumbered those from American literature, but schools had managed to introduce a large body of modern literature into the curriculum; appreciation and sensitivity were regarded as goals equal in importance to knowledge about literature; prescribed lists of titles had given way to suggested lists; and many schools were organizing literature in thematic units of study which were closely related to pupil interest. Until recently then, most school programs have been organized without direct concern for many effects on the reader. Literary criticism as a response to reading was often seen as the paramount concern. In 1968, Purves could assemble considerable evidence to support his statement that, "despite its importance to the teaching of English . . . response as content has not yet entered the literature curricula of this country."[20]

Concern with the impact of literature on readers has been evident in research for many years as the discussion earlier in this volume indicates, and individual specialists on teaching literature to young people have long advocated that teachers concern themselves with providing literary

[18] Lynch, James J. and Bertrand Evans. *High School English Textbooks: A Critical Examination.* Boston: Little, Brown, 1963.

[19] Rosewell, Paul Truman. *A Historical Survey of Recommendations and Proposals for the Literature Curricula of American Secondary Schools Since 1892.* Unpublished doctoral dissertation (University of Nebraska, Lincoln, 1965).

[20] Purves, Alan C. "Testing in Literature," *Summative and Formative Evaluation of Student Learning.* (Benjamin Bloom, J. Thomas Hastings, and George Madaus, eds.). New York: McGraw-Hill, 1969.

experiences to which young people can respond. Moreover, developments of the last few years indicate growing concern with the reaction between book and reader. In separate statements on the Anglo-American Seminar on the teaching and learning of English held at Dartmouth College in 1966, Muller[21] and Dixon[22] stressed the concern of the conferees with the imaginative development of young people. Active, emotional engagement in the literary experience was seen as a major goal and not one in conflict with the genuine critical response. Concern was expressed lest direct instruction in literary criticism and literary history inhibit the reader's personal involvement. "The content-centered emphasis of the Basic Issues Conference has been replaced by an emphasis upon experience and involvement," writes Albert Marckwardt, Director of the Seminar.[23] "As Arthur Eastman has described it in a comment on the seminar, this amounts to 'a preference for power rather than knowledge, for experience rather than information, for engagement rather than criticism.' " The conferees at Dartmouth put it even more bluntly: "The dryness of schematic analysis of imagery, symbols, myth, structural relations, *et al.*, should be avoided passionately at school and often at college. *It is literature, not literary criticism, which is the subject.*"[24] According to Marckwardt, the new development represents not a return to the experience curriculum and a rejection of the idea of English as discipline, but an awareness that the concept of discipline was a matter of operation rather than contentive. "All of this does imply that the sensitivity to literature and the adroitness in the use of language that we seek cannot be achieved by pouring them into empty vessels, that they will come about only through engagement and exercise, and that the idea of exercise without engagement is fruitless." Certainly a new concern with the impact of literature on the pupil is very much a charge to the literature teacher today.

The most complete contemporary statement of the purposes of literary education was prepared by Stafford[25] for the Commission on Literature, reflecting the views of scholars, critics, writers, and teachers. Emphasizing the significance of imaginative experiences for individuals in our society, Stafford called for a reemphasis on the power of literature to offset the continual blunting of student sensibilities in our culture though overemphasis on the factual, the trite, and the trivial. Although

[21] Muller, Herbert J. *The Uses of English.* New York: Holt, 1967.

[22] Dixon, John. *Growth through English.* Reading, England: National Association for the Teaching of English, 1967.

[23] Marckwardt, Albert H. "From the Basic Issues Conference to the Dartmouth Seminar: Perspectives on the Teaching of English," *PMLA,* 82:8–13, September 1967.

[24] Squire, James R. (ed.). *Response to Literature.* Champaign, Ill.: National Council of Teachers of English, 1968, p. 26.

[25] Stafford, William. *Friends to This Ground.* Champaign, Ill.: National Council of Teachers of English, 1967.

some acquaintance with the structure of literature, with literary history, and literary biography was seen as contributing to student understanding and appreciation, the ultimate test is the power of the imaginative experience itself. Writing about this new conception of literary education, Miller clearly expressed the growing concern:[26]

> . . . there is a new realization that imaginative growth involves both receptivity and creativity, both witnessing and making, both intake and output. In short, there is realization that the creative impulse is an inherent part of the imagination, and that deep engagement with literature will naturally involve the creative act.

## *Contemporary School Programs*

The content of instruction in literature in the high school as well as the college has concentrated on four dimensions of study: literary works, contextual information about the author and the work, literary theory and terminology, and cultural information (mythology, folklore, and common symbols).[27] Most programs seek a sound balance among these factors, as they also do in studying the linguistic, rhetorical, and content properties of any literary work. Few total curricular programs are organized to stress involvement of the individual reader, his personal responses and associations, and his experience in literature, although many teachers continue to see such experience as central in any cumulative program and a paramount concern of the teacher within whatever external course framework he is operating. Some go so far as to stress that whatever the overall program, some of the student's attention must be directed to the experience of literature itself.

During recent years the most influential developments in the secondary curriculum in literature have been the pilot programs created by the English Curriculum Centers supported by the United States Office of Education. Described by Bennett[28] and by Shugrue,[29] the centers have created model units of instruction, course outlines, and selected units of instruc-

[26] Miller, James E., Jr. "Literature in the Revitalized Curriculum," *Bulletin of the National Association of Secondary School Principals, 51,* No. 1:33, April 1967.

[27] A classification based on a study of recent statements of purposes as reported in Alan C. Purves, "Testing in Literature," *Summative and Formative Evaluation of Student Learning.* (Benjamin Bloom, J. Thomas Hastings, and George Madaus, eds.). New York: McGraw-Hill, 1969.

[28] Bennett, Robert A. (ed.). *Progress Report of English Curriculum Study and Demonstration Centers.* Champaign, Ill.: National Council of Teachers of English, 1966.

[29] Shugrue, Michael F. "New Materials for the Teaching of English: The English Program of the USOE," *PMLA, 41:*1–36, May 1966. See also Shugrue, Michael. *English in A Decade of Change.* New York: Western Publishing Co., 1968.

tion. The centers varied in their concern with the purposes, approaches, and content of instruction and in their interest in educational level; some concentrated on developing material for pupils; others prepared guides for the teacher. Together, however, their contributions present a rich body of pilot curricula from which new secondary programs are emerging. And in the range of their interest they reflect the scholarly and professional concerns of the past decade in education.

The center at Carnegie–Mellon University developed a high school literature program for average and above average students organized on a thematic basis. Themes like "The American Puritan Attitude" or The American Social Conscience" served as the basis for grouping literary selections around basic human problems. Young people thus were asked to respond to ideas.

A six-year program at the University of Oregon focused on the sequential study of concepts of literary form and craft, with individual units concerned with such problems as point of view, form, and the author's choice of subject. Here the concern of today's critics and teachers with the rhetorical analysis of literature is especially apparent, and the program seems organized to elicit an educated pattern of response to literary works not unlike the articulated responses of today's critics. At the University of Nebraska, a kindergarten to twelfth grade literature program focused on developing understanding of the structure of literature and has been strongly influenced by both theories of genres and the archetypal criticism of Northrop Frye. The reading of legends and folktales and the "reservoir literature" needed to understand allusions is an essential aspect of this program. The curriculum at Purdue University is "opus-centered," concentrating upon single major works and relating student work in language, composition, and literary perception to an understanding of the complete selection. The junior high school center at Florida State University tested different ways of organizing classroom literary experiences for adolescents – through thematic, typological, or conceptual arrangements. Curriculum specialists at Indiana University concentrated on the teaching of contemporary genres. Of the recent pilot centers developing materials on literature, only two have been primarily concerned with student reaction rather than with literary content or the analysis of literature. The Gateway English program of Hunter College saw its task as involving disadvantaged pupils in meaningful reading experiences. High impact, urban-oriented literary selections relevant to problems faced by the pupils were organized in units of instruction on such topics as "A Family Is a Way of Feeling" or "Coping" and taught through inductive, discovery methods to help young people develop "emotional independence and maturity" and satisfying "personal codes and values."

The "English in Every Classroom" project of Elton McNeil and Daniel

Fader[30] has focused even more on changing attitudes toward reading of disadvantaged pupils. To motivate general readers from kindergarten through junior college, classrooms were saturated with appropriate, attractive paperback books, newspapers, and magazines. The approach to literature was social, the emphasis on relevance to the student's immediate situation, and the ultimate effect, according to the project director, was a significant gain for pupils both in verbal proficiency and in teacher ratings of pupil self-esteem. The program, described in detail by Fader and Shaevits in *Hooked on Books,*[31] differs from other recent experimental curriculum projects in the emphasis it places on wide reading and personal response.

For the most part, however, the curricula in American high schools, like the pilot literature programs, are concerned less with the personal responses of individual readers than with the organization of literary content, whether it be thematical or topical as appear primarily in grades seven through ten, American literature in grade eleven, or English literature or world literature in grade twelve. A recent national study of schools with outstanding English programs,[32] reports some 52 per cent of all class time in English devoted to the teaching of literature, more than half of all departments claiming "the student's development through literature" to be a primary objective, but few classroom teachers who have reached a clear consensus about the purposes of the program.

Purves reached a similar conclusion in commenting on the lack of emphasis on affective goals after examining all major curricular statements on literary education printed before 1967:

> In part this may be explained by the fact that these goals are more often stated as assumptions or hopes rather than as educational objectives. To a certain extent the kind of commitment they describe is unteachable and not readily measurable. A second partial explanation may be that these goals are not seen as consonant with the prevailing informal educational philosophy that school is a time for work and the intellect, and that it is not particularly important to see literature as pleasurable. The professional study of literature, be it philological, historical, or critical, is thought of – to use the phrase of Matthew Arnold and R. P. Blackmur – as a "job of work." This conception has permeated the American school, which sees literature as a serious enterprise from which we gain wisdom and skill in critical thinking.[33]

[30] McNeil, Elton B. and Daniel Fader. *English in Every Classroom,* Final Report of USOE Project No. 07215. University of Michigan, Ann Arbor, November, 1967. (ERIC No. ED 016 673).

[31] Fader, Daniel N. and Morton H. Shaevits. *Hooked on Books.* New York: Berkeley Publishing Co., 1966.

[32] Squire, James R. and Roger K. Applebee. *High School English Instruction Today.* New York: Appleton-Century, 1968. pp. 93–138.

[33] Purves, Alan C. "Testing in Literature," *Summative and Formative Evaluation of Student Learning.* (Benjamin Bloom, J. Thomas Hastings, and George Madaus, eds.). New York: McGraw-Hill, 1969.

The programs observed in the National Study varied considerably in the quality of the books taught, in the ways in which instruction was organized, and in many of the approaches used in teaching. More important than any particular pattern of organization seemed to be the extent to which the programs provided for the careful study and close reading of individual texts and supported this close reading with a broadly based program of guided individual reading. The Study provided additional evidence suggesting a lack of general agreement on a fixed literary canon of works to be taught in secondary programs today, and on the freedom allowed individual schools and teachers in choosing selections with high impact for their pupils. Indeed in 1964, Anderson[34] reported only nine major titles taught by as many as 30 per cent of all public secondary schools and only a few more in most Catholic and independent schools.

Literary education in secondary schools today thus remains torn between the obligations to teach literature as knowledge or structure and literature as human experience. Within the overall curricular framework, teachers vary considerably in their concern with the effects of reading. Commenting on the need to synthesize "English as experience and English as cognitive structure" in program planning, George Henry[35] suggests a four-tiered approach to curriculum building. Initially he suggests that teaching concern itself with the motives and acts of men toward each other – with "reality" or "life" or "existence." Secondly, teaching should deal with the work of the literary art – poem, play, novel – "that clarifies, orders, and passes judgment on these acts and events, and that has an internal structure or form of its own which evokes a response to the author's comment 'on life.' " At a third level, he suggests that teaching deal with the theoretical concepts and structures from small to large extracted from these numerous works, inferred by critics and theorists. The fourth level, according to Henry, is curriculum building or course-making, a fusion of the other three. "It draws on the existential reality of the pupils and the conditions of the times; it selects hundreds of literary works as comments on human existence in many ages and periods; it taps the resources of cognitive structures, small- middle- and large-scale, created by critics and scholars; it organizes all these to probe literary experience, and then to ask what the undertaking means." The concerns of curriculum specialists like George Henry and the experimental literary programs of the pilot centers of the sixties should lead American secondary education toward more purposeful programs in the future, but at best they will only provide richer, more meaningful learning environments in which reader response can be deepened and extended.

[34] Anderson, Scarvia B. *Between the Grimms and 'The Group': Literature in American High Schools.* Princeton, N.J.: Educational Testing Service, 1964.

[35] Henry, George. "The Place of Logical Structure in Teaching Literature," *College English, 30,* No. 3: 241–49, December 1968.

## *College and University English Programs*

Achieving a balance between structure of subject and experience of individual, between acquisition of knowledge and refinement of skill, between the contemporary and the traditional, the casual and the formal – all problems in today's secondary school programs – affects college English teaching to an even greater degree. The confusion partially results from the multiple purposes of college English programs. Over 40 per cent of the total college English department effort is devoted to teaching Freshman English, an offering required on 93.2 per cent of all campuses which traditionally focuses on the processes of composition whatever the literary content.[36] With 8 per cent of all undergraduates majoring in English, and with English majors among the three largest groups of students in 75 per cent of the schools, over half of the students in English courses beyond the freshman level still are students *not* majoring in English.[37] Of the undergraduate majors, some one-quarter go on to graduate work in the field, even more complete requirements for school teaching. Thus, many college programs almost inevitably reflect the cleavages between "service" courses and courses for specialists, between programs for prospective scholars and those for prospective teachers, between "general" offerings in literature and specialized courses for the advanced student.

Even so, curricula among departments of English have a remarkable quality of sameness: standard introductory courses, standard individual author courses, standard period courses. In 1965, Gerber[38] edited a descriptive report on *The College Teaching of English,* indicating that in literature at least, the general nature of course offerings did not vary greatly with the size and nature of an institution or the population of the student body, although larger institutions can make available a greater number of electives and 95 per cent of all undergraduate institutions use the elective as one way of permitting students to choose those courses of greatest interest.[39] Presumably adjustments are made by instructors in relation to individual students or to method within rather traditional patterns. To be sure, departments differ on the exact nature of requirements and, particularly, on the extent to which they provide special opportunities through seminars, tutorials, and independent study for students to

[36] Wilcox, Thomas. "More Findings from the National Study of Undergraduate Programs in English," *ADE Newsletter,* No. 20: 27, January 1969.

[37] Leggett, Glenn. "Final Progress Report on the National Study of Undergraduate English Programs." Address presented to the Modern Language Association, New York City, December 1968. *PMLA,* in press.

[38] Gerber, John C. (ed.). *The College Teaching of English.* New York: Appleton-Century, 1965.

[39] Dressel, Paul L. and Frances H. DeLisle. *Undergraduate Curriculum Trends.* Washington, D.C.: American Council on Education, 1969, p. 36.

study limited topics in depth, with correspondingly less coverage or breadth.

Some recent developments suggest somewhat greater concern today than in the past with student response to literature. The National Survey of Undergraduate English Programs[40] notes a movement toward greater emphasis on literature for freshman students. Rowland[41] and others, summarizing 180 articles on the college teaching of English appearing from 1957 through 1963, reported heightened interest in critical rather than historical approaches to literary study. Allen's[42] report on improving the doctoral programs for prospective college and university teachers of English places considerable stress on teaching responsibilities.

Contrary to some frequently expressed assumptions, the conditions under which literature is taught in the colleges are not such as to discourage discussion, conferences, seminar presentation, and even independent study. Traditionally, Freshman English, whether in two-year or four-year institutions, is taught in unusually small classes, frequently enrolling fewer than 25 students. According to the National Survey of Undergraduate Programs, 40 per cent of all classes above the freshman level have less than twenty students.[43] Large lecture classes, in short, are not prevalent among college departments of English.

Of particular interest to those concerned with the impact of reading on the college student is the growing concern of scholars with the relationship of criticism and teaching to social and humane values.[44] In higher education as in the lower schools, it is the relationships of reader to book and student to teacher that can stimulate a deepening response; it is the approach to the work rather than the course organization, which seems the most crucial. The New Criticism of the thirties and forties turned college teachers and teaching away from the historical factualism associated with Germanic scholarship, and substituted detached scientific analysis of individual works. As Muscatine states,

[40] Leggett, Glenn. "Final Progress Report on the National Study of Undergraduate English Programs." Address presented to the Modern Language Association, New York City, December 1968. *PMLA,* in press.

[41] Rowland, J. Carter and others. *An Annotated Bibliography on the College Teaching of English, 1957–1963.* Champaign, Ill.: National Council of Teachers of English, 1966.

[42] Allen, Don Cameron. *The Ph.D. in English and American Literature.* New York: Holt, 1968.

[43] Wilcox, Thomas. "More Findings from the National Study of Undergraduate Programs in English," *ADE Newsletter,* No. *20:*27, January 1969.

[44] See, for example: Arrowsmith, William. "The Future of Teaching," *Improving College Teaching* (C. B. T. Lee, ed.). Washington, D.C.: American Council on Education, 1967; Kampf, Louis. *On Modernism: The Prospects for Literature and Freedom.* Cambridge, Mass.: Massachusetts Institute of Technology Press, 1967; Ohmann, Richard. "The Size and Structure of An Academic Field: Some Perplexities," *College English, 36:*259–367, February 1967.

This has yielded us splendid results in the techniques of close reading and in the appreciation of formal structure. But the effort to eliminate historical irrelevance and personal idiosyncrasy from literary interpretation has ended up in a kind of estheticism that is frequently just as far from commitment to human values as is the production of the chemist and of the logician.[45]

The contemporary critical movement perhaps led college readers to see detached critical reactions as the only appropriate response to literature. Now concern with feeling, experience, and moral significance is reasserting itself. "Only in [the English teacher's] classroom are details of immediate, living, individual thought and feeling and response legitimate areas of interest and speculation," writes DeMott.[46] As Miller states:

[The teacher] should not become didactic and attempt to inculcate beliefs; rather he should question, discuss and explore with his students. . . . Literature so explored should open to the student a variety of possibilities of values and visions, confront him – like life itself – with a multiplicity of ethical systems or moral perspectives. This expansion and deepening of the student's moral awareness constitutes the education of this moral imagination.[47]

Thus, college teaching, like instruction in the schools, is moving increasingly toward the use of discussion, inductive approaches, and the cultivation of discovery, as distinct from formal presentation and indoctrination. Like the new discovery methods being used in the schools, the approaches suggest an expanded role of the teacher as guide, explicator, counselor, and critic rather than as formal lecturer. They also suggest that far greater opportunities may occur to guide the responses of readers than in many classrooms of the past.

## *Extending and Deepening Response*

### The Nature of Response

As the discussion of literary and research backgrounds earlier in this volume indicates, response to literature is not passive but implies active involvement; it includes not only immediate response but subsequent effects; and the overt responses of a reader may indicate little of the inner response. Moreover, studies continue to demonstrate that literary response is a highly personal phenomenon affected by emotional factors and by the experience, sex, age, and degree of sophistication of the reader.

[45] Muscatine, Charles. "The Future of University Education as an Idea," *Knowledge and the Future of Man.* (Walter J. Ong. S.J., ed.). New York: Holt, 1968, p. 49.

[46] DeMott, Benjamin. "Reading, Writing, Reality, Unreality . . . ," *Response to Literature* (James R. Squire, ed.). Champaign, Ill.: National Council of Teachers of English, 1968, p. 39.

[47] Miller, James E., Jr. "Literature in the Revitalized Curriculum," *Bulletin of the National Association of Secondary School Principals, 51,* No. 1:33, April 1967.

This being true, it is not surprising that the range of responses which have interested researchers and specialists in the teaching of literature encompasses many different kinds of behaviors. Nor is it surprising to find the responses appropriate for, say, a reader in the seventh grade to differ widely from those of a college student.

Several attempts have been made to describe the range of responses to literature by high school and adult readers. Pioneer efforts by Waples and others[48] in 1940 suggested that reading had five social effects: instrumental; acquisition of useful information; increased self-esteem and prestige; reinforcement of personal views; distraction from anxieties; and enriched aesthetic experience. As later refined by Russell,[49] this view sees 19 possible effects of reading classified in four major categories:

## *Possible Effects of Reading*

Instrumental

1. Enrichment of experience.
2. Acquisition of knowledge, facts.
3. Increased understanding of human relationships.
4. Encouraged writing or imitation activities (dramatic).
5. Encouraged reading of the same or related authors.
6. Increased abilities in reading (general).
7. Resulted in greater liking (for animals, and so on).

Reenforcement

8. New or changed attitudes.
9. Helped general personality adjustment or development of philosophy of life.

Respite

10. Identification with character or characters.
11. Enjoyment of fantasy.
12. Wish fulfillment.
13. Escape and relaxation.

Esthetic

14. Enjoyment of humor, adventure, romance.
15. Appeal to imagination.
16. Appreciation of character.

[48] Waples, Douglas, Bernard Berelson, and Franklyn R. Bradshaw. *What Reading Does to People*. Chicago: University of Chicago Press, 1940.

[49] From an unpublished manuscript by David H. Russell.

17. Enjoyment of illustrations.
18. Portrayal or arousal of emotions.
19. Literary appeal (criticism, rhythm, vocabulary, and so on).

A comprehensive approach to categorizing responses, rather than effects, has been undertaken by Purves.[50] In a report which sought to describe American goals of education for comparison with those of other countries to form the specifications for a cross-national study of achievement in literature, Purves examined 23 major documents describing the literature curricula in secondary schools and classified stated aims with respect to student behavior. He found that the behaviors could be grouped under the headings of knowledge, application, response, expressed response, and participation, and that they did not fall neatly into the taxonomical domains of the cognitive and the affective. "One reason for this is that the central behavior, *Respond to,* is jointly cognitive, affective, perceptual, and psychomotor; a second is that much of critical analysis involves an admixture of feeling and attitude." Based on his study, Purves suggested the following classification of primary behaviors:

*Behaviors in Literature*

KNOWLEDGE — To recall.
To recognize.

APPLICATION — To apply knowledge of specific literary texts.
To apply biographical information.
To apply literary, cultural, political, or intellectual history.
To apply literary terms.
To apply critical systems.
To apply cultural information.

RESPONSE — Those "unteachable" and "unmeasurable" covert and overt behaviors which occur during the process of reading, hearing, or watching a performance of a literary work.

EXPRESSIONS OF RESPONSE — To recreate the work in some oral, dramatic, or artistic form.
To talk or write about the work:
- To express one's engagement with.
- To perceive (to analyze the parts of, to analyze the relationships in).

[50] Purves, Alan C. "Testing in Literature," *Summative and Formative Evaluation of Student Learning.* (Benjamin Bloom, J. Thomas Hastings, and George Madaus, eds.). New York: McGraw-Hill, 1969.

To express one's evaluation of.
To express a pattern of preference for.
To express one's interpretation of.
To express a pattern of response to.
To express a variety of responses to.

PARTICIPATION To be willing to respond to.
To take pleasure in responding to.
To accept the importance of.

Purves' distinction between *response*, which he considers a primary concern of teachers of literature, and *expressions of response*, the articulated reactions with which teachers deal, seems important. He further notes that the recreative response, such as dancing a poem, drawing illustrations to a story, or acting out a play, tends to be somewhat suspect in secondary schools because it strikes many teachers as too close to play and too far from learning, even though proponents see major creative, linguistic, and educational values in such work. Certain recent publications, such as the recommendations of Barnes[51] and the study of British teaching by Squire and Applebee,[52] suggest that recreative responses may receive more emphasis in the curriculum in literature in the future. Nevertheless, the expressed response is likely to continue to receive pedagogical emphasis in the secondary schools because it is more closely associated with cognition and, therefore, more amenable to teaching.

In a separate study, Purves[53] provides a comprehensive analysis of 70 elements of expressed response, as identified through an analysis of the writings of critics, students, and teachers. Grouped under the four major categories of expressed response – engagement, perception, interpretation, and evaluation – are scores of typical responses indicating the range and complexity of literary reactions. Each of the major categories, Purves believes, is a distinct goal in teaching. The responses of *engagement*, of course, deal with the emotional and personal impact of a work, with the processes of identification, and with the writer's surrender to the work. Often highly subjective, it appears as a reader tries to express the ways he has experienced a literary work in its various aspects. Engagement with literature is both necessary and desirable, but its excess can lead to a complete disassociation of the reader from reality.

[51] Barnes, Douglas. *Drama in the Classroom.* Champaign, Ill.: National Council of Teachers of English, 1968.

[52] Squire, James R., and Roger K. Applebee. *A Study of the Teaching of English in Selected British High Schools.* USOE Cooperative Research Project 6-1849. Urbana: University of Illinois, 1968, pp. 263–83.

[53] Purves, Alan C., and Victoria Rippere. *The Elements of Writing About a Literary Work: A Study of Response to Literature.* Champaign, Ill.: National Council of Teachers of English, 1967.

Under *perception,* Purves classifies those analytic, synthetic, or classificatory reactions which deal with a work either in isolation or in historical context. Closely analogous to "understanding," responses of this kind are empirically verifiable and encompass the ways in which a reader looks at any work as apart from his own experience of it.

Responses classified as *interpretation* are those embracing attempts to find meaning in a literary selection, to generalize about it, to draw inferences, and to relate the work to the reader's experiences and understanding. Interpretative responses may be either to the form or to the content of a literary work.

The final category of responses is *evaluation,* those statements dealing with the worth of a literary work whether based on personal or external criteria. Quite frequently, Purves reports, such evaluative responses are based on the other kinds of reactions.

The Purves categorization is useful to researchers and teachers in suggesting the range and complexity of response to literature. He notes that the elements "exist in no particular order of logic, psychology, or theory" and that in any individual's expressed response "one category may precede any other."[54] Not all elements will appear in any reader's expressed response to a particular work and not all need be formal concerns of the teacher of literature. Yet in using these categories in a pilot study of reactions to reading, Purves found important differences in the reactions of thirteen-year-old American, British, German, and Belgian students, differences which he attributed to varying educational and cultural patterns.[55] Formal training in a particular approach to literary analysis seemed to have shaped the responses of Belgian boys, whereas the absence of emphasis on any particular approach in the school programs of American students may have contributed to the diffusion and lack of consistency of their reactions.

Commenting on present curricular emphasis as suggested by available instructional guides, Purves notes,

> Interpretation is by far the most important, receiving a third again as much emphasis as its nearest competitor, engagement, and twice as much as evaluation, yet at the same time there is [in the examined curriculum guides] virtually no mention of inculcating a pattern of response. This might be explained by the fact that although the curriculum writers are deeply concerned that students learn how to derive meaning from works of literature, they are careful not to announce that they wish this to be the only acceptable mode of response.[56]

[54] *Ibid.,* p. 8.

[55] Purves, Alan C. "An Examination of the Varieties of Criticism," *College Composition and Communication, 17:*94–99, May 1966.

[56] Purves, Alan C. "Testing in Literature," *Summative and Formative Evaluation of Student Learning.* (Benjamin Bloom, J. Thomas Hastings, and George Madaus, eds.). New York: McGraw-Hill, 1969.

These observations seem to be supported by the work of Hirshfield.[57] He classified the classroom experiences of 31 teachers in five schools in accordance with Bloom's *Taxonomy of Educational Objectives* (knowledge, comprehension, application, analysis, synthesis, and evaluation) and found only analysis, comprehension, and knowledge consistently appearing, and more classroom time was devoted to knowledge than to comprehension. If richness in response and the development of appropriate patterns of response are important instructional goals, teachers would do well to examine their current programs in the light of the Purves findings.

## The Stance of the Teacher

High school and college teachers concerned with student response to literature are aware that the way in which literary selections are approached, whether inside or outside the classroom, is fundamental in guiding reactions. Miller[58] believes that informality, flexibility, and improvisation are essential in the classroom, with the teacher concentrating on two major goals (often "approached so obliquely as perhaps to appear hidden") – trying to meet each student wherever he is, to engage honestly his understanding, his interest, his imagination, his emotional energies; trying by every means at his disposal to provide the experience that will grow into the lasting commitment. In this view, vitality, drama, and creativity are essential elements requiring stress; close reading, particularly "lively sessions of critical controversy, arousing interest as well as passion in questions of value," may ultimately help the student-reader learn that there are many ways of seeing, many ways of entering, and many ways of understanding any piece of literature.

How to accomplish these aims tends to be more controversial than the ends themselves. Many high school and college teachers would agree with Wimsatt,[59] who suggests that the process of teaching a literary work should involve *explanation* of the explicit and clearly ascertainable, *description* of the structure of the work and its historical relations, *explication* which "turns description as far as possible into meaning," and finally the activity of *appreciation*, "which shows most in the explication of the poem." Several recent textbooks on the teaching of literature, such as those by Murphy,[60] Ryan,[61] and Knapton and Evans,[62] are in general

[57] Hirshfield, George. *A Taxonomic Approach to the Evaluation of Secondary School English Programs.* Unpublished doctoral dissertation (University of New Mexico, Albuquerque, 1967).

[58] Miller, James E., Jr. "Literature in the Revitalized Curriculum," *Bulletin of the National Association of Secondary School Principals, 51,* No. 1:33, April 1967.

[59] Wimsatt, W. K. "What to Say About A Poem," *College English, 24:*377–83, February 1963.

[60] Murphy, Geraldine. *The Study of Literature in the High School.* Waltham, Mass.: Blaisdell, 1969.

agreement with Wimsatt's point of view. Other widely-read discussions of method stress somewhat different approaches. Burton[63] emphasizes relating the content of literature to the personal needs and interests of adolescents; Rosenblatt[64] stresses the personal nature of the literary experience; and Rosenheim[65] attempts to relate critical concerns with the dynamic processes involved in literary engagement. Similar differences can be found in most journal articles and in the practices to be observed in classrooms in this country.

Growing in influence, however, are those concerned lest too great an emphasis on analysis and explication and too much attention to literary history limit and restrict the responses of the reader. The scholars and teachers participating in the Dartmouth Seminar on the Teaching and Learning of English stated their reservations in a blunt reminder to teachers that the experience of art is a thing of the individual's own making, an activity in which each individual is his own interpretive artist:

> At the present time, there is too much learning about literature in place of discriminating enjoyment, and many students arrive at and leave universities with an unprofitable distrust of their personal responses to literature. At the university, as in the secondary school, the explicit analysis of literature should be limited to the *least* required to get an understanding of the work, within the student's limits, and the aim should be to return as soon as possible to a direct response to the text.[66]

Those who view literature in this way reject the idea of a literary content to be "handed over" to pupils or a subject which can only be approached through methods of critical analysis. They feel that knowledge of form, critical method, or historical fact may be a help or a hindrance to the student reader, and that affective response is an integral part of a reader's experience with literature. They are committed to classroom approaches which stimulate the complex totality of response, recognizing that the reactions of a mature reader should be conditioned both by an intellectual grasp of the literary work, its parts and principles of organization, and by knowledge of the world the work refers to both in relation to the student's own experience and to other works of literature.

---

[61] Ryan, Margaret. *Teaching the Novel in Paperback.* New York: Macmillan, 1963.

[62] Knapton, James and Bertrand Evans. *Teaching A Literature-Centered English Program.* New York: Random House, 1967.

[63] Burton, Dwight L. *Literature Study in the High School* (rev. ed.). New York: Holt, 1964.

[64] Rosenblatt, Louise M. *Literature as Exploration* (rev. ed.). New York: Noble and Noble, 1968.

[65] Rosenheim, Edward R., Jr. *What Happens in Literature.* Chicago: University of Chicago Press, 1960.

[66] Squire, James R. (ed.). *Response to Literature.* Champaign, Ill.: National Council of Teachers of English, pp. 26–27.

### The Effects of Content

Continuously over the past four decades, the reading preferences of adolescents and young people have been surveyed in a series of studies, many referred to earlier in this volume, which have provided schools with abundant evidence concerning the choices exercised in adolescent reading. Reviewing the impact of such studies, Meckel[67] observed that they have guided the choice of selections for both basic and supplementary reading programs in the junior and senior high schools. For example, early in the junior high school, readers are likely to erect defenses against emotional disturbances, particularly those associated with heightened sexual responsiveness, and thus against the direct expression of emotion that may be found in literary works. Thus, works like *Evangeline* or *Romeo and Juliet* seem singularly inappropriate for reading at this level. Similarly, at fifteen and sixteen many young people become uneasy about expressing their personal emotional experiences; they seek the safety of conformity to mass attitudes or of participating in mass responses. It is not that they refuse to respond, but rather they refuse to express overtly what they may be feeling underneath. Method must be adjusted accordingly, and works of literature to be discussed in class must be chosen both for their quality as literature and their potential effect on the reactions of young people.

The development of a body of literature written for and about adolescents has also influenced high school reading programs. Junior novels are frequently used with twelve- to fifteen-year-olds as "transitional" literature suitable for young people not yet interested in mature adult reading. Alm[68] and Dunning[69] have analyzed the asumptions in these books concerning human experience and the role of such books in the educative process. Although finding that many junior novels tend to present unrealistic, didactic views of human behavior, reflecting middle-class values, Dunning recommended their use as effective bridges to adult reading. Magaliff[70] has completed a full-length assessment of the genre.

Evidence, too, suggests that literature written for adolescents can contribute to teaching objectives. Evans,[71] in a compared group experiment,

[67] Meckel, Henry C. "Research on Teaching Composition and Literature," *Handbook of Research on Teaching*. (N. L. Gage, ed.). Chicago: Rand McNally, 1933, pp. 966–1006.

[68] Alm, Richard S. *A Study of the Assumptions Concerning Human Experience Underlying Certain Works of Fiction Written for and About Adolescents.* Unpublished doctoral dissertation (University of Minnesota, Minneapolis, 1955).

[69] Dunning, Arthur S. *A Definition of the Role of the Junior Novel Based on Analyses of Thirty Selected Novels.* Unpublished doctoral dissertation (Florida State University, Tallahassee, 1959).

[70] Magaliff, Cecile. *The Junior Novel.* Port Washington, N.Y.: Kennikat Press, 1964.

[71] Evans, William H. *A Comparison of the Effects of a Superior Junior Novel and "Silas Marner" on the Ability of Tenth Grade Students to Read the Novel.* Unpublished doctoral dissertation (Florida State University, Tallahassee, 1961).

found *Swiftwater*, which he regarded as a superior junior novel, as effective as *Silas Marner* in preparing tenth grade students to read *The Pearl*. Blount[72] compared the students' concepts of the novel genre with the concepts held by selected experts, and found that study of three junior novels brought student perceptions of the genre closer to the perceptions of specialists than did reading and discussion of three adult novels.

The most extensive study of the reactions of young people to titles included in school programs was conducted by Norvell,[73] whose work has proven helpful in determining which standard works to require in the curriculum. Useful suggestions are also offered by Whitman's[74] report on the titles which superior college students recall as their most memorable reading experiences in secondary schools and by a similar report from Squire and Applebee[75] as part of the National Study of High School English Programs.

Specialized studies also assist teachers in selecting literature for school programs. Simpson and Soares[76] asked 4,250 junior high school students to rate 862 short stories, then analyzed the 77 least-liked and best-liked selections. Among the factors of high appeal were physical action, conflict, suspense, a single unifying action, and concrete and clear language. Nelms[77] attempted to determine the characteristics of poetry that might be significantly related to the evaluative responses of adolescents. He found that students preferred poems with narrative interest and that high evaluations were related to a combination of masculine interest, realism, and emotional versus rational appeal. Clarity and comprehension were also influential in the judgments, but the quality of the poetry seemed unrelated.

Teachers of literature in American schools and colleges select literature to be studied both in relation to the preferences of readers and to the purposes of the literary programs. These purposes vary somewhat from institution to institution but are inevitably related to literary values and to fostering a literary education. However, an indication of the potential effect of selecting literature to achieve social and political ends may be gleaned

[72] Blount, Nathan S. *The Effect of Selected Junior Novels and Selected Adult Novels on Student Attitudes toward the "Ideal" Novel.* Unpublished doctoral dissertation (Florida State University, Tallahassee, 1963).

[73] Norvell, George W. *The Reading Interests of Young People.* Boston: Heath, 1950.

[74] Whitman, Robert S. "Significant Reading Experiences of Superior English Students," *Illinois English Bulletin, 51:*1–24, January 1964.

[75] Squire, James R. and Roger K. Applebee. *High School English Instruction Today.* New York: Appleton-Century, 1968, pp. 99–106.

[76] Simpson, Roy H. and Anthony Soares. "Best and Least-Liked Short Stories in Junior High School," *English Journal, 54:*108–111, February 1965.

[77] Nelms, Frank Benny. *Characteristics of Poetry Associated with Preferences of A Panel of Tenth-Grade Students.* Unpublished doctoral dissertation (University of Iowa, Iowa City, 1967).

from studying the programs developed in Nazi Germany where literature was selected, taught, and read to inculcate "the consciousness of being a German and to develop a human awareness of duty of party, fatherland, and people, all of whom had made sacrifices for the common good."[78] Stories of German heroes, German families, and Germanic racial experiences were subtly emphasized throughout organized school programs for the acknowledged purpose of "strengthening the heart" of German youth. The recent study by Daigh of the long-range effects of the Nazi program reveals that literature was used as a valuable pedagogical instrument by both the state and the Nazi party and that sufficient circumstantial evidence exists to suggest that the Nazi pedagogical program was "reasonably successful." The selection and teaching of literature can indeed have serious effects.

## Methods and Approaches to Literature

Good teaching at different educational levels depends as much on the mode of presentation (and the mode of response consequently implied) as on the selection of materials. Early[79] has suggested that the maturity of the reader affects both the appropriate presentation and the nature of response and has hypothesized that as readers grow older they pass through three stages of response: from unconscious enjoyment to self-conscious appreciation to conscious delight. Whitehead[80] has commented that as students grow older they should "increasingly undertake their reading of literature 'in context' . . . the context being that provided by knowledge about the author and his other works, about the conditions of the time in which he writes, and about his relationship to other writers." Other age differences have been discussed earlier in this volume.

Regardless of the educational level, however, certain modes of approach to literature remain central, although they find different kinds of expression and amplification. The Dartmouth Seminar report identified three of the basic modes:[81]

**The Individual Child with the Individual Book:** The teacher's task in assisting the reader to find "the right book at the right time," a program of individual reading requiring the availability of a wide variety of appropriate titles.

**Literature as Group Experience:** Storytelling, dramatization, folksongs

[78] Daigh, Charles F. *The Role of Literature in the Education of Youth in the Third Reich.* Unpublished doctoral dissertation (University of Illinois, Urbana, 1967).

[79] Early, Margaret. "Stages of Growth in Literary Appreciation," *English Journal, 41:*161–67, March 1960.

[80] Whitehead, Frank. *Response to Literature* (James R. Squire, ed.). Champaign, Ill.: National Council of Teachers of English, 1968, p. 65.

[81] *Ibid.*, pp. 16–17.

and ballads, and other corporate possessions through which an individual relates his response to the responses of others.

**Presentation of Literary Material Accompanied by Discussion:** The common classroom approach during which the reading of a work of literature, with assistance from the teacher, is followed by informal or structured discussion.

All three approaches may be found in today's secondary school and college classrooms, although wide reading, informal discussion, and communal experience tend to be characteristic of the junior high school years, with structured discussion and formalized drama experience increasing in the high school and college. During the later years, particularly, an individual's interest in literary experience may be satisfied by forms other than the book – by recorded literature, by films, or theatrical experience. The wise teacher attempts to continue a program of individual reading but expands the program to include discussion of other kinds of literary experience.

Research and experience suggest certain emphases which require attention in any sound program designed to stimulate more mature responses:

**Discussion and Oral Approaches:** Specialists seem to agree that informal discussion involving pupils and teachers is particularly conducive to formulating responses to literary works. However, Squire and Applebee reported that only 19.5 per cent of all classroom time in English is devoted to discussion, compared with 22.2 per cent emphasizing recitation, and 21.1 per cent emphasizing lectures or teacher presentation.[82] Hoetker[83] examined teacher questioning behavior in nine junior high school English classes and found a questioning rate per minute of 5.17 questions, or one teacher question every 11.8 seconds. The continued lack of emphasis on real discussion in many classrooms only substantiates the concerns of Taba[84] who, in examining the discussion responses of high school students to literature, reported that factual restatement of ideas predominated. Only 12 per cent of the students generalized about the meaning of the narrative. Taba noted, however, that group discussion tended to push the level of thinking beyond the level which individuals reach on their own. Additional support for discussion methods has been provided by Casper,[85] who found that adult-led junior Great

[82] Squire, James R. and Roger K. Applebee. *High School Instruction Today.* New York: Appleton-Century, 1968, p. 45.

[83] Hoetker, James. "Teacher Questioning Behavior in Nine Junior High School English Classes," *Research In the Teaching of English, 2:*99–106, Fall 1968.

[84] Taba, Hilda. *With Perspective on Human Relations.* Washington, D.C., American Council on Education, 1955.

[85] Casper, Thomas, Rev. *Effects of Junior Great Books Programs at the Fifth Grade Level on Four Intellectual Operations and Certain of Their Component Factors as Defined by J. P. Guilford.* Unpublished doctoral dissertation (St. Louis University, St. Louis, 1964).

Book discussions encouraged divergent thinking and the ability to form new ideas, and by Steinberg and others,[86] who pressed for an inductive approach to the teaching of literature which encourages pupils to make their own discoveries in literature.

Oral interpretation of literature by teacher or pupils has been strongly supported by the Dartmouth Seminar. The use of classroom drama for this purpose has been advocated by Moffett.[87] Britton[88] found that student reaction to particular poems improves with planned rereading of the poems orally, and similar results were reported by Rees and Peterson.[89] The importance of oral approaches in extending the responses of young people thus continues to be reaffirmed, even though the skill of teachers in using such approaches remains less than effectively demonstrated.

**Skill in Interpreting** I. A. Richards[90] was the first to demonstrate that the misinterpretations of college readers interfere with adequate understanding and appreciation. He emphasized the difficulties in comprehension resulting in large part from stereotyped thinking and critical and technical prejudgments. Squire,[91] Wilson,[92] and, more recently, Ducharme[93] have reported similar problems which high school and college readers encounter in interpreting different kinds of works. Squire discovered six sources of misinterpretation in adolescent responses:

Failure to grasp the essential meaning.

Reliance upon patterns of stereotyped thinking.

Unwillingness to accept unpleasant facts in interpreting characters and their actions.

Critical predispositions.

Irrelevant associations.

Unwillingness to suspend judgment until a story is completed.

Wilson found that these tendencies decrease somewhat among college students responding to a novel, but even at this level logically formulated

[86] Steinberg, Erwin and others. "The Inductive Teaching of English," *English Journal, 55:*139–57, February 1966.

[87] Moffett, James. *Drama in the Classroom.* Champaign, Ill.: National Council of Teachers of English, 1967.

[88] Britton, J. N. "Evidence of Improvement in Poetic Judgment," *British Journal of Psychology, 45:*196–208, March 1954.

[89] Rees, Richard D. and Darhl M. Peterson. "A Factorial Determination of Points of View in Poetic Evaluation and Their Relation to Various Determinants," *Psychological Reports, 16:*31–39, 1965.

[90] Richards, I. A. *Practical Criticism: A Study in Literary Judgment.* New York: Harcourt Brace, 1929.

[91] Squire, James R. *The Responses of Adolescents While Reading Four Short Stories.* Champaign, Ill.: National Council of Teachers of English, 1964.

[92] Wilson, James R. *Responses of College Freshmen to Three Novels.* Champaign, Ill.: National Council of Teachers of English, 1966.

[93] Ducharme, Edward Robert. *Close Reading and the Teaching of Poetry in English Education and in Secondary Schools.* Unpublished doctoral dissertation (Columbia University, New York, 1968).

responses emerge only after careful analysis. Ducharme reported an alarming lack of skill in close reading and critical analysis among 200 liberal arts graduates enrolled in teacher education programs, and little or no material on critical analysis in existing methods books for teachers. His recommendation that prospective teachers receive systematic training in the close reading of literature tends to be supported by the findings of Madsen,[94] who found that undergraduate course work in criticism produces a systematic and significantly greater understanding of critical theory among prospective teachers.

Studies of this kind suggest that better teacher preparation and more attention to close critical reading is needed to assist pupils with difficulties in interpreting literature. Moreover, Squire,[95] Rogers,[96] and Schubert[97] have independently demonstrated that skill in interpretation is not significantly related to overall reading ability as measured by standardized tests; hence, interpretation must be taught independently.

***Creative Writing and Literary Response:*** The upsurge in interest in creativity education seems to have awakened specialists to an awareness that imaginative written response to human experience may precede, follow, or be inextricably linked to imaginative response to literature. "In this conception of English, focusing on the faculty of the imagination, there is a new realization that imaginative growth involves both receptivity and creativity, both witnessing and making, both intake and output.[98] Some specialists such as James E. Miller, Jr. believe that every course in English should become a course in both imaginative reading and creative composition. The publications emerging from the Dartmouth Seminar reflect these insights into the relationship of writing and reading, particularly the reports written by Dixon[99] and Summerfield.[100] Moffett's curricular handbook for teachers[101] suggests specific ways to

[94] Madsen, Alan L. *Responses of Prospective English Teachers to A Test on Theories of Literary Criticism.* USOE Project No. HE-145. Urbana: University of Illinois, 1968.

[95] Squire, James R. *The Responses of Adolescents While Reading Four Short Stories.* Champaign, Ill.: National Council of Teachers of English, 1964.

[96] Rogers, Charlotte. *Individual Differences in Interpretative Responses to Reading Short Stories at the Eleventh Grade Level.* Unpublished doctoral dissertation (University of Arizona, Tucson, 1965).

[97] Schubert, Delwyn G. "The Relationship between Reading and Literary Appreciation," *California Journal of Educational Research, 4:*201–202, November 1953.

[98] Miller, James E., Jr. "Literature in the Revitalized Curriculum," *Bulletin of the National Association of Secondary School Principals, 51,* No. 1: 33, April 1967.

[99] Dixon, John. *Growth through English.* Reading, England: National Association for Teaching of English, 1967.

[100] Summerfield, Geoffrey (ed.). *Creativity in English.* Champaign, Ill.: National Council of Teachers of English, 1968.

[101] Moffett, James. *A Student-Centered Language Arts Curriculum, Grades K–13: A Handbook for Teachers.* Boston: Houghton Mifflin, 1968.

relate the writing and reading of dialogue, monologue, narrative, poetry, journals, and diaries. Research evidence concerning the interrelationship of creative writing and reader reaction must await further exploration. In a pilot study, Richard Smith[102] suggests that the kind of writing task used to orient student readers to reading matter will influence attitudinal development toward that matter, but evidence is far from conclusive concerning the nature of the attitudinal shift. According to observers, teachers in the schools of the United Kingdom have experimented widely with ways of relating creative written and oral expression to literary response, and student enthusiasm for both reading and writing appears to be one positive result.[103]

***Impact of Wide Reading:*** For forty years, empirical evidence has indicated that extensive reading of literature results in the reading of more books, in the development of more favorable attitudes toward books, and in growth in reading skill. LaBrant,[104] for example, has discussed the contributions of wide reading to the expansion of reading interests and, in a follow-up study of subjects conducted some twenty-five years later, found that as adults the subjects who had completed a six-year free reading program were doing significantly more reading than most other groups with which they were compared. Norvell[105] found wide reading contributing to pupils' growth in overall reading ability. Appleby[106] found that students in a one-semester English elective using an individual reading approach were more inclined to derive certain satisfactions from the study of literature than are students in a required English course. Among the satisfactions mentioned were attitudes to reading fiction for characterization, style, and technique and satisfactions in the possible contributions of literature to their self-improvement. Certain problems inherent in wide reading are also known. Handlan[107] has indicated that such reading must be guided carefully by the teacher lest

[102] Smith, Richard J. *The Effects of Reading A Short Story for Creative Purpose on Student Attitudes and Writing.* University of Wisconsin, Madison: Center for Cognitive Learning, 1967.

[103] Squire, James R. and Roger K. Applebee. *A Study of the Teaching of English in Selected British Schools.* USOE Cooperative Research Project 6-1849. Urbana: University of Illinois, 1968, pp. 157–203.

[104] LaBrant, Lou L. *An Evaluation of the Free Reading Program in Grades Ten, Eleven, and Twelve.* Columbus: Ohio State University, 1936. Also LaBrant, Lou L. "The Use of Communication Media," *The Guinea Pigs after Twenty Years.* (Margaret Willis, ed.). Columbus: Ohio State University, 1961, pp. 127–64.

[105] Norvell, G. W. "Wide Individual Reading Compared with the Traditional Plan of Studying Literature," *School Review, 26:*606–13, 1941.

[106] Appleby, Bruce Charles. *The Effects of Individualized Reading on Certain Aspects of Literature Study with High School Seniors.* Unpublished doctoral dissertation. (University of Iowa, Iowa City, 1967).

[107] Handlan, Bertha. "The Fallacy of Free Reading." *English Journal, 25:*182–87, March 1946.

young people continue to read at their present level of quality and interest and not progress to more mature experiences. Successful programs in independent reading also demand classroom book collections and the availability of appropriate titles. In 1965, LaCampagne[108] presented the recommendations of two national conferences of high school English chairmen calling for better library collections and for classroom collections of 500 separate titles.

***Evaluating Growth in Literary Response:*** Teachers, like researchers, have depended largely upon observation, expressed reading preferences, and other indirect methods to evaluate growth in student responses to literature. Researchers have intermittently attempted to develop adequate instruments for measuring the impact of reading, but the subjectivity of most judgments on appreciation and a lack of knowledge about the nature of responses have prevented creation of valid measurement tools. The Carroll Prose Appreciation test is one of the few standardized instruments available for school use.[109] It is based on the assumption that appreciation correlates highly with ability to judge short stories in terms of sensitivity to style, understanding of multiple meanings, and emotional capacity to respond to fine shades of feeling. More helpful to classroom teachers has been a series of paper and pencil devices suggested by Loban,[110] including the use of cumulative reading records, a plot completion test, a "Grasp of Human Conduct Test" in which the reader is asked to predict the action of a character in another situation; a social distance scale; and other devices. Although no one of the measures adequately assesses growth in a pupil's ability to respond, the employment of a variety of such measures, however rough, does offer the teacher a variety of insights to supplement his own observations.

An attempt to develop a test of literary appreciation was reported by Forehand,[111] who was concerned with the understanding, interpretation, and evaluation of a short story. Understanding was measured by factual multiple-choice items; interpretation by free response items coded into ten categories; attitude by the use of semantic differential scales applied to diverse concepts. Forehand also required readers to choose a "preferred" statement from several related to the short story.

The most recent and comprehensive statement on testing in literature

[108] LaCampagne, Robert (ed.). *High School Departments of English: Their Organization, Administration, and Supervision.* Champaign, Ill.: National Council of Teachers of English, 1965.

[109] Carroll, Herbert A. "A Method of Measuring Prose Appreciation," *English Journal, 22:*184–89, March 1933.

[110] Loban, Walter. "Evaluating Growth in the Study of Literature," *English Journal, 37:*277–87, May 1948.

[111] Forehand, G. A. "Problems of Measuring Response to Literature," *Clearing House, 40:*369–75, October 1966.

instruction has been contributed by Purves.[112] After analyzing the various understandings and behaviors involved in literary study, he suggests ways in which each may be examined. He finds that a comprehensive program would require three main types of testing: literary acquaintance; literary analysis and interpretation; and attitudes toward literature and literary response. The three, Purves believes, should be concerns of teachers throughout the year, embedded in continuous interwoven, teaching-and-testing approaches. "Formative evaluation is a microcosm of summative evaluation," writes Purves, "in that it deals with a single work or a small group of works and usually with a smaller segment of the spectrum of behaviors." Only by touching all the behaviors involved in the study of literature can the teacher be assured that he is not restricting himself or his students to a limited set of behaviors involved in the study of literature.

As the discussion in this chapter makes clear, the teaching of literature in high school and college is influenced by many factors. Concern with knowledge, literary tradition, professional education, and with general cultural concerns influence the choices made by teachers within the classroom. Fundamentally, however, the teacher's approach to student and to literary selection will govern the effect which the instructional program has on the individual reader. The dynamics of reading are to be found in the interaction of book and reader, but the stance of the teacher can do much to block or facilitate this interaction.

## *Aids in Selecting Literature*

To guide the personal reading of young people, most teachers depend upon the recommendations of professional colleagues. Few teachers find time to read extensively from among the hundreds of new titles for young people which are published annually. The American Library Association, the Children's Book Council, International Reading Association, and National Council of Teachers of English publish helpful reviews in current professional journals and regularly revise annotated booklists. Among the more helpful of the many lists which constantly appear are the following:

Perkins, Ralph. *Book Selection Media* (rev. ed.). Champaign, Ill.: National Council of Teachers of English, 1967. An annotated index to the many lists of books currently available.

Willard, Charles B. (ed.). *Your Reading.* New York: Bantam Books, 1966. A list of books for readers in the junior high school.

[112] Purves, Alan C. "Testing in Literature," *Summative and Formative Evaluation of Student Learning.* (Benjamin Bloom, J. Thomas Hastings, and George Madaus, eds.). New York: McGraw-Hill, 1969.

Alm, Richard S. (ed.). *Books for You.* New York: Washington Square Press, 1964. A list for senior high school readers.

Lueders, Edward (ed.). *Books in Literature and the Fine Arts.* New York: Washington Square Press, 1962. An interdisciplinary list of titles for college and adult readers.

Crosby, Muriel (ed.). *Reading Ladders for Human Relations* (4th ed.). Washington, D.C.: American Council on Education, 1963. Annotated lists of selections for readers of varying age levels grouped under human relations themes.

O'Neal, Robert. *Teacher's Guide to World Literature for the High School.* Champaign, Ill.: National Council of Teachers of English, 1966. This list is particularly strong in literature from non-Western cultures.

Weber, J. Sherwood (ed.). *Good Reading.* New York: New American Library, 1960. A standard reference tool for college students.

Carlsen, G. Robert. *Books and the Teen-Age Reader.* New York: Bantam Books, 1967. Written for parents, but useful to teachers, this book provides extensive discussion of literature of many kinds.

Rollins, Charlemae (ed.). *We Build Together.* Champaign, Ill.: National Council of Teachers of English, 1967; and Dodd, Barbara. *Negro Literature for High School Students.* Champaign, Ill.: National Council of Teachers of English, 1968. These two titles suggest many selections by and about black Americans.

# Index

# Author Index

# *Topic Index*

A B C D E F G H I J 5 4 3 2 1 7 0